A Practitioner's Guide to UK Money Laundering Law and Regulation

Third Edition

A Practitioner's Guide to UK Money Laundering Law and Regulation

Third Edition

Consultant Editor

Ben Kingsley
Slaughter and May

SWEET & MAXWELL

 THOMSON REUTERS

First Edition	2004
Second Edition	2009
Third Edition	2015

Published in 2015 by Thomson Reuters (Professional) UK Limited trading as Sweet & Maxwell, Friars House, 160 Blackfriars Road, London, SE1 8EZ (Registered in England & Wales, Company No.1679046.
Registered Office and address for service: 2nd floor, 1 Mark Square, Leonard Street, London, EC2A 4EG.).

Sweet & Maxwell ® is a registered trademark of Thomson Reuters (Professional) UK Limited.

For further information on our products and services, visit *http://www.sweetandmaxwell.co.uk.*

Typeset by Letterpart Limited, Caterham on the Hill, Surrey, CR3 5XL.

Printed and bound by CPI Group (UK) Ltd, Croydon, CR0 4YY.

No natural forests were destroyed to make this product: only farmed timber was used and replanted.

A CIP catalogue record of this book is available for the British Library.

ISBN: 978-0-414-05257-4

Thomson Reuters and the Thomson Reuters logo are trademarks of Thomson Reuters.

Crown copyright material is reproduced with the permission of the Controller of HMSO and the Queen's Printer for Scotland.

Biographies

Ben Kingsley has been a partner at Slaughter and May since 2008. He provides regulatory consultancy and transactional advice to both financial institutions and non-regulated firms on the UK and EU financial regulatory aspects of a broad range of matters and projects across the full waterfront of regulated products and markets. Ben is listed as a leading individual in the *Financial Services: Non-contentious* section of Chambers UK for 2013.

Highlights of Ben's work in recent years have included advising the Central Bank of Cyprus on the EU regulatory aspects of the resolution of Bank of Cyprus and HM Treasury on a range of matters arising out of the financial crisis, including on the governmental interventions in the UK banking sector.

Ben has considerable experience in advising on the UK and international anti-money laundering and financial sanctions regimes and, as a member of Slaughter and May's Global Investigations Group, he has also advised a range of financial sector firms on the conduct of internal regulatory investigations and on the management of regulator-led enquiries and investigations.

Paul Marshall is a barrister practising commercial and financial services law at No.5 Chambers, specialising in dispute resolution. He has been instructed by banks, law firms and individuals on money laundering issues and is author of the Chancery Bar Association's guidance on AML law and the Regulations. He was educated at Magdalene College Cambridge, the LSE and Sandhurst.

Ben Hammond is a partner in Ashurst's financial services regulatory group. He leads the firm's non-contentious regulatory practice in Hong Kong, where he is currently based, and advises clients in a broad range of transactional and non-transactional regulatory areas, including anti-money laundering and sanctions issues. Ben has particular expertise in cross-jurisdictional regulatory advice; reconciling Asian regulatory regimes with European and UK regulatory requirements. Ben joined Ashurst in January 2015 from Slaughter and May, where he had worked since 2004.

Stephen Gentle is a partner in the Crime, Fraud and Investigations group at Simmons & Simmons LLP. He specialises in assisting corporate and individual clients on complex fraud and financial regulatory matters, generally in an international context. He also has particular expertise in advising in Financial Conduct Authority matters with an emphasis on insider dealing, market misconduct and international regulatory issues.

Cherie Spinks is a supervising associate in the Crime, Fraud and Investigations group at Simmons & Simmons LLP. She has significant experience in advising on internal investigations and on criminal investigations run by the UK Serious Fraud Office. She also advises professionals and corporations based in the UK and off-shore on anti-money laundering and sanctions compliance issues.

Elizabeth Richards is a lawyer by background, having trained with the Crown Prosecution Service. She has worked on financial crime issues for a number of regulatory bodies and professional associations, including the Law Society, Gambling Commission and National Federation of Property Professionals. She led a Financial Action Task Force (FATF) project relating to the designated non-financial businesses and professions. She later chaired the money laundering working group of the International Consortium of Real Estate Agents and represented the property sector at the FATF private sector forum. Elizabeth successfully completed an internship at the

United Nations Counter Terrorism Executive Directorate, and in her spare time she sits on the board of the United Nations Association.

James London is a lawyer by background; he has worked for nearly 20 years in the financial crime area with the Financial Conduct Authority, the Financial Services Authority and the Securities and Investment Board. During that time, he has had secondments to HM Treasury and the Home Office working, largely, on aspects of the FSMA dealing with financial crime and, at the Home Office, terrorist financing. During his time with the FSA he has been responsible for introducing the *Money Laundering Sourcebook* and managing the project that looked at Money Laundering Themes, the first such project of its kind. Since his return to the FCA/FSA from his last secondment, he has managed various financial crime intelligence liaison, assessment, whistle-blowing and triage teams and now runs the FCA's Financial Crime Policy and Risk Team and is the Co-ordinator of the Financial Crime Information Network.

Debbie Ward is an EY Partner based in their London office. She is a financial crime professional specializing in anti-money laundering. Debbie has worked with major institutions in the development and implementation of global anti-money laundering and "know your customer" policies and procedures. Debbie spent 18 months on secondment to the FSA within the enforcement division, and is also a member of the Association of Certified Fraud Examiners and the Institute of Chartered Accountants.

Colin Pickard is a director at EY based in their London office. He is a financial crime professional whose work focuses on the implementation of financial crime risk assessment, control processes and reporting. Colin has spent over 15 years working and consulting for investment banks in London and New York. Before working in the financial services sector, Colin was a UK police officer specializing in investigations and data control.

Gabriela Grosicka is a manager at EY based in their London office. She is a financial crime professional specializing in anti-money laundering. She has eight years of financial crime experience gained in retail banking, card acquiring, private equity. She has also performed a role of a Deputy MLRO in one of the leading UK investment management firms.

Richard Jones QC practises at No.5 Chambers, London and Birmingham. His main field of practice is business law, and he has a special interest in compliance issues and in the practical aspects of money laundering on which he has lectured extensively. He is a Fellow of the Society of Advanced Legal Studies, and the co-author of "Investigation and Enforcement". He sits as a Recorder.

Denis J. McInerney is a member of Davis Polk's Litigation Department and Global Enforcement and Investigations Group. He recently returned to the firm after serving as Chief of the Fraud Section (2010–2013) and Deputy Assistant Attorney General (2013–2014) of the Department of Justice's Criminal Division where he played a leadership role in, among other matters, DOJ's investigations into the alleged manipulation of LIBOR and the foreign exchange market by various financial institutions and the preparation of *A Resource Guide to the Foreign Corrupt Practices Act*, published by DOJ and the SEC in 2012. Denis's practice focuses on grand jury, regulatory, cross-border and internal investigations, and he has regularly advised clients concerning AML matters. He has conducted over a dozen jury trials as a prosecutor, criminal defense attorney and civil plaintiff's attorney, including representing Arthur Andersen in federal court in Texas on obstruction of justice charges.

James L. Kerr is a graduate of Yale College and the University of Pennsylvania Law School, where he was on the law review. His practice includes complex commercial litigation and arbitration, with a particular focus on banking litigation. He regularly advises and represents U.S. and foreign banks, financial intermediaries, foreign central and government banks, multilateral financial institutions and foreign states in a variety of international controversies arising in the context of the emerging markets, the swap markets, and sovereign debt restructurings, in particular with respect to provisional remedies and the cross-border enforcement of judgments. James is a frequent participant in emerging market symposia on sovereign debt and sovereign immunity litigation, and a regular panelist in programs on letters of credit and bank guarantees. James is actively engaged in TRIA and related terrorist enforcement litigation, letter of credit litigation, and proceedings implicating OFAC and AML compliance.

Michael J. Russano is a counsel in Davis Polk & Wardwell's Litigation Department whose practice includes general commercial, accounting, bankruptcy and securities litigation. He has also represented numerous U.S. and foreign banks and other corporate institutions in regulatory and internal investigations, including money laundering investigations, and has advised clients concerning AML and SAR matters.

Sarah Breslow is an associate in Davis Polk & Wardwell's Litigation Department. She has represented U.S. and foreign banks in regulatory and internal investigations, including providing advice on AML matters.

Contents

1   The UK Statutory Framework

Ben Kingsley
Partner
Slaughter and May

2   Civil Liability and Money Laundering

Paul Marshall
Barrister, No.5 Chambers

3   International Considerations

Ben Hammond
Partner
Ashurst LLP

4   The Money Laundering Regulations 2007

Stephen Gentle
Partner

Cherie Spinks
Supervising Associate
Simmons & Simmons LLP

7   The Role of the Financial Conduct Authority

Elizabeth Richards
Consultant, Policy and Risk Team, Specialist Supervision Division

James London
Manager, Policy and Risk Team, Specialist Supervision Division

8   Practical Systems and Controls

Debbie Ward
Partner, Financial Crime Team

Colin Pickard
Director, Financial Crime Team

Gabriela Grosicka
Manager, Financial Crime Team
Ernst & Young LLP

10 The Extra-Territorial Effects of US Anti-Money Laundering Law

Denis J. McInerney
Partner

James L. Kerr
Counsel

Michael J. Russano
Counsel

Sarah Breslow
Associate
Davis Polk & Wardwell LLP

Chapter 1

The UK Statutory Framework

Ben Kingsley
Partner
Slaughter and May

1.1 Introduction

Since the second edition of this text was published in 2009, the UK's domestic anti-money laundering (AML) statutory framework has remained largely unaltered. Reasonably significant changes have nevertheless been taking place at EU level, in particular the formulation of a new Money Laundering Directive and an updated Wire Transfer Regulation. These European legal developments, coupled with a number of developments in the guidance and approach of the various UK law enforcement agencies and national supervisors, have prompted this updated text.

In particular, key developments in recent years have been:

- The adoption of the Fourth EU Money Laundering Directive (the Fourth Directive)[1]
- The adoption of the Second EU Wire Transfer Regulation (WTR2)[2];

---

[1] Directive (EU) 2015/849 of the European Parliament and of the Council of 20 May 2015 on the prevention of the use of the financial system for the purposes of money laundering or terrorist financing, amending Regulation (EU) No 648/2012 of the European Parliament and of the Council, and repealing Directive 2005/60/EC of the European Parliament and of the Council and Commission Directive 2006/70/EC [2015] OJ L141/73.

[2] Regulation (EU) 2015/847 of the European Parliament and of the Council of 20 May 2015 on information accompanying transfers of funds and repealing Regulation (EC) No 1781/2006 [2015] OJ L141/1.

- The reorganisation of UK financial crime investigatory and enforcement agencies, including the creation of the National Crime Agency (NCA) and the absorption of the Serious Organised Crime Agency (SOCA) into that body;
- The enactment of the Terrorist Asset-Freezing etc. Act 2010 (TAFA 2010) in response to Supreme Court challenges to the UK's domestic terrorist asset-freezing regime; and
- Significant regulatory enforcement decisions relating to AML control failings.

1.1.1 UK legislative developments

At the time of publication, the Fourth Directive and WTR2 had been adopted but the UK had not adopted legislation to implement necessary modifications to its domestic legislative regime.[3] That implementing legislation, once adopted, is unlikely to make materially significant changes to the UK regime, which had for many years applied a higher standard than that strictly required by the Third EU Money Laundering Directive[4] (the Third Directive).

As far as UK domestic legislation is concerned, in the period since the prior edition of this text, TAFA 2010 has been the most significant single piece of UK legislation to impact on the AML statutory framework. That piece of legislation is discussed in more detail later in this Chapter (see section 1.6.3.1).

It is worth mentioning that the UK Government's broader commitment to identifying and tackling financial crime has

---

[3] On 28 August 2015 HM Treasury and the Department for Business Industry and Skills issued a call for evidence as part of a review to improve the effectiveness of rules designed to prevent money laundering and terrorist financing. This review will provide context to the Government's work to complete the implementation of the Fourth Directive, which it has confirmed it will do by means of updating the Money Laundering Regulations by June 2017. The deadline for responses to the call for evidence was 23 October 2015. Business Secretary Sajid Javid was quoted as saying that "This new review is about making sure the rules we have to protect our strong financial services industry from abuse are not unintentionally holding back new and existing British business."

[4] Directive 2005/60/EC of the European Parliament and of the Council of 26 October 2005 on the prevention of the use of the financial system for the purpose of money laundering and terrorist financing [2005] OJ L309/15.

also been evident in other areas of policy-making, for example in relation to bribery and corruption with the introduction of new corporate offences of bribery under the Bribery Act 2010, and developments in the approach to ensuring compliance with EU and international sanctions regimes.

The recent introduction of the legal framework for a public register of beneficial owners of UK companies, introduced by the Small Business, Enterprise and Employment Act 2015 (SBEEA 2015), is another interesting example of AML-inspired measures entering the legislative space indirectly via developments in other policy areas.

From January 2016, SBEEA 2015 requires all UK-registered companies to maintain a publicly available register of people with significant control over the company (a PSC register). Among other things, the PSC register will record the relevant person's name, service address and date of birth. From April 2016, this information will also have to be filed at Companies House, although only the month and year from the recorded date of birth will be available to the public.

Companies traded on the London Stock Exchange or the Alternative Investment Market (defined in SBEEA 2015 as "DTR5 issuers"), or those otherwise subject to broadly similar disclosure regimes, will not be required to keep a PSC register—the principle being that they are already subject to adequate equivalent transparency obligations. For wholly owned subsidiaries of those exempted companies, the only information required to be included in the PSC register are the details of the direct parent.

The PSC register will thus enhance the level of information available to firms carrying out know your customer (KYC) processes on UK registered companies. The PSC register shares some similarities with the beneficial owner tests set out in the Money Laundering Regulations 2007 (the 2007 Regulations, SI 2007/2157), under which UK AML KYC obligations arise, although differences exist. For example, SBEEA 2015's definition of "significant control" introduces a third test not found in the 2007 Regulations, namely the concept of controlling the right to appoint or remove a majority of the board. Statutory guidance will be produced on the meaning of "significant influence or control" in the context of SBEEA 2015.

1.1.2 Developments relating to enforcement agencies

In 2013, the UK financial regulatory landscape was altered materially with the division of the Financial Services Authority into two successor organisations, the Prudential Regulation Authority (PRA) and the Financial Conduct Authority (FCA).

In the context of the AML regime, the FCA has essentially become the direct successor to the FSA as an AML supervisor for regulated firms and certain others. The Office of Fair Trading continued to play a supervisory role in the AML sphere until its responsibilities were divided on 1 April 2014 between the Competition and Markets Authority (in relation to competition matters), the FCA (consumer credit matters, including AML supervisory role for such firms) and HMRC (AML supervisory role for estate agents).

Also notable in the AML context, the Serious Organised Crime Agency (SOCA) was absorbed into the newly-created National Crime Agency (the NCA) with effect from 7 October 2013. The Government explained the main thrust behind this organisational change came from the need to co-ordinate a response to organised crime at a national level. In its policy paper presented to Parliament in June 2011,[5] the Government noted that despite the formation of SOCA, the UK's response to serious and organised crime had remained "patchy". The NCA is responsible for a broad remit of intelligence, analysis and enforcement work across a range of specialisms, including border policing and child exploitation alongside economic crime.

Other agencies continue to perform their roles within the supervisory and enforcement matrix. In particular, HMRC

---

[5] Home Office, *The National Crime Agency: A plan for the creation of a national crime-fighting capability* (June 2011).

continues to perform a significant AML supervisory role alongside the FCA, and, along with the Joint Money Laundering Steering Group, has published Treasury-approved guidance.

1.1.3 Enforcement

The Proceeds of Crime Act 2002 (POCA 2002) and the Terrorism Act 2000 (TA 2000) continue to dominate the AML and counter-terrorist finance legislative landscape in the UK.

However, while enforcement activity under those two key pieces of legislation have tended to be relatively low level in terms of enforcement targets, that is by no means an indication that AML has slipped down the political and regulatory agenda. Significant fines have also been levied by the FSA and FCA under their respective regulatory jurisdictions in respect of AML control failures.

For example, in March 2012, the FSA fined Coutts & Co £8.75 million for failing to take reasonable care to establish and maintain effective AML systems and controls relating to high risk customers, including Politically Exposed Persons (PEPs). The failings were characterised by the FSA as serious, systemic and persistent. The penalty would have amounted to £12.5 million if Coutts had not obtained a 30 per cent discount for agreeing to settle at an early stage.

Then, in January 2014, the FCA fined Standard Bank plc £7.6 million for failings in its AML policies relating to corporate customers connected to PEPs. This was the first case brought by the FCA with a focus on commercial banking activity. It was also the first case using the FCA's updated penalty regime, applicable to regulatory infringements that occurred on or after 6 March 2010. Under that revised penalties regime, the FCA assesses penalties based on five steps: disgorgement; the seriousness of the breach; mitigating and aggravating factors; adjustment for deterrence; and settlement discount.[6]

---

[6]   DEPP 6.5A in the FCA Handbook.

1.1.4 EU developments

At the EU level, in February 2013, the Commission adopted a legislative proposal for a Directive to amend and replace the Third EU Money Laundering Directive after a review had concluded that it was necessary to update the existing framework.

The Fourth Directive was seen as a response to evolving threats of money laundering and terrorist financing, as well as a means to implement the February 2012 AML and counter-terrorist financing standards published by the Financial Action Task Force (FATF). The Fourth Directive was published in the Official Journal of the EU on 5 June 2015 and came into force 20 days after its publication.

Like its predecessor, the Fourth Directive is a minimum harmonising Directive: it does not prescribe the details of the measures that Member States must take to detect and prevent money laundering. However, the new regime sets a higher level of common standards, for example by enhancing the required clarity and accessibility of beneficial owner information, tightening the rules on simplified due diligence and strengthening the sanctioning powers of national supervisors.

The Fourth Directive thus extends the scope of the EU-AML regime in a number of ways, including broadening the categories of individuals falling within the definition of a PEP. The focus of third-country equivalence is also amended, moving from a positive equivalence framework to instead listing non-equivalent third countries.

Other changes in emphasis introduced by the Fourth Directive include a risk-based approach to identifying and mitigating money laundering and terrorist financing (an approach that is of course already very familiar to practitioners in the UK). There is also a requirement for Member States to identify, assess, understand and mitigate the AML risks they face and to keep their assessments up to date.[7] The emphasis on ensuring compatibility of national AML regimes with data protection requirements is also strengthened.

Member States were given two years to implement national legislative measures to give effect to the Fourth Directive (i.e. by 26 June 2017). Given that the UK's legislative position has been super-equivalent to the requirements of the Third Directive for some time, the extent of the changes required to implement the Fourth Directive in the UK are inevitably not as great as in other Member States.

The 2007 Regulations, which gave effect to the Third Directive in the UK, were subject to a post-implementation review by HM Treasury. A call for evidence in October 2009 led to responses on topics including guidance, supervisory arrangements, industry practice and the effectiveness and proportionality of the 2007 Regulations.

In April 2010, HM Treasury published a summary of responses to the call for evidence, followed by its formal response to the review in June 2011. A consultation was subequently launched by HM Treasury in June 2011, which focused on proposals to revise the 2007 Regulations to implement some of the reforms suggested by respondents to the call for evidence. A summary of consultation responses was published in November 2011.

As a result of that review, in July 2012, HM Treasury published its decision to make amendments to the 2007 Regulations with a view to reducing the regulatory burden that they imposed, whilst strengthening the overall regime. The majority of the changes came into force on 1 October 2012, implemented by the Money Laundering (Amendment) Regulations 2012.

At the review's conclusion in 2012, HM Treasury identified a number of amendments to be considered or implemented at a later date. Those issues were due to be reviewed as part of the legislative amendment package triggered by the adoption of the Fourth Directive.

---

[7] Fourth Directive art.7.

The impact of the adoption of WTR2 is addressed in para.1.5 of this Chapter.

1.1.5 Summary

This Chapter outlines the current statutory framework for AML in the UK, focusing on the primary statutory offences relating to money laundering and terrorist financing but also considering the enforcement and asset tracing processes which are available to the UK's investigatory and prosecuting authorities.

Though the remainder of this Chapter focuses on the key statutory provisions contained in POCA 2002 and TA 2000, references are made to those other sources of law, regulation and guidance which affect or contribute to the UK's broader AML framework. References to regulated sector firms are to those firms which carry on a business in the regulated sector, as set out in Sch.9 to POCA 2002, which is intended to correspond to those categories of firms which are subject to the 2007 Regulations or any successive Regulations.[8]

The implications of the Fourth Directive for the 2007 Regulations are addressed in Ch.4, and the FCA's *Senior Management Arrangements, Systems and Controls Sourcebook* is covered in Ch.6, but readers should appreciate that these sources of AML law and regulation are also key constituents of the statutory framework in the UK.

1.2 Statutory offences

POCA 2002 and TA 2000 set out a range of criminal offences, the effect of which is to require businesses, in particular businesses in the regulated sector, to monitor for and to report

---

[8] Including credit institutions; investment firms; long-term insurers and their intermediaries; collective investment undertakings; auditors, insolvency practitioners, accountants and tax advisers; many (but not all) lawyers; trust or company service providers; estate agents; dealers in high-value goods; and casino operators.

potential money laundering and terrorist financing. Those statutory measures also provide legal tools, including court-issued disclosure orders, for the UK's investigating and prosecuting authorities to pursue and disrupt organised criminals and terrorist organisations.

The primary statutory offences relating to money laundering are contained in Pt 7 of POCA 2002 and ss.15–22 and 39 of TA 2000. These offences superseded the money laundering offences under the Criminal Justice Act 1988, the Prevention of Terrorism (Temporary Powers) Act 1989, the Drug Trafficking Act 1994 and the equivalent statutes applicable in Scotland and Northern Ireland. In July 2005, a number of supplemental amendments were made to POCA 2002 by the Serious Organised Crime and Police Act 2005 (SOCPA 2005) and, in 2007, POCA 2002 and TA 2000 were further amended by the Terrorism Act 2000 and Proceeds of Crime Act 2002 (Amendment) Regulations 2007 (the Terrorism Act and POCA Amendment Regulations).

Under POCA 2002 and TA 2000, there are essentially three "principal" money laundering offences. A person (including a firm or an individual) commits a money laundering offence if he:

(a) conceals, disguises, converts or transfers the proceeds of criminal conduct or of terrorist property;
(b) becomes concerned in an arrangement to facilitate the acquisition, retention or control of, or to otherwise make available, the proceeds of criminal conduct or of terrorist property; or
(c) acquires, possesses or uses property while knowing or suspecting it to be the proceeds of criminal conduct or of terrorist property.

There are also three "secondary" or third-party offences:

(a) failure to disclose any of the above offences;
(b) tipping-off of persons engaged in money laundering or terrorist financing as to any investigation; and

(c) prejudicing an investigation in relation to money laundering or terrorist finance offences.

The provisions of POCA 2002 and TA 2000 apply in principle to
all legal persons, individual and corporate, so that fines could
potentially be imposed on both corporate entities and individual directors, managers and officers—who can also be
imprisoned.[9] The personal liability aspect of the statutory
money laundering offences gives senior officers in regulated
sector firms ample reason to be cautious in this area.

Apart from the personal liability for individuals working in the
regulated financial services industry, and in particular senior
management and compliance staff, the reputational damage
which a conviction and fine is likely to cause at a corporate
level must also be a serious concern for any firm. The 2007
Regulations (and, when applicable to a regulated sector firm,
the FCA's *Senior Management Arrangements, Systems and Controls Sourcebook*) impose regulatory obligations on firms to train
their staff in AML procedures but, regulatory obligations aside,
it is quite clearly both in the personal and corporate best
interests of firms and their management to ensure that staff at
all levels of the business are aware of their statutory obligations
and liabilities and are adequately equipped to face them.

1.3   Proceeds of Crime Act 2002

Part 7 of POCA 2002, which contains the primary offences
relating to money laundering, came into force on 24 February
2003. Transitional provisions applied so that the principal
offences under ss.327–329 and 333 of POCA 2002 could only be
committed if the conduct constituting the offence was committed after 24 February 2003.[10] Similarly, the s.330 "failure to
disclose" offence under POCA 2002 (see para.1.3.2 below) may

---

[9]   When a fine is imposed upon conviction for any offence under POCA 2002 or TA
  2000, the level of the fine is determined by the court, taking into account the
  seriousness of the offence and the financial circumstances of the offender.
[10] Proceeds of Crime Act 2002 (Commencement No. 4, Transitional Provisions and
  Savings) Order (SI 2003/120) art.3.

only be committed if the information which gives rise to the requisite knowledge, suspicion or reasonable grounds for knowledge or suspicion came to a person after 24 February 2003.

1.3.1 The principal money laundering offences

Sections 327–329 of POCA 2002 constitute the principal money laundering offences—concealment, acquisition and assisting the retention of the proceeds of crime, defined in POCA 2002 as "criminal property".

Criminal conduct is conduct which constitutes an offence in any part of the UK, or would do so if the conduct occurred in the UK.[11] Criminal property means, for the purposes of these offences, property of all forms (including, of course, money) which constitutes or represents, in whole or in part, directly or indirectly, a person's benefit from criminal conduct.[12] In a series of Court of Appeal decisions, including most recently a 2011 case[13], followed in April 2015 by a Supreme Court decision[14], it has been determined that the property in question must be criminal *before* a relevant POCA 2002 offence occurs. The facts before the courts in both of those cases concerned the offence of becoming involved in arrangements prohibited by s.328. The court has held consistently that it is not sufficient for property to become criminal by virtue of the arrangements taking place: it must be criminal property at the time the relevant arrangement begins to operate on it.

If a person obtains what is referred to, somewhat arcanely, as a "pecuniary advantage" as a result of or in connection with criminal conduct, he is treated as having obtained a benefit as a result of or in connection with that criminal conduct.[15] In other words, it is not necessary for a person actively to receive "proceeds" from an offence in order for his assets to constitute

---

[11] POCA 2002 s.340(2).
[12] POCA 2002 s.340(3)(a).
[13] *R. v Akhtar (Urfan)* [2011] EWCA Crim 146; [2011] 1 Cr. App. R. 37 (p.464).
[14] *R. v GH* [2015] UKSC 24; [2015] 1 W.L.R. 2126; [2015] 2 Cr. App. R. 12 (p.195).
[15] POCA 2002 s.340(6).

or represent the benefit of criminal conduct. The savings that a person makes as a result of tax evasion are, therefore, treated as criminal property albeit perhaps without there being any specifically identifiable "proceeds" from that criminal conduct.

Significantly, an alleged offender must know or suspect that property constitutes or represents a benefit from criminal conduct, so property will not be treated as criminal property in determining whether an offence has been committed under ss.327, 328 or 329 if the alleged offender is genuinely unaware that the property involved is or might be the proceeds of criminal conduct.[16]

Unless, therefore, a firm's employee knowingly engages in business with a suspected money launderer or otherwise intentionally assists a money launderer, both the firm and the employees are unlikely to be at significant risk of committing these offences as principal offenders—all three offences require a degree of intent, or at least wilful blindness.

All firms should, however, be familiar with the nature and extent of those principal money laundering offences; and a regulated sector firm must additionally ensure that its employees receive appropriate training in relation to money laundering, including as to the scope of these principal offences.

In particular, relevant employees of a regulated sector firm must be trained to identify potentially disclosable offences for the purposes of the failure to disclose offence under POCA 2002: if employees in the regulated sector, and hence potentially also the firms which employ them, know,suspect or have reasonable grounds to know or suspect that a customer, counterparty or other person is engaged in money laundering activities (collectively herein "suspicious persons"),[17] they may commit a criminal offence if they fail to disclose that

---

[16] POCA 2002 s.340(3)(b).
[17] The disclosure obligations under POCA 2002 relate to all persons of whom an individual or firm has knowledge or suspicion of involvement in money laundering.

information (see para.1.3.2 below for a more detailed explanation of the failure to disclose offences).

If a regulated sector firm or any of its employees can be shown to have known or suspected that a person was engaged in money laundering activities, but nevertheless entered into a particular course of conduct with that suspicious person, that firm and any relevant employees could have committed one of the principal money laundering offences under POCA 2002 unless the limited defence of making an after-the-event disclosure of the course of conduct to the NCA and having a "reasonable excuse" for not having made the disclosure before the event applies.

In general, firms should, as a policy matter, not engage in any activity with a suspicious person unless a request for consent to the NCA has been submitted and confirmation received that the NCA consents to the particular course of conduct (see para.1.3.4 below on the consent regime).

The three principal money laundering offences are set out in POCA 2002 as follows:

1.3.1.1 Concealing the proceeds of crime

Section 327 of POCA 2002 provides that:

" (1) A person commits an offence if he –
    (a) conceals criminal property;
    (b) disguises criminal property;
    (c) converts criminal property;
    (d) transfers criminal property;
    (e) removes criminal property from England and Wales or from Scotland or from Northern Ireland.
    ...

(3) Concealing or disguising criminal property includes concealing or disguising its nature, source, location, disposition, movement or ownership or any rights with respect to it."

That is the basic "money laundering" offence, criminalising conduct which enables criminals to conceal, disguise or move the proceeds of their crimes. The offence can be committed by the predicate offender, though it is presumably more likely to be used against a money laundering intermediary.

An offence under s.327 is punishable by a fine and up to 14 years' imprisonment.

1.3.1.2   *Assisting money laundering*

Section 328 of POCA 2002 provides that:

> "(1)   A person commits an offence if he enters into or becomes concerned in an arrangement which he knows or suspects facilitates (by whatever means) the acquisition, retention, use or control of criminal property by or on behalf of another person."

There is perhaps greater potential for a regulated sector firm to commit an assistance offence under s.328 than the basic concealment or acquisition offences under ss.327 and 329, but, as previously mentioned, for the offence to be committed, any alleged offender under s.328 must know or suspect that the relevant property is criminal property[18] as well as knowing or suspecting that the arrangement into which he enters, or becomes concerned in, facilitates the retention or control of that criminal property.

In practice, therefore, the assistance offence cannot be committed without a degree of knowledge or suspicion on the part of the persons involved. The offence is, of course, a disclosable offence for the purposes of the s.330 "failure to disclose" offence and as such, it remains important for regulated sector firms and their employees to be aware of and to understand the crime.

---

[18] POCA 2002 s.340(3)(b).

An offence under s.328 is punishable by a fine and up to 14 years' imprisonment.

1.3.1.3   *Acquiring criminal property*

Section 329 of POCA 2002 provides that:

> "(1) A person commits an offence if he –
>   (a)   acquires criminal property;
>   (b)   uses criminal property;
>   (c)   has possession of criminal property."

In effect, this is a form of "handling stolen goods" offence in a money laundering context. A person may be convicted under s.329 if it is established that he knew or suspected that property which he had acquired, used or taken possession of constituted or represented the benefit of criminal conduct. This crime is presumably intended to apply to persons who are not necessarily involved in the underlying criminal conduct or subsequent laundering activities, but nonetheless knowingly enjoy the benefits of criminal activity. Unknowing possession of the proceeds of criminal conduct, however, is not within the offence.

It is a defence for a person who acquires, uses or has possession of criminal property to show that he acquired, used or had possession for adequate consideration. "Adequate" is, perhaps unsurprisingly, not a defined term, but most probably should be interpreted in terms of "market-rate" consideration rather than "peppercorn" consideration, which in some other legal contexts may be construed as adequate.

An offence under s.329 is punishable by a fine and up to 14 years' imprisonment.

1.3.1.4   *The scope of the primary offences*

The nature of the underlying offences of which a person's knowledge or suspicion can give rise to a primary offence (and consequently also the secondary offences discussed below) under POCA 2002 is widely drafted. Criminal property is defined in POCA 2002 as any property which constitutes or represents the benefit of criminal conduct. Criminal conduct is conduct which constitutes any offence in the UK or, subject to the limited territorial carve-out discussed below, would do so if it occurred in the UK. There is no time limit to the test, so the proceeds of criminal conduct which occurred prior to POCA 2002 coming into force are nevertheless criminal proceeds for the purposes of POCA 2002 even though, as noted above, conduct in relation to those proceeds can only constitute an offence under POCA 2002 if it occurred after POCA 2002 came into force.

Under the previous legislation, the money laundering offences were concerned only with the proceeds of serious crime, which in essence meant offences punishable in the Crown Court by at least one year of imprisonment. As noted above, however, under POCA 2002, the proceeds of any conduct which constitutes (or would constitute) a criminal offence in the UK can be the subject of laundering for the purposes of the statutory money laundering offences.

The broad scope of the definition of criminal conduct in POCA 2002 has, however, raised some difficult practical issues for firms, and particularly those in the regulated sector: will a firm risk committing a serious primary money laundering offence under POCA 2002 if it deals with another person when it knows or suspects that person has obtained a "pecuniary advantage" from criminal conduct even if the underlying "criminal conduct" concerned is merely a minor breach of health and safety or employment regulations?

Under the original wording of POCA 2002, conduct which constituted an offence in any part of the UK *or would constitute an offence in any part of the UK if it occurred there* was treated as giving rise to criminal property which could then be laundered for the purposes of POCA 2002. This test is known as the "single-criminality test" because it characterises conduct occurring outside the UK as criminal conduct without taking into account whether the conduct is an offence in the jurisdiction in which it is carried out. The peculiar result of the single-criminality test as originally drafted was that it meant conduct which was entirely lawful in the country in which it actually occurred, but which would be criminal if carried on in the UK, could amount to criminal conduct for POCA 2002 purposes.

In recognition of the problems cause by that definition, SOCPA 2005 introduced two key amendments to POCA 2002 in relation to the primary money laundering offences which took effect in 2006.

The first set of amendments specifically addressed the single-criminality issue. Defences were introduced[19] so that, subject to certain qualifications, a person charged with a primary money laundering offence who knows or believes on reasonable grounds that the relevant criminal conduct (in relation to which relevant knowledge or suspicion of money laundering has arisen) occurred outside the UK will not commit a primary money laundering offence in the UK if the relevant conduct was not, at the time it occurred, unlawful in the jurisdiction in which it occurred and was not otherwise conduct of a description prescribed for this purpose by the Government; a double-criminality override defence to the single-criminality test.

The Government then made an order, which came into force in May 2006, which prescribed for the purposes of the double-criminality override defence to the primary money laundering offences[20] conduct which would be punishable in the UK by more than one year of imprisonment[21] had the conduct occurred; but that order carved out:

- conduct which would constitute an offence under certain gaming legislation; and
- conduct which would constitute an offence under ss.23 or 25 of the Financial Services and Markets Act 2000 (FSMA

---

[19] POCA 2002 ss.327(2A), 328(3) and 329(2A)
[20] But not for the s.330 failure to disclose offence.
[21] The Proceeds of Crime Act 2002 (Money Laundering: Exceptions to Overseas Conduct Defence) Order 2006 (SI 2006/1070).

2000) (i.e. carrying on regulated activities by way of business without authorisation in breach of the general prohibition, or communicating an unlawful financial promotion).

The result is that a person will not commit a primary money laundering offence if the criminal conduct potentially giving rise to such an offence is conduct which a person knows or believes on reasonable grounds occurred overseas and which, had it occurred in the UK, would be punishable by one year or less of imprisonment or would have constituted an offence under the relevant gaming legislation or FSMA 2000 ss.23 or 25.

An equivalent defence was introduced in relation to the secondary failure to disclose an offence discussed in para.1.3.2 below, but the order described above does not apply to that defence; as a consequence, a person does not commit an offence under s.330 if he fails to make a report in relation to conduct which he knows or believes on reasonable grounds to be money laundering occurring in a jurisdiction outside the UK in which that conduct is not unlawful, regardless of the fact that the money laundering offences in the UK are punishable by substantially more than one year of imprisonment.

The second set of amendments[22] addressed limited categories of de minimis transactions which would otherwise have been caught by the primary offences. The Government introduced a de minimis carve-out from the primary money laundering offences, available only to deposit taking institutions, with the effect that a money laundering offence will not be committed by those institutions if the acts which would have given rise to the offence occur in the course of operating a customer account, and the value of the funds concerned is less than £250 (or such higher limit as may from time to time be agreed by those authorised under POCA 2002). This carve-out enables banks to permit de minimis standing orders and direct debits to continue to be drawn out of a bank account—for example, utility and other lifestyle-essential payments—without specific

---

[22] POCA 2002 ss.327(2C), 328(5), 329(2C) and 339A.

consent from the NCA, even after the bank has become suspicious of its customer and filed a suspicious activity report (SAR).

1.3.1.5 Prior consent of the NCA as a defence

If a firm or any of its officers or employees knows or suspects that a suspicious person is engaged in money laundering activities and that a particular course of conduct with which they (or their firm) are asked to become involved would or could therefore involve the commission of an offence under ss.327, 328 or 329 POCA 2002, that person may avail itself of a statutory defence by seeking the prior consent of the NCA in respect of the relevant proposed conduct. Unless there is a reasonable excuse for not doing so, the request for consent must be submitted *prior* to the relevant conduct being undertaken by the firm.

There is a distinction between:

(a) a request for consent, known in POCA 2002 as an "authorised disclosure",[23] made by a firm or any of its employees in order to trigger the defence to the offences set out in ss.327–329 POCA 2002; and

(b) an SAR, which may be filed by a regulated sector firm, or in principle by any of its employees, as required by ss.330 or 331 POCA 2002.

A request for consent is made by or on behalf of a firm which is seeking consent from the NCA to enable it to carry out a proposed course of action without committing a primary money laundering offence. A *regulated sector* firm may in addition need to submit a SAR to the NCA if the firm or any of its key officers or employees has knowledge, a suspicion, or reasonable grounds for knowledge or a suspicion, that another person is engaged in money laundering, whether or not the firm has been asked to or intends to become involved in a transaction with that person. To avoid confusion, in this

---

[23] Under POCA 2002 s.338.

chapter we differentiate between the terms "authorised disclosure" and "SAR" in accordance with these interpretations.

However, in practice the term "SAR" is commonly used interchangeably to refer to either situation. Furthermore, NCA guidance now requires both authorised disclosures and SARs in the technical sense to be submitted via an SAR.[24]

An authorised disclosure should normally be made to the NCA by a firm's Money Laundering Reporting Officer (MLRO). POCA 2002 stipulates that the NCA must respond to an authorised disclosure seven working days after the disclosure is made at the latest[25]; the response will be either to grant or refuse consent for the firm to proceed any further with the proposed course of conduct. If a firm makes an authorised disclosure and does not receive a response from the NCA within that seven working-day period, consent is deemed to have been given.[26]

When the NCA receives an authorised disclosure, it will either refer the case to a law enforcement agency for a decision to be made, or make a decision itself as to whether the proposed conduct or the suspicious person involved should be investigated further, and will then grant or refuse consent accordingly.

If the NCA refuses consent to proceed with a particular course of conduct, the enforcement authorities have 31 days (calendar rather than working days) from the date of the refusal to investigate the proposed conduct or the suspicious person and, if appropriate, take action to freeze or seize assets or take some other action.[27] Upon the expiry of that 31-day period, and in the absence of an interim restraining action, the firm which made the authorised disclosure is deemed to have received consent to proceed with the particular course of action.

---

[24] NCA UK Financial Intelligence Unit Guidance Note, *Obtaining consent from the NCA under Part 7 POCA or Part 3 Terrorism Act 2000, section 2 – The Process.*
[25] POCA 2002 s.335(5).
[26] POCA 2002 ss.335(2)–(3).
[27] POCA 2002 s.335(6).

By way of a practical example, if an MLRO reports a suspicion of money laundering to the NCA on Tuesday 1 March, the NCA has seven working days from Wednesday 2 March to respond. If, therefore, the firm has not received a response by the end of Friday 10 March, consent to proceed with a particular transaction is deemed to have been given. If consent is refused by the NCA on Thursday 3 March, for instance, law enforcement authorities have 31 calendar days from and including 3 March (that is, until 2 April) in which to investigate the proposed conduct and the suspicious person.

In September 2014, the NCA issued guidance implementing a new regime to speed up the processing of SARs. The Consent Team in the UK Financial Intelligence Unit (UKFIU) at the NCA noted a significant increase in the average turnaround time for all requests for consent, due in part to the non-inclusion of the information required. The NCA's "Suspicious Activity Reports Regime, Annual Report 2014" showed that in the year to end–September 2014, the average turnaround time for all authorised disclosures (both those dealt with only by the NCA and those referred to another law enforcement agency) was 4.3 days, up from 3.5 days the previous year.[28] Consequently, from 1 October 2014, where SARs requesting consent are submitted which are missing the reason for suspicion or fail to identify the nature of the criminal property, the case will be closed without further engagement from the UKFIU. The reporter will be sent a letter from the UKFIU explaining which parts of the information are missing and confirming that the case is closed.[29]

If an MLRO makes an authorised disclosure to the NCA as a result of having received an internal disclosure from another employee, but gives consent for the activity to proceed before receiving formal consent from the NCA, the MLRO may be guilty of a criminal offence under s.336 POCA 2002 and liable to a fine and up to five years' imprisonment. An employee who innocently carries out the (prohibited) course of conduct

---

[28] NCA, *Suspicious Activity Reports (SARs) Annual Report 2014*.
[29] NCA/UK Financial Intelligence Unit Guidance Note, *Closure of cases requesting consent* (September 2014).

having relied on that MLRO's consent, however, will maintain a defence by virtue of having made an internal disclosure to the MLRO (presumably provided that he does not have knowledge of the MLRO's offence).

The Serious Crime Act 2015 (SCA 2015) inserted a new subsection into s.338 of POCA 2002 from 1 June 2015 which confirms that "where an authorised disclosure is made in good faith, no civil liability arises in respect of the disclosure on the part of the person by or on whose behalf it is made".[30]

1.3.2 The failure to disclose offences

Section 330 POCA 2002 provides that:

" (1) A person commits an offence if each of the following three conditions is satisfied.
   (2) The first condition is that he –
     (a) knows or suspects, or
     (b) has reasonable grounds for knowing or suspecting,
    that another person is engaged in money laundering.
   (3) The second condition is that the information or other matter –
     (a) on which his knowledge or suspicion is based, or
     (b) which gives reasonable grounds for such knowledge or suspicion,
    came to him in the course of a business in the regulated sector.
  (3A) The third condition is –
     (a) that he can identify the other person mentioned in subsection (2) or the whereabouts of any of the laundered property, or
     (b) that he believes, or it is reasonable to expect him to believe, that the information or other matter mentioned in subsection (3) will or may assist in identifying that other person or the whereabouts of any of the laundered property.

---

[30] POCA 2002 s.338(4A), inserted by Serious Crime Act 2015 s.37.

(4) The fourth condition is that he does not make the required disclosure to –
(a) a nominated officer, or
(b) a person authorised for the purposes of this Part by the Director General of the National Crime Agency,
as soon as is practicable after the information or other matter mentioned in subsection (3) comes to him."

Money laundering means, for these purposes, the offences under ss.327, 328 or 329 POCA 2002.[31] The "laundered property" is the property forming the subject matter of the money laundering known, suspected, or in respect of which there are reasonable grounds for knowing or suspecting that another person has been engaged. Practitioners will be aware that the obligation to file SARs with the NCA in order to avoid committing an offence applies not only in relation to knowledge or suspicions concerning a regulated sector firm's own customers, but also any person with whom it has dealings in the course of its business in the regulated sector (e.g. including counterparties to transactions, lenders, agents, advisers to those parties and prospective customers).

The "failure to disclose" offence is something which the financial services industry in the UK became accustomed to dealing with over a period of many years in relation to terrorist financing and drug trafficking-related offences.[32] One of the key features of the s.330 failure to disclose offence, however, is that it applies not only in relation to dealings with the proceeds of serious offences, but rather to dealings with the proceeds of *all* crimes. The formal reporting obligation is, therefore, rather broader than the predecessor regimes.

The other key feature of the failure to disclose offence under POCA 2002 is that it utilises an objective test and thereby effectively criminalises negligence in the regulated sector.

---

[31] POCA 2002 s.340(11).
[32] Failure to disclose offences existed prior to POCA 2002 in the Drug Trafficking Act 1994 s.52 and ss.18 and 18A of the Prevention of Terrorism (Temporary Powers) Act 1989, subsequently replaced by s.19 and later s.21A TA 2000.

If an individual employed in the regulated sector fails to detect or suspect that a suspicious person is engaged in money laundering activities, but a court determines that objectively, in the given circumstances, he should have done so, that individual (and potentially therefore also the firm) may be guilty of a criminal offence punishable by a fine and up to five years' imprisonment. The fact that the individual was genuinely not suspicious will not be a defence if a court determines, with the benefit of hindsight, that there were circumstances which should have led him, or the firm, to be suspicious.

By virtue of s.340(11)(d), money laundering includes, for these purposes, not only conduct which constitutes a primary money laundering offence in the UK, but also conduct which would constitute such an offence if done in the UK.

As noted above, in May 2006, a double-criminality override defence was introduced in relation to the failure to disclose offence in POCA 2002 s.330(7A) in the following terms:

> "(7A) Nor does a person commit an offence under this section if –
> (a) he knows, or believes on reasonable grounds, that the money laundering is occurring in a particular country or territory outside the United Kingdom, and
> (b) the money laundering –
> (i) is not unlawful under the criminal law applying in that country or territory, and
> (ii) is not of a description prescribed in an order made by the Secretary of State."

The Government has still not prescribed any description of money laundering for the purposes of s.330(7A)(b)(ii). Consequently, a person will not commit a s.330 offence if he fails to disclose money laundering which he knows or believes on reasonable grounds to be occurring in a jurisdiction outside the UK in which that activity is not unlawful, regardless of the fact that the money laundering offences in the UK are serious offences carrying substantial penalties.

1.3.2.1 Required disclosures for employees in the regulated sector

Individuals working for regulated sector firms can discharge their disclosure obligations and thereby avoid committing an offence under s.330 by making a "required disclosure". The required disclosure will most often be an internal report to the firm's MLRO in accordance with that firm's established reporting procedures rather than a direct report (a SAR) to the NCA.

If an individual working in the regulated sector does not make a required disclosure concerning a suspicious transaction or other activity and a court determines that the individual concerned knew or suspected, or had reasonable grounds for knowing or suspecting, that the transaction or other activity involved money laundering, only two general defences are available:

(a) where the individual has a "reasonable excuse" for not making a required disclosure – the legal meaning of reasonable excuse is not clear and has not yet been tested in the courts; the prudent view must be that the term will be construed narrowly and should not be relied upon in practice, except in very special circumstances, to determine whether a disclosure should be made; or

(b) where the individual has not been provided with suitable training by his employer and did not have actual knowledge or suspicion of money laundering. (Under the 2007 Regulations, employers are required to provide their employees with adequate training on how to identify potential money laundering and on their legal duties and liabilities under, inter alia, POCA 2002).[33]

The latter defence emphasises the obligation for senior management under the 2007 Regulations to ensure that staff are properly trained.

If an individual is thought to have committed a s.330 offence but can successfully demonstrate that the firm has failed to

---

[33] See Ch.4.

provide adequate training, the inevitable conclusion to be drawn is that senior management, either individually or collectively, are responsible for that regulatory failure (although not necessarily for the commission of a primary statutory offence). Under the 2007 Regulations, any director or other senior officer who has contributed to the firm's failure to comply with training requirements may be liable to prosecution and, on conviction, to up to two years' imprisonment.[34]

Lawyers and certain other "relevant professional advisers" are not required to make a disclosure to the NCA if the information or other matter on which their knowledge or suspicion of money laundering is based, or which gives reasonable grounds for knowledge or suspicion, came to them in privileged circumstances.[35] Originally, this defence was available only to lawyers, but following representations made to the Treasury by accountants (through the Institute of Chartered Accountants in England and Wales) and other professional bodies the defence was extended to accountants, auditors and tax advisers who are members of certain professional bodies.

1.3.2.2 The MLRO offence

In addition to the general failure to disclose offence under s.330, if an employee makes an internal report in accordance with that firm's reporting procedures, the firm's MLRO may commit a separate failure to disclose offence if he then fails to deliver a SAR to the NCA.

Section 331 provides that:

> "(1) A person nominated to receive disclosures under Section 330 commits an offence if the conditions in subsections (2) to (4) are satisfied.
> (2) The first condition is that he –
> (a) knows or suspects, or
> (b) has reasonable grounds for knowing or suspecting,

---

[34] Money Laundering Regulations 2007 (SI 2007/2157) regs 21, 45 and 47.
[35] POCA 2002 s. 330(6)(b) and (10).

that another person is engaged in money laundering.

(3) The second condition is that the information or other matter –

(a) on which his knowledge or suspicion is based, or

(b) which gives reasonable grounds for such knowledge or suspicion,

came to him in consequence of a disclosure made under Section 330.

(3A) The third condition is –

(a) that he knows the identity of the other person mentioned in subsection (2), or the whereabouts of any of the laundered property, in consequence of a disclosure made under Section 330,

(b) that that other person, or the whereabouts of any laundered property, can be identified from the information or other matter mentioned in subsection (3), or

(c) that he believes, or it is reasonable to expect him to believe, that the information or other matter will or may assist in identifying that other person or the whereabouts of any of the laundered property.

(4) The fourth condition is that he does not make the required disclosure to a person authorised for the purposes of this Part by the Director General of the National Crime Agency as soon as is practicable after the information or other matter mentioned in subsection (3) comes to him."

If an employee makes a required disclosure report to the MLRO in accordance with the firm's reporting procedures, and the MLRO then fails to disclose that information to the NCA after having determined (or negligently failed to determine) that it was a justified report, he may have committed an offence unless he had a "reasonable excuse".

The MLRO failure to disclose offence is punishable by a fine and up to five years' imprisonment

1.3.2.3   Limited value SARs

In July 2005, the Government amended s.330 with the specific aim of "easing the money laundering reporting requirements on the regulated sector".[36]

The introduction of subsection (3A) to s.330 has narrowed the scope of the failure to disclose offence by requiring a person working in the regulated sector to make a required disclosure or file a SAR with SOCA *only* if either the identity of the person committing the money laundering, or the whereabouts of the laundered property, can be identified, or it is reasonable to believe that the information which the person possesses would enable such matters to be established.

The practical effect of this amendment is that if a person working in the regulated sector becomes aware that another person has committed an offence, but is not in a position either to identify the offender or to know where the proceeds of the criminal conduct could be found, it may not be necessary to make a required disclosure or file a SAR.

A similar qualification applies in relation to the MLRO failure to disclose offence under s.331.

This qualification is particularly relevant if the underlying offence is a remote or anonymous offence such as credit card fraud, where the financial institutions involved in detecting the offence have a limited (if any) ability to interact with or identify the offender.

The amendment provided some relief for firms which might otherwise have needed to file "limited intelligence value" SARs with SOCA, but it is critical to note that the (objective) second limb to subsection 3A somewhat diluted the effect of the new subsection. The possibility that a court could determine after the fact that a subjective assessment of the relevance of particular information was wrong means that individual employees may not wish to make (and perhaps

---

[36] Explanatory notes to SOCPA 2005.

should be encouraged not to make) an assessment of whether a required disclosure is in fact required; it is probably best reserved for the MLRO to make that assessment in light of any other information of which the firm is aware which might have a bearing on a decision to file a SAR.

It is one thing for an MLRO to conclude that, on the basis of all of the information available to the MLRO (and therefore the firm), it is not reasonable to believe that information will or may assist in identifying a person or laundered property; there would be a risk to the firm involved, however, if the internal reporting policy permitted individual employees to make that assessment. Firms may not therefore wish to emphasise this element of the offence in the context of internal training sessions and reporting procedures.

Ultimately the consequences of being second-guessed by an investigatory authority or a court in relation to the relative value of the information possessed by a firm may outweigh the relatively minor administrative inconvenience for an MLRO in filing a SAR.

The NCA phased out SOCA's legacy "limited intelligence value" reporting form and associated guidance.

1.3.2.4 Relevance of guidance

Section 330(8) of POCA 2002 provides that:

> "(8) In deciding whether a person committed [a failure to disclose offence] the court must consider whether he followed any relevant guidance which was at the time concerned –
> (a) issued by a supervisory authority or any other appropriate body,
> (b) approved by the Treasury, and
> (c) published in a manner it approved as appropriate in its opinion to bring the guidance to the attention of persons likely to be affected by it."

The effect of this provision is that certain pieces of industry guidance may be given statutory recognition by the Treasury so that firms which are subject to the UK AML regime, regulated sector firms in particular, are provided a degree of comfort that compliance with widely recognised industry standards should, in general, be viewed positively by the courts (and consequently also by relevant supervisory authorities). Section 330(8) does not, however, go as far as to establish a safe harbour for firms complying with approved guidance.

In May 2013, HM Treasury published an updated list of approved guidance (the Approved Guidance), which now includes:

- Guidance for the UK Financial Sector produced by the Joint Money Laundering Steering Group (the JMLSG Guidance). The JMLSG Guidance, which is set out in three parts, is regularly reviewed and updated. The most recent revisions to Pts I and II in November 2014 are awaiting formal approval from HM Treasury; and
- AML guidance from HMRC (the HMRC Guidance), including advice for high value dealers, trust or company service providers, currency exchange offices, money transmission businesses and cheque encashment businesses.

Different sector-specific guidance publications for accountants, tax practitioners, legal professionals and the property sector have also been approved, alongside a guidance note from the Gambling Commission aimed at casinos.

Guidance contained in the FCA's *Senior Management Arrangements, Systems and Controls Sourcebook* which applies to FCA-authorised firms (addressed in more detail in Ch.6) does not constitute relevant guidance for the purpose of s.330(8), although it is, of course, relevant to those authorised firms in a more general sense.

The Approved Guidance, and in particular the JMLSG Guidance and HMRC Guidance, probably has greater relevance in the context of compliance with the 2007 Regulations (which deal more with procedural AML requirements) than with POCA 2002; they contain a great deal of helpful information, both generic and sector-specific, in relation to the customer identification and verification processes requirements in the 2007 Regulations.

Nevertheless, the guidance also sets out practical tips for firms on the circumstances in which transactions may (or ought to) attract suspicion for the purposes of POCA 2002, to assist regulated sector firms in particular in their assessment of the more onerous objective test for the s.330 offence.

Whilst the Approved Guidance has no legal force per se, evidentially it has become important as a result of s.330(8) POCA 2002 and equivalent provisions in TA 2000 and the 2007 Regulations.[37] Regulated sector firms should therefore be aware of the best practice standards which are set out in the Approved Guidance and, where appropriate, use them as a benchmark against which to measure the firm's compliance.

If a firm finds itself in the position of having failed to detect or disclose potential money laundering activities, it will doubtless find itself in a more comfortable position if it can demonstrate that it has in place systems and controls to detect and prevent money laundering which meet or exceed the standards suggested by the Approved Guidance, notwithstanding that potential money laundering may nevertheless have passed undetected or undisclosed.

1.3.3 The tipping-off offences

The tipping-off offences in POCA 2002 were substantially revised in December 2007 (along with certain aspects of TA 2000 which are addressed in the following sections) in order to give effect to certain of the requirements of the Third Directive.[38]

---

[37] TA 2000 s.21A(6) and Regulation 45(2) of the 2007 Regulations.
[38] By the Terrorism Act 2000 and Proceeds of Crime Act 2002 (Amendment) Regulations 2007 (SI 2007/3398).

Section 333A applies only to the regulated sector and provides that:

"(1) A person commits an offence if –
    (a) the person discloses any matter within subsection (2),
    (b) the disclosure is likely to prejudice any investigation that might be conducted following the disclosure referred to in that subsection, and
    (c) the information on which the disclosure is based came to the person in the course of a business in the regulated sector.

(2) The matters are that the person or another person has made a disclosure under this Part –
    (a) to a constable,
    (b) to an officer of Revenue and Customs,
    (c) to a nominated officer, or
    (d) to a National Crime Agency officer authorised for the purposes of this Part by the Director General of that Agency,
of information that came to that person in the course of a business in the regulated sector.

(3) A person commits an offence if –
    (a) the person discloses that an investigation into allegations that an offence under this Part has been committed is being contemplated or is being carried out,
    (b) the disclosure is likely to prejudice that investigation, and
    (c) the information on which the disclosure is based came to the person in the course of a business in the regulated sector."

Each of the two offences described above carry a penalty of a fine and up to two years' imprisonment.[39]

Effectively, therefore, POCA 2002 contains two separate tipping-off offences for persons carrying on business in the regulated sector: tipping-off in relation to reports of suspicion,

---

[39] POCA 2002 s.333A(4).

and prejudicing an investigation. The first offence involves disclosing that a report has been made either internally (to an MLRO) or externally to the NCA or another relevant authority. The second offence involves disclosing that an investigation is being contemplated or is being carried out.

While there may be some scope for overlap between these two offences, there are also some significant differences between them and, accordingly, it is necessary for all those working in the regulated sector to be aware of the conditions precedent to each. The first offence requires that an internal report of suspicion to an MLRO, or an external SAR or authorised disclosure has been filed; the second offence requires that an investigation into an alleged money laundering offence under POCA is being carried out or is contemplated (note that the investigation must relate to an offence under POCA 2002 and not to the underlying criminal conduct, although in practice it may not be easy to make a clear distinction).

In either case, however, an offence will only be committed if the disclosure of information by the firm or individual in the regulated sector *is likely to prejudice* any investigation which may ensue, is being contemplated, or is being carried out.

In circumstances where an individual employed by a regulated sector firm has suspicions about a particular person or activity, it can be difficult to determine how best to deal with that suspicion in practice. To avoid committing a criminal offence under s.330, the individual must make an internal report to his firm's MLRO. The MLRO must then determine whether a SAR needs to be filed with the NCA or, if the firm is asked to engage in activities which would involve it dealing with the suspicious person, whether an authorised disclosure needs to be submitted to the NCA and consent obtained before proceeding.

If the MLRO seeks a consent from the NCA, the firm and individuals involved could potentially commit an offence under any of ss.327, 328 or 329 POCA 2002 if the firm then engages in any further activity with the suspicious person. At the same time, however, the firm will be concerned to ensure that a tipping-off offence is not committed by either expressly or impliedly confirming to the customer that the firm cannot proceed with a requested transaction, or must wait before engaging in certain activities, because a request for consent has been submitted.

Failing to follow a customer's instructions in relation to a transaction while a report is processed may alert that customer to the fact that the firm has become suspicious of the customer's activities. Could the fact that the customer could draw his own conclusion that the firm had submitted an authorised disclosure and was waiting for consent to proceed as a result of the firm refusing to complete a requested transaction (or seeking to delay completion without giving the customer a clear explanation) amount to tipping-off? This seems unlikely; the offence requires that a person *discloses* relevant information, indicating that an *active* disclosure is contemplated.

In any event, ss.333D(3) and (4) go further by confirming that a person will not commit an offence under s.333A if he did not know or suspect that the disclosure would *be likely to prejudice* an investigation. In other words, it is not sufficient that a firm or individual simply disclosed relevant information to another person: a prosecuting authority would need also to demonstrate that the firm or individual knew or suspected that making that disclosure would be likely to prejudice any subsequent (or ongoing) investigation. The offence seemingly therefore requires the person or firm concerned to know or suspect that there is an investigation, or the possibility of an investigation, and to have an intention to prejudice, or at least a reckless disregard as to whether prejudice would follow.

In the absence of evidence that a firm or individual officer or employee sought tacitly to confirm the understanding of a suspicious person that a relevant disclosure had been made, or an investigation commenced, it seems unlikely that either offence would be committed if there is no active communication of those matters. Perhaps more importantly, however, unless it can be shown that the firm or individual knew or suspected that the disclosure would be likely to prejudice an investigation, the offence should not arise. Section 333A does not therefore prohibit any communication between a firm and its customer once an authorised disclosure has been submitted to the NCA. When considered in this light, the tipping-off offences are, perhaps, not quite as substantial a bear-trap as some firms have in the past feared.

It is possible, though, that more difficult situations may arise from time to time and so one must continue to tread carefully. If a firm of auditors forms a suspicion in the course of an audit that its client may have been involved in money laundering, that firm may be required to cease acting for its client and to provide a full and clear explanation to its client; auditors are required to explain their reasons if they cease to act for a client.[40] Would any such explanation amount to tipping-off? It seems at least possible that it could.

It is likely that in some situations, refraining from dealing with a suspicious person will prompt questions which could put the firm at risk of being forced into making a statement of some nature, thereby risking an active tipping-off "disclosure". That will be more likely if the suspicious person concerned is a customer or client of the firm. Banks in particular have found it difficult to reconcile the tensions inherent in POCA 2002 between the failure to disclose offence and the tipping-off offences.

In its February 2015 guidance,[41] the NCA states that it does not provide or approve standard wording for firms to use in circumstances that may amount to tipping-off. Firms are instead advised by the NCA to discuss an appropriate approach with its relevant supervisor or professional body. The courts have also been required to consider the difficulties faced by firms in the regulated sector in this context and have sought to provide some comfort (in relation to which see the commentary in the following section).

---

[40] Companies Act 2006 ss.517 and 519.
[41] NCA/UK Financial Intelligence Unit Guidance Note, *Submitting A Suspicious Activity Report (SAR) within the Regulated Sector* (February 2015).

In practice, it seems unlikely that a prosecuting authority would pursue a firm for tipping-off if it had complied in all respects with its disclosure obligations under POCA 2002, had taken no active steps to tip off the suspicious person in question and had followed any instructions from a relevant professional body after making its disclosure.

There are also limited safe harbours from the tipping-off offences in the form of "permitted disclosures", the scope of which are set out in ss.333B–333E. The permitted disclosures regime carves out from the s.333A offences, inter alia, the following disclosures:

- a disclosure of relevant information between employees or officers within the same undertaking[42];
- a disclosure by a credit or financial institution[43] to another credit or financial institution in the same consolidated group which is subject to the Third Directive or equivalent requirements[44];
- a disclosure between two credit institutions, between two financial institutions, between two professional legal advisers or between two firms of accountants of relevant information relating to a client or former client of both firms, a transaction involving both firms or the provision of a service by both firms, in each case in order to prevent a money laundering offence being committed under POCA 2002 and provided that the recipient of the disclosure is subject to the Third Directive or equivalent requirements and that both firms are subject to the Data Protection Act 1998 or equivalent duties of professional confidentiality and protection of personal data[45]; and

---

[42] POCA 2002 s.333B(1).
[43] The terms "credit institution" and "financial institution" are defined in POCA 2002 s.333E(2) by reference to the regulated sector as described in Sch.9 POCA 2002.
[44] POCA 2002 s.333B(2).
[45] POCA 2002 s.333C.

- a disclosure of relevant information by a professional legal adviser or other professional adviser (including accountants) to a client in order to dissuade the client from engaging in conduct which would amount to an offence.[46]

In addition to the tipping-off offences for the regulated sector, a general offence of prejudicing an investigation remains relevant for non-regulated sector firms. Section 342 provides that:

> "(1) This section applies if a person knows or suspects that an appropriate officer or (in Scotland) a proper person is acting (or proposing to act) in connection with a confiscation investigation, a civil recovery investigation, a detained cash investigation or a money laundering investigation which is being or is about to be conducted.
> (2) The person commits an offence if –
> (a) he makes a disclosure which is likely to prejudice the investigation,
> (b) he falsifies, conceals, destroys or otherwise disposes of, or causes or permits the falsification, concealment, destruction or disposal of, documents which are relevant to the investigation."

The s.342 offence may only be committed by non-regulated sector firms, and applies in slightly narrower, although nevertheless egregious, circumstances than the s.333A offences (namely making a disclosure which prejudices an investigation which is known or suspected to be underway or about to be commenced, or falsifying or destroying documents which are relevant to an investigation), but remains a serious money laundering offence punishable by a fine and up to five years' imprisonment.

Section 342(3)(a) provides that a person does not commit the offence if he does not know or suspect that a relevant disclosure is likely to prejudice an investigation. The s.342 offence therefore again requires an intention to prejudice, or at

---

[46] POCA 2002 s.333D(2).

least show reckless disregard, as to whether prejudice will follow from a relevant disclosure.

1.3.4   Practical issues associated with the consent regime

As previously discussed, where a regulated sector firm or any of its employees knows or suspects that a suspicious person is engaged in money laundering activities and that a particular course of conduct with which they are asked to become involved would or could involve the commission of an offence under any of ss.327, 328 or 329 POCA 2002, that firm should make an authorised disclosure to the NCA in order to avoid committing that offence.

The firm is then required to allow up to seven working days for the NCA to respond to the request for consent, refusing consent or declaring that a 31-day moratorium period (during which the firm may not engage in any activity with the suspicious person) has commenced. This process, known as the consent regime, has come under close scrutiny since POCA 2002 was enacted due to the difficulties that it causes for firms, particularly in relation to the tipping-off offences.

The key issue that has been raised by firms in respect of the consent regime is the difficulty in suspending all activity in relation to a particular customer for the period between the making of an authorised disclosure and the time at which consent to proceed is granted by the NCA. During such periods of suspension it is not uncommon for the firm to have to deal with difficult questions as to why a transaction has not proceeded in accordance with instructions; in some cases customers of firms which have sought consent and in effect frozen customer accounts in the meantime have begun legal proceedings to force the firm to process the transactions.

In these circumstances, firms find themselves in a difficult position. Explaining to a customer that a transaction cannot be processed due to the firm's suspicion of money laundering and consequent disclosure to the NCA could in some circumstances amount to a "tipping-off" offence (if the firm considers that any subsequent investigation is likely to be prejudiced as a result). On the other hand, offering no explanation as to why a transaction or payment instruction is being delayed could damage relationships and reputations and, potentially, give rise to contractual or tortious liabilities for the firm.

1.3.4.1 Judicial guidance

The courts have been asked to consider such circumstances and, accordingly, we now have some useful judicial commentary on the appropriate way to address that particular difficulty.

In *Squirrell Ltd v National Westminster Bank plc*,[47] the customer, Squirrell, had brought legal proceedings against NatWest to force it to process a transaction. NatWest, suspecting that monies received by Squirrell could be criminal property, had made an authorised disclosure in respect of the customer and had therefore concluded that it was unable to process the transaction. NatWest had blocked Squirrell's account without providing an explanation to Squirrell. Squirrell made an application to the court requesting that its account be unblocked and for the bank to give reasons as to why it had been blocked.

The High Court dismissed Squirrell's application on the grounds that the test under POCA 2002 required NatWest to cease processing transactions and make a disclosure as soon as it had a suspicion of money laundering. There did not need to be any actual evidence of money laundering for that suspicion to arise. Accordingly, the course of action taken by NatWest was "unimpeachable", as it had done what was required of it by legislation.

The court had sympathy for customers in Squirrell's position in respect of whom no evidence of criminal conduct had been provided, whose business had possibly suffered serious detriment as a result of the account having been frozen, but

---

[47] *Squirrell Ltd v National Westminster Bank Plc* [2005] EWHC 664 (Ch); [2006] 1 W.L.R. 637.

who could not expect to receive damages from the bank or the authorities. Despite its sympathy, however, on the basis that Parliament had clearly laid out in POCA 2002 the mechanism to deal with the issue of consent, the court held that it was powerless to intervene for Squirrell.

The *Squirrell* case also highlighted the importance of liaising at an early stage with the NCA. Once the application to the court had been made by Squirrell, NatWest found itself in the difficult position of not being able to offer a defence to the court for fear of committing the offence of tipping-off. This dilemma was resolved by the intervention of HM Customs and Excise (now part of HMRC) which enabled the court to be informed of the reasons for NatWest's refusal to operate Squirrell's account.

Similar circumstances were considered by the Court of Appeal in *K Ltd v National Westminster Bank plc*.[48] In that case the customer, K, wished to process two large business transactions through its account with NatWest, and a director of K gave pre-warning of these transactions to the account manager at NatWest. At the time of the second transaction, however, NatWest suspected that the monies could amount to criminal proceeds and, accordingly, refused to process the transaction and filed a SAR in relation to K. NatWest then wrote to K, informing it that it could not process the transaction, but without offering any reason.

K made an application to the court for a mandatory injunction to force NatWest to comply with its instructions. At first instance K's application was rejected and K appealed to the Court of Appeal arguing, inter alia, that by refusing to process its instructions, NatWest was in breach of its mandate and, accordingly, that the judge should have restrained the bank from continuing to act in breach of contract.

The Court of Appeal agreed with the decision in *Squirrell* that Parliament had struck a "precise and workable balance of

---

[48] *K Ltd v National Westminster Bank Plc* [2006] EWCA Civ 1039; [2007] 1 W.L.R. 311; [2007] Bus. L.R. 26.

conflicting interests" in POCA 2002 by considering that a limited amount of interference was to be tolerated in preference to allowing money laundering to be carried on in the commercial community. The court ruled that NatWest had followed the correct procedure laid out in POCA 2002 by refusing to carry out the transaction, and that as the bank held a suspicion, it was prohibited as a matter of criminal law from carrying out the customer's mandate. Accordingly, the mandate with K had been temporarily suspended until the illegality was removed and so NatWest could not be held by the court to be in breach of contract.

Similar issues were again considered in *Shah v HSBC Private Bank UK Ltd*,[49] where the reasoning above was maintained. On four occasions over a seven-month period, Mr Shah instructed HSBC to transfer monies, totalling more than US $28 million, from his account. HSBC suspected that the funds were criminal property and filed a SAR with SOCA on each occasion, causing delays. Although HSBC made the transfers once permission had been granted, Mr Shah claimed that the delays had caused suspicion resulting in the seizure of his assets and the loss of over US $330 million. He claimed that HSBC was in breach of contract by failing to process his payment instructions promptly and in failing to explain the delays. He argued that he should have been given the primary facts leading HSBC to contact SOCA, and SOCA's reference numbers.

The court held that in circumstances where a bank suspects money laundering, an implied term in the bank-customer contract permitted it to refuse to execute a payment instruction pending permission from the relevant authority under POCA 2002. Moreover, the bank was not obliged to provide its customer with details of its disclosure to SOCA/the NCA. Moreover, if the provision of that information might amount to a "tipping-off" offence, the bank was obliged to refuse to provide it.

---

[49] *Shah v HSBC Private Bank (UK) Ltd* [2012] EWHC 1283 (QB); [2013] Bus. L.R. D38.

More controversially, an earlier Court of Appeal judgment in the same case[50] has opened up the possibility of challenges to the validity of suspicions triggering the filing of a SAR. The Court of Appeal's decision suggests that a person who is the subject of a SAR is entitled to require the basis of the suspicion that gave rise to the SAR to be disclosed in court and the nature of the suspicion itself then to be investigated and established.

The threshhold for suspicion is unchanged: "more than fanciful"[51] but falling short of "reasonable grounds".[52] However, a failure to establish an appropriate suspicion when subject to legal challenge opens up the possibility of damages being sought by a SAR subject for losses suffered as a result of a "wrongful suspicion" having prompted the SAR.

The courts have clearly recognised the difficulties for a firm that risks committing a criminal offence if, having identified a suspicion of money laundering, it does not freeze relevant accounts or transactions and file a SAR. A practical consequence is that any adversely affected person may then apply to court for assistance or to enforce contractual rights, but encouragingly, the courts have consistently shown that they will not assist or otherwise require the firm concerned to perform specific actions if to do so would be to require the firm to commit the criminal offence which it seeks to avoid. That said, the Court of Appeal has at least indicated that it may not be enough for a firm simply to assert that it had a suspicion to avail itself of the court's protection; the existence of a genuine suspicion may be tested by the court.

Thus, when assessing the legal risks around SAR reporting, firms are now arguably required to weigh the relative risks of the possibility of prosecution for failure to report a suspicion on the one hand against a claim for damages for breach of contract stemming from a wrongful suspicion on the other. In general, though, it must be right that firms should file rather

---

[50] *Shah v HSBC Private Bank (UK) Ltd* [2010] EWCA Civ 31; [2010] Bus. L.R. 1514.

[51] *R. v Da Silva (Hilda Gondwe)* [2006] EWCA Crim 1654; [2007] 1 W.L.R. 303; [2006] 2 Cr. App. R. 35 (p.517).

[52] *K Ltd v National Westminster Bank Plc* [2006] EWCA Civ 1039. See also JMLSG Guidance paras 6.11–6.14.

than not file whenever there is a genuine suspicion, and thus prioritise their obligations under POCA 2002 (and TA 2000) over contractual obligations and other duties owed to customers and counterparties.

1.3.4.2   Reform of the consent regime

A Home Office consultation in 2007[53] proposed three options for developing the POCA consent regime, namely:

- *Build on the current regime*—that is, keeping the regime much as it currently stands, but with more official guidance on acceptable behaviour in relation to the tipping-off risk, fungibility etc.
- *Twin track approach*—this would give firms the option of either freezing a transaction and asking for consent as in the current regime or alternatively, avoiding liability by making a pre-event notification to the relevant agency of their suspicion that an offence may be committed in the future (e.g. where a transaction is contemplated but not yet completed) and then proceeding with the transaction unless restrained.
- Addressing the issue of fungibility (i.e. the fact that a bank account contains indistinguishable mixed funds) through specific statutory amendments—this option was intended as a supplement to either of the first two options. It would clarify that obtaining consent in relation to an initial suspicious transaction would cover any subsequent so-called "technical" offences (i.e., those involving funds thought to have been tainted by the original suspicious transaction) so that there would be no need to separately report each such suspicion.

The consultation closed in March 2008. SOCA, *Suspicious Activity Reports Regime Annual Report 2008*, published on 20 November 2008, subsequently confirmed that following a consideration of responses to the consultation, the Home Office and SOCA had reached the conclusion that the responses

---

[53] Home Office consultation document, *Obligations to Report Money Laundering: the Consent Regime*, December 2008.

demonstrated that there was "no clear way forward on this issue as regards to further amendments to the current legislation".

On 28 August 2015, the Government published a call for evidence on the effectiveness of rules designed to prevent money laundering and terrorist financing as part of its Cutting Red Tape review. The consent regime may be revisited as part of the output of that review.

1.4 The Terrorism Act 2000

With effect from 19 February 2001, the majority of the UK's anti-terrorism legislation was repealed and replaced by TA 2000. Among other things, it criminalises the financing and supporting of terrorists and terrorism through a number of offences, which for convenience are collectively described here as the terrorist finance offences. The offences under TA 2000 mirror to a large extent the money laundering offences under POCA 2002.

The terrorist finance offences, each punishable by a maximum of 14 years' imprisonment and/or a fine, are:

(a) fund-raising, receiving or providing money or other property knowing or having reasonable cause to suspect that it will or may be used for the purposes of terrorism;

(b) using or possessing money or other property knowing or having reasonable cause to suspect that it will or may be used for the purposes of terrorism; or

(c) entering into or becoming concerned in an arrangement as a result of which money or other property is made available to another while having reasonable cause to suspect that it will or may be used for the purposes of terrorism.

A separate terrorist money laundering offence is committed by a person who enters into or becomes concerned in an arrangement which facilitates the retention or control of

terrorist property by concealment, removal from the jurisdiction, transfer to nominees or in any other way.

In addition to these offences, TA 2000 also contains failure to
disclose and tipping-off offences on equivalent terms to the
offences under POCA 2002 ss.330, 333A and 342.

1.4.1 The terrorist finance offences

As with the principal POCA 2002 offences, if a firm knowingly
engages in business with, or otherwise intentionally assists, a
suspected terrorist or terrorist fundraising organisation, it
could in principle commit one of the three principal terrorist
finance offences – fundraising, terrorist treasury or assistance
to terrorists – as a principal offender.

Additionally, in contrast to the primary POCA 2002 offences
which, as discussed above, require an element of subjective
intent (i.e., conducting business with knowledge or suspicion
of money laundering), TA 2000 applies a second limb objective
test to the terrorist finance offences, so that a person may also
commit one of the three principal terrorist finance offences by
negligently engaging in business with or assisting a suspected
terrorist money launderer.

Specifically, TA 2000 s.15—the fundraising offence—provides
that:

> "(1) A person commits an offence if he –
>   (a) invites another to provide money or other prop-
>   erty, and
>   (b) intends that it should be used, or has reasonable
>   cause to suspect that it may be used, for the
>   purposes of terrorism.
> (2) A person commits an offence if he –
>   (a) receives money or other property, and
>   (b) intends that it should be used, or has reasonable
>   cause to suspect that it may be used, for the
>   purposes of terrorism.
> (3) A person commits an offence if he–

(a) provides money or other property, and
(b) knows or has reasonable cause to suspect that it will or may be used for the purposes of terrorism."

Section 16 of TA 2000—the terrorist treasurer's offence—provides that:

"(1) A person commits an offence if he uses money or other property for the purposes of terrorism.
(2) A person commits an offence if he–
    (a) possesses money or other property, and
    (b) intends that it should be used, or has reasonable cause to suspect that it may be used, for the purposes of terrorism."

Section 17 of TA 2000—the assistance offence—provides that:

"A person commits an offence if–

(a) he enters into or becomes concerned in an arrangement as a result of which money or other property is made available or is to be made available to another, and
(b) he knows or has reasonable cause to suspect that it will or may be used for the purposes of terrorism."

In each case, the alleged offender must at least know (intent) or have reasonable cause (negligence) to suspect that money or other property will be used for the purposes of terrorism.

Terrorism means, for these purposes, the use or threat of serious violence or other specified action to persons or property which is designed to influence a government or an international governmental organisation or to intimidate a section of the public for the purpose of advancing a political, religious, racial or ideological cause.[54] There is no jurisdictional

---

[54] TA 2000 s.1(1) and (2), as amended by TA 2006 s.34 and CTA 2008 s.75(2)(a).

limit to "terrorism" so that the terrorist finance offences may be committed in relation to entirely non-UK terrorist activities.[55]

In addition, pursuant to s.63, if a person does anything outside the UK which would have constituted the commission of an offence under any of ss.15 to 17 if it had been done in the UK, he will be treated as having committed that offence (in the UK). There is no double-criminality override in relation to TA 2000, as there is in relation to POCA 2002 offences.

The Counter-Terrorism and Security Act 2015[56] (CTSA 2015) inserted a new offence under s.17A of TA 2000, making it illegal for reinsurers or insurers to reimburse ransom payments made to terrorists (whether in relation to terrorist demands inside or outside the UK). It does not prohibit reimbursement payments in respect of non-terrorism related criminality, where there is no reasonable cause to suspect terrorist activity at the time the reimbursement payment is made.

An offence under each of ss.15, 16, 17 or 17A is punishable by a fine and up to 14 years' imprisonment.

1.4.1.1   *The terrorist money laundering offence*

The terrorist money laundering offence is essentially the fourth terrorist finance offence, although in one sense it sits apart from ss.15 to 17A because it is a strict liability offence. Section 18 provides that:

> "(1) A person commits an offence if he enters into or becomes concerned in an arrangement which facilitates the retention or control by or on behalf of another person of terrorist property–
> (a) by concealment,
> (b) by removal from the jurisdiction,
> (c) by transfer to nominees, or
> (d) in any other way.

---

[55] TA 2000 s.1(4).
[56] CTSA 2015 s.42(1) with effect from 12 February 2015.

(2) It is a defence for a person charged with an offence under subsection (1) to prove that he did not know and had no reasonable cause to suspect that the arrangement related to terrorist property."

An offence under s.18 is punishable by a fine and up to 14 years' imprisonment.

Terrorist property means money or other property which is likely to be used for the purposes of terrorism, the proceeds of acts of terrorism and the proceeds of acts carried out for the purposes of terrorism.[57]

Again, pursuant to s.63, if a person does anything outside the UK which would have constituted the commission of an offence under s.18 if it had been done in the UK, he will be treated as having committed that offence (in the UK).

The terrorist money laundering offence can be described as a strict liability offence because it can be committed without establishing intention or suspicion of a terrorist purpose on the part of the alleged offender. The reason it is not a strict liability offence in practice, however, is the existence of the specific defence in subsection (2) that a person may show that he did not know and had no reasonable cause to suspect that the arrangement in question related to terrorist property. The end result may appear to be the same for this offence as for the ss.15–17 offences —if there is no intention or suspicion, there is no offence—but in practice the burden of proof is reversed. A firm or individual MLRO charged with a s.18 offence must establish the defence in order to defend the charge, whereas the prosecuting authorities must establish intention or reasonable cause for suspicion before they can charge for a s.15, 16 or 17A offence.

As with the principal POCA 2002 offences, most firms may rightly consider the possibility of being charged with a principal terrorist finance offence to be remote in the absence of some degree of intention or recklessness on the part of their

---

[57] TA 2000 s.14.

employees. However, firms and their employees clearly need to be familiar with the nature and extent of all the terrorist finance and money laundering offences so that they are in a position to avoid being reckless as regards those offences and to identify potentially disclosable offences for the purposes of the regulated sector failure to disclose offence under TA 2000, discussed at para.1.4.2 below.

The 2007 Regulations impose a general requirement on firms to take appropriate measures to ensure that all relevant staff are "made aware of the law relating to ... terrorist financing", which is defined to include all of the offences under ss.15 to 18.[58]

1.4.1.2 Co-operation with the police and the NCA (the TA 2000 consent regime)

If a firm or an individual officer or employee of the firm knows or suspects that a suspicious person is engaged in terrorist activities, but nevertheless engages in activity with that suspicious person, that firm and the individuals involved may commit one of the terrorist finance offences if there is knowledge or reasonable cause to suspect that money or other property will as a result be used or made available for the purposes of terrorism.

The "authorised disclosure" regime discussed at para.1.3.1 above in relation to the principal POCA 2002 offences is broadly reflected in TA 2000 ss.21, 21ZA and 21ZB.

Pursuant to s.21(1), a person does not commit a terrorist finance offence, or the terrorist money laundering offence, if he acted with the express consent of *a constable*[59] (which in this case means the police rather than the NCA, although the constable is then required to notify the disclosure under this section to the NCA).[60]

---

[58] Money Laundering Regulations 2007 (SI 2007/2157) reg.21.
[59] TA 2000 s.21(1).
[60] TA 2000 s.21C.

Pursuant to ss.21(2) and 21ZB (introduced into TA 2000 in December 2007),[61] a person does not commit a terrorist finance offence, or the terrorist money laundering offence, if he disclosed to *a constable or SOCA*, on his own initiative and as soon as reasonably practicable *after having become involved* in a transaction or arrangement (and in relation to a disclosure to the NCA under s.21ZB, there is a reasonable excuse for having failed to make a disclosure prior to becoming involved), his suspicion or belief that money or other property involved in that transaction or arrangement is terrorist property, and he did not subsequently act contrary to the instructions of the constable or the NCA.[62]

It is also a defence to any those offences[63] for a person to prove that he intended to make such a disclosure and there is a reasonable excuse for his failure to do so.[64]

Under s.21ZA, also introduced into TA 2000 in December 2007, a person does not commit a terrorist finance offence, or the terrorist money laundering offence, if *before becoming involved* in any transaction or arrangement, he discloses to *the NCA* his suspicion or belief that money or other property involved in that transaction is terrorist property and the information on which that suspicion or belief is based and he obtains consent to become involved in the transaction or arrangement con-cerned.

There are no prescribed time limits within which a constable may be required to give "express consent" for the purposes of s.21(1), but the NCA has seven working days after the day on which a disclosure is made to it under s.21ZA in which to deny that consent, after which the person making the disclosure is entitled to construe consent as having been given.[65]

---

[61] By Terrorism Act 2000 and Proceeds of Crime Act 2002 (Amendment) Regulations (SI 2007/3398).

[62] TA 2000 s.21(2)–(4) and s.21ZB(3).

[63] Though not for the offence under s.15(1) of inviting another person to provide money or other property and intending or having reasonable cause to suspect that it may be used for the purposes of terrorism.

[64] TA 2000 ss.21(5) and 21ZC.

[65] TA 2000 s.21ZA(2)–(4).

These disclosures and consent requests are equivalent to "authorised disclosures" under POCA 2002, and can be distinguished from the SARs regime which arises by virtue of the failure to disclose offences.

1.4.2 The failure to disclose offences

The TA 2000 contains two failure to disclose offences. The first, set out in s.19, applies to businesses other than regulated sector firms and uses a basic subjective test, that is, does the person concerned believe or suspect that another person has committed a terrorist finance or money laundering offence? An offence under this section is punishable by a fine and up to five years' imprisonment.

The second, at s.21A, introduced to TA 2000 on 20 December 2001 by the Anti-Terrorism, Crime and Security Act 2001 (ATCSA 2001), applies only to regulated sector firms[66] and uses the objective negligence test which POCA 2002 has also subsequently applied to the regulated sector.

The history of the s.21A failure to disclose offence is interesting, not least because of the speed at which it passed through Parliament (a matter of a few days), receiving Royal Assent in the early hours of 13 December 2001 and coming into force a week later—all part of the UK's legislative response to the terrorist activities in New York and Washington DC in September of that year.

In fact, the objective negligence test for failing to disclose knowledge or suspicion of money laundering was a concept first proposed in the Proceeds of Crime Bill (as it then was). After September 2001, the objective test element of that Bill was essentially cut-and-pasted into ATCSA 2001 in respect of terrorist finance offences and accelerated into the statute book.

Section 21A provides that:

---

[66] Defined in Sch.3A to TA 2000, but equivalent to the regulated sector for POCA 2002 purposes as defined in Sch.9 POCA 2002.

"(1) A person commits an offence if each of the following three conditions is satisfied.

(2) The first condition is that he–
   (a) knows or suspects, or
   (b) has reasonable grounds for knowing or suspecting,

that another person has committed or attempted to commit [a terrorist finance or money laundering offence].

(3) The second condition is that the information or other matter–
   (a) on which his knowledge or suspicion is based, or
   (b) which gives reasonable grounds for such knowledge or suspicion,

came to him in the course of a business in the regulated sector.

(4) The third condition is that he does not disclose the information or other matter to a constable [including a NCA officer] or a nominated officer as soon as is practicable after it comes to him."

The s.21A failure to disclose offence is punishable by a fine and up to five years' imprisonment.

The introduction of the objective test for regulated sector firms by ATCSA 2001 was, like POCA 2002 s.330(2)(b), one of the most significant changes in AML law in recent years because it effectively criminalises negligence. As with POCA 2002 s.330, if an individual employed in the regulated sector knows or suspects that a person is engaged in terrorist finance activities, or if a court determines that objectively he should have done, and he fails to notify the NCA or his MLRO, that individual may have committed a serious criminal offence.

The obligation to disclose is in respect of knowledge or suspicion of conduct which constitutes a terrorist finance or money laundering offence or would do so if relevant conduct occurred in the UK.[67] As noted above, the double-criminality override test under POCA 2002, which carves out from the

---

[67] TA 2000 s.21A(11).

definition of criminal conduct certain conduct which is lawful in the jurisdiction in which it occurs even if unlawful in the UK, does not apply under TA 2000.

As under POCA 2002, an individual officer or employee of a firm can discharge his TA 2000 disclosure obligations, and thereby avoid committing a criminal offence, by making a disclosure to his firm's MLRO in accordance with the firm's internal reporting procedures.

Again, the Approved Guidance has statutory recognition under TA 2000 as it does under POCA 2002 (see para.1.3.2.4 above) so that a court "must" take into account a person's compliance with the Approved Guidance in considering whether a terrorist finance offence has been committed. The JMLSG Guidance contains specific advice on how regulated sector firms can assess the objective test in the context of terrorist financing activity disclosures.[68]

As under POCA 2002, legal advisers and certain other professional advisers may, in limited circumstances, rely on a defence of privilege to avoid committing a failure to disclose offence under TA 2000. It is also a defence for an individual charged with a failure to disclose offence under s.21A to show that he had a "reasonable excuse" for not having made a disclosure.[69] Again, the legal meaning of reasonable excuse in this context has not yet been tested in the courts and the prudent view is that the term will be construed narrowly. Legal professional privilege may be raised as a defence by lawyers charged with failing to disclose knowledge or suspicion of terrorist finance offences.

---

[68] JMLSG Guidance at paras 6.15–6.17 of Pt I.
[69] TA 2000 s.21A(5)(a).

1.4.3 The tipping-off offence

As a result of legislative amendments made in December 2007,[70] the tipping-off regime under TA 2000 is now on an equal footing with the tipping-off regime under POCA 2002 (see para.1.3.3 above).

The main tipping-off offence under TA 2000 s.21D only applies to the regulated sector; it is largely the same as the POCA 2002 s.333A offence, save that it applies in respect of persons who tip off others about the fact that a disclosure has been made to the police or the NCA or that an investigation is being contemplated or carried out in relation to TA 2000 offences.

Section 21D of TA 2000 provides that:

" (1)   A person commits an offence if –
  (a)   the person discloses any matter within subsection (2);
  (b)   the disclosure is likely to prejudice any investigation that might be conducted following the disclosure referred to in that subsection; and
  (c)   the information on which the disclosure is based came to the person in the course of a business in the regulated sector.
 (2)   The matters are that the person or another person has made a disclosure under a provision of this Part –
  (a)   to a constable,
  (b)   in accordance with a procedure established by that person's employer for the making of disclosures under that provision,
  (c)   to a nominated officer, or
  (d)   to a [National Crime Agency officer] authorised for the purposes of that provision by the Director General of that Agency,
  of information that came to that person in the course of a business in the regulated sector.
 (3)   A person commits an offence if–

---

[70] By Terrorism Act 2000 and Proceeds of Crime Act 2002 (Amendment) Regulations (SI 2007/3398).

     (a)   the person discloses that an investigation into allegations that an offence under this Part has been committed is being contemplated or is being carried out;

     (b)   the disclosure is likely to prejudice that investigation; and

     (c)   the information on which the disclosure is based came to the person in the course of a business in the regulated sector."

Like its equivalent in POCA 2002 s.333A, the s.21D tipping-off offence is punishable by a fine and up to two years' imprisonment.

The commentary in para.1.3.3 on the POCA 2002 tipping-off offences for the regulated sector applies in essentially the same terms to the TA 2000 tipping-off offences, with appropriate substituted references to the underlying terrorist offences. The TA 2000 also provides limited safe-harbours from the tipping-off offences in the form of permitted disclosures which mirror those permitted disclosures set out in ss.333B–333E POCA 2002.[71]

The tipping-off offence in TA 2000 s.39, which is equivalent to the offence under POCA 2002 s.342, applies to non-regulated sector firms.

Section 39 provides that where a person knows or has reasonable cause to suspect that law enforcement authorities are conducting or propose to conduct an investigation in connection with the commission of terrorist offences, that person commits an offence if he:

    "(2) ...

     (a)   discloses to another anything which is likely to prejudice the investigation, or

     (b)   interferes with material which is likely to be relevant to the investigation".

---

[71] At ss.21E–21H TA 2000.

and further that if a person knows or has reasonable cause to suspect that disclosure of a suspected terrorist finance offence has been made to the NCA, that person commits an offence if he:

> "(4) ...
>> (a) discloses to another anything which is likely to prejudice an investigation resulting from the disclosure [...], or
>> (b) interferes with material which is likely to be relevant to an investigation resulting from the disclosure [...]".

The s.39 offences are punishable by a fine and up to five years' imprisonment.

It is a defence to the s.39 tipping-off offences for an alleged offender to show that he "did not know and had no reasonable cause to suspect that the disclosure or interference was likely to affect a terrorist investigation"[72] or that he had a "reasonable excuse" for the disclosure or interference.[73]

1.4.4 Practical issues associated with the consent regime

The same issues associated with the tension between seeking appropriate consents and avoiding tipping-off offences arise under TA 2000 as under POCA 2002. If a regulated sector firm has suspicions about a particular customer or counterparty, it must disclose those suspicions and seek consent from the NCA to avoid committing a terrorist finance or money laundering offence (and a s.21A failure to disclose offence). At the same time, the firm must seek to avoid committing a tipping-off offence under s.21D.

At the time of writing, no specific guidance on the difficulties firms may face in respect of the TA 2000 consent regime has been produced, however it is assumed that the principles applicable in respect of the POCA 2002 consent regime as set

---

[72] TA 2000 s.39(5)(a).
[73] TA 2000 s.39(5)(b).

out in the cases of *Squirrell Ltd, K Ltd* and *Shah* (see para.1.3.4.1 above) will apply equally in respect of TA 2000.

On 28 August 2015, the Government published a call for evidence on the effectiveness of rules designed to prevent money laundering and terrorist financing as part of its Cutting Red Tape review. The TA 2000 consent regime may be revisited as part of the output of that review.

1.5 The Wire Transfer Regulation

On 5 June 2015, the Second EU Wire Transfer Regulation[74] (WTR2) was published and its substantive provisions will have effect from 26 June 2017. It amends and replaces the original EU Wire Transfer Regulation[75] that was adopted by the EU Parliament and Council in November 2006 to implement Financial Action Task Force (FATF) Special Recommendation VII on information that should be included in electronic funds transfers.

The WTR2 is designed to address transparency gaps in the original regime. The regulation also aligns the EU framework with new FATF Recommendations set out in FATF's February 2012 international standards on AML and counter-terrorist financing[76] (the FATF Standards). The WTR2 has direct effect in the UK and all other EEA Member States and applies to all legal or natural persons whose business includes the transfer of funds services.

Under the regime, Payment Service Providers (PSPs) must include certain specified information in all electronic funds transfers and must have in place measures to verify this information. Formerly, the key information that was required

---

[74] Regulation (EU) 2015/847 of the European Parliament and of the Council of 20 May 2015 on information accompanying transfers of funds and repealing Regulation (EC) No 1781/2006 [2015] OJ L141/1.

[75] Regulation 1781/2006 of the European Parliament and of the Council of 15 November 2006 on information on the payer accompanying transfers of funds [2006] OJ L345/1.

[76] FATF Standards Recommendation 16 and Interpretive Notes.

to be included in a wire transfer instruction was the payer's name, address and account number, subject to exceptions in certain circumstances. Under the WTR2, this requirement is extended to also include the payee's name and account number or unique transaction identifier.[77]

The verification requirement is likewise extended. In circumstances where there is a transfer of funds of more that EUR 1,000 and the PSP of the payer is established outside of the EU, the PSP of the payee must verify the identity of the payee if this has not already been verified. If the PSP of the payer is established outside of the EU, but the transfer of funds is less than EUR 1,000, the PSP of the payee will only be required to verify the identity of the payee if there is a suspicion of money laundering or terrorist financing.[78]

Given the increasing prevalence of technology in banking, WTR2 aims to clarify the regime's application in this area. Payments using credit or debit cards, mobile telephones or any other digital or information technology device will be excluded from the regulation's scope where certain conditions are met, but will be subject to the regulation if they are used in person-to-person transfers.[79] This is defined as a transaction between natural persons acting, as consumers, for purposes other than a trade, business or profession.[80]

The WTR2 also introduces a risk-based approach to dealing with transfers for which required information is missing. Both the PSP of the payee and intermediary PSPs must establish effective risk-based procedures for determining when to execute, reject or suspend a transfer of funds lacking the required payer or payee information, and for taking appropriate follow-up action.[81]

More attention is given to the role of national supervisors under the WTR2. Articles 17–21 of WTR2 augment the original

---

[77] WTR2 art.4(2).
[78] WTR2 art. 7(3) and (4).
[79] WTR2 art.2(3).
[80] WTR2 art.3(10).
[81] WTR2 arts.8(1) and 12(1).

provision on penalties and monitoring by detailing specific minimum measures and the circumstances in which they apply, setting out co-ordination and publication requirements, and stipulating that Member States must establish effective mechanisms to encourage the reporting of breaches to the relevant national supervisors.

The growing importance of data protection is also recognised under the new regime. After feedback from the European Data Protection Supervisor and the Article 29 Working Party,[82] WTR2 incorporates specific data protection provisions in art.15a and detailed record-keeping procedures in art.16.

Pursuant to WTR2, once the standard legislative five-year data retention period expires, PSPs will have to delete personal data, unless otherwise provided for in national law. Member states can only allow or require further retention if the time extension is proportionate and necessary for the prevention, detection or investigation of money laundering and terrorist financing, but the maximum retention period must not exceed 10 years.[83] There is also now an explicit prohibition on processing data obtained for the purposes of compliance with WTR2 for commercial purposes.[84]

Financial service sector businesses will still need to consider which role they are fulfilling during their involvement in a payment chain, in order to comply with WTR2. The new regulation maintains essentially the same definitions, namely:

- *"Payer"* means a natural or legal person who holds a payment account and allows a transfer of funds from that payment account, or, where there is no payment account, a natural or legal person who gives a transfer of funds order;
- *"Payee"* means a natural or legal person who is the intended recipient of the transfer of funds;

---

[82] An independent advisory body charged with helping the Commission with data protection.
[83] WTR2 art.16(1) and (2).
[84] WTR2 art.15(2).

- *"Payment Service Provider"* means bodies and natural persons, as referred to in specified EU legislation, who provide transfer of funds services; and
- *"Intermediary Payment Service Provider"* means a payment service provider of neither the payer nor the payee who receives and transmits a fund transfer on behalf of a payment service provider of a payer or payee or of another intermediary payment service provider.

To aid the interpretation of the definitions, the JMLSG Guidance[85] cites the example of a bank or building society which effects an electronic funds transfer on a customer's instructions to debit that customer's account. In such a case, the bank or building society will be a PSP whether it undertakes the payment itself (in which case it must provide its customer's details as the payer), or via an intermediary PSP. If the transfer is carried out through an intermediary PSP, the bank or building society must provide the required information on its customer to that intermediary PSP. This would include circumstances in which the bank or building society processes the payment through an electronic banking product supplied by the intermediary PSP.

Where, however, a financial sector business processes a transaction through an account in its own name, it would be reasonable for it to consider itself as the payer, rather than the PSP, even where the transaction ultimately relates to a customer, for example in respect of mortgages, insurance claims or financial markets trades. (At the time of writing, the JMLSG Guidance comments on the original Wire Transfer Regulation but, as noted above, the definitions are largely the same.)

In order to allow for enforcement of the original Wire Transfer Regulation in the UK, the Treasury made the Transfer of Funds (Information on the Payer) Regulations 2007 (the 2007 Transfer Regulations) in November 2007.[86] The 2007 Transfer Regulations make provision for:

---

[85] JMLSG Guidance Paras 5.2.11–5.2.13 of Pt I.
[86] Transfer of Funds (Information on the Payer) Regulations (SI 2007/3298).

(i)   the enforcement of the obligations placed on UK financial sector businesses under the Wire Transfer Regulation;
(ii)   the supervision of PSPs; and
(iii) enforcement powers for the supervisors.

There has not yet been an indication of when the 2007 Transfer Regulations will be amended or superseded in order to give effect to WTR2. In the meantime, the effect of the 2007 Transfer Regulations is that PSPs in the UK which are authorised by the FCA will be supervised by the FCA for wire transfer purposes. Other PSPs in the UK will be supervised by HMRC which has included guidance on the Wire Transfer Regulation in its money laundering guidance. The HMRC Guidance is approved by the Treasury for the purposes of the Wire Transfer Regulation.

Failure to comply with the Wire Transfer Regulation can be a criminal offence punishable by a fine and up to two years' imprisonment.[87]

1.6   Investigations, confiscation and asset freezing

To assist the investigatory and enforcement processes involved in tackling money laundering and terrorist financing, law enforcement authorities and the Treasury have a range of powers to enable wide-ranging and effective investigations of money laundering and to undermine criminal and terrorist enterprises through asset freezing, seizure and confiscation. The most significant of these are contained in POCA 2002, TA 2000 and ATCSA 2001, with further freezing and confiscation powers made available under the Serious Crime Act 2007 (SCA 2007) and the Counter-Terrorism Act 2008 (CTA 2008). Since the second edition of this publication, TAFA 2010 has introduced a legislative framework to support the asset-freezing regime that was challenged by the Supreme Court in 2010.

This Chapter does not cover the specific application of the investigatory powers, legislative and court processes involved

---

[87] Transfer of Funds (Information on the Payer) Regulations (SI 2007/3298) reg.14.

in obtaining and serving the variety of orders available to law enforcement authorities and the Treasury. It is sufficient that firms are aware that they must comply with a valid court order or Treasury order, subject to serious criminal sanctions either for direct breach of the order or under contempt of court proceedings.

It is useful, however, for firms to recognise some of the key orders which may be obtained by law enforcement authorities in connection with the investigation and enforcement of money laundering and terrorist financing offences and subsequent asset confiscation proceedings.

1.6.1 Investigatory orders

Investigations into money laundering and terrorist finance offences can often involve the analysis of otherwise confidential customer records held by financial institutions. Some law supervisory and enforcement authorities have for some time had the benefit of specific enhanced powers to order or procure disclosure of confidential information,[88] but it is only since ATCSA 2001 and POCA 2002 that these powers have become part of the basic toolkit of investigatory measures available to all law supervisory and enforcement authorities.

The key investigatory orders provided for by ATCSA 2001 and POCA 2002 are account monitoring orders and customer information orders.[89] Account monitoring orders require ongoing disclosure of information in relation to specific accounts

---

[88] The Serious Fraud Office (SFO), for instance, has had extensive investigatory powers since 1988: under Criminal Justice Act 1987 s.2, on its own initiative (i.e., without involving the courts) the SFO has been able to order any person to answer questions, furnish information or produce documents with respect to any matter relevant to the investigation of a serious or complex fraud; the FCA also has extensive powers to compel persons to answer questions, disclose information and produce documents in pursuance of their statutory functions. The Coroners and Justice Act 2009 amended SOCPA 2005 s.71, giving the FSA (and now FCA, PRA and Bank of England) powers to grant immunity from prosecution to individuals who are prepared to provide evidence of serious misconduct to the regulator.

[89] ATCSA 2001 introduced the account monitoring order into TA 2000 in December 2001; prior to that, TA 2000 made provision for customer information orders to be

whereas customer information orders require one-off disclosures of information in relation to specific persons.

1.6.1.1 Account monitoring orders

Account monitoring orders enable law enforcement authorities to monitor individual bank accounts for investigatory purposes. Investigators can apply to the court for an account monitoring order under TA 2000 in pursuance of an investigation into terrorist finance activities or terrorist organisations. The applicant must show that "the tracing of terrorist property is desirable for the purposes of the investigation" and that granting the order "will enhance the effectiveness of the investigation".[90]

POCA 2002 makes provision for an equivalent order in relation to non-terrorist-related money laundering investigations.[91] There are four circumstances in which an account monitoring order may be obtained under POCA 2002, namely in pursuance of:

(1) a money laundering investigation (i.e. investigating whether a money laundering offence has been committed);
(2) a confiscation investigation (i.e. investigating whether a person has benefited from his criminal conduct and identifying property which might be confiscated);
(3) a civil recovery investigation (i.e., investigating whether property is recoverable under the civil recovery process discussed at para.1.6.2 below); or
(4) an exploitation proceeds investigation (i.e., investigating whether money can be recovered by the courts from a person who has benefitted from the exploitation of accounts about their crimes, for example by selling their memoirs, or receiving payments for public speaking or media interviews).[92]

---

made, though on a slightly more restricted basis (s.38A and Sch.6A TA 2000, introduced by Sch.2 and Pt 1 ATCSA 2001).
[90] TA 2000 Sch.6A para.2(1).
[91] POCA 2002 ss.370–375.
[92] Part 7 Coroners and Justice Act 2009.

Orders in relation to civil recovery and exploitation proceeds investigations may only be granted by the High Court.

In each of these four circumstances, the applicant authority must show that there are reasonable grounds for making the order, that the information required to be disclosed by the order "is likely to be of substantial value (whether or not by itself) to the investigation for the purposes of which the order is sought", and that it is in the public interest for that information to be disclosed.[93]

An account monitoring order under either Act requires a specific institution to provide specified information relating to all or any accounts held by a specified person for a continuous period of up to 90 days.

An institution (including its controlling officers) which is served with an account monitoring order but fails to comply is likely to be held in contempt of court.

1.6.1.2 *Customer information orders*

Unlike account monitoring orders which require financial institutions to give investigators access to customer information for a period of time, customer information orders obtained under TA 2000[94] or POCA 2002[95] require institutions simply to deliver up a snapshot of the information which they hold in relation to specified customers.

An order may be sought in respect of all financial institutions, a group of institutions or a specific institution.

Customer information orders will only be granted in pursuance of a terrorist investigation, a money laundering investigation, a confiscation investigation, a civil recovery investigation or an exploitation proceeds investigation. Orders in relation to civil recovery and exploitation proceeds investigations may

---

[93] POCA 2002 s.371.
[94] TA 2000 s.38 and Sch.6, as amended by Sch.2 Pt 4 ATCSA 2001.
[95] POCA 2002 ss.363–369.

only be granted by the High Court. The judge must be persuaded either that "the tracing of terrorist property is desirable" and that granting the order "will enhance the effectiveness of the investigation"[96] or, in the case of a POCA 2002 order, that there are reasonable grounds for making the order, that the information required to be disclosed by the order "is likely to be of substantial value (whether or not by itself) to the investigation for the purposes of which the order is sought", and that it is in the public interest for that information to be disclosed.[97]

If given, an order will require the financial institutions specified in the order to provide "any customer information" held in relation to the specified person or persons. Customer information, for these purposes, includes confirmation that a specified person holds or has held an account with the institution and the details of any such account (names, addresses, date of birth or incorporation details, evidence of identity obtained by the institution, signatories to the customer's accounts and any other accounts for which the customer is a signatory).

An institution will commit a specific offence, punishable by fine, if it fails to comply with a customer information order[98] or, in the case of a POCA 2002 order (but not a TA 2000 order) provides false or misleading information in response to an order.[99] Specific provision is made in TA 2000 for officers of institutions who consent to or connive in an institution's failure to comply with a customer information order—an offence punishable by a fine and up to six months' imprisonment.

1.6.2 Asset recovery and other remedies

Since February 2001, TA 2000 has enabled a court to seize property following the commencement of proceedings in respect of a terrorist finance offence, and then to confiscate that

---

[96] TA 2000 Sch.6 para.5.
[97] POCA 2002 s.365.
[98] TA 2000 Sch.6 para. 1(3) and 1(5) and POCA 2002 s.366(1) and (2).
[99] POCA 2002 s.366(3) and (4).

property following a conviction, if the property is intended to be used for the purposes of terrorism.[100] Those powers were enhanced by ATCSA 2001 by enabling law enforcement authorities to apply to the court for property to be seized at the commencement of an investigation, even before proceedings were begun.[101]

POCA 2002 introduced even wider powers in the context of other criminal investigations and proceedings – enabling courts to confiscate the proceeds of general as well as specific criminal conduct – and established the Assets Recovery Agency (ARA) with the objective to identify and confiscate criminal property and otherwise to ensure that criminals are deprived of the benefits of their crimes. The responsibilities of the ARA were absorbed by SOCA and then by the NCA's Economic Crime Command where asset recovery operations currently reside.

The key orders which the NCA and certain other authorities may seek in pursuance of their asset seizure and confiscation objectives are disclosure orders, restraint orders, forfeiture orders and serious crime prevention orders.

1.6.2.1 Disclosure orders

A disclosure order granted under POCA 2002 s.357 enables a prosecutor or an appropriate director or member of staff at the NCA to require "any person whom the appropriate officer considers has relevant information" to answer questions and/or provide information and/or produce documents in connection with an investigation to establish whether particular property may be confiscated or made the subject of a civil recovery action or exploitation proceeds investigation.

The judge must be persuaded that there are reasonable grounds for making the order, that the information required to be disclosed by the order "is likely to be of substantial value (whether or not by itself) to the investigation for the purposes

---

[100] TA 2000 s.23 and Sch.4.
[101] TA 2000 Sch.4 para.5, introduced by ATCSA 2001 s.3 and Sch.2.

of which the order is sought", and that it is in the public interest for that information to be disclosed.[102]

Failure to comply with a disclosure order can be punished with a fine and up to six months' imprisonment. Supplying false or misleading information in response to a disclosure order is punishable by a fine and up to two years' imprisonment.

A disclosure order cannot require a lawyer to disclose information which is subject to legal professional privilege, except to confirm the name and address of a particular client.

1.6.2.2   Restraint orders

A restraint order prohibits specified persons from dealing with specified property—essentially, it is a form of freezing order. The court can make a restraint order under TA 2000 or under POCA 2002 (in respect of a terrorist finance offence or other criminal offences, respectively) on its own account, or on the application of law enforcement authorities, at any time after an investigation has been commenced.[103] The court will grant the order if it appears that a forfeiture or confiscation order may be made in any proceedings for the offence.

Once a restraint order is made, property subject to the order can be temporarily seized to prevent it being dealt with or removed from the jurisdiction of the court.

1.6.2.3   Forfeiture and confiscation orders

The powers of forfeiture under TA 2000 have been extended by CTA 2008.[104] The amended forfeiture provisions under TA 2000 provide that upon conviction for a terrorist finance offence or terrorist money laundering offence, a court may order the forfeiture (i.e. confiscation) of any money or other property which was, at the time of the offence, in the offender's possession or control and which had been used, which they

---

[102] POCA 2002 s.358.
[103] TA 2000 Sch.4 Pt.1 para.5 and POCA 2002 s.40(2).
[104] CTA 2008 ss.34–38.

intended should be used, or (in certain cases) which they had reasonable cause to suspect might be used, for the purposes of terrorism;[105] the court may also order the forfeiture of any money or other property which either wholly or partly, directly or indirectly, is received by the offender as a payment or other reward.[106]

Under POCA 2002, the court has a much wider power to order the confiscation of criminal property when a person is convicted of any offence in, or committed for sentencing to, the Crown Court. The order is discretionary, but if a court is satisfied on the balance of probabilities that the person concerned has either benefited from the commission of that particular offence or benefited from "general criminal conduct", it must generally order the proceeds of that criminal conduct to be seized (if it has not already been seized pursuant to a restraint order) and confiscated.[107]

The ability to confiscate criminal property, even though it cannot be proven to be the proceeds of particular criminal conduct, was a significant development for law enforcement. In essence, it lowered the standard of proof required in order to confiscate assets. Under POCA 2002, assets of a person convicted of an offence may now be seized on a burden of the balance of probabilities, whereas previously it had been necessary to demonstrate that assets represented the benefit of specific criminal conduct for which a conviction had been secured.

If a court determines that it is appropriate to grant a confiscation order following a conviction, it is required to assess the level of benefit which an offender has received from general or particular criminal conduct (the recoverable amount) and to order that the offender pay that amount. Since 1 June 2015, the court's ability to order payment of the recoverable amount has been subject to a proportionality consideration. The order can be made only "if, or to the extent

---

[105] TA 2000 s.23 as substituted by CTA 2008 s.34.
[106] TA 2000 s.23(7), as substituted by CTA 2008 s.34.
[107] POCA 2002 s.6.

that, it would not be disproportionate to require the defendant to pay the recoverable amount".[108]

If the court decides that an offender has a criminal lifestyle, in determining whether he has benefited from general criminal conduct, and in assessing the level of that benefit, it is required to assume that property which came into the offender's possession up to six years before the date on which criminal proceedings were commenced (and any time after the date of conviction) represents the proceeds of his general criminal conduct.

Criminal lifestyle is defined in POCA 2002 s.75 by reference to the nature of the offence of which the offender has been convicted. A conviction for drug trafficking, money laundering or any other prescribed lifestyle offence is conclusive evidence that the offender has a "criminal lifestyle".[109] Otherwise, a criminal lifestyle is deemed where the offence is one of at least three offences of which the offender has been convicted in the past six years and from which he has obtained a benefit, or where the offence was committed over a period of at least six months. An offender will not be deemed to have a criminal lifestyle unless the benefit obtained from those offences is at least £5,000.[110]

The Serious Crime Act 2015 (SCA 2015) inserted a new s.13A into POCA 2002, which became effective from 1 June 2015 and enables a prosecutor to apply to the court for any compliance order that the court considers to be appropriate for the purpose of ensuring that the confiscation order is effective. This application can be made at any time while the confiscation order is in effect. The court may also make a compliance order of its own initiative at the time the confiscation order is made.

---

[108] POCA 2002 s.6(5) as amended by SCA 2015.
[109] POCA 2002 Sch.2 contains a full list of offences conviction for which will be conclusive evidence of a criminal lifestyle.
[110] POCA 2002 s.75(4).

1.6.2.4 *Serious crime prevention orders*

The serious crime prevention order (SCP Order) was introduced by SCA 2007 s.1 with effect from 6 April 2008. The NCA and other law enforcement agencies can apply to the High Court for an SCP Order to be imposed on an individual pursuant to which conditions, restrictions or reporting requirements will apply with the purpose of restricting that individual's involvement in serious crime.

For the purposes of imposing an SCP Order, a person has been involved in serious crime if he:

* has committed a serious offence (whether in England and Wales or elsewhere);
* has facilitated the commission by another person of a serious offence (whether in England and Wales or elsewhere); or
* has conducted himself in a way that was likely to facilitate the commission by himself or another person of a serious offence (whether in England and Wales or elsewhere and whether or not such an offence was committed).

A serious offence in England and Wales means an offence under the laws of England and Wales which, at the time when the court is considering the matter in question, falls within a description specified in SCA 2007 or which the court considers sufficiently serious to be treated as such. The offences specified in the Act include, inter alia, various drug offences, people trafficking offences, arms trafficking offences, prostitution and child sex offences and the primary money laundering offences under POCA 2002. Section 47 of SCA 2015 adds to the list of specified offences, set out in Pt 1 of Sch.1 to SCA 2007, to include offences relating to cyber crime, possession of firearms and the cultivation of cannabis plants.

An offence is treated as having been committed outside England and Wales if it is an offence in that other jurisdiction and, had it been committed in England and Wales, would have been a serious offence here, or is considered by the court to be sufficiently serious to be treated as if it would have been a serious offence here.

Section 1 of SCA 2007 is drafted widely and enables the High Court to make an order containing "such prohibitions, restrictions or requirements; and such other terms; as the court considers appropriate for the purpose of protecting the public". An SCP Order can only be made if the High Court is satisfied that the relevant individual has been involved in serious crime, and if the High Court has reasonable grounds to believe that the order would protect the public by preventing, restricting or disrupting involvement by the individual in serious crime.

An SCP Order may only be imposed on individuals who are over the age of 18 and who are represented at the proceedings at which the SCP Order is made. A notice setting out the terms of any SCP Order which is made must be served in person on the individual concerned.

Typically, SCP Orders are used to restrict the ability of an individual to travel, or the persons with whom an individual may associate, as well as to restrict their ability to access certain assets or financial services.

In an early example, the first SCP Order used in an SFO prosecution in March 2009 saw a twice-convicted fraudster banned from conducting investment and financial management business for four years after release from prison. As at 31 March 2014, a total of 182 SCP Orders had been obtained by the NCA and its predecessor, SOCA. A further 136 had been obtained by police forces or other agencies and notified to the NCA/SOCA.[111]

---

[111] This number may not be the complete picture of SCP Orders secured by other law enforcement agencies, as some may not have been reported to the NCA/SOCA. Home Office Fact Sheet, *Improvements to Serious Crime Prevention Orders* (March 2015).

The Government's Serious and Organised Crime Strategy, published in October 2013, made a commitment to enable law enforcement agencies to make better use of SCP Orders. A number of changes were consequently made by SCA 2015 to strengthen the effectiveness of the regime:

- Additions to the indicative offences (as mentioned above) to include offences relating to cyber crime, possession of firearms and the cultivation of cannabis plants;
- Extension of the SCP Orders framework to Scotland;
- Provisions enabling a new SCP Order to be imposed when a person has been convicted of breaching an existing SCP Order; and
- Consolidation of the financial reporting orders (FROs) into the SCP Order.

The FROs were introduced by SOCPA 2005 as a post-conviction order that imposed financial reporting requirements. However, the effectiveness of the orders were limited by the fact that breaching the order only amounted to a summary offence. Because the breach of an SCP Order is an either way offence, meaning it can be dealt with by a magistrates' court or the Crown Court, the SCP Orders do not have the same enforcement drawbacks as FROs. The policy decision was therefore made to impose financial reporting requirements through SCP Orders going forward, and SCA 2015 made provision for this.

1.6.2.5   *Civil recovery and taxing powers*

In addition to powers of seizing and confiscating the property of suspected and convicted criminals, the NCA has standing to bring a civil action to recover property which is or represents the proceeds of criminal conduct regardless of whether a criminal prosecution has been brought for an offence in connection with that property, and to exercise a taxation function in respect of income or gains which it reasonably believes to have arisen or accrued as a result of criminal conduct.

Part 5 of POCA 2002 sets out the civil recovery regime, which enables the enforcement authority to apply to the High Court for a recovery order against any person whom "the authority thinks holds recoverable property".[112]

A property freezing order may also be applied for before or during the recovery proceedings.[113] In July 2012, a majority decision of the Supreme Court[114] upheld a challenge against a worldwide property freezing order on the basis that the legislative context restricts references to property in POCA 2002 Pt 5 to property within the UK, despite the overall definition of property as "all property wherever situated" set out in s.316(4). The majority held that a civil recovery order (and related property freezing order) can only be made in respect of property that is within the territorial jurisdiction of the court making it. The dissenting judges argued that POCA 2002 was poorly drafted but the objective is clearly to deprive criminals of the proceeds of their crimes, whether in the UK or abroad.

The NCA may wish to undertake civil recovery proceedings against a person's property because that person cannot be tried for a criminal offence in the UK (and as such the court could not issue a confiscation order), for example because the person has died since the commission of the offence giving rise to the recoverable property, or because the person had no direct connection with the commission of the offence (for instance, organised criminals may procure others to commit offences from which they ultimately obtain the benefit).

Essentially, the process of civil recovery involves an application to the court, pre-empted, if necessary, by an application for the appointment of an interim receiver over particular assets.[115] The court may appoint an interim receiver if it is satisfied that "there is a good arguable case" that the property to which the application relates "is or includes recoverable property" or an

---

[112] POCA 2002 s.243.
[113] POCA 2002 s.245A.
[114] *Serious Organised Crime Agency v Perry* [2012] UKSC 35; [2013] 1 A.C. 182; [2013] 1 Cr. App. R. 6 (p.61).
[115] POCA 2002 s.246.

interest in recoverable property.[116] The function of the interim receiver is to prevent persons dealing with that property and, where necessary, to investigate whether particular property is recoverable property.

If an interim recovery order is subsequently given by the court, it must appoint a trustee for civil recovery, nominated by the enforcement authority, whose function is to secure and preserve any recoverable property vested in him by the recovery order and to realise non-cash recoverable property. The proceeds of the recovery process are held by the trustee ultimately for the benefit of the enforcement authority. The Policing and Crime Act 2010 amended the Limitation Act 1980, increasing the amount of time available to enforcement authorities, so that property now ceases to be recoverable 20 years (rather than 12 years) after the date on which it was obtained.[117]

POCA 2002 enables the NCA to apply tracing provisions to recoverable property so that, for instance, the proceeds of a sale of recoverable property can in some circumstances be recoverable even if those proceeds do not themselves directly represent the proceeds of criminal conduct.[118]

Part 6 of POCA sets out the NCA's revenue functions. Section 317 provides that if the NCA has reasonable grounds to suspect that "income arising or a gain accruing to a person in respect of a chargeable period is chargeable to income tax or is a chargeable gain (as the case may be) and arises or accrues as a result of the person's or another's criminal conduct (whether wholly or partly and whether directly or indirectly)" it may notify HMRC that it intends to exercise revenue functions in respect of that person. The NCA can then exercise the revenue powers which could otherwise be exercised by HMRC and demand that an individual pay tax on particular income or

---

[116] POCA s.246(4)–(6).
[117] Limitation Act 1980 s.27A, as amended by Policing and Crime Act 2009 s.62(1)(a).
[118] POCA 2002 ss.304–310.

capital gains. The NCA's assumption of revenue powers can be undertaken in respect of corporate entities as well as individuals.[119]

The NCA has additionally been empowered to make an application for an exploitation proceeds order introduced by the Coroners and Justice Act 2009.[120] The order essentially applies to the money raised by publicising a serious offence (the "book deal" scenario). The order requires the respondent to pay the exploitation proceeds to the NCA.

1.6.3 Freezing orders etc.

Financial institutions operating in the EU will be familiar with the orders which the Treasury has for some time issued to implement sanctions imposed by UN Security Council Resolutions against particular governments and regimes and the individuals and corporates that support them.[121]

The Government is also required to give effect to EU measures imposing economic sanctions or other restrictive measures. Such measures are typically made pursuant to EU Regulations, which are directly effective in each Member State but require implementation into domestic legislation in order to impose criminal sanctions (European legislation cannot impose criminal sanctions into national laws). The EU typically implements sanctions imposed by the UN Security Council, but can and does also impose restrictive measures which go beyond those imposed at UN level. Perhaps the most notable recent example of this has been the EU's sanctions in relation to Russia and the Ukraine.[122]

---

[119] POCA 2002 s.317(1)(b).

[120] Coroners and Justice Act 2009 Pt.7.

[121] HM Treasury has powers under the United Nations Act 1946 to implement resolutions of the United Nations Sanctions Committee by statutory instrument. HM Treasury provides firms with a consolidated list of all subjects of sanctions currently in force.

[122] For further information on the EU sanctions regime, see *http://eeas.europa.eu/cfsp/sanctions/index_en.htm* [Accessed 21 September 2015].

Asset freezes are commonly imposed on a range of individuals and organisations as part of coordinated UN and EU economic sanctions regimes, but powers have also been granted to HM Treasury to impose asset freezes in other circumstances, including on its own initiative, in particular in relation to the assets of terrorists or terrorist organisations. The detail of the general UN, EU and UK economic sanctions regimes are beyond the scope of this guide, but three key UK asset freezing powers are described in the following sections.

1.6.3.1   The Terrorist Asset-Freezing etc. Act 2010

The Government introduced terrorist asset freezing legislation in high profile circumstances following a 2010 Supreme Court decision[123] that quashed two of HM Treasury's existing terrorist asset freezing orders.

The Terrorism (United Nations Measures) Order 2006 (the TO) and the Al-Qaida and Taliban (United Nations Measures) Order 2006 (the AQO) were made without a vote in Parliament by HM Treasury in response to a UN Security Council Resolution requiring member states to take steps to freeze the assets of organisations involved in international terrorism. The orders were made pursuant to the United Nations Act 1946 s.1, which authorises the making of measures "necessary or expedient" to give effect to United Nations Security Council Resolutions.

On 27 January 2010, the Supreme Court held that the TO and elements of the AQO should be quashed after finding that the measures went beyond the scope of the power provided for under the 1946 Act. A subsequent ruling of the Supreme Court denied the Government a stay and the judgment consequently took immediate effect on 4 February 2010.

In response to the rulings, the Government fast-tracked temporary legislation through Parliament using emergency

---

[123] *A v HM Treasury*; sub nom. *HM Treasury v Ahmed* [2010] UKSC 2; [2010] 2 A.C. 534; [2010] H.R.L.R. 204.

procedures. The Terrorist Asset-Freezing (Temporary Provisions) Act 2010 came into force on 10 February 2010 and provided retroactive validation of the Terrorism (United Nations Measures) Orders 2009, 2006 and 2001, enabling financial institutions to maintain the applicable parts of the asset-freezing regime which the court had voided.

Ahead of the temporary legislation's expiry date of 31 December 2010, the Government consulted on primary legislation designed to establish permanently the underlying legality of the asset-freezing regime. On 16 December 2010, TAFA 2010 came into force, repealing the temporary statute.

Under TAFA 2010 Pt 1, a person must not engage in the prohibited activities listed below in circumstances where they know or have reasonable cause to suspect that they would be carrying out one of the following:

- Dealing with funds or economic resources owned, held or controlled by a designated person. This includes using, altering, moving, allowing access to, transferring or dealing in any other way that would result in any change in volume, amount, location, ownership, possession, character or destination of funds; or making any other change that would enable use, including portfolio management. Dealing with economic resources means exchange or use in exchange for funds, goods or services[124];
- Making funds or financial services available (directly or indirectly) to a designated person[125];
- Making funds or financial services available to any person for the benefit of a designated person[126];
- Making economic resources available (directly or indirectly) to a designated person, if that designated person would be likely to exchange the economic resources, or use them in exchange, for funds, goods or services[127]; or

---

[124] TAFA 2010 s.11.
[125] TAFA 2010 s.12.
[126] TAFA s.13.
[127] TAFA 2010 s.14.

- Making economic resources available to any person for the benefit of a designated person.[128]

Designated persons are placed into two categories by TAFA 2010 s.1: those designated by the Treasury and those designated by the European Council under EC Regulation 2580/2001.[129] Article 2(3) of the Regulation gives the Council the power to establish, review and amend the relevant list of designated persons, which is then set out in the Annex to a new Council Implementing Regulation each time changes are made.

Designations made by the Treasury can be final (lasting for one year) or interim (lasting for 30 days or until a final designation is made, whichever is earliest), and the detail of this distinction is set out in TAFA 2010 ss.2–9, along with provisions for variation or revocation of Treasury designations. The Treasury is required to take steps to generally publicise both its interim and final designations, and to give written notice of such designations to the designated person. These notification requirements, set out in ss.3(1) and 7(1) of TAFA 2010, are modified in specific circumstances.

The Treasury does not have to take steps to publicise an interim or final designation generally if the Treasury believes the designated person is an individual under the age of 18, or the Treasury considers that the disclosure of the designation should be restricted in the interests of national security, for reasons connected with the prevention or detection of serious crime, or in the interests of justice.[130] For the duration of time that one or more of these conditions is met, the Treasury can limit disclosure of the designation to "only such persons as they consider appropriate", but the requirement to generally publicise the designation is reinstated once the circumstances in the conditions cease to exist.[131] Where the Treasury has the

---

[128] TAFA 2010 s.15.
[129] Council Regulation (EC) No 2580/2001 of 27 December 2001 on specific restrictive measures directed against certain persons and entities with a view to combating terrorism [2001] OJ L344/70.
[130] TAFA 2010 s.3(2)-(4) and s.7(2)-(4).
[131] TAFA 2010 s. 3(4)-(5) and s.7(4)-(5).

power to limit disclsoure of a designation, it can also specify that the designation is confidential.[132] It is an offence to disclose a confidential designation without lawful authority.[133]

The prohibited activities above are subject to exceptions and/or licences, as set out in ss.16 and 17 TAFA 2010. Broadly, the exceptions make it permissible for a financial institution to continue to credit interest payments to an account and to perform contractual payments under agreements made prior to an asset freeze having been imposed. If otherwise prohibited activities are conducted under the authority of a licence granted by the Treasury, those actions should not constitute an offence. However, a person who purports to act under the authority of a licence but fails to comply with any conditions set out in it commits a separate offence under s.17. It is also an offence to enter into arrangements that circumvent an asset freeze.[134]

Conduct outside of the UK can still constitute an offence under TAFA 2010 Pt 1 if committed by a UK national or a UK-constituted or UK-incorporated body.[135]

The offences of breaching confidentiality or the terms of a licence are punishable, on conviction on indictment, by imprisonment for a term not exceeding two years or by a fine or both. Other offences under TAFA 2010 are punishable, on conviction on indictment, by imprisonment for a term not exceeding seven years or by a fine or both.[136] Liabilities exist for officers of a body corporate where that individual's consent or negligence has caused the body corporate to commit the offence in question.[137]

Under TAFA 2010, relevant firms have an obligation to inform the Treasury as soon as practicable if, during the course of their business, they have or obtain information which causes the

---

[132] TAFA 2010 s.10(1).
[133] TAFA 2010 s.10(2)-(7).
[134] TAFA 2010 s.18.
[135] TAFA 2010 s.33.
[136] TAFA 2010 s.32.
[137] TAFA 2010 s.34.

institution to know or suspect that a person is a designated person or has committed one of the offences outlined above.[138] The Treasury also has the power to request information from designated persons and others, including to request the production of documents.[139] It is an offence to fail to comply with the reporting obligations or to fail to comply with a request for information.

The Act has been independently reviewed by David Anderson QC on an annual basis since February 2011. The fourth report on the year ending 16 September 2014 noted the "remarkably low" amount of assets frozen (£61,000 under both lists) and the limited but increasing use of the power (eight new designations in the year reviewed, which is more than the total number of designations over the previous three years). The report noted that:

> "For the fourth year in succession, as recorded in the Treasury's quarterly reports, there were no prosecutions during the reporting period of designated persons or of third parties for breaching prohibitions imposed under the Act. However, a caution was issued in the quarter to June 2014, and breaches or possible breaches were investigated during the period under review."[140]

Amongst other things, the report also discussed the "seemingly intractable" problems of financial institutions refusing to extend their services to individuals and entities which have been de-listed. The issue has been raised in all four reports to date and highlights the cautious approach being taken by banks citing regulatory and reputational risks as a justification for categorising the provision of services as outside the banks' risk appetite. Mr Anderson has urged banks to "acknowledge duties to their customers and to the principle of financial inclusion", and it is possible that this will prompt the production of some guidance on the point.

---

[138] TAFA 2010 s.19.

[139] TAFA 2010 s.20.

[140] David Anderson QC, *Fourth report on the operation of the Terrorist Asset-Freezing etc. Act 2010*, para.5.2, March 2015.

The Government publishes responses to the independent reviewer reports and in principle adjustments can be made to the TAFA 2010 framework as a consequence of the reviews.

1.6.3.2 Orders under the Anti-Terrorism, Crime and Security Act 2001

The UN sanctions powers were built on by ATCSA 2001 by giving the Treasury the power to issue freezing orders on its own initiative.[141]

The ATCSA 2001 freezing orders prevent UK persons (including UK nationals and bodies corporate situated outside the UK) from making funds available to or for the benefit of a specified resident or government of a country or territory outside the UK.

The Treasury may make an ATCSA 2001 freezing order if it reasonably believes that "action to the detriment of the United Kingdom's economy (or part of it)" or "action constituting a threat to the life or property" of one or more nationals or residents of the UK "has been or is likely to be taken by a person or persons".[142]

A freezing order could, for instance, require a bank to prevent withdrawals and block cheques or a broker-dealer to prevent further dealings in investments by its customers. An order could also extend to the overseas branches of a UK-incorporated regulated sector firm, and could potentially even require the freezing of the assets of an overseas entity which are held in an overseas jurisdiction by the overseas branch of a UK-incorporated firm.

Although the provisions have now been in place for a number of years, at the time of writing, the Treasury has only used its

---

[141] ATCSA 2001 s.4 and Sch.3.
[142] ATCSA 2001 s.4(2).

power to make one ATCSA 2001 freezing order: the Landsbanki Freezing Order 2008[143] which was used to freeze the UK branch assets of Landsbanki Islands hf, the Icelandic bank which ran into difficulties in 2008. The purpose of the Landsbanki Freezing Order was to freeze the UK assets of Landsbanki Islands hf on the grounds that action to the detriment of the UK's economy had been or was likely to be taken by the government of Iceland or persons resident in Iceland. The action was taken in order to protect the depositors of the UK internet banking operations of Landsbanki known as Icesave.

The Landsbanki Freezing Order was amended and then revoked by subsequent orders.[144]

Though each order made under ATCSA 2001 must specify the consequences of breach, failure to comply with a freezing order is likely to give rise to criminal liability with an ultimate punishment of up to two years' imprisonment. This was the case in the Landsbanki Freezing Order.

1.6.3.3 *Directions under the Counter-Terrorism Act 2008*

The CTA 2008 confers on the Treasury the power to make directions in connection with terrorist financing, money laundering and certain other activities, together with a provision for enforcement.

The AML provisions contained in CTA 2008 were a late addition during the passing of the Counter-Terrorism Bill and were introduced without consultation. The reason for this addition was, reportedly, to cure a perceived defect in the Treasury's powers to implement recommendations made in 2009 by the Financial Action Task Force (FATF) in relation to Iran.

---

[143] Landsbanki Freezing Order 2008 (SI 2008/2668) and subsequent licences made thereunder.

[144] Landsbanki Freezing (Amendment) Order (SI 2008/2766) and Landsbanki Freezing (Revocation) Order (SI 2009/1392).

The Treasury went on to make the Financial Restrictions (Iran) Order 2009[145] aimed at hindering the pursuit of nuclear weapons programmes by Iran. The order effectively shut down the United Kingdom operations of Bank Mellat and its subsidiary. The bank successfully challenged the order and directions made under it by the Treasury in the Supreme Court, where the measures were held to be disproportionate and procedurally flawed.[146]

Two further orders have been made under CTA 2008, both in relation to Iran.[147]

A direction may be made by the Treasury under Sch.7 to CTA 2008 if one or more of the following conditions is satisfied:

- the FATF has advised that measures should be taken against a country because of the risk of terrorist financing or money laundering being carried on in that country, by the government of that country or by persons resident in that country;
- the Treasury reasonably believes that terrorist financing or money laundering is being carried on in a country, by the government of that country or by persons resident in that country; or
- the Treasury reasonably believes that either (i) the development or production of nuclear, radiological, biological or chemical weapons, or (ii) the doing in the country of anything that facilitates the development or production of such weapons, poses a significant risk to the national interests of the UK.

If one or more of those conditions is satisfied, the Treasury may issue a direction which applies to a particular person operating

---

[145] Financial Restrictions (Iran) Order (SI 2009/2775).

[146] *Bank Mellat v HM Treasury* [2013] UKSC 38 and 39; [2014] A.C. 700; [2013] H.R.L.R. 30.

[147] Financial Restrictions (Iran) Order (SI 2011/2775) and Financial Restrictions (Iran) Order (SI 2012/2904).

in the UK financial sector, any description of persons operating in that sector, or all persons operating in that sector[148] (for these purposes "affected persons").

A CTA 2008 direction can apply requirements in relation to transactions or business relationships with a particular person carrying on business in a specified country, the government of that country, or a person resident or incorporated in that country[149] (for these purposes "prescribed persons"). Such a direction may also impose requirements in relation to a particular prescribed person, any description of prescribed persons or all prescribed persons.[150] The Treasury may not for these purposes prescribe a person in another EEA Member State.

Requirements can be imposed as follows:

- to require affected persons to carry out increased customer due diligence (either generally, or in a specified manner) in relation to prescribed persons; and/or
- to require affected persons to perform additional ongoing monitoring (either generally, or in a specified manner) in relation to prescribed persons; and/or
- to require affected persons to provide specified information or documentation to a person specified in the direction on a periodic or regular basis; and/or
- to prohibit affected persons from dealing with prescribed persons.

Failure to comply with an order made under CTA 2008 will constitute an offence punishable by a fine and up to two years' imprisonment.

Amendments to the CTA 2008 directions regime made by TAFA 2010 emphasised the scope of the CTA framework, for example by ensuring that directions can apply to the branches of a relevant person wherever they are located and allowing

---

[148] CTA 2008 Sch.7 para.3.
[149] CTA 2008 Sch.7 para.9(1).
[150] CTA 2008 Sch.7 para.9(2).

requirements to be imposed in relation to subsidiaries of targetted organisations. The TAFA 2010 amendments also introduced an offence of knowingly and intentionally circumventing the requirements of a direction under Sch.7.[151]

1.6.3.4 EU developments

In March 2012, the Commission proposed new rules for a more effective and widespread confiscation of funds and other property acquired through crime. As a result, Directive 2014/42/EU[152] came into force on 19 May 2014. However, the UK decided not to opt into the Directive.

1.7 Conclusion

Since the previous edition of this publication, the UK statutory framework has remained broadly unchanged. Significant legislative developments at the EU level will necessitate some amendments to the UK regime, but the impact of these changes is lessened by the fact that UK has legislated ahead of the rest of Europe to maintain a broader scope and greater intensity for its AML and counter-terrorist financing measures.

Organisational restructurings have led to new enforcement agencies designed to improve effectiveness, but the overall powers and remit remains largely unaltered.

The output of the Government's published review of the effectiveness of rules designed to prevent money laundering and terrorist financing launched in 2015 as part of the Cutting Red Tape project is likely to lead to changes, and hopefully improvements, in the way that this important anti-crime and terrorism legislative framework interacts with business.

---

[151] TAFA 2010 Pt 2.

[152] Directive 2014/42/EU of the European Parliament and of the Council of 3 April 2014 on the freezing and confiscation of instrumentalities and proceeds of crime in the European Union [2014] OJ L127/39.

Chapter 2

Civil Liability and Money Laundering

Paul Marshall[1]
Barrister, No.5 Chambers

> "International fraud is a growth business. Electronic transfer of funds; the widespread use of nominee companies and offshore accounts; the increased sophistication of legitimate financial transactions; and the reluctance of bankers and professional men to inquire into their clients' affairs; all contribute to the ease and speed with which fraudsters can transfer substantial sums from one country to another and conceal their source and the identity of those who control them."[2]

2.1 Introduction

Money laundering law in its suppressive role for the most part engages with the criminal jurisdiction, both in relation to the substantive law, now codified under the Proceeds of Crime Act 2002 (POCA 2002, as amended) and also in connection with the widespread and draconian sanctions that back the (preventive) regulatory provisions under the Money Laundering Regulations 2007[3] (the 2007 Regulations), to be replaced in response to the EU Fourth Money Laundering Directive[4] (the Fourth Directive). Nevertheless, money laundering, both as an activity

---

[1] BA (Cantab); BSc. (Econ.) (Lond. (LSE)); MCIArb.
[2] Sir Peter Millett, "Tracing the Proceeds of Fraud" (1991) 107 L.Q.R. 71.
[3] Money Laundering Regulations 2007 (SI 2007/2157).
[4] Directive (EU) 2015/849 of the European Parliament and of the Council of 20 May 2015 on the prevention of the use of the financial system for the purposes of money laundering or terrorist financing, amending Regulation (EU) No 648/2012 of the European Parliament and of the Council, and repealing Directive

engaged in by criminals seeking to wash the taint of criminality from property and as an activity that governments require professionals to police, report on, and prevent, ineluctably engages with the civil law. If that proposition required to be illustrated, it is put beyond contention by new legislative provisions that give effect to transparency principles that require registers to be established of beneficial ownership of company shares and trusts. As *The Economist* suggested on 17 February 2007, while cash is anonymous,[5] "the suspicion clings that where you find anonymity you find drugs, fraud, money laundering, terrorist financing, and a huge amount of humdrum tax evasion".[6] Much of the impetus of "soft" law initiated by the Financial Action Task Force (FATF) has been directed toward increasing transparency with a correlative decrease, wherever possible, in anonymity.[7]

This Chapter firstly considers ways in which the money laundering regime engages with the civil law, in the first instance discussing ways in which criminal property may give rise to civil liability, and be recovered from those who hold it. Second, consideration is given to how those engaged in implementing the regime and policing the financial system are exposed to risk of civil liability in doing so by measures designed to encourage conscientious and vigilant application of procedures to detect and prevent money laundering. That is of fundamental importance because the reporting regime is at the heart of the policing function now imposed on the financial sector under POCA 2002 and it abrogates traditional (legal) concepts and duties of client confidentiality. The effect of reporting (on transactions (or arrangements)) has for some time given rise to considerable difficulty in legal analysis but

---

2005/60/EC of the European Parliament and of the Council and Commission Directive 2006/70/EC [2015] OJ L141/73.

[5] Or as the Emperor Vespasian more pithily put it to Titus when a tax on urine from public urinals (used for dyeing) was imposed in Rome in about AD 70 *"pecunia non olet"*—money doesn't stink—money laundering law may be said to be concerned with establishing *per contra* that it can and does.

[6] Cited by Tim Bennett, *Money Laundering Compliance*, 3rd edn (Haywards Heath: Bloomsbury, 2014) at para.1.6.

[7] The abolition of bearer shares under the Fourth Directive and the registration of beneficial interests in companies and trusts are striking illustrations with far-reaching implications.

has to some extent been recently clarified, both by the court in 2012 and more recently still by s.37 of the Serious Crime Act 2015, given Royal Assent on 3 March 2015. Section 37 (the requirement for which impliedly suggests that the courts have provided insufficient certainty on the point) came into force on 1 June 2015.[8] Third, brief consideration is given to the scheme of civil sanctions provided for under the 2007 Regulations. Discussion is brief because, as noted, it is likely that the entire sanctions regime under the 2007 Regulations will be substantially revised under the forthcoming Regulations that will implement the Fourth Directive. The existing regulatory structure is widely considered, both by those subject to it and by the relevant authorities, to have engendered an excessively defensive response by businesses.

If a person is the victim of fraud, he will wish to recover the money that he has lost. In such a case it will be scant comfort that the fraudsters are apprehended and tried by a criminal court. Neither will it help him if a bank or financial institution through which the funds were successfully laundered is fined or prosecuted for a failure to carry out proper identity checks, or to report suspicious transactions to the National Crime Agency (NCA).[9] He is out of pocket and wants his money back.

There will be a claim against the original wrongdoers. However, in practice, fraudsters tend to be impecunious, or else to disappear taking their gains with them, preferably to a jurisdiction without an extradition treaty, or whose courts will not permit recovery of the proceeds of crime.[10] Hence attempts

---

[8] Serious Crime Act 2015 (Commencement No.1) Regulations (SI 2015/820) reg.3(k).

[9] In what may seem a process of continual reorganisation and change, the Serious Crime Act 2007 abolished the Asset Recovery Agency (ARA) and transferred its responsibilities and powers to the Serious Organised Crime Agency (that had replaced the National Criminal Intelligence Service or NCIS in 2006) that was itself replaced in 2013 by the National Crime Agency.

[10] In *Baden v Société Générale Pour Favoriser le Developpement du Commerce* [1993] 1 W.L.R. 509 Ch.D, fraudsters succeeded in extracting over $100 million from various mutual funds. A significant amount of this was siphoned off to Costa Rica through a number of unauthorised investments made by the funds, including investments in companies connected with the president of Costa Rica. When the fraud was discovered, the wrongdoers fled there. In *Polly Peck International Plc v Nadir (No.2)* [1992] 4 All E.R. 769 CA, the defendant was

by victims to recover their money from third parties alleged to be implicated in the fraud, or to have facilitated it in some way. Banks and other financial institutions are prime targets for such claims. There are many reasons for this. First, the theft and concealment of large sums of money will almost inevitably involve payments being made through such institutions. It is therefore relatively easy to allege that a bank or other financial institution was involved in laundering the proceeds. Secondly, such institutions have "deep pockets" and are therefore worth pursuing for the large sums involved. Finally, unlike the original wrongdoers, they have a fixed location, and cannot disappear to avoid judgment being entered against them.

The purpose of this Chapter is to provide an overview of the civil law claims that may be made against a bank or financial institution that is alleged to have assisted in laundering the proceeds of fraud. The focus is on fraud, as opposed to other forms of money laundering, as only such claims have given rise to civil actions for damages. That is unsurprising, as in other forms of money laundering there is unlikely to be a victim capable of bringing a civil claim, or else the person will be involved in the underlying criminal conduct. Thus, in the case of drug money laundering, individual drug users cannot sue a bank that is alleged to have laundered the proceeds of drug dealing both on the grounds that the drug users have suffered no financial loss and also because they are party to the underlying criminal activity.[11] Similarly, in the case of terrorism, the victims of terrorist attacks are unlikely to be able to establish a claim against financial institutions alleged to have held money under terrorist control owing to the lack of any nexus or causal link between holding such funds and subsequent terrorist atrocities.[12] In the case of other crimes,

---

accused of stealing large sums of money from Polly Peck and diverting them to northern Cyprus. Before trial, he jumped bail and fled there.

[11] Contracts for the sale of drugs are illegal and in buying drugs, the purchaser will commit the offence of possession under the Misuse of Drugs Act 1971. The principle that money paid for drugs is irrecoverable follows from the wider principle that money paid under an illegal or immoral contract cannot be recovered: *Holman v Johnson* (1775) 1 Cowp. 341 at 343.

[12] A bank that assisted in planning terrorist attacks would be liable as a joint tortfeasor. However, should such a situation ever arise, the appropriate response

there is unlikely to be any causal link between the use of a bank account and the underlying criminal conduct.

This Chapter does not cover the disgorgement of the profits of criminal conduct under the confiscation regime established by POCA 2002. That is covered in Ch.1. Instead, the focus is on claims under the general law. The conclusion is that the civil law has generally provided an effective tool for the recovery of the proceeds of fraud, and is therefore a significant source of potential liability for banks and financial institutions.

2.1.1   Some important distinctions

A victim of fraud has a wide range of potential claims open to him, depending on what happened to his money and the involvement of the persons alleged to have participated in laundering it. These include claims in tort for conversion, conspiracy and unlawful interference in trade as well as claims in restitution on the basis that the defendant has been unjustly enriched. Equity provides personal remedies against third parties that interfere with trust property (which includes money stolen by directors or employees from a company).[13] The type of claim that a claimant may bring depends on the facts of the case (Did the defendant receive the money? Was such receipt for his own benefit or for the account of others? Did he assist in paying it to third parties? Was he dishonest in doing so?), and the type of remedy that the claimant wants (Are damages sufficient or does the claimant need a propri-etary remedy, for example because the defendant is insolvent?).

In understanding the potential liability of a bank or financial institution, it is necessary to make a few distinctions at the outset as these determine the nature of the remedy that a claimant may obtain. The most important are those between

---

would be criminal prosecution of those involved, withdrawal of authorisation and seizure of the funds under terrorist control.

[13] Whether equity provides a remedy for assistance in a breach of fiduciary duty not involving the misapplication of trust funds is controversial. See the cases referred to in fn.105 below.

common law rights and equitable causes of action, and between personal rights and property rights.

2.1.1.1   Common law and equity

The nature of the rights that may be asserted at common law and in equity are often different. Briefly, equity was a body of rules developed by the Court of Chancery in England before 1873 to correct, supplement and reform the common law.[14] It did this by modifying the effect of certain legal rules (e.g. by holding that it was unconscionable in certain cases for a plaintiff to rely on common law rights), and by developing new remedies (e.g. rescission, specific performance, specific delivery). The characteristic institution of equity is the trust, and when equity wishes to impose liability on a person, it typically does so by declaring that person to be a trustee, or else treating him as if he were a trustee (i.e. as a constructive trustee).[15]

How this works in practice was vividly demonstrated in the Supreme Court's recent (July 2014) review of constructive trusts in connection with bribes and secret commissions in *FHR European Ventures LLP v Cedar Capital Partners LLC*.[16] Though not in issue in the proceedings, the Bribery Act 2010 makes such payments offences predicate for money laundering and, accordingly, criminal property under POCA 2002 s 34. Thus payments of bribes will engage both the AML legislative regime and trust law.

FHR v Cedar is both a leading decision and a paradigm instance of unlawful (illegal) payment. FHR purchased the issued share capital of Monte Carlo Grand Hotel SAM from Monte Carlo

---

[14] John D. Heydon, Mark J. Leeming and Peter G. Turner (eds), *Meagher, Gummow and Lehane's Equity: Doctrines and Remedies*, 5th edn (London: Lexis Nexis, 2014).

[15] There are exceptional cases where a person would incur direct personal liability. Further, where equity acted in its concurrent or auxiliary jurisdiction in support of common law claims, there was no need to rely on an actual or notional trust. An example of the former is equity's jurisdiction to grant rescission for fraud. An example of the latter is the equitable remedy of discovery (now available in all proceedings under the Civil Procedure Rules).

[16] *FHR European Ventures LLP v Cedar Capital Partners LLC* [2014] UKSC 45; [2015] A.C. 250; [2014] 2 B.C.L.C. 145.

Grand Hotel Ltd (the Vendor) for €211.5m. The purchase was a joint venture between the claimants for whom FHR was the vehicle. Cedar Capital Partners provided consultancy services to the hotel industry, and it had acted as the claimants' agent in negotiating the purchase. Cedar accordingly owed fiduciary duties to the claimants. Cedar had also entered into an agreement with the vendor which provided for the payment to Cedar of a €10m fee following a successful conclusion of the sale and purchase of the issued share capital. The Vendor paid Cedar €10m on or about 7 January 2005. FHR claimed the €10m received by Cedar from the Vendor.

There were inconsistent lines of authority that included, most importantly, *Tyrrell v Bank of London*[17] (a decision of the House of Lords), *Lister & Co v Stubbs*[18] and a more recent decision of the Court of Appeal *Sinclair Investments Ltd v Versailles Trade Finance Ltd (In Administration).*[19] At first instance in *FHR v Cedar*, Simon J held himself bound by the judgment given by Lord Neuberger MR in *Sinclair Investments* but the Court of Appeal distinguished that case on appeal. In the Supreme Court, Lord Neuberger, giving the judgment of the Court,[20] overruled *Sinclair*, concluding that the law had taken a wrong turn. He observed that:

> "[t]here can clearly be different views as to what require-
> ments have to be satisfied before a proprietary interest is
> created. More broadly, it is fair to say that the concept of
> equitable proprietary rights is in some respects somewhat
> paradoxical. Equity, unlike the common law, classically
> acts in personam ... yet equity is far more ready to accord
> proprietary claims than common law. Further, two general
> rules which law students learn early on are that common
> law legal rights prevail over equitable rights, and that
> where there are competing equitable rights the first in time
> prevails; yet, given that equity is far more ready to
> recognise proprietary rights than common law, the effect

---

[17] *Tyrrell v Bank of London* (1862) 10 H.L. Cas. 26; 11 E.R. 934 HL.
[18] *Lister & Co v Stubbs* (1890) 45 Ch. D. 1 CA.
[19] *Sinclair Investments (UK) Ltd v Versailles Trade Finance Ltd (In Administration)* [2011] EWCA Civ 347; [2012] Ch. 453; [2011] Bus. L.R. 1126.
[20] *FHR European Ventures* [2014] UKSC 45 at [32].

of having an equitable right is often to give priority over common law claims—sometimes even those which may have preceded the equitable right. Given that equity developed at least in part to mitigate the rigours of the common law, this is perhaps scarcely surprising. However, it underlines the point that it would be unrealistic to expect complete consistency from the cases over the past 300 years."

Resolving long uncertainty and occasionally hot debate, the Supreme Court concluded that a bribe or secret commission accepted by an agent is held on trust for his principal.[21] Accordingly, the Supreme Court clarified the law, affirming the Court of Appeal's decision that FHR had a proprietory claim to the money received by Cedar (reversing Simon J on the point).

2.1.1.2   Personal and property rights

This distinction is often crucial. Property rights are rights in relation to a thing (a *res*).[22] The distinguishing characteristic of property rights is that they are enforceable against the world generally. A person that interferes with property rights will incur liability to the owner of the property.[23] Personal rights, on the other hand, are rights against a particular person, or a class of persons. An example of a property right is ownership of land. An example of a personal right is a debt which gives the right to sue the debtor for non-payment. Property rights may also give rise to personal rights. Thus, if D deceives me into transferring my shares in company X to him, then he will be personally liable in the tort of deceit for interference with my property rights.

The most important characteristic of property rights is that they endure. They will not normally be defeated by a third party's interference with my property. Thus, if D steals my car and sells it, I can recover the car, or its value, from a purchaser

---

[21] *FHR European Ventures* [2014] UKSC 45 at [46].
[22] This derives from Roman law. See *Gaius' Institutes 1.8* and *Justinian's Institutes 1.2.12.38*.
[23] Many exceptions exist.

from D. Further, and of particular relevance in a money laundering context, property rights will not be lost if the defendant becomes insolvent. So long as I can still identify my property (or, in certain cases, its traceable proceeds) I will be entitled to recover it, or its value, even if the defendant is insolvent. If, on the other hand, my property has been dissipated or destroyed, then I will be limited to a personal claim for damages.

There are reasons other than priority in insolvency why a claimant may wish to assert a property right. Thus, if a fraudster has invested my money successfully, I may wish to strip him of his gains. If I have a proprietary interest in the money used to make the investment I may do so.[24] Equally, there may be procedural advantages in bringing a proprietary claim. If the property is located within England, the defendant may be prevented by an injunction from dissipating the property until the claim is heard. Thus, banks may be subjected to an order preventing them from permitting transactions on an account which is alleged to be subject to a constructive trust: see generally *Paragon Finance plc v D.B. Thakerar & Co*[25] and *Foskett v McKeown.*[26]

2.1.1.3 *Common law and equitable property rights*

At common law there are two types of property right. You either own something outright, or you have a security interest in it. The range of security interests is limited (e.g. a mortgage, a pledge, a lien).[27] In general, at common law, ownership follows possession,[28] and remedies for interference with legal rights are usually based on interference with possession.[29] As

---

[24] *Trustee of the Property of F.C. Jones & Sons (A Firm) v Jones* [1997] Ch. 159; [1996] 3 W.L.R. 703 CA.

[25] *Paragon Finance Plc v D.B. Thakerar & Co* [1998] EWCA Civ 1249; [1999] 1 All E.R. 400 CA.

[26] *Foskett v McKeown* [2001] 1 A.C. 102; [2000] 2 W.L.R. 1299 HL (see further at fn.145 below) and see also *Polly Peck International Plc v Nadir (Asil) (No.2)* [1992] 4 All E.R. 769 CA.

[27] The range of encumbrances that can be created on land are ignored for these purposes (e.g. an easement or *profit à prendre*).

[28] *Armory v Delamirie* (1722) 1 Str. 505; 93 E.R. 664.

[29] There are exceptions. In the case of land, the true owner could always seek to

possession is open and transparent, liability for interference with legal rights is generally strict.[30]

Equity was able, through the institution of the trust, to recognise a much wider range of property rights. The main technique was to say that although a person may have legal ownership of property it is subject to the beneficial interest of another person. In this way, equity carved a wide range of equitable interests out of the legal title. It follows that the holder of the legal title may be subject to claims from a number of other persons who are or claim to be beneficially interested in the property. In the case of a bank account, the legal owner is the account holder. However, in equity, an account may be subject to a number of third-party interests in favour of persons beneficially entitled to the money.

The consequence of that is that equitable interests in property are often hidden, and it may be difficult for persons dealing with the legal owner to discover them. Hence, the law has developed protections for persons dealing with the legal owner, of which the most important is that an equitable interest cannot be enforced against a purchaser from the legal owner who acts in good faith without notice of such equitable interests (the bona fide purchaser rule). For the same reason, equity generally requires either "fault" or "notice" before imposing liability on a person for interference with equitable rights. A person who receives property subject to another's equitable rights is not, without more, liable to the beneficiary, even if the person deals with the property in such a way as to cause the equitable interest to be lost. This is expressed in the maxim that equity operates on the "conscience" of the legal owner.[31] This distinction between the traditional fault-based

---

recover the land itself. Equally, a person with a better claim for possession (the owner) could recover against a person with a more limited right (e.g. a thief or a purchaser from the thief).

[30] *Hollins v Fowler* (1874–1875) L.R. 7 H.L. 757 HL (conversion) and *Lipkin Gorman v Karpnale Ltd* [1991] 2 A.C. 548; [1991] 3 W.L.R. 10 HL (money had and received).

[31] *Westdeutsche Landesbank Girozentrale v Islington LBC* [1996] A.C. 669 HL at 705. There are historical reasons for this as it enabled Chancery judges to state that they were not negating the relevant common law rule, but precluding the defendant from relying on it if it would be unconscionable to do so.

approach of equity, and the strict common law position, will be seen in the different remedies that the common law and equity make available for money laundering.

2.1.1.4 Common law and equitable remedies

The common law provides a range of remedies for interference with legal rights. However, they normally only give rise to personal rights (i.e. a right to damages for interference with the right). As the law now stands, a person is not able to assert a direct common law claim to identifiable property other than land, although the court has a discretionary power to order the return of specific property that has been misappropriated. However, even if a person is not seeking a proprietary remedy he may need to show that he had a common law proprietary right at a point in time in the past in order to bring a personal claim against the defendant (e.g. a claim for damages for conversion depends on the claimant having had title to the property when the defendant interfered with it. However, the claimant need not still own the property when the action is brought).

Equity, on the other hand, provides both personal and proprietary claims in respect of misapplied property. If the victim can identify his property (or its traceable proceeds) in the defendant's hands then he may be able to assert a direct proprietary claim. Such a claim will be available even if the defendant is insolvent as property rights are not defeated by insolvency.[32] Equity also provides personal remedies against persons that interfere with equitable rights although, as stated above, such claims currently require proof of fault. Thus, a defendant will be liable if he dishonestly assists in a breach of fiduciary duty, or if he "knowingly" receives property that is beneficially owned by other people. The standard of knowledge required for these causes of action is controversial and it has been argued that a person should be strictly liable for

---

[32] *Chase Manhattan Bank N.A v Israel-British Bank (London) Ltd* [1981] Ch. 105; [1980] 2 W.L.R. 802 Ch.D. Again there are exceptions (e.g. preferences, transactions entered into at an undervalue or in fraud of creditors). These are not relevant in the present context.

interference with equitable property rights. It is unclear whether the law will develop in this direction, although if it did this could have significant consequences in expanding the potential liability of financial institutions that receive money which represents the proceeds of crime.

2.1.2 Organisation of the Chapter

This Chapter provides an overview of the main claims that can be brought to recover the proceeds of fraud. To set the context, the next section describes, briefly, the duties that a bank or financial institution owes to its customer, and how this interrelates with the institution's potential criminal liability for money laundering. The third section deals with common law claims and covers liability for conversion, deceit, conspiracy and unlawful interference in trade as well as for money had and received. The latter term is used instead of the more common term "restitution" as there exists a wide range of different causes of action that may lead to restitution. In this section, the focus is solely on the common law personal claim to reverse unjust enrichment.

The fourth section deals with equitable causes of action. This addresses the liability of persons who assist in a breach of trust or fiduciary duty. The section also analyses the liability of banks and financial institutions for the receipt of monies paid away in breach of trust or fiduciary duty. The fifth section considers property claims where the victim is able to assert continuing ownership of his property. The final section describes the circumstances in which a person whose property has been misapplied may assert rights in substitute assets that were acquired with the proceeds of his property.

2.2   The financial institution and its customer

The duties of a bank or other financial institution to its customer are briefly described below. There is a potential conflict between the institution's duty to its customer (e.g. to honour a cheque, to transfer funds, to sell shares, etc.) and its potential liability to third parties for money laundering if it suspects that its customer may be acting unlawfully. The dilemma for the institution (in addition to the difficult questions it will face in relation to its potential liabilities under statute) is whether to comply with its customer's instructions, and hence potentially expose itself to liability to third parties, or else refuse to do so and so risk action against it by its customer.

2.2.1 Duties of a bank to its customer

The primary duty of a bank is to comply with the terms of a customer's mandate.[33] This is a contractual duty, and a bank will incur liability for breach of contract if it fails without a proper reason to give effect to its customer's instructions.[34] A bank is therefore exposed to a claim for damages if it refuses to repay a deposit, or to honour cheques drawn on an account.[35] Alliott J, in *Lipkin Gorman v Karpnale Ltd*, stated the traditional law as follows[36]:

(1) the bank is entitled to treat the customer's mandate at its face value save in extreme cases;
(2) the bank is not obliged to question any transaction which is in accordance with the mandate, unless a reasonable banker would have grounds for believing that the authorised signatories are misusing their authority for the purpose of defrauding their principal or otherwise defeating his true intention;
(3) it follows that if the bank does not have reasonable grounds for believing that there is fraud it must pay;
(4) mere suspicion or unease do not constitute reasonable grounds and are not enough to justify the bank in failing to act in accordance with a mandate; and
(5) the bank is not required to act as an amateur detective.

---

[33] *Lipkin Gorman* [1992] 4 All E.R. 409 CA.
[34] *N. Joachimson (A Firm) v Swiss Bank Corporation (Costs)* [1921] 3 K.B. 110 CA.
[35] *Hilton v Westminster Bank Ltd* (1926) 135 L.T. 358 CA.
[36] *Lipkin Gorman* [1987] 1 W.L.R. 987 QBD at 1006.

That analysis must now be read subject to a bank's duties under POCA 2002.

2.2.2 Other financial institutions

Although the case law has mainly been concerned with the duties of banks, other financial institutions can face the same dilemmas. A stock broker, fund manager or financial adviser owes contractual duties including a duty of care to its customers, and will be liable to its customers for breach of contract if it fails to give effect to the terms of its customer agreement. If, however, the customer is using the financial institution to carry out a fraud, or to launder the proceeds of crime, then it may incur liability to the victims for facilitating the fraud. In such a case the institution will need to assess the level of the risk, and then reach a judgment in the same way as a bank would.

2.2.3 Money laundering offences and the position of the financial institution

A further concern is the possibility of criminal liability where a financial institution suspects wrongdoing. A financial institution must not give effect to instructions from its customer if to do so would involve the institution committing a money laundering offence.

The key statutory money laundering offences have been discussed in Ch.1. Financial institutions, and banks in particular, can find themselves in the difficult position of having to notify the NCA of a suspicion about a customer, and to avoid committing a primary assistance offence by giving effect to that customer's instructions, whilst at the same time seeking to avoid committing a tipping-off offence as a result of refusing to deal in accordance with the customer's mandate.

Under POCA 2002, it is an offence for a bank to enter into or become concerned in an arrangement known or suspected to facilitate by whatever means the acquisition, retention, use or control of criminal property:

> "Thus a bank would commit an offence if it allowed ordinary banking business to be conducted in respect of funds suspected to be criminal property unless the bank had made an authorised disclosure under s. 338 and received the appropriate consent under s. 335."[37]

It is no defence to a charge of money laundering that the bank was contractually obliged to obey its customer's instructions. In such circumstances the court said in *K Ltd v National Westminster Bank plc*[38]:

> "If the law of the land makes it a criminal offence to honour the customer's mandate in these circumstances there can, in my judgment, be no breach of contract for the bank to refuse to honour its mandate and there can, equally, be no invasion (or threatened invasion) of a legal right on the part of the bank such as is required before a claimant can apply for an injunction."

It follows that, in the absence of relevant consent, it is illegal for the bank to process transactions on the customer's account. The difficulties that arose under previous legislation, where customers sued their bank for non-performance of the terms of the mandate, accordingly have been resolved in favour of the bank.

The practical effect of a bank suspecting money laundering and reporting its suspicions to the NCA is therefore to suspend the bank's obligations to its customer under the mandate.[39]It is not necessary for the bank to have to justify its suspicion through providing evidence. Nor will the court permit the cross-examination of an employee who entertained such suspicion. In the court's view, the existence of suspicion is a subjective fact. There is no requirement that there should be reasonable grounds for the suspicion.[40] It may be doubted whether this

---

[37] *R. (on the application of UMBS Online Ltd) v Serious Organised Crime Agency* [2007] EWCA Civ 406, [2007] Bus. L.R. 1317 at [4].

[38] *K Ltd v National Westminster Bank Plc* [2006] EWCA Civ 1039; [2007] 1 W.L.R. 311; [2007] Bus. L.R. 26 at [10].

[39] *K Ltd v National Westminster Bank Plc* [2007] Bus. L.R. 26 at [11].

[40] *K Ltd v National Westminster Bank Plc* [2007] Bus. L.R. 26 at [16].

legislation has struck a fair balance between the interests of the Government in the suppression of financial crime and the rights of individuals to access their accounts and perform financial transactions without proof of actual wrongdoing.

2.3   Common law claims

This section sets out certain common law causes of action that are available to the victim of fraud. Apart from money had and received, these claims are likely to be mainly relevant to the original wrongdoers, as opposed to a bank or financial institution. They will therefore be considered briefly. The reason for considering them is that the liability of a bank or other financial institution is normally predicated on the existence of wrongdoing by the primary offender.

2.3.1   Conversion

Conversion is the unlawful appropriation of another person's property,[41] whether for that party's own benefit or for the benefit of a third party. A defendant guilty of conversion is liable to pay damages equal to the value of the property converted.[42] There is also a statutory power to order the return of the property where an award of damages would not be an adequate remedy. This is unlikely to be relevant in a money laundering context, as the claimant will be adequately compensated through repayment of the money with interest.

2.3.1.1   Types of conversion

Conversion covers the deliberate taking, receipt, purchase, sale, disposal or consumption of another's property. Anyone who without authority receives or takes possession of another's

---

[41] Michael A. Jones, Anthony M. Dugdale and Mark Simpson (eds), *Clerk & Lindsell on Torts*, 21st edn (London: Sweet & Maxwell, 2014), para.17-09. The essence of the wrong was the unauthorised dealing with the claimant's chattel so as to question or deny his title to it, para.17-06.
[42] *Kuwait Airways Corp v Iraqi Airways Co (No.6)* [2002] UKHL 19; [2002] 2 A.C. 883; [2003] 1 C.L.C. 183.

goods with the intention of asserting some right over them, or deals with them in a manner inconsistent with the right of the true owner, is prima facie guilty of conversion.[43]

2.3.1.2 *What property can be converted?*

Conversion applies to interference with the ownership of chattels and money, but not things in action.[44]It follows that it is impossible to bring a claim in conversion for the misappropriation of a debt, or of money held in a bank account, as these are things in action.[45] This seriously restricts the use of the tort of conversion in combating money laundering, as this will usually involve the making of payments into and out of bank accounts. However, it may be possible to bring a claim in conversion in respect of a misappropriated banker's draft, a cheque or a bill of exchange. Definitive bearer securities and money market instruments held in physical bearer form may also be converted. This will not be possible, however, if the instruments are dematerialised, or are held through an intermediary or a clearing system.[46]

As conversion is based on an interference with property rights, it is only possible to maintain a claim if it can be shown that the defendant converted identifiable property. This presents a practical difficulty in the case of money as it will be very difficult to identify through whose hands individual notes and coins have passed (although each bank note has a unique serial number, it is very uncommon to keep a record of this number and to trace its subsequent ownership). Further, even if it is possible to show that the claimant's notes and coins ended up being paid across the counter of X Bank it is likely that the claimant's title to the money will by then have been lost. This is

---

[43] *Lancashire & Yorkshire Railway v MacNicoll* (1918) 88 L.J. K.B. 601; [1918] All E.R Rep. 537.

[44] That is the definition of "goods" under s.14 of the Torts (Interference with Goods) Act 1977.

[45] *OBG Ltd v Allan; Mainstream Properties Ltd v Young, Douglas v Hello! Ltd;* sub nom. *OBG Ltd v Allen* [2007] UKHL 21; [2008] 1 A.C. 1; [2007] Bus. L.R. 1600.

[46] In the (unlikely) event of the custody arrangement involving a bailment of physical instruments, the bailee may be guilty of conversion if he misappropriates the claimant's property or detinue if he fails to return it.

because the original owner's title to money is extinguished once it has been paid as currency to a third party acting in good faith.[47]

2.3.2 Deceit

It is in the nature of fraud to induce persons to part with their money by false representations. Most frauds will involve at some stage the making of dishonest statements. Examples include fraudulent representations in a company prospectus, ponzi schemes, boiler rooms, etc.

Deceit involves the making of a false statement which is intended to be relied on and is relied on by a person to his detriment. The statement must also be made fraudulently. A statement is made fraudulently if it is made knowingly, without belief in its truth, or recklessly or carelessly as to whether it is true or false.[48] It follows that a statement believed to be true, no matter how implausible, is not fraudulent (in such circumstances, a person may be liable for negligence, although in that case it would be necessary to show the existence of a relationship of sufficient proximity between the parties).[49]

A person who has lost money or other property as a result of fraud may sue the fraudsters for deceit. If he has been induced by fraud to enter into a contract, he will also be able to avoid the contract and recover any money or property transferred under it.[50] The problem with a claim in deceit, however, is that it only lies against the parties to the fraud. A bank or financial

---

[47] *Derry v Peek* (1889) 14 App. Cas. 337 at 376 HL.

[48] *Derry v Peek* (1889) 14 App. Cas. 337 at 376 HL.

[49] The case law on liability for negligent misstatement is enormous. See, e.g. *Hedley Byrne and Co Ltd v Heller and Partners Ltd* [1964] A.C. 465; [1963] 3 W.L.R. 101 HL; *Caparo Industries Plc v Dickman* [1990] 2 A.C. 605; [1990] 2 W.L.R. 358; [1990] B.C.C. 164 HL and *Williams v Natural Life Health Foods Ltd* [1998] 1 W.L.R. 830; [1998] B.C.C. 428 HL.

[50] Unless the right to rescind has been lost, e.g. because third parties have acquired rights in property transferred under the agreement.

institution used by fraudsters will not be liable unless the institution itself has made fraudulent statements or was a willing party to the fraud.

2.3.3 *Conspiracy*

For a conspiracy, there must be concerted action between two or more persons. For concerted action, there must be an agreement or understanding between the combiners.[51] The agreement may be formal or informal, express or tacit.[52] There must be a meeting of minds in the sense that the parties knew the essential facts and entertained the same object.[53] It is necessary for defendants to have knowledge of facts that make the proposed conduct unlawful, even if they do not appreciate the legal significance.[54] An overt act by one or more, but not necessarily all, of the conspirators is an essential element of the tort of unlawful means conspiracy.[55]

Conspiracies may be criminal or civil (and indeed both). In both kinds of conspiracy the mischief (the essence of the tort and offence respectively) is in the combining or combination with the relevant unlawful (or criminal) intention. Importantly, agreement need not be express but may be tacit and agreement may be inferred from actions. Conspiracies, whether civil or criminal, are by their nature hidden.[56] It will be apparent that money laundering of any complexity may readily additionally involve both criminal and civil conspiracies. The ambit of unlawful means (civil) conspiracy remains to be fully worked

---

[51] *Mulcahy v The Queen* (1868) L.R. 3 H.L. 306 HL at 317.

[52] *Kuwait Oil Tanker Co SAK v Al-Bader* [2000] 2 All E.R. (Comm) 271 CA at 312 per Nourse LJ (a modern leading decision on civil conspiracy).

[53] *Crofter Hand Woven Harris Tweed Co v Veitch* [1942] A.C. 435 HL at 479—the leading authority on the law in this area, as further recently clarified in *Customs and Excise Commissioners v Total Network SL* [2008] UKHL 19; [2008] 1 A.C. 1174; [2008] 2 W.L.R. 711 (below).

[54] *Belmont Finance Corp v Williams Furniture Ltd (No.2)* [1980] 1 All E.R. 393 CA at 404 per Buckley LJ.

[55] *Crofter Hand Woven Harris Tweed Co v Veitch* [1942] A.C. 435 HL.

[56] See the judgment of Nourse LJ in *Kuwait Oil Tanker Co SAK v Al-Bader* [2000] 2 All E.R. (Comm) 271 CA, approving propositions of O'Connor LJ to that effect in the Court of Appeal decision in *R. v Siracusa* (1990) 90 Cr. App. R. 340 CA at 349.

out following the very important House of Lords' (liberalising) decision in *HM Commissioners of Revenue and Customs v Total Network Services*.[57]

There are two separate forms of the civil wrong (tort), though in practice only "unlawful means conspiracy" is likely to have application in this context because money laundering, necessarily of its very nature, is an illegal activity.

An unlawful means conspiracy is a combination to do an unlawful act thereby causing loss to the victim. There must be an agreement, combination or understanding between the parties to do the relevant acts and capable of being inferred from the circumstances. Of great importance is that the conspirators need not all join in at the same time, nor need they have exactly the same aim in mind.[58] Conspirators may therefore move in and out of a conspiracy but still remain liable for the loss caused to the victim.

In *Commissioners of Revenue and Customs v Total Network Services SL*[59] the House of Lords overruled the Court of Appeal's decision in *Powell v Boladz*[60] and held that the tort of conspiracy to use unlawful means (contrary to the Court of Appeal's decision in *Powell*) does not require that the unlawful means must be independently actionable (that is to say, give rise to separate independent civil liability—even if, say, otherwise a crime) at the suit of the claimant. At first sight, that may not appear to be of particularly wide importance, but it is. *Total Network* involved a so-called "carousel fraud" where HMRC was defrauded of VAT. It was alleged by HMRC in civil proceedings that the defendants had operated such a fraud committing the offence of cheating the Revenue. It was alleged

---

[57] *Customs and Excise Commissioners v Total Network SL* [2008] UKHL 19; [2008] 1 A.C. 1174; [2008] 2 W.L.R. 711.

[58] *Kuwait Oil Tanker Co SAK v Al-Bader* [2000] 2 All E.R. (Comm) 271 CA at [111]: "it is not necessary for the conspirators all to join the conspiracy at the same time, but we agree with the judge that the parties to it must be sufficiently aware of the surrounding circumstances and share the same object for it properly to be said that they were acting in concert at the time of the acts complained of".

[59] *Total Network SL* [2008] UKHL 19; [2008] 1 A.C. 1174; [2008] 2 W.L.R. 711.

[60] *Powell v Boladz* [1998] Lloyd's Rep. Med. 116; (1998) 39 B.M.L.R. 35 CA.

that that constituted "unlawful means" for the purpose of a cause of action in conspiracy. That was accepted by the judge at first instance and freezing orders were granted. The Court of Appeal held[61] that it was bound by its earlier decision in *Powell* and there was no cause of action because the unlawful means alleged were not *independently* actionable by HMRC. The House of Lords held *Powell* to have been wrongly decided. Thus a cause of action in conspiracy can arise where the unlawful means relied upon is only a crime (and not itself a tort). The Court of Appeal in *Powell* had the effect of very severely limiting the ambit of the tort of unlawful means conspiracy. That limit has now been removed and it remains somewhat uncertain how wide-ranging the tort of unlawful means conspiracy is in practice. But it has peculiar and obvious relevance to money laundering because provided the con-spiracy (i.e. the combination) is directed at the victim, and the unlawful conduct is the means of intentionally harming him, a claim for conspiracy will be available (though subject to damage having been suffered[62] as damages in conspiracy are assessed on similar generous principles (remoteness of loss) to those that apply to damages for fraud/deceit).

It will be immediately apparent that the decision in *Total Network* is of great potential importance given the enormous expansion of the criminal law in recent years, including the development of money laundering law, almost all of which is the product of statutory development since 1980. Other crimes that may give rise to claims for civil conspiracy may include a conspiracy to defraud, fraud under the Fraud Act 2006, insider dealing and market manipulation[63] and bribery under the Bribery Act 2010.

---

[61] *Total Network SL* [2007] EWCA Civ 39, [2007] 2 W.L.R. 1156.
[62] *Lonrho v Al-Fayed (No.5)* [1993] 1 W.L.R. 1489 CA at 1494 and 1501 per Dillon and Stuart Smith LJJ.
[63] It is unclear if market abuse would constitute "unlawful conduct" if it did not involve the commission of an insider dealing or market manipulation offence.

The second type of conspiracy involves an agreement to use lawful means to harm the claimant. In this case, it is necessary to show that the *predominant purpose* of the conspirators is to injure the victim.[64]

The tort of conspiracy may provide a remedy against the underlying wrongdoers. Indeed, there may be clear procedural and substantive advantages to a claimant in bringing a claim in conspiracy, rather than relying on individual unlawful acts.[65] Further, "[t]o allege a conspiracy to defraud may describe the events in the fairest and most sensible way".[66] However, it is unlikely to provide a remedy against banks or financial institutions unless they are actively party to the fraud. A bank or financial institution that negligently fails to appreciate that its customers are intent on fraud will not be liable as a co-conspirator. Liability in equity as a constructive trustee will depend upon particular facts and the relevant state of knowledge.

2.3.4 Unlawful interference in trade

This is a further claim that may be brought against the underlying wrongdoers. It is unlikely to be relevant to a bank or financial institution. The tort consists of:

(a) wrongful interference with the actions of a third party in which a claimant has a financial interest; and
(b) an intention thereby to cause loss to the claimant.[67]

---

[64] *Quinn v Leathem* [1901] A.C. 495 HL; *Crofter Hand Woven Harris Tweed Co v Veitch* [1942] A.C. 435 HL; *Lonrho v Shell Petroleum (No.2)* [1982] A.C. 173; [1981] 3 W.L.R. 33 HL.
[65] Where the conspiracy is effected outside of England, a claim in conspiracy may simplify the conflict of laws analysis as the claimant will rely on the single tort of conspiracy rather than sue separately in respect of each of the individual unlawful acts carried out pursuant to the agreement. It will also enable liability to be imposed on those parties to the underlying agreement who do not carry out any of the illegal acts (e.g. a mafia boss or leader of a crime syndicate).
[66] *Kuwait Oil Tanker v Al-Bader* [2000] 2 All E.R. (Comm) 271 at [131].
[67] *OBG Ltd v Allan*; sub nom. *Mainstream Properties Ltd v Young*; *Douglas v Hello! Ltd* [2007] UKHL 21; [2008] 1 A.C. 1; [2007] Bus. L.R. 1600 at [47].

The essence of the tort "is deliberate interference with the plaintiff's interests by unlawful means".[68] In this context the "unlawful means" must be civilly, as opposed to criminally, actionable.[69]

2.3.5 *Money had and received (restitution)*

The final common law claim is the action for money had and received. This claim exists to reverse a defendant's unjustified enrichment. It is therefore available to reverse the enrichment of the original wrongdoers although in practice there will be a range of other causes of action available. It is also available against third parties that are unjustly enriched. Thus it is possible in this way to recover misapplied money from an innocent donee. Equally, a bank or financial institution that beneficially receives stolen money will be liable unless it can rely on a relevant defence. It is therefore a significant potential source of liability for banks and financial institutions.

A person is liable if:

(a)   he has been enriched;
(b)   that enrichment was at the expense of the plaintiff;
(c)   there is no legal reason for him to retain the enrichment; and
(d)   no defence is available.[70]

A person will always be enriched by the payment of money. This applies as much to a bank or financial institution as to any other person who receives the proceeds of crime. This is because money that is paid into a bank account becomes the property of the bank. However, as is explained below, a bank may be able to invoke the defences of "ministerial receipt" or change of position where it has received money and has accounted for it to its customer.

---

[68]   *Barretts & Baird (Wholesale) Ltd v Institution of Professional Civil Servants* [1987] I.R.L.R. 3 QBD.
[69]   *OBG Ltd v Allan* [2007] Bus. L.R. 1600 HL.
[70]   *Banque Financière de la Cité v Parc (Battersea) Ltd* [1999] 1 A.C. 221; [1998] 2 W.L.R. 475; [1998] C.L.C. 520 HL.

The making of a mistaken payment, or the non-consensual transfer of funds, are paradigm examples of enrichment "at the expense of the plaintiff". A large body of case law has developed setting out the situations in which the defendant may not retain an enrichment (referred to as "unjust factors"). These include payments made by mistake, under duress, as a result of an unconscionable bargain, or straightforward cases of theft. In practice it will be easy in a money laundering context to show that the misapplication was induced by an unjust factor, thereby triggering a prima facie obligation on the recipient to repay.

Where the money has passed through one or more bank accounts, or through payments made via a clearing system, then the original debt represented by the bank account will have ceased to exist. If the claimant wishes to bring a claim against a recipient whose account is credited with the proceeds of the fraud, he will need to rely on the doctrine of tracing to show that the money that ended up in the defendant's account represents the proceeds of the money taken from his account. Tracing is considered in the final section of this Chapter.

It should be noted that unlike equitable claims (see below), liability at common law for money had and received is strict.[71] It follows that a defendant will be liable from the moment of receipt. It is no defence that the defendant did not know or suspect that the money was stolen. A bank or financial institution may therefore be liable even if it acts in complete good faith in crediting a customer's account with money that turns out, on examination, to represent the proceeds of crime. Neither need the bank still retain the money, or any traceable proceeds, at the time that the claimant brings his action. This is because the bank's liability is a personal liability to make restitution for value that it should never have received as opposed to a property claim or a claim for damages for wrongdoing. Equally, a defendant may be liable even though the account holder became legally entitled to the money. This is illustrated by *Lipkin Gorman v Karpnale Ltd*.[72] A partner in a

---

[71] *Kelly v Solari* (1841) 9 M & W 54; 152 E.R. 24.
[72] *Lipkin Gorman v Karpnale Ltd* [1991] 2 A.C. 548; [1991] 3 W.L.R. 10 HL.

firm of solicitors drew a number of cheques on the firm's client account in order to fund his gambling. It was held that as the partner had actual authority to draw cheques on the client account he became entitled to the drafts. Nonetheless, the club at which the stolen money was gambled away was held liable in restitution (money paid under a wager being treated under English law at the time as a gift by the unsuccessful gambler to the club).

2.3.5.1 Defences

Given the scope of potential liability where a customer pays money into his account that represents the proceeds of crime, it is important for financial institutions to know the circumstances in which they will be able to rely on defences to mitigate the scope of this prima facie liability. Unfortunately, this area of law is complex and is likely to be subject to further refinement by the courts.

2.3.5.1.1 Ministerial receipt

It is a defence for an agent that has received money in his capacity as agent if he has paid it over to his principal before acquiring notice of a third party's claim to the money. In this case, the third party must sue the principal and the agent drops out of the picture. This is referred to as "ministerial receipt" as the agent receives the money as minister for his principal. The same principle applies to banks that receive money as agent for their customer. However, so long as the account between the bank and its customer is provisional, and is capable of being reversed, the bank is not able to rely on the defence.[73] In *Kleinwort & Sons v Dunlop Rubber*[74] the House of Lords indicated that there needed to be some element of detriment before a bank could rely on this defence. Merely crediting a customer's account was not enough, as in that case the bank "had only got to run a pen through some private entries in

---

[73] *Bavins & Sims v London & South Western Bank Ltd* [1900] 1 Q.B. 270 CA.
[74] *Kleinwort & Sons v Dunlop Rubber Co Ltd* (1907) 97 L.T. 263 HL. See also *Kerrison v Glyn, Mills, Currie & Co* (1912) 81 L.J.K.B. 465 HL.

their own books and the matter then would have stood in precisely the same position as it stood in before the mistake was made".[75]

However, once payment over to the customer has taken place then the defence will be available. In *Agip (Africa) Ltd v Jackson*,[76] the defendant accountants set up a shelf company to facilitate the laundering of money stolen from the claimants. A cheque was fraudulently altered, resulting in payment being made to the shelf company. The defendants received the money through their client account and then paid it on to the beneficiaries of the fraud overseas. The defendants were sued, amongst other claims, for money had and received. The court held that they had received the money as agent for the ultimate beneficiaries in accordance with whose instructions they had paid it on. They were therefore not liable for money had and received. Millett J. said that they "must be treated as being in the same position as an agent who has accounted to his principal. Money paid by mistake to such an agent cannot afterwards be recovered from the agent but only from the principal".[77] Equally, where the bank has altered its position on the faith of the payment then it will be able to rely on the defence.[78]

2.3.5.1.2 Change of position

This is a defence "available to a person whose position has so changed that it would be inequitable in all the circumstances to require him to make restitution".[79] In *Lipkin Gorman*, referred to above, the liability of the club to repay money stolen from the solicitors' client account was limited to the club's net winnings. As the club had paid out in respect of those bets that were successful it would be inequitable to require the club to repay to the solicitors the gross sum gambled away by the dishonest partner.

---

[75] *Colonial Bank v Exchange Bank of Yarmouth, Nova Scotia* (1885) 11 App. Cas. 84 at 89 PC(Can).
[76] *Agip (Africa) Ltd v Jackson* [1990] Ch. 265; [1989] 3 W.L.R. 1367 Ch.D.
[77] *Agip (Africa) Ltd* [1990] Ch. 265 at 268.
[78] *Kerrison v Glyn, Mills, Currie & Co* (1911) 81 L.J.K.B. 465 at 472 HL.
[79] *Lipkin Gorman v Karpnale Ltd* [1991] 2 A.C. 548 at 580 HL.

In the case of a bank or financial institution, the defence should be available where the bank has made payments to, or to the order of, a customer and the bank is no longer able to reverse those entries. Where a bank can, without detriment, reverse a credit entry to reflect the fact that it has made restitution to the claimant, the defence of change of position will not be available.[80]

2.3.5.1.3 Bona fide purchase

Bona fide purchase is also a defence to a claim for money had and received. The effect of the defence is to give the purchaser a better title than the seller himself possessed.[81] The circumstances in which a bank can raise a bona fide purchase in respect of monies credited to an account are, however, unclear. There is no authority on whether payment into an overdrawn account will support a defence of bona fide purchase by the bank. However, there would appear to be no reason in principle why such a defence should not be available, and the defence is recognised in respect of equitable claims.[82] Where the account is in credit, the possibility of the bank being able to rely on this defence by crediting its customer's account was rejected, albeit without detailed discussion, by Lord Templeman and Lord Goff in the House of Lords in *Lipkin Gorman*.[83]

2.4   Equitable claims

This section describes equitable claims that may be made against banks and financial institutions. After briefly setting out the remedies available against defaulting fiduciaries, the two main remedies for dishonest assistance and knowing receipt will be examined.

---

[80] Jonathon P. Moore, *Restitution from Banks*, unpublished D.Phil thesis (Oxford University, 2000), p.140.

[81] *Barclays Bank v Boulter* [1999] 1 W.L.R. 1919; [2000] C.P. Rep. 16; (2000) H.L.R. 170 HL.

[82] Moore, *Restitution from Banks* (2000), p.332.

[83] *Lipkin Gorman* [1991] 2 A.C. 548 HL at 562 and 577.

2.4.1 Remedies against defaulting fiduciaries

In the case of fraud against a company, the wrongdoers, if directors or senior employees, are likely to owe fiduciary duties to the company. It follows that a company whose property has been misapplied will, in all probability, have a claim against the principal wrongdoers for breach of fiduciary duty. The identification of a breach of fiduciary duty is important if the victim wishes to bring a claim in equity against third parties (e.g. a financial institution) for having assisted in that breach of duty. This is because such a claim will only be available where there has been a breach of fiduciary duty. It follows that where all that is alleged (or can be proved) is negligence or a breach of contract then there will be no claim against a third party in equity for dishonest assistance or for knowing receipt in "laundering" the proceeds.

Company directors are in a fiduciary relationship with the company. The same applies to agents of the company. Employees and managers may also owe fiduciary duties if they are in a position of trust and confidence and are given particular powers or discretions such that the company is in a position of vulnerability towards them.[84]

The law imposes a number of duties on fiduciaries of which the most important are the following:

(a) a fiduciary must not place himself in a position where his own interest conflicts with that of his beneficiary (the "no conflict" rule);
(b) a fiduciary must not profit from his position at the expense of his beneficiary (the "no profit" rule); and
(c) a duty of confidentiality.

In the case of company directors, the scope of the directors' duties is further subject to modification under company law and is often restricted by the company's constitution. This falls outside the scope of this Chapter. However, as a general matter,

---

[84] Patrick Parkinson, "Fiduciary Obligations", in Patrick Parkinson (ed), *The Principles of Equity*, 2nd edn (2003), p.345.

company directors are required to exercise their powers in good faith to promote the success of the company, to exercise independent judgment, to obey the company's constitution and not to place themselves in a position where there is a conflict between their duties to the company and their personal interest.[85]

If directors or employees of a company perpetrate a fraud on the company they will incur personal liability for breach of fiduciary duty as well as any criminal liability. Although in most cases the directors or employees will be acting dishonestly there is no requirement that this is the case for a director to incur liability. Thus in *Belmont Finance Corporation v Williams Furniture Ltd (No.2)*,[86] directors honestly believed that a takeover was at a fair price and in the interests of the company. However, although honest, as the directors had used the company's own money, in breach of the prohibition on financial assistance in the Companies Act, they were found to have acted in breach of fiduciary duty. Equally, if a director has a personal interest in a transaction and fails to disclose it, then this will be a breach of duty even if he otherwise considers the transaction to be beneficial to the company.[87] On the other hand, mere negligence by the directors or employees in the performance of their duties is not a breach of fiduciary duty.[88]

Where a director acts in breach of fiduciary duty, he will be personally liable to the company for any losses caused by the breach.[89] In the case of a director misapplying the company's property he will be liable to repay that money. If he has made a profit from the breach of duty, then he will be liable to account

---

[85] See ss.171–173 and 175 of the Companies Act 2006. The consequences of a breach of duty are the same as applied to the corresponding equitable rules: Companies Act 2006 s.178.

[86] *Belmont Finance Corporation v Williams Furniture Ltd (No.2)* [1980] 1 All E.R. 393 CA.

[87] Compare with *Swindle v Harrison* [1997] P.N.L.R. 641 CA.

[88] *Bristol & West Building Society v Mothew (t/a Stapley & Co)* [1998] Ch. 1; [1997] 2 W.L.R. 436; [1997] P.N.L.R. 11 CA.

[89] *Target Holdings Ltd v Redferns* [1996] A.C. 421; [1995] 3 W.L.R. 352; [1995] C.L.C. 1052 HL.

to the company for the profit.[90] Further, any property acquired by him that is derived from the misapplied funds will be held by him on constructive trust for the company.[91] The rules on tracing (see below) determine when property is "derived" from other property. Examples of a breach of fiduciary duty include a director receiving payments from the company that have not been properly authorised,[92] misusing confidential information disclosed to him in his capacity as director to personally profit at the expense of the company,[93] or the theft of the company's property which is then invested in an asset that increases in value.[94]

2.4.2 Liability for dishonest assistance

Equity provides a remedy against third parties who assist in a breach of trust or breach of fiduciary duty. Such persons are said to be liable as "constructive trustees". However, this is merely a label and there is no requirement that the assistant receives or holds any property that has been misapplied.[95] Neither is such a person a trustee in the proper sense, and he does not owe fiduciary duties to the victim of the breach of trust. His liability is instead to make good the loss that his assistance has caused.[96]

Originally, a claim was available only against those who "assist with knowledge in a dishonest and fraudulent design on the part of the trustees".[97] There were therefore two separate requirements. First, the breach of trust had to be "dishonest" and "fraudulent". It followed that if the fiduciary had not acted dishonestly then the third party would escape liability no

---

[90] *Regal (Hastings) Ltd v Gulliver* [1967] 2 A.C. 134 HL; *Boardman v Phipps* [1967] 2 A.C. 46; [1966] 3 W.L.R. 1009 HL; *Guinness Plc v Saunders* [1990] 2 A.C. 663; [1990] 2 W.L.R. 324; [1990] B.C.C. 205 HL.

[91] *Attorney-General for Hong Kong v Reid* [1994] 1 A.C. 324; [1993] 3 W.L.R. 1143 PC.

[92] *Guinness Plc v Saunders* [1990] B.C.C. 205 HL.

[93] *Boardman v Phipps* [1967] 2 A.C. 46 HL; *Canadian Aero Services v O'Malley* (1973) 40 D.L.R. (3rd) 371.

[94] Compare with *Foskett v McKeown* [2001] 1 A.C. 102 HL.

[95] *Royal Brunei Airlines Sdn Bhd v Tan* [1995] 2 A.C. 378; [1995] 3 W.L.R. 64; [1995] B.C.C. 899 PC.

[96] *Paragon Finance Plc v D.B. Thakerar & Co* [1999] 1 All E.R. 400 CA.

[97] *Barnes v Addy* (1873–74) L.R. 9 Ch. App. 244 CA at 251–252.

matter how dishonest he had been himself.[98] Secondly, the third party had to have acted with "knowledge" of the relevant breach of trust. What amount of knowledge was required remained controversial, although broadly two lines of authority developed. Under the first line of cases, a person would be liable if he had actual or constructive notice of the breach of trust.[99] A separate line of authority insisted on something more, requiring either actual knowledge of the breach of trust, or at least a want of probity on the part of the third party.[100] This was generally equated with dishonesty.[101]

This controversy seemed to be resolved by the judgment of the Privy Council in *Royal Brunei Airlines v Tan.*[102] The Privy Council decided that it was not necessary that the breach of trust or fiduciary duty be dishonest or fraudulent. It was sufficient that the third party had assisted in the breach of duty. Secondly, the standard of liability for the third party was one of dishonesty:

> "... dishonesty is a necessary ingredient of accessory liability. It is also a sufficient ingredient. A liability in equity to make good resulting loss attaches to a person who dishonestly procures or assists in a breach of trust or fiduciary obligation. It is not necessary that, in addition, the trustee or fiduciary was acting dishonestly, although

---

[98] *Belmont Finance Corp Ltd v Williams Furniture Ltd* [1979] Ch. 250; [1978] 3 W.L.R. 712 CA.

[99] *Selangor United Rubber Estates v Cradock (No.3)* [1968] 1 W.L.R. 1555 Ch.D; *Karak Rubber Co Ltd v Burden (No.2)* [1972] 1 W.L.R. 602 Ch.D; *Baden v Société Générale Pour Favoriser le Developpement du Commerce et de l'Industrie en France SA* [1993] 1 W.L.R. 509 Ch.D.

[100] *Belmont Finance Corporation v Williams Furniture (No.2)* [1979] Ch. 250 CA at 267 and 275; *Agip (Africa) Ltd v Jackson* [1990] Ch. 265 Ch.D at 293; *Eagle Trust Plc v SBC Securities Ltd* [1993] 1 W.L.R. 484 Ch.D at 495.

[101] *Agip v Jackson,* above.

[102] *Royal Brunei Airlines Sdn Bhd v Tan* [1995] B.C.C. 899 PC. Strictly, Privy Council judgments are not binding authority. See *Attorney-General v Blake* [1997] Ch. 84 at 96; [1996] 3 W.L.R. 741; [1996] E.M.L.R. 382 Ch.D and *Jyske Bank (Gibraltar) Ltd v Spjeldnaes* unreported, Ch.D, 4 September 1997, Evans-Lombe J, transcript p.313. However, *Tan* has been repeatedly applied, including by the House of Lords in *Twinsectra Ltd v Yardley* [2002] UKHL 12; [2002] 2 A.C. 164; [2002] P.N.L.R. 30.

117

this will usually be so where the third party who is assisting him is acting dishonestly."[103]

It is therefore necessary to show: (i) a breach of trust or fiduciary duty; (ii) assistance; (iii) dishonesty; and (iv) a sufficient causal connection.

2.4.2.1 A breach of trust or fiduciary duty

There must be a breach of trust or fiduciary duty.[104] It is unclear whether the breach must involve a misapplication of property.[105] In the context of money laundering, that is irrelevant as laundering the proceeds of fraud will inevitably involve the misapplication of property.[106]

2.4.2.2 Assistance

Again, this is unlikely to give rise to much difficulty in practice. A bank that launders the proceeds of crime is assisting in the relevant breach of fiduciary duty. That is because a breach of fiduciary duty involving the misapplication of money is not fully implemented until the funds have been successfully concealed.[107] In appropriate cases, the receipt of

---

[103] *Tan* [1995] 2 A.C. 378 at 392.

[104] *Goose v Wilson Sandford (No.2)* [2001] Lloyd's Rep. P.N. 189 CA.

[105] *Bankgesellschaft Berlin AG v Makris* unreported, 22 January 1999 per Cresswell J; *Petrotrade Inc v Smith (Vicarious Liability)* [2000] C.L.C. 916 QB (Comm); *Goose v Wilson Sandford & Co (No.2)* unreported, 25 January 1999 Ch.D per Rimer J, and *Satnam Investments Ltd v Dunlop Heyward & Co Ltd* [1999] F.S.R. 722 CA suggest that there must be a misapplication of trust property. Earlier cases appear to have assumed that that is not the case: see *Selangor United Rubber Estates Ltd v Cradock (No.3)* [1968] 1 W.L.R. 1555 Ch.D and *Cowan de Groot Properties v Eagle Trust* [1992] 4 All E.R. 700 Ch.D. However, more recent cases have left the point open: see *Brown v Bennett* [1999] B.C.C. 525 CA; *Fyffes Group Ltd v Templeman* [2000] 2 Lloyd's Rep. 643 QB (Comm) and *Goose v Wilson Sandford & Co (No.2)* [2001] Lloyd's Rep. P.N. 189 CA. See Charles Mitchell, "Assistance" in Peter Birks and Arianna Pretto (eds), *Breach of Trust* (Oxford: Hart Publishing, 2002), p.139.

[106] Dishonesty not involving a misapplication of property may attract criminal liability. However, such behaviour (e.g. deceiving or bribing a public officer to act contrary to his duty) does not involve money laundering. Deceit causing loss, but not involving the misapplication of property, is actionable at common law.

[107] *Heinl v Jyske Bank (Gibraltar) Ltd* [1999] Lloyd's Rep. Bank 511 CA at 523.

money may also amount to assistance. Whether the bank has acted dishonestly is another matter.

2.4.2.3   Dishonesty

This is the area that has given rise to most difficulty in practice. In establishing a requirement for dishonesty, Lord Nicholls seemed to lay down a "jury" test. In *Royal Brunei*, he explained it as follows:

> "acting dishonestly, or with a lack of probity, which is synonymous, means simply not acting as an honest person would in the circumstances. This is an objective standard. …. The standard of what constitutes honest conduct is not subjective. Honesty is not an optional scale, with higher or lower values according to the moral standards of each individual. If a person knowingly appropriates another's property, he will not escape a finding of dishonesty simply because he sees nothing wrong in such behaviour.
>
> In most situations there is little difficulty in identifying how an honest person would behave. Honest people do not intentionally deceive others to their detriment. Honest people do not knowingly take others' property. Unless there is a very good and compelling reason, an honest person does not participate in a transaction if he knows it involves a misapplication of trust assets to the detriment of the beneficiaries. Nor does an honest person in such a case deliberately close his eyes and ears, or deliberately not ask questions, lest he learn something he would rather not know, and then proceed regardless."[108]

A person is liable if he fails to act in the way that an honest and reasonable person would have acted in the circumstances. This does not mean that the person's knowledge or beliefs are irrelevant. If a defendant believes that the transaction concerned is legitimate, then it is not dishonest to proceed unless an honest man would have appreciated that it was fraudulent.

---

[108] *Royal Brunei* [1995] 2 A.C. 378 at 389.

Thus in *Heinl v Jyske Bank (Gibraltar) Ltd*,[109] the defendant escaped a finding of dishonesty in respect of a complex money laundering scheme where he transferred funds through different accounts on the instructions of a rogue. He admitted that he did not know the purpose of the transactions and acted simply on the orders of the rogue. As all the transfers were effected at the same bank, nothing was being concealed.[110] On the facts, that would appear to be a generous finding, although the principle is surely sound.

In *Twinsectra Ltd v Yardley*[111] the House of Lords held that a subjective approach must be taken to the question of dishonesty. For a person to incur liability for dishonest assistance:

> "it must be established that the defendant's conduct was dishonest by the ordinary standards of reasonable and honest people and that he himself realised that by those standards his conduct was dishonest."[112]

Subsequently, in *Barlow Clowes International Ltd (in liquidation) v Eurotrust International Ltd*[113] the Privy Council considered that the House of Lords had not intended to reach such a conclusion:

> "Their Lordships accept that there is an element of ambiguity in these remarks which may have encouraged a belief, expressed in some academic writing, that the *Twinsectra* case had departed from the law as previously understood and invited inquiry not merely into the defendant's mental state about the nature of the transaction in which he was participating but also into his views about generally acceptable standards of honesty. But they do not consider that this is what Lord Hutton meant. The reference to 'what he knows would offend normally accepted standards of honest conduct' meant only that his

---

[109] *Heinl* [1999] Lloyd's Rep. Bank. 511 CA.
[110] Despite the fact that the Court of Appeal found that he had lied serially on oath.
[111] *Twinsectra Ltd v Yardley* [2002] UKHL 12; [2002] 2 A.C. 164; [2002] P.N.L.R. 30.
[112] *Twinsectra Ltd* [2002] 2 A.C. 164 HL at 172.
[113] *Barlow Clowes International Ltd (in liquidation) v Eurotrust International Ltd* [2005] UKPC 37; [2006] 1 W.L.R. 1476; [2006] 1 P. & C.R. DG16.

knowledge of the transaction had to be such as to render his participation contrary to normally acceptable standards of honest conduct. It did not require that he should have had reflections about what those normally acceptable standards were."[114]

The Privy Council approved the approach of the trial judge that:

"Although a dishonest state of mind is a subjective mental state, the standard by which the law determines whether it is dishonest is objective. If by ordinary standards a defendant's mental state would be characterised as dishonest, it is irrelevant that the defendant judges by different standards."[115]

Further:

"Such a state of mind may consist in knowledge that the transaction is one in which he cannot honestly participate (for example, a misappropriation of other people's money), or it may consist in suspicion combined with a conscious decision not to make inquiries which might result in knowledge."[116]

In the view of the Privy Council, it seems that a person may be "dishonest" as a result of making a mistake as to what ordinary people regard as honest, or simply by giving no thought to the matter.

This raises an apparent conflict of authority between the House of Lords and the Privy Council.[117] In *Abou-Rahmah v Abacha*,[118] Arden LJ considered that the Court of Appeal (and by implication other courts) should follow the Privy Council. Rix and Pill LJJ held that it was not necessary to resolve this issue.

---

[114] *Barlow Clowes* [2005] UKPC 37 at [15].

[115] *Barlow Clowes* [2005] UKPC 37 at [10].

[116] *Barlow Clowes* [2005] UKPC 37 at [10].

[117] Adverted to by the Court of Appeal in [2008] EWCA Civ 1007, 31 July 2008, although the case was decided on factual issues.

[118] *Abou-Rahmah v Abacha* [2006] EWCA Civ 1492; [2007] Bus. L.R. 220.

In *Mullarkey v Broad*,[119] Lewison J at first instance followed Arden LJ. However, in *Attorney General for Zambia v Meer, Care & Desai (A Firm)*[120] Peter Smith J considered the discussion in *Abou-Rahmah* to be obiter dicta and adopted the view of Lord Clarke MR, who wrote extra-judicially, that:

> "'the test is an objective one, but an objective one which takes account of the individuals in question's [sic] characteristics'. I agree (as he really said) it is not appropriate to draw analogies with other areas. He went on to say: 'it is a test which requires a court to assess an individual's conduct according to an objective standard of dishonesty. In doing so, the court has to take account as to what the individual knew; his experience, intelligence and reasons for acting as he did. Whether the individual was aware that his conduct fell below the objective standard is not part of the test.'"[121]

Peter Smith J considered that the majority and minority in *Twinsectra* had been at cross purposes and "did not believe that there was anything other than a misunderstanding as between the effect of the various judgments in *Twinsectra* which spawned a huge unnecessary debate".[122] In his view, "[e]ssentially it is a jury question as to dishonesty to be assessed in the light of all the material".[123] That test was also followed by Teare J, with the agreement of counsel, in *Markel International Insurance Co Ltd v Surety Guarantee Consultants Ltd*.[124]

If a bank knows that funds are being transferred to conceal their origin, then in the absence of special facts, it will act dishonestly. In other cases, the transaction is likely to appear as

---

[119] *Mullarkey v Broad* [2007] EWHC 3400 (Ch).

[120] *Attorney-General of Zambia v Meer Care & Desai (A Firm)* [2007] EWHC 952 (Ch) at [340]. An appeal to the Court of Appeal was only concerned with issues of fact: [2008] EWCA Civ 1007.

[121] Anthony Clarke, "Claims against professionals: negligence, dishonesty and fraud" (2006) 22 P.N. 70.

[122] *Meer Care & Desai (A Firm)* [2007] EWHC 952 (Ch) at [366].

[123] *Meer Care & Desai (A Firm)* [2007] EWHC 952 (Ch) at [368].

[124] *Markel International Insurance Co Ltd v Surety Guarantee Consultants Ltd* [2008] EWHC 1135 (Comm).

a legitimate transition. It is only if the institution is put on inquiry that there will be any duty to inquire. In such a case, as Millett J. stated in *Agip*:

> "Mr Jackson and Mr Griffin are not to be held liable for the misapplication of the plaintiffs' funds because they failed to make inquiries which would have discovered the fraud, but because they dishonestly assisted in the misapplication. Their failure to make the inquiries which honest men would have made to satisfy themselves that they were not engaged in furthering a fraud is merely the evidence from which their dishonesty is inferred."[125]

2.4.2.4   A causal connection

The defendant's actions must have some causative effect. However, in this case it "is no answer, either to say that he only participated in a part of a chain of events all of which led to the breach of trust, or to assert that the breach of trust would probably have occurred without his assistance".[126] In an earlier case, it was held that a wife who accompanied her husband on trips to Switzerland to launder the proceeds of the Brinks Mat gold robbery did so in her spousal capacity and did not render any material assistance to the underlying money laundering operations.[127]

2.4.3   Liability for knowing receipt

The second head of equitable liability is for "knowing" receipt. As will become clear, both the role and scope of this claim remain subject to debate, and it is likely that the law will be subject to reconsideration and possible reformulation in the future. This cause of action has been one of the main means of pursuing banks and financial institutions which are alleged to have become involved in money laundering schemes.

The requirements for liability under this heading are

---

[125] *Agip (Africa) Ltd v Jackson* [1990] Ch. 265 Ch.D at 296.
[126] *Balfron Trustees Ltd v Petersen* [2001] I.R.L.R. 758 Ch.D at [21].
[127] *Brinks Ltd v Abu-Saleh (No.3)* [1996] C.L.C. 133 Ch.D.

"first, a disposal of [the claimant's] assets in breach of fiduciary duty; secondly, the beneficial receipt by the defendant of assets which are traceable as representing the assets of [the claimant]; and thirdly, knowledge on the part of the defendant that the assets he received are traceable to a breach of fiduciary duty".[128]

2.4.3.1 Breach of fiduciary duty

The requirement is the same as for dishonest assistance. In practice, it is unlikely to be difficult to show a breach of duty where the claimant's money has been paid away for an unauthorised purpose. Examples include a partner using partnership property to pay his private debts[129] or an agent using the proceeds of sale of his principal's property to discharge his personal overdraft.[130]

2.4.3.2 Beneficial receipt

The defendant must have received the claimant's property (or other property that represents the traceable proceeds of the claimant's property) beneficially.[131] If the defendant never received any property, or did so as agent, then he can only be liable for dishonest assistance. Whilst this requirement is easy to state it is more difficult to assess when in fact it is met. "[A] defendant must have received [the property] in his or her own right, must have enjoyed the property beneficially. There is, thus, no cause of action in knowing receipt against a person who holds trust property merely as agent for a third party".[132] The difficulty that has arisen in practice is in determining whether a bank that is sued for knowing receipt received the

---

[128] *El-Ajou v Dollar Land Holdings Plc (No.1)* [1994] B.C.C. 143 at 154 per Hoffmann LJ.

[129] *Lankshear v ANZ Banking Group (New Zealand) Ltd* [1993] 1 NZLR 481.

[130] *Westpac Banking Corp v Savin* [1985] 2 N.Z.L.R. 41.

[131] *Agip (Africa) Ltd v Jackson* [1990] Ch. 265 at 292; *Eagle Trust Plc v SBC Securities Ltd* [1993] 1 W.L.R. 484 at 490 and 501; *El-Ajou v Dollar Land Holdings Plc* [1993] 1 All E.R. 717 at 738; *Nimmo v Westpac Banking* [1993] 3 N.Z.L.R. 218; *Air Canada v M&L Travel Ltd* [1993] 3 S.C.R. 787 and *Citadel General Assurance v Lloyd's Bank Canada* [1997] 3 S.C.R. 805.

[132] *Gold v Rosenberg* [1997] 3 S.C.R. 767 at [40].

money beneficially (in which case it may be liable) or as agent for its customer (in which case the claimant must sue the bank's customer).

It is well established that the relationship between a bank and its customer is that of debtor and creditor.[133] It follows that where money is paid into an account, the money becomes the bank's own money, and the customer is entitled to be repaid an equivalent sum in accordance with the terms of the mandate. It could therefore be argued that in all cases where money is paid into a bank account, the bank receives the money beneficially, with the result that the bank is potentially liable if it turns out that the money was misappropriated.[134] In fact, the courts have refused to endorse such an approach because it would impose extensive potential liability on banks.

In most cases, the courts have drawn a distinction between the situation where money is paid into an account in credit and where money is paid into an overdrawn account. In the former case, the bank is considered to receive the money as agent with the result that the victim must sue the account holder, and not the bank, for knowing receipt. Where the account is overdrawn, however, the bank is said to receive the money beneficially and so is potentially liable. Millett J explained the distinction as follows:

> "[t]he essential feature ... is that the recipient must have received the property for his own use and benefit. This is why neither the paying nor the collecting bank can normally be brought within it. In paying or collecting money for a customer the bank acts only as his agent. It is otherwise, however, if the collecting bank uses the money to reduce or discharge the customer's overdraft. In doing so, it receives the money for its own benefit."[135]

---

[133] *Foley v Hill* (1848) 2 H L Cas. 28; 9 E.R. 1002.

[134] Compare Simon Gleeson, "The Involuntary Launderer" in Peter Birks (ed), *Laundering and Tracing*, (Oxford: Clarendon Press, 1995) and Bryan, "Recovering Misdirected Money from Banks" in Francis Rose (ed), *Restitution and Banking Law*, (Routledge, 1998).

[135] *Agip (Africa) Ltd v Jackson* [1990] Ch. 265 at 292 Ch.D.

Thus a bank will receive money paid into an account as agent when the account is in credit. Where, however, the account is overdrawn, the bank is treated as having received the money beneficially.[136]

2.4.3.3 Is the crediting of an overdrawn account always beneficial receipt?

The distinction referred to above is clear, and however arbitrary it may be, is capable of giving a clear answer and provides a measure of protection to banks. However, a number of commentators have argued that the protection is insufficient and that mere receipt of money into an overdrawn account should not amount to beneficial receipt. There should be something more before a bank can incur liability for knowing receipt. Suggested requirements are that the bank was pressing for payment,[137] or that there was some conscious act of appropriation by the bank in reducing the overdraft.[138]

Either suggestion is difficult to accept. It is strange that a bank's liability should turn on whether or not it was pressing for payment.[139] The bank's position is the same regardless of whether or not it was pressing for payment. Equally, a requirement that the bank make a conscious appropriation is

---

[136] See, for example *Agip, Stephens Travel Services International Pty Ltd v Qantas Airways Ltd* (1988) 13 N.S.W.L.R. 331; *Box v Barclays Bank* [1998] Lloyd's Rep. Bank 185 Ch.D; *Lankshear v ANZ Banking Group*[1993] 1 N.Z.L.R. 481 and *Cigna Life Insurance NZ v Westpac Securities* [1996] 1 N.Z.L.R. 80 at 87. See also Ali Malek QC and John Odgers QC (eds), *Paget's Law of Banking*, 14th edn (London: LexisNexis, 2014), paras 28.18 and 28.28 and J.D. Heydon and M.J. Leeming (eds), *Jacobs' Law of Trusts in Australia*, 7th edn (2006), p.339.

[137] Ross Cranston QC, *Principles of Banking Law*, 2nd edn (Oxford University Press, 1997), p.208. See *Gray v Johnson* (1868) L.R. 3 H.L. 1 at 13; *Foxton v Manchester and Liverpool District Banking Co* (1884) 44 L.T. 406 at 408; *Coleman v Bucks and Oxon Union Bank* [1897] 2 Ch. 243 at 254 Ch.D; *Westpac Banking v Savin* [1985] 2 N.Z.L.R. 41 at 53 and *Stephens Travel Services v Qantas Airways* (1988) 13 N.S.W.L.R. 331 at 365.

[138] P.J. Millett, "Tracing the Proceeds of Fraud" (1991) 107 L.Q.R. 71 at 83 fn.46. For tentative support, see *Westpac Banking Corp v MM Kembla* [2001] 2 N.Z.L.R. 298 at 316–317, where the court concluded that "[t]his area of the law is marked by present confusion".

[139] Moore, *Restitution from Banks* (2000), p.221.

problematic as a bank has little choice in whether or not to credit a payment made to an overdrawn account.[140]

2.4.3.4   Credits made in foreign currency

There is some authority that a different rule applies depending on whether the account is credited in the same currency or in a different currency. In *Polly Peck International Plc v Nadir (No.2)*[141] the defendant caused large sums of the plaintiff company's money to be transferred to a company, IBK, controlled by him. IBK then deposited the money in an account with Midland Bank in the name of the Central Bank of Northern Cyprus (the Central Bank). In exchange, the Central Bank credited two accounts of IBK in Northern Cyprus. One of the accounts was denominated in sterling and the other in Turkish lire. It was argued for the plaintiff that the Central Bank was liable for knowing (i.e. dishonest) assistance or, alternatively, for knowing receipt. At first instance, Millett J was inclined to consider the case as one of knowing assistance. This is consistent with his judgment in *Agip*, as the Central Bank had credited the account of IBK in Northern Cyprus and had therefore given value for the deposit. On appeal, Scott LJ in the Court of Appeal drew a distinction between the sterling and the lire deposits. In respect of the sterling deposits, the Central Bank received the money as banker and therefore as agent for its customer, IBK. In respect of the lire deposits the position was different as "the Central Bank was exchanging Turkish lire for sterling and became entitled to the sterling not as banker for IBK but in its own right. IBK became entitled to the Turkish lire".[142]

The Court of Appeal therefore treated the credits in respect of Turkish lire in the same way as if the bank had sold goods (or travellers cheques) to IBK in exchange for the sterling deposits. The bank had not received the money as agent, but beneficially.

---

[140] Moore, *Restitution from Banks* (2000), p.213.
[141] *Polly Peck International Plc v Nadir (No.2)* [1992] 4 All E.R. 769 CA.
[142] *Nadir (No.2)* [1992] 4 All E.R. 769 at 777.

This approach has been criticised by most commentators.[143] It is inconsistent with the modern approach that views foreign currency as money and not as a commodity.[144] It also fails to recognise that the bank had given full value for the Turkish lire deposits in the same way as it had with the sterling deposits. In *Nimmo v Westpac*[145] Blanchard J did not "pretend to understand the point of distinction". The better view is that it makes no difference whether the account is credited in domestic currency or in a foreign currency.

2.4.3.5 The level of knowledge required

The defendant must "know" that the property is attributable to a breach of trust or fiduciary duty. What level of knowledge will suffice? Clearly, a bank with actual knowledge will be liable. Equally, if the institution believes the money to be stolen, or deliberately closes its mind to this fact, it will be liable. Such behaviour is dishonest. Where there has been more controversy is whether a defendant that acts carelessly can be liable as a knowing recipient.

Broadly, two approaches can be seen in the cases. On the one hand, many cases have insisted on conscious wrongdoing, or dishonesty, for the recipient to be liable. The contrary view, that constructive knowledge, or negligence, suffices for liability, has also attracted judicial support, although the trend of authority in recent years was in favour of requiring conscious wrongdoing. The whole issue was reconsidered by the Court of Appeal in *B.C.C.I. (Overseas) Ltd v Akindele*[146] where the court concluded that

> "just as there is now a single test of dishonesty for knowing assistance, so ought there to be a single test of

---

[143] Bryan, "Recovering Misdirected Money from Banks" in Francis Rose (ed), *Restitution and Banking Law* (Routledge, 1998) and Moore, *Restitution from Banks* (2000), pp.178–180.

[144] *Camdex International Ltd v Bank of Zambia (No.2)* [1997] 1 W.L.R. 632; [1996] C.L.C. 1945 CA.

[145] *Nimmo v Westpac* [1993] 3 NZLR 218 at 225–226.

[146] *Bank of Credit and Commerce International (Overseas) Ltd v Akindele* [2001] Ch. 437; [2000] 3 W.L.R. 1423; [2000] B.C.C. 968 CA.

knowledge for knowing receipt. The recipient's state of knowledge must be such as to make it unconscionable for him to retain the benefit of the receipt. A test in that form, though it cannot, any more than any other, avoid difficulties of application, ought to avoid those of definition and allocation to which the previous categorisations have led. Moreover, it should better enable the courts to give common sense decisions in the commercial context."[147]

It is questionable whether a test formulated in such abstract terms will survive as it is difficult to see how an appeal to "unconscionability" will enable the court to give predictable answers.[148] A number of the difficulties with the new test were discussed by the High Court in *Criterion Properties Plc v Stratford UK Properties LLC*.[149] As Hart J explained:

"[i]t is clear ... that the single test of unconscionability now applicable in knowing receipt cases is intended to be something different from the 'dishonesty by an objective standard' test applicable in a knowing assistance case. It is not obvious, simply as a matter of the language being used, whether making out a case of unconscionability (in the sense of the recipient's conscience being affected) is supposed now to be easier, or harder, to make out than a case of .... dishonesty. The latter is unquestionably an objective standard, albeit with subjective elements. But 'unconscionability' might be thought to be a wholly subjective standard."[150]

The judge concluded that unconscionability is a lower standard than dishonesty:

"That accords with one's intuition: a person who has actually received stolen goods should be more vulnerable to being held accountable to the true owner for their value

---

[147] *Akindele* [2001] Ch. 437 CA at 455.
[148] Which is why it was rejected in the case of dishonest assistance by Lord Nicholls.
[149] *Criterion Properties Plc v Stratford UK Properties LLC* [2002] EWHC 496 (Ch); [2002] 2 B.C.L.C. 151.
[150] *Criterion Properties* [2002] EWHC 496 (Ch) at [33].

than someone whose actions have merely facilitated the theft ... In my judgment, therefore, what *Belmont* and *Akindele* decide for present purposes is that actual knowledge of circumstances which make the payment a misapplication is sufficient to bind the conscience of the recipient. What is left open and undecided by either of these cases is the case where the recipient knows of circumstances which may on the one hand make the payment a misapplication but which may on the other hand be consistent with perfect propriety. Such a case might be determined on its particular facts by the principle that a party to a commercial agreement should not be fixed with notice simply because in a loose sense he has been put on inquiry. Close examination of the particular facts might in such a case be necessary."[151]

On appeal, the Court of Appeal stated that "the purpose of the new formulation was to give greater flexibility for the application of common sense in commercial situations".[152] The court stressed each case had to be viewed in the context of the commercial relationship between the parties. The case was appealed to the House of Lords[153] which held that the dispute turned on ordinary principles of agency law. Knowing receipt was accordingly not relevant. However, because of its inherent uncertainty, it is unlikely that the unconscionability standard will be accepted by the House of Lords or Privy Council when the issue arises for decision in a future case. That said, judges at first instance have so far been able to apply *Akindele* without difficulty.[154]

2.4.3.6 Should liability be strict?

A number of influential academic commentators have argued that the requirement for knowledge, or fault, on the part of the

---

[151] *Criterion Properties* [2002] EWHC 496 (Ch) at [33] and [38].

[152] *Criterion Properties* [2002] EWCA Civ 1883 at [31] per Carnwath LJ.

[153] *Criterion Properties* [2004] UKHL 28; [2004] 1 W.L.R. 1846; [2004] B.C.C. 570.

[154] *Primlake Ltd (in liquidation) v Matthews Associates* [2006] EWHC 1227 (Ch); *Ali v Al-Basri* [2004] EWHC 2608 (QB); *Quarter Master UK v Pyke* [2004] EWHC 1815 (Ch). See Paul McGrath QC, *Commercial Fraud in Civil Practice*, 2nd edn (Oxford University Press, 2014), paras 5.83, 5.120 and 5.141.

recipient should be abolished, and that a recipient of misapplied money should be strictly liable subject to defences. The result would be that a bank that receives money beneficially would be liable even if it neither knows nor ought to have known that the money was stolen. This argument, if accepted, would significantly increase the potential liability of banks and financial institutions. It would then be for an institution that receives the proceeds of crime honestly to raise a defence to the claim. Suggested defences include change of position, ministerial (i.e., non-beneficial) receipt and bona fide purchase. These defences were considered, briefly, above when discussing claims for money had and received.

There have been signs that a number of judges in the higher courts favour a strict liability approach.[155] Courts have on several occasions accepted that the basis of knowing receipt is restitutionary.[156] In *El-Ajou v Dollar Land Holdings*,[157] Millett J. stated that "I do not see how it would be possible to develop any logical and coherent system of restitution if there were different requirements in respect of knowledge for the common law claim for money had and received, the personal claim for an account in equity against a knowing recipient and the equitable proprietary claim".[158] The Royal Court of Jersey has accepted the argument for strict liability.[159] However, the contrary view has been expressed, both academically and by the judiciary.[160] The Court of Appeal, in *Akindele*, doubted "whether strict liability coupled with a change of position defence would be preferable to fault-based liability in many

---

[155] P.J. Millett, "Tracing the Proceeds of Fraud" (1991) 107 L.Q.R. 71 at 82.

[156] *Polly Peck v Nadir (No.3)* unreported, 17 March 1993 CA; *Royal Brunei Airlines v Tan* [1995] 2 A.C. 378 at 386 and *Dubai Aluminium Co Ltd v Salaam* [2002] 3 W.L.R. 1913 at 1933.

[157] *El-Ajou v Dollar Land Holdings Plc (No.1)* [1993] B.C.C. 698 Ch.D.

[158] *El-Ajou* [1993] B.C.C. 698 Ch.D at 718.

[159] *In re Esteem Settlement and the Number 52 Trust (Abacus (C.I.) Ltd as Trustee)* [2002] J.L.R. 53 at 113; [242] of transcript.

[160] Lionel Smith, "W(h)ithor Knowing Receipt?" (1998) 114 L.Q.R. 394; Lionel Smith, "Unjust Enrichment, Property, and the Structure of Trusts" (2000) 116 LQR 412; Jaffey, "The Nature of Knowing Receipt" (2001) 15 Tru L. I. 151, and Margaret Halliwell, "Assistance in a Breach of Trust and Receipt of Trust Property" in Steve Hedley, Margaret Halliwell, Neil Allen, Joanna Bird, Peter McDermott (eds), *The Law of Restitution* (LexisNexis, 2002), p.97.

commercial transactions".[161] Similarly, Commonwealth courts,[162] whilst accepting the restitutionary basis of the claim, have consistently insisted on fault,[163] a position recently confirmed by the High Court of Australia.[164]

2.5 Proprietary remedies

A victim may desire or need a proprietary remedy. The reasons for doing so include obtaining priority in an insolvency, taking the benefit of an increase in the value of an asset that represents the traceable proceeds of misapplied property, or obtaining an order for specific delivery of property. As mentioned above, proof of a proprietary interest may also be necessary to bring a claim in conversion or to provide the basis for a tracing claim. As in other areas of the law, it is necessary to distinguish between common law and equitable claims.

2.5.1 Common law proprietary claims

The range of remedies available at common law is very limited. This follows from the limited class of third-party rights that exist at common law. Basically, at common law you either own something or you do not. A common law proprietary claim is therefore a claim to ownership of the asset. Further, common law property rights are generally protected indirectly by a claim in tort for interference with ownership (i.e., conversion). Such claims lead to a money judgment against the defendant,

---

[161] *Akindele* [2001] Ch. 437 CA at 456 per Nourse LJ.

[162] But not Jersey. See *In re Esteem Settlement and the Number 52 Trust (Abacus (C.I.) Ltd as Trustee)* [2002] J.L.R. 53.

[163] *Citadel General Assurance Co v Lloyd's Bank Canada* (1997) 152 D.L.R. (4th) 411 at 434–436; *Gold v Primary Developments Ltd* (1997) 152 D.L.R. (4th) 385 at 396–400 (Canada); *Powell v Thompson* [1991] 1 N.Z.L.R. 597 at 607–609; *Nimmo v Westpac Banking Corp* [1993] 3 N.Z.L.R. 218 at 224–225; *Springfield Acres Ltd (in liquidation) v Abacus* [1994] 3 N.Z.L.R. 502; *Cigna Life Insurance NZ Ltd v Westpac Securities Ltd* [1996] 1 N.Z.L.R. 80; *Equiticorp Industries Group (in statutory management) v The Crown* [1998] 2 N.Z.L.R. 481 at 631–639 (New Zealand). Australian courts also require fault. See *Consul Development Pty Ltd v DPC Estates Pty Ltd* (1975) 132 C.L.R. 373.

[164] *Farah Constructions Pty Ltd v Say-Dee Pty Ltd* (2007) 81 A.L.J.R. 1107.

but do not give title to any property in the defendant's possession. It follows that the scope for common law proprietary remedies is quite limited.

For example, a bank balance is a chose in action representing a debt owed by the bank to the account holder. It can therefore be owned and be subject to a proprietary claim. However, as a debt owed by the bank it ceases to exist if the money is repaid to the account holder, or if the funds are transferred (properly or not) to third parties. Thus, the effect of misapplication of the money will be that the original property will cease to exist.[165] Whether the victim can assert common law or equitable rights in the proceeds is a matter for the law of tracing.

Money and bearer securities are negotiable instruments. It follows that they may be the subject of a common law claim although any proprietary rights will be lost once the money has passed as currency, or the bearer instrument has been acquired by a holder in due course.[166]

2.5.2 Equitable proprietary claims

Unlike the common law, equity has never had any difficulty in protecting proprietary rights directly. If I receive property in which you have a beneficial interest, then generally I will hold that property on a constructive trust. Fault, or notice, is irrelevant in this context, and the difficulties that the courts have faced in analysing the knowledge requirement in cases of knowing receipt do not apply. Similarly, if I buy property that is subject to an equitable proprietary interest then I will hold it subject to such interest unless I am a bona fide purchaser for value. Of course, such rights are precarious as a person without knowledge or notice of the claimant's rights is generally free to deal with such property and will not incur liability for doing so.

---

[165] *R. v Preddy (John Crawford)* [1996] A.C. 815; [1996] 3 W.L.R. 255; [1996] Cr. App. R. 524 HL.
[166] *Miller v Race* (1758) 1 Burr. 452; 97 E.R. 398.

It follows that if money to which I am beneficially entitled is diverted to a third party, then I will be able to follow that money and assert any continuing property rights I have against any recipient other than a third party who acquired it for value and without notice.[167] Equally, equity is able to recognise lesser proprietary interests than full ownership. Thus a person who has a lien or charge over property will be able to assert the same right against a recipient of the property.

Where property has been obtained by fraud then the court may impose a constructive trust in favour of the victim.[168] If the fraudster did not hold the property on constructive trust, the victim would have to prove alongside ordinary creditors because the assets would belong to the fraudster and therefore be available for such creditors.[169] This underlines the importance of being able to bring a proprietary claim.

2.6 Tracing

This section describes the circumstances in which a person is able to assert a proprietary interest in a substitute asset that was acquired with the proceeds of the claimant's property. In almost all cases involving the misapplication of money, it will not be possible to identify the original notes to assert a continuing proprietary right to them as there will be no record of the serial numbers and the money will in any event have passed as currency. Further, in the case of the diversion of funds from a bank account, there is no "transfer" of property; rather the debt owed by the bank to the customer whose account is debited is reduced or extinguished and in its place a new debt is created, either at the same bank, or another bank,

---

[167] *Chase Manhattan Bank NA v Israel-British Bank (London) Ltd* [1981] Ch 105; [1980] 2 W.L.R. 202 Ch.D.

[168] *Westdeutsche Landesbank Girozentrale v Islington LBC* [1996] A.C. 669 at 715. The better view is that such a trust is not automatic, and that where property is obtained under a contract induced by fraud, the contract remains valid and enforceable until the victim seeks to rescind it: see *Shalson v Russo* [2005] Ch. 281 Ch.D at 317–318. See also *Reese River Silver Mining Company Ltd v Smith* (1869) L.R. 4 H.L. 64 HL and *Newbigging v Adam*(1886) 34 Ch. D. 582 CA.

[169] *Re Esteem Settlement and the Number 52 Trust* [2002] J.L.R. 53 at 93; [175] of transcript.

in favour of the recipient of the money.[170] In this case, the person whose account has been debited will need to trace the value represented by the debit from his account to the recipient's account.[171]

Often, a person will seek to trace in order to assert a proprietary right in an asset. Thus, in *Trustee of the Property of F.C. Jones & Sons (A Firm) v Jones*,[172] the creditors of a bankrupt partnership were able to assert that money that had been wrongfully taken by a partner from the firm, and given by him to his wife to engage in a successful speculation in commodities futures, was an asset of the partnership. The wife had paid the proceeds of the speculation into a new bank account opened for that purpose. The court declared that the bank account belonged to the partnership's creditors.

However, it is not invariably the case that tracing will be used to support a proprietary claim. Thus, if the claimant seeks to bring a personal claim which depends on his having had a proprietary interest at some point in the past, then he will need to trace the money until receipt by the defendant. Examples are a claim for money had and received or for knowing receipt.

Traditionally, there have been two different tracing rules: one at common law and another in equity. It has been suggested by the House of Lords that the maintenance of two different sets of rules is unprincipled and that the same requirements should apply to common law and equitable tracing[173]. Such a development seems likely to occur when a suitable case reaches the higher courts. However, at first instance, the courts continue to apply the traditional rules.[174]

---

[170] *Preddy* [1996] A.C. 815 HL.

[171] *Lipkin Gorman v Karpnale Ltd* [1991] 2 A.C. 548 HL at 572–573. See *Foskett v McKeown* [2001] 1 A.C. 102 HL at 127–128.

[172] *Trustee of the Property of F.C. Jones & Sons (A Firm) v Jones* [1997] Ch. 159; [1996] 3 W.L.R. 703 CA.

[173] *Foskett v McKeown* [2001] 1 A.C. 102 HL at 109, 113 and 128.

[174] *Shalson v Russo* [2005] Ch. 281 Ch.D at 314–315. In Jersey, the Royal Court has expressed the view that the rules of equitable tracing should apply to all tracing actions: *In re Esteem Settlement* [2002] J.L.R. 53 at 97; [190] of transcript. It must be admitted that Jersey law is not based on English common law and differs in significant respects from it.

2.6.1 The nature of tracing

Tracing is a process, not a legal remedy. It "is the process by which the plaintiff traces what has happened to his property, identifies the persons who have handled or received it, and justifies his claim that the money which they handled or received (and if necessary which they still retain) can properly be regarded as representing his property". [175] It "identifies the traceable proceeds of the claimant's property. It enables the claimant to substitute the traceable proceeds for the original asset as the subject matter of his claim. But it does not affect or establish his claim. That will depend on a number of factors including the nature of his interest in the original asset."[176]

Generally, a claimant will seek to assert the same rights or interest in the substitute asset that he had in respect of the original asset. Thus, if the claimant owned the original asset he will be entitled to ownership of all (or part) of the asset representing the traceable proceeds depending on the amount of his contribution to the substitute asset. In *Foskett v McKeown*[177] the defendant misused the claimants' money to pay part of the premiums on his life assurance policy, and subsequently committed suicide. The beneficiaries under the policy were his children. The amount of the claimants' money that had been wrongfully paid in premiums was significantly less than the percentage share of the total death benefit paid out by the insurance company that had been paid for by those premiums. The House of Lords held that the claimants could trace their money into the payment made by the insurance company and were entitled to a proportionate share of the proceeds of the policy.

2.6.2 Tracing at common law

Tracing at common law enables a person to assert proprietary rights in a substitute asset. It may also be necessary to trace at common law to bring a claim for conversion or for money had

---

[175] *Boscawen v Bajwa* [1996] 1 W.L.R. 328 CA at 334 per Millett LJ.
[176] *Foskett v McKeown* [2001] 1 A.C. 102 at 128 per Lord Millett.
[177] *Foskett* [2001] 1 A.C. 102; [2000] 2 W.L.R. 1299 HL.

and received. Common law tracing is traditionally subject to a number of important limitations. As these limitations do not apply to equitable tracing, a plaintiff will only rarely seek (or be able) to trace at common law.

First, a person cannot trace through a mixed substitution. The common law "could only appreciate what might almost be called the 'physical' identity of one thing with another. It could treat a person's money as identifiable so long as it had not become mixed with other money. It could treat as identifiable with the money other kinds of property acquired by means of it, provided that there was no admixture of other money".[178] It follows that it is impossible at common law to trace money through a bank account when that account is credited with both the claimant's money and money from some other source.[179] Equally, if money is paid across the counter to a bank, then it will not be possible to trace at common law against the bank as the individual notes and coins will have been mixed with other money.

Secondly, it is not possible to trace money through a clearing system. This is because when money is paid through a clearing system, it is inevitably mixed with other money.[180]

Thirdly, there is some authority that there must be a physical substitution with the result that the common law cannot trace through a telegraphic transfer. In this case there is only a "stream of electrons".[181] Tracing is, however, possible in respect of payments made by cheque provided that no mixing occurs.[182]

None of these limitations apply in equity. Common law tracing does, however, have one advantage over equitable tracing in that there is no requirement that there exists a fiduciary

---

[178] *Ministry of Health v Simpson*; sub nom. *Re Diplock's Estate* [1948] Ch. 465 CA at 518 per Lord Greene MR.

[179] *Agip (Africa) Ltd v Jackson* [1990] Ch. 265 Ch.D at 285.

[180] *Agip (Africa) Ltd v Jackson* [1990] Ch. 265 Ch.D at 286; [1991] Ch. 547 CA at 566.

[181] *Agip (Africa) Ltd* [1990] Ch. 265 Ch.D at 286. This "requirement" was not considered by the Court of Appeal on appeal.

[182] *Banque Belge pour l'Etranger v Hambrouck* [1921] 1 K.B. 321 CA.

relationship between the parties.[183] Thus in the case of straightforward theft, the better view is that a plaintiff can only trace at common law.[184] Equally, where tracing is being used to support a claim in conversion or for money had and received, the plaintiff will be able to trace his value provided that it can be shown that the defendant received it through a series of clean substitutions. Thus in *Lipkin Gorman*[185] the solicitors were able to trace the money stolen from the firm's client account and gambled away at the defendant club as there had been no mixing of money, and the defendants were treated as donees (the gambling contracts then being void).

2.6.3 Tracing in equity

A person may wish to trace in equity in order to assert equitable ownership of, or a lien over, property held by the defendant. If the defendant has disposed of the property so as to leave no traceable proceeds then the claimant may trace his property to receipt by the defendant in order to bring a claim for knowing receipt.

The merit of equitable tracing is its flexibility. There is no restriction on the types of assets that may be traced or on the transactions through which the tracing process may be

---

[183] Scott, "The Right to 'Trace' at Common Law" (1966) 7 U.W.A.L.R. 463.

[184] In Australia it has been held that a thief is a trustee and owes fiduciary duties: "where money has been stolen, it is trust money in the hands of the thief and he cannot divest it of that character" *Black v S Freeman & Co* (1910) 12 C.L.R. 105 at 110. In *Westdeutsche Landesbank Girozentrale v Islington LBC* [1996] A.C. 669 at 715, Lord Browne-Wilkinson opined that the victim could trace in equity on the basis that the thief was subject to an immediate constructive trust in favour of the victim. However, the better view is that this is not the law in England. As Rimer J pointed out in *Shalson v Russo* [2003] EWHC 1637 (Ch) at [110], a thief ordinarily acquires no property in what he steals. Accordingly, he cannot be a trustee of it. "The fact that, traditionally, equity can only trace into a mixed bank account if [the precondition that there exists a fiduciary relationship] is satisfied provides an unsatisfactory justification for any conclusion that the stolen money must necessarily be trust money so as to enable the precondition to be satisfied. It is either trust money, or it is not. If it is not, it is not legitimate artificially to change its character so as to bring it within the supposed limits of equity's power to trace: the answer is to develop those powers so as to meet the special problems raised by stolen money."

[185] *Lipkin Gorman* [1990] 2 A.C. 548 HL.

conducted.[186] However, under the traditional rules, equitable tracing has one major limitation: the requirement that there must be a fiduciary relationship.[187] That requirement has been subject to extensive criticism,[188] and it is unlikely that it will survive examination by the House of Lords. It is, however, readily satisfied in most cases of corporate fraud, as the theft of a company's money will almost inevitably involve a breach of fiduciary duty on the part of the company's employees or agents.[189]

The requirement for a fiduciary relationship will be met in three situations. The first is where the property already belongs in equity to the claimant (e.g. the theft of trust property). The second is where the property is misappropriated by a person in a fiduciary relationship with the claimant (e.g. the embezzlement of a company's property by a director).[190] Thirdly, the requirement will also apparently be satisfied where the recipient receives the property subject to a constructive trust arising as a result of the receipt of the property.[191]

Unlike the common law, equity will permit a person to trace through a mixture, and has developed detailed rules to determine the ownership of mixtures of value. These rules differ depending on whether the claimant is tracing against a person who wrongfully created the mixture or against an innocent third party whose money was mixed with the claimant's. Unsurprisingly, the rules are more onerous when tracing against a wrongdoer.

---

[186] *El-Ajou* [1993] B.C.C. 698 Ch.D.
[187] *Agip (Africa) Ltd* [1991] Ch. 547 CA at 566. The requirement is derived from *Sinclair v Brougham* [1914] A.C. 398 HL and *Ministry of Health v Simpson*; sub nom. *Re Diplock's Estate* [1948] Ch. 465 CA.
[188] For example, Lionel D. Smith, *The Law of Tracing* (Oxford: Clarendon Press, 1997), pp.120–130, 340–347.
[189] *Agip (Africa) Ltd* [1990] Ch 265 Ch.D at 290.
[190] Craig Rotherham, "Tracing", in Hedley (ed), *The Law of Restitution* (London: Butterworths, 2002), p.65.
[191] *Chase Manhattan Bank v Israel-British Bank (London) Ltd* [1981] Ch 105; [1980] 2 W.L.R. 202 Ch.D. The correctness of this case has been doubted, and it seems inconsistent with established principles.

For banks and financial institutions, the equitable tracing rules are a potent source of liability. That is because banks and financial institutions will frequently receive money or other property beneficially (e.g. shares or money market instruments) that become mixed with the bank's own property.[192] Thus, whenever cash is paid over the counter to a bank, the money becomes mixed with the bank's money, bringing the equitable tracing rules into play. The same applies if a bank receives a telegraphic transfer, clears a cheque or buys shares from a customer. If the original money was subject to third-party equitable interests, the bank or institution may be at risk of a claim for knowing receipt or dishonest assistance. If the claimant's original property is still held by the bank, then it may be at risk of a proprietary claim for a constructive trust over that property.

2.6.3.1   Tracing against a wrongdoer

Where the claimant's money is mixed with the money of a wrongdoer, then the interests of the wrongdoer are subordinated to those of the innocent contributor.[193] That principle has a number of aspects.

First, if it is not possible to identify the share of the mixture contributed by the claimant from that of the person who wrongfully created the mixture, then the claimant is entitled to the whole.[194] In the case of money, that is unlikely to be the case unless the relevant records have been destroyed. Any doubt as to the size of the parties' shares will also be resolved against the wrongdoer.[195]

Secondly, an innocent contributor is entitled, at his option, to claim either a proportionate share of the mixture, or else a lien for the amount of his contribution.[196] If the asset has risen in value then the claimant will seek a proportionate share. If, on

---

[192] Smith, *The Law of Tracing* (1997), pp.231–234.

[193] *Foskett v McKeown* [2001] 1 A.C. 102 HL at 132 per Lord Millett.

[194] *Firth v Cartland* (1865) 2 Hem. & M. 417 at 420; 71 E.R. 525 and *Jones v De Marchant* (1916) 28 D.L.R. 561.

[195] *Lupton v White* (1808) 15 Ves. Jr. 432; 33 E.R. 817.

[196] *Firth* (1865) 2 Hem. & M. 417 and *Jones* (1916) 28 D.L.R. 561.

the other hand, the asset has depreciated, the claimant will want a charge over any remaining value. This could be relevant where the claimant's money has been used to acquire an asset, for example, land or shares that have fallen in value.

Thirdly, any losses are borne in the first instance by the wrongdoer, that is, drawings are deemed to be made against the wrongdoer's share.[197] Although said to be a presumption of honesty, that is in fact a rule of law and it is not open to a wrongdoer to argue that he intended to dissipate the claimant's share.

Fourthly, an innocent contributor can trace out of the mixture into any other asset that was acquired with the proceeds of the mixture. In *Re Oatway*[198] a trustee mixed £3,000 of trust money with £4,000 of his own. The money was frittered away apart from £2,137 which was used to buy shares. The court held that the beneficiary could claim the shares as representing £2,137 of the trust monies. The rest of the money had necessarily been dissipated. Thus, if a money launderer mixes money in his account and then buys shares that rise in value, the defrauded victim can trace his value through the account into the shares and then claim, at his choice, either ownership or a lien over the shares. Where the proceeds are used to acquire a number of assets, then the victim can choose whichever of those assets he wishes to trace into.

Fifthly, where money is withdrawn from the account, and subsequent payments are made into the account, the claimant is restricted to the lowest intermediate balance. That can be illustrated by *James Roscoe (Bolton) Ltd v Winder*.[199] The defendant collected a debt owed to the plaintiff and wrongfully paid it into his own account. He subsequently made withdrawals leaving a balance of £25 before making further deposits, leaving a credit balance at his death of £358. The plaintiff claimed the £358. The court held that he could only identify £25 as the proceeds of the debt. The withdrawals from the account

---

[197] *Re Hallett's Estate* (1880) 13 Ch. D. 696 CA.
[198] *Re Oatway* [1903] 2 Ch. 356 Ch.D.
[199] *James Roscoe (Bolton) Ltd v Winder* [1915] 1 Ch. 62 Ch.D.

meant that the rest of the plaintiff's money had been dissipated. The result will only be different if it can be shown that subsequent payments into the account were *intended* by the payer to make good previous withdrawals. That is hardly likely to occur in the case of money laundering. The result may operate harshly but it is the necessary consequence of the rule that property rights must be rights in respect of something. If the thing is destroyed, or the account ceases to hold any value, then there is nothing left which the claimant can identify as representing *his* property. Neither will the court engage in an artificial exercise of combining different accounts that are in credit with an overdrawn account to create a notional credit balance into which a person can trace.[200]

2.6.3.2 *Tracing against innocent third parties*

The rules are different in this case as there is no reason to subordinate the interests of third parties to those of the claimant. All have contributed to the mixture and as against each other, none is a wrongdoer. This is most likely to be the case where the claimant's value is mixed with the property of a bank or financial institution. Equally, where value is mixed by a third party in an account held with a bank, the account holder may find that he is subject to a tracing claim by persons who allege that their value was mixed in the account.

The basic rule is that where the value of several persons has been mixed, then each is entitled to a proportionate share. As between themselves, they have a joint co-ownership interest.[201] This is a property right that can be enforced against the bank where the money is held[202] (although not in the bank's own insolvency).

More difficult questions arise when money has been withdrawn from the account.

---

[200] *Shalson v Russo* [2005] Ch. 281 Ch.D at 327–328.
[201] *Re Tilley's Will Trusts* [1967] Ch. 1179 Ch.D.
[202] *Re Hallett's Estate* (1880) 13 Ch. D. 696 CA.

2.6.3.3   *Withdrawals by a wrongdoer from the mixture*

If the money is held in a deposit account, then the parties will share rateably in proportion to their contributions. Any withdrawals will result in the shares of each of the contributors being reduced rateably, although in that case, the contributors may be able to trace into any value acquired with the proceeds of a withdrawal, e.g. a purchase of shares.[203]

A different approach has been taken in respect of money held in a current account. In this case, the courts have generally applied the "first in, first out" rule in *Clayton's Case*.[204] This is a presumption, derived from banking practice, that where money is paid out of an active bank account, the first money paid in is the first to be paid out. The effect is to prioritise the last claimant whose money is paid into the account, and who will therefore be paid in full (if sufficient value remains). The same rule has been applied by the courts in the case of the mixing of the claimant's money with the money of an innocent donee (e.g. money given by a money launderer to his wife or children). In that case, as both the donee and the victim of the fraud are innocent of any wrongdoing, the "first in, first out" rule applies, and not the harsher rule where the mixing was with the wrongdoer's own money.

Clayton's Case provides a solution to a factual problem of how to allocate losses in an active bank account. However, its rough and ready nature, and its prioritising of the claims of later contributors, has lead to it being widely criticised.[205] It "apportions a common misfortune through a test which has no relation whatever to the justice of the case".[206] In *Barlow Clowes International Ltd Vaughan*[207] the Court of Appeal, whilst accepting its correctness as a general rule, held it to be inapplicable on the facts of the case.

---

[203] *Ministry of Health v Simpson*; sub nom. *Re Diplock's Estate* [1948] Ch. 465 CA.

[204] *Devaynes v Noble*; sub nom. *Clayton's Case* (1816) 1 Mer. 529; 35 E.R. 767. See *Ministry of Health v Simpson* [1948] Ch. 465 CA.

[205] See, e.g. Smith, *The Law of Tracing* (1997), pp.185–194.

[206] *Re Walter J. Schmidt & Co* (1923) 298 F. 314 at 316 per Learned Hand J.

[207] *Barlow Clowes International Ltd (In Liquidation) v Vaughan* [1992] 4 All E.R. 22 CA.

A large number of investors had paid money to Clowes to invest in various mutual funds. Few investments were actually made and a significant percentage of the money was dissipated by Clowes to fund a lavish lifestyle. At first instance the judge decided that *Clayton's Case* applied. On appeal, the court decided that if the application of the rule would be impractical, or would result in injustice, or would be contrary to the intention of the investors, it would not apply if an alternative method of distribution was available. In the case, the court decided that the remaining proceeds should be divided amongst the investors *pari passu* without regard to the order in which contributions were made.

2.6.3.4 *Withdrawals by innocent contributors*

If neither party is a wrongdoer, the better view is that a contributor to the mixture is entitled to withdraw his share. The effect of such a withdrawal is that the mixture is separated (unless the claimant takes more than his share) with the result that any further losses will be apportioned amongst those whose contributions remain mixed.[208]

> "A volunteer who mixes what turns out to be trust money with his own can surely 'unmix' it subsequently if he thinks fit to do so. And as the operation of equity is directed to preventing the volunteer doing what is unconscionable, surely it would be unconscionable for the volunteer who, for his own purposes, has earmarked the trust money to assert that what he has earmarked is not trust money."[209]

A similar result has been reached in recognising the effectiveness, for tracing purposes, of the internal allocation of funds through ledgers.[210]

---

[208] Smith, *The Law of Tracing* (1997), pp.212–215.
[209] *Simpson* [1948] Ch. 465 CA at 552 per Lord Greene MR.
[210] *Re Moffitt, Zwerling & Kemler (No.3)* (1995) 875 F. Supp. 1152 (E.D. Va); *Boscawen v Bajwa* [1996] 1 W.L.R. 328; (1995) 70 P. & C.R. 391 CA.

2.6.3.5   *Tracing into payment of a debt (backward tracing)*

A further problem is the effect on tracing where the claimant's value is used to pay a debt (or, which is the same thing, is paid into an overdrawn bank account). In *Ministry of Health v Simpson*, the Court of Appeal held that where money was used to pay a debt, the "debt was extinguished" leaving no traceable proceeds.[211]

That approach has been convincingly criticised by Smith.[212] In his view, when money is used to pay a debt, then the claimant should be able to trace into whatever value was acquired in return for incurring the debt. A debt is simply deferred payment. Thus, when payment of the debt is made, the proceeds of the payment are whatever was originally acquired in consideration for the debt. That is an attractive argument and avoids the conclusion reached in *Ministry of Health v Simpson* that where the claimant's money is used to pay an existing debt, then the claimant's value is treated as having disappeared, with the result that the defendant remains unjustly enriched.[213]

However, the courts have so far been unwilling to accept this analysis, and unless the matter is reconsidered by the House of Lords, the position laid down in *Simpson* remains the law. *Bishopsgate Investment Management v Homan*[214] concerned the theft of pension fund monies by Robert Maxwell. The monies were paid into accounts of Maxwell Communications Corporation (MCC) that either were, or subsequently became, overdrawn. The Court of Appeal held that equitable tracing could not be pursued through an overdrawn account. Neither was it

---

[211] *Ministry of Health v Simpson*; sub nom. *Re Diplock's Estate* [1948] Ch. 465 CA at 549.
[212] Smith, "Tracing into the Payment of a Debt" (1995) C.L.J. 290; *The Law of Tracing* (1997), pp.146–152, 215–217.
[213] Compare with Craig Rotherham, "The Metaphysics of Tracing", pp.122–125 in Craig Rotherham (ed), *Proprietary Remedies in Context*, (Oxford: Hart Publishing, 2002). According to Rotherham, "Tracing should be available in this context only if the transactional link in question is likely to indicate that that part of the defendant's estate that is available for distribution in bankruptcy continues to be swollen at the plaintiff's expense."
[214] *Bishopsgate Investment Management Ltd (in liquidation) v Homan* [1995] Ch. 211; [1994] 3 W.L.R. 1270; [1994] B.C.C. 868 CA.

possible to trace misappropriated money into assets acquired before the money was received as *"ex hypothesi* it cannot be followed into something which existed and so had been acquired before the money was received and therefore without its aid".[215] There was therefore no causal connection between the purchased asset and the theft.

At first instance, Vinelott J accepted that there might be circumstances where there was a close connection between a particular misappropriation of Bishopsgate's money and the acquisition by MCC of an asset. One instance was where an asset was acquired by MCC with monies borrowed from an overdrawn (or loan) account where when the borrowing was incurred it was intended that it would be repaid by misappropriations of Bishopsgate's money. A second example was where monies misappropriated from Bishopsgate were paid into an overdrawn MCC account in order to reduce the overdraft so as to make finance available, within the overdraft limits, for MCC to purchase some other asset.

Dillon LJ stated in the Court of Appeal that "if the connection [the judge] postulates between the particular misappropriation ... and the acquisition by MCC of a particular asset is sufficiently clearly proved, it is at least arguable, depending on the facts, that there ought to be an equitable charge in favour of [Bishopsgate] on the asset in question of MCC".[216] Leggatt LJ however disagreed, considering that it was never possible to trace through an overdrawn bank account. Henry LJ, unhelpfully, agreed with both judgments.

Subsequently, in *Foskett v McKeown*,[217] Scott VC considered "the point as still open", and stated that

> "I do not regard the fact that an asset is paid for out of borrowed money with the borrowing subsequently repaid out of trust money as being necessarily fatal to an equitable tracing claim by the trust beneficiaries. If in such

---

[215] *Homan* [1995] Ch. 211 CA at 221 per Leggatt LJ.
[216] *Homan* [1995] Ch. 211 CA at 217.
[217] *Foskett v McKeown* [1998] Ch. 265 CA at 283–284.

a case, it can be shown that it was always the intention to use the trust monies to acquire the asset, I do not see why the order in which the events happen should be regarded as critical to the claim."

The other two members of the court reiterated that it was not possible to trace into an already acquired asset.[218] First instance judges have continued to follow *Homan* and *Simpson*,[219] whilst expressing a preference in principle for Dillon LJ's approach.[220]

2.6.4 *The future of tracing*

The above analysis has been based on the existence of two separate sets of tracing rules, one for tracing at common law and one in equity. However, the justification for maintaining two separate sets of tracing rules, each with their own limitations, has increasingly been challenged. Smith, in his study of the law of tracing, concludes that the development of two different sets of rules was unjustified in principle and based on a misinterpretation by the courts of the relevant case law. Birks has argued in favour of the amalgamation of the two sets of rules distinguishing clearly between tracing (a process of identification of what has happened to property) with claiming (asserting ownership rights in property).[221] The real difference, he argues, lies not in the process of tracing but in the nature of rights that a person can assert. If a claimant has a common law right, then tracing will give rise to common law remedies, whereas if the claimant's interest in the property is equitable, then equitable remedies will be available.

---

[218] *Foskett* [1998] Ch. 265 CA at 289 (Hobhouse LJ) and 296 (Morritt LJ).
[219] *Box v Barclays Bank* [1998] Lloyd's Rep. Bank. 185 at 203 per Ferris J; *Shalson v Russo* [2003] EWHC 1637 (Ch).
[220] *Jyske Bank (Gibraltar) Ltd v Spjeldnaes* unreported, 23 July 1997, Ch.D per Evans Lombe J at 333 334; *Shalson v Russo* [2005] Ch. 281 Ch.D at 320.
[221] See P. Birks "Tracing, Subrogation and Change of Position" (1995) 9 Tru. L. Int. 124; "On Taking Seriously the Difference Between Tracing and Claiming" (1997) 11 Tru L Int 2 and "The Necessity of a Unitary Law of Tracing" in Ross Cranston (ed), *Making Commercial Law* (Oxford: Clarendon Press, 1997).

In *Foskett v McKeown*, Lord Steyn cited with approval Birks' analysis.[222] Lord Millett considered that

> "there is nothing inherently legal or equitable about the tracing exercise. There is thus no sense in maintaining different rules for tracing at law and in equity. One set of tracing rules is enough ... There is certainly no logical justification for allowing any distinction between them to produce capricious results in cases of mixed substitutions by insisting on the existence of a fiduciary relationship as a precondition for applying equity's tracing rules."[223]

It is considered that when a suitable case reaches the House of Lords (or, possibly, a bold Court of Appeal),[224] the view that there is a single law of tracing will prevail.[225] However, until this happens it will continue to be necessary to refer to the traditional rules.

2.7 Civil law risks to gatekeepers reporting suspicion

One of the greatest difficulties faced by those persons and institutions loyally doing their best to apply money laundering law as (largely) codified under POCA 2002 was the difficulty created by the consent regime and the way that this cut across contractual duties and duties of confidentiality, notably those owed by banks to their customers. In an article, the author of this Chapter suggested that there was insufficient legislative protection afforded to banks (and analogous undertakings) against litigation risk of claims arising out of consent SARs that interfered with transactions with foreseeable consequential loss where the report turned out to have been unjustified.[226] It is to

---

[222] *Foskett* [2001] 1 A.C. 102 HL at 113.

[223] *Foskett* [2001] 1 A.C. 102 HL at 128.

[224] See Sir Robert Walker, "Tracing After *Foskett v McKeown*" [2001] R.L.R. 573.

[225] This appears already to be the law in Jersey: *In re Esteem Settlement* [2002] J.L.R. 53 at 97.

[226] Paul Marshall, "*Shah v HSBC Private Bank (UK) Ltd*: filling the legislative gaps" (2012) 7 J.I.B.F.L. 407.

be remembered that there is no statutory requirement for suspicion to be reasonable, merely that the requisite suspicion be held.[227]

That the possible effects of the disclosure requirements and the working of the disclosure regime as a whole on commercial relationships were insufficiently evaluated at the Committee stage prior to the enactment of POCA 2002 in February 2003 was vividly revealed in the *HSBC v Shah* litigation (below), and by the fact that Parliament considered that protective provisions needed to be introduced under the Serious Crime Act 2015 (below). The problem faced by banks (and other similar customer-facing entities) in effect, was finding themselves in the invidious position between the *Scylla* of the draconian criminal penalties for failing to report suspicion and the *Charybdis* of risk of being sued for damages by their client for making a report on insufficient grounds (as Mr Shah sued HSBC).

The Court of Appeal, to widespread surprise, declined to accede to HSBC's application for summary judgment on its defence—that it was simply complying with the statutory requirements imposed by POCA 2002. Longmore LJ said that "Any claim by a customer that his bank has not executed his instructions is, on the face of it, a strong claim if the instructions have not in fact been executed."[228]

It is worth explaining in some detail how and why the bankers' dilemma arose. It did so as (presumably) an unintended consequence of the unique approach that POCA 2002 adopts to suspicious transactions. (As is explained in further detail below, the problem is peculiarly engaged in connection with transactional suspicion, typically in relation to the provisions of POCA 2002 s.328, as distinct from more generic suspicion under s.330—though that is not to thereby suggest that the latter is free from risk).

---

[227] As explained by Longmore LJ in *K Ltd v National Westminster Bank* [2006] EWCA Civ 1039 at [21].

[228] *Shah v HSBC Private Bank (UK) Ltd* [2010] EWCA Civ 31; [2010] Bus. L.R. 1514 at [25].

A curious and unique feature of the AML regime as implemented in the UK is the so-called "consent regime". It is illegal for a person to proceed with a transaction (arrangement) that involves property that is suspected of representing (wholly or partly) the benefit from (any) criminal conduct and where the property in question does represent such a benefit. Such conduct need not be serious criminal conduct and, further, the relevant property may be derived from conduct that occurred overseas but which would constitute an offence had the relevant conduct occurred in the UK. All that is necessary is that the state of mind necessary to constitute suspicion should have existed at the relevant time in point of fact.

The key to the consent regime is that each of the three substantive money laundering offences (ss.327–329) are provided with a specific statutory defence where a report of suspicion is made to the National Crime Agency (NCA) as soon as practicable (i.e. an authorised disclosure) and *before* proceeding with the transaction (the prohibited act) consent is given by the NCA to do so. There are two periods in which a transaction may be effectively sterilised as a result of delay pending such consent being given. The first is an initial period of seven days (the notice period), within which the NCA must either give or refuse consent: if that is not done, consent is deemed to have been given. The second is a further 31-day "moratorium period" where nothing may be done to progress the arrangement if within the notice period the NCA declined to consent to the transaction proceeding. That period runs from the date on which consent is declined by the NCA. In the absence of a court (restraint) order after the expiry of that further period, consent to the transaction is deemed to be given. (In practice, in the overwhelming number of cases, consent has been given within a few days of a report being made.)

A maximum penalty of 13 years' imprisonment for conviction on indictment for money laundering (where the transaction later turns out, as was suspected, to have involved property that represented a benefit from criminal conduct) operates as encouragement to banks and others involved in financial and other property transactions to report their suspicions and to wait for the "appropriate consent" to be given. The legal effect of the requirement to report suspicion, together with the statutory prohibition on proceeding with a transaction ("arrangement" under POCA 2002 s.328) involving a benefit suspected of being derived from any criminal conduct is that the transaction in question, pending consent, is frustrated by supervening statutory illegality. Both parties, *pro tem*, are relieved of any further contractual obligation. The point is that it is an offence to proceed with a transaction suspected of representing a benefit from criminal conduct but *only* where the property is not only suspected of representing a benefit from criminal conduct but also does *in fact* represent such a benefit. As the Court of Appeal has explained, it is not the suspected transaction that taints the property but rather the original underlying (or predicate) offence.[229] If the property in question is untainted by crime, however much the facts may give rise to suspicion of money laundering, it is not unlawful under POCA 2002 (i.e. it will not be an offence) to proceed with a transaction. The corollary of this is that in the absence of any statutory defence being provided, and until March 2015 there were none, contractual obligations are *not suspended under the legislation* where a transaction is incorrectly/unjustifiably suspected of involving property derived from criminal conduct. The simple rationale for this odd position is that money laundering can only involve criminal property. (While seemingly obvious, it is a proposition that from time to time has been lost sight of.)

The foregoing, that is, the result of the unique way in which the United Kingdom has implemented the Vienna Convention and EU legislation on money laundering under the "consent regime", gave rise to the extraordinary consequence that, until amendments were introduced in March 2015 to POCA 2002, anyone who participated in a transaction by advising, or otherwise acting for, a client, was:

---

[229] *R. v Geary (Michael)* [2010] EWCA Crim 1925; [2011] 1 W.L.R. 1634, approved by the Supreme Court in *R. v GH* [2015] UKSC 24; [2015] 1 W.L.R. 2126; [2015] 2 Cr. App. R. 12 (p.195).

(a) on the one hand, subject to draconian criminal penalties had they proceeded, without the requisite consent, with a suspected transaction which turned out, as suspected, to involve criminal property; but,
(b) on the other, if the property in question was untainted by crime, (that is, it did not represent a benefit from criminal conduct within the meaning of POCA 2002 s.340) and a report was made with the effect of suspending the transaction, the reporter was exposed to a claim for damages should the suspension of a transaction have caused loss or damage to the person subject of suspicion.

Given that (contrary to what was previously thought to be the position) a bank or other reporter could be required to prove at trial the fact of suspicion,[230] the invidious choice for banks (and other reporters) involved the balancing of risk between committing a criminal offence if suspicion was entertained but no suspicious activity report (SAR) was made, with suspicion subsequently shown to have been well-founded, and being sued if a suspicion was reported, but it turned out to be unfounded. That that position—and attendant exposure to criminal and civil liability—was determined by the difficult concept of suspicion has been the source of much difficulty and confusion, and it is one reason for the high cost to business of implementing AML procedures.

It was to that conundrum, and the (unsatisfactory) absence of any statutory protection against a claim for breach of contract afforded to a person whose suspicion turns out to have been unfounded, that was considered by Supperstone J (after years of interlocutory skirmishing including several trips to the Court of Appeal), in *Shah v HSBC Private Bank*.[231]

Supperstone J's approach can be dealt with briefly, because the issue has largely been resolved by statutory amendment to POCA 2002 under s.37 of the Serious Crime Act 2015 (SCA 2015). Nevertheless, the court's approach remains of interest. HSBC contended for the existence of an obvious or necessary

---

[230] Noted by the author of this Chapter in (2010) 5 J.I.B.F.L. 287.
[231] *Shah v HSBC Private Bank (UK) Ltd* [2012] EWHC 1283 (QB); [2013] Bus. L.R. D38.

contractual term to be implied into the contract of a mandate to the effect that the bank was entitled to refuse to execute payment instructions in the absence of appropriate consent from the Serious Organised Crime Agency (predecessor to the NCA) where it suspected the transaction in question constituted money laundering. Supperstone J referred to the principles for implying a contractual term from a judgment in the same litigation where Hamblen J said that:

> "... where the bank has a relevant suspicion that the property is criminal property it has no alternative but to seek appropriate consent under POCA [2002]. The bank is most unlikely to be in a position to know whether or not the property is criminal property, but, if it suspected that it is, then in order to avoid potential criminal liability under POCA [2002] it must make a disclosure and seek appropriate consent. Analytically this may be legally permissible as the result of an obvious and/or necessarily implied restriction on or qualification of the bank's duties rather than on grounds of illegality, but the end result is the same."[232]

Supperstone J concluded his short consideration of the arguments in relation to an implied term:

> "... I am led to the conclusion that the term for which the Defendant contends is to be implied by reason of the statutory provisions. In my judgment the 'precise and workable balance of conflicting interests' in POCA [2002] that Longmore LJ noted in *K Ltd v National Westminster Bank Plc (Revenue and Customs Comrs intervening) (Practice Note)* [2007] Bus. L.R. 26 at [22] [that] Parliament has struck requires the implication of this term in the contract between a banker and his customer."[233]

It was common ground that there was no precedent for implying a term to this effect.

---

[232] *Shah v HSBC Private Bank (UK) Ltd* [2009] EWHC 79 (QB) at [39].
[233] *Shah v HSBC Private Bank (UK) Ltd (No.2)* [2012] EWHC 1283 (QB); [2013] Bus. L.R. D38 at [45].

For reasons beyond the scope of this Chapter, it may be respectfully doubted whether the proposition that Parliament, under POCA 2002, struck a "precise and workable balance", was justified or correct. (In barest summary, the authorised disclosure regime never received detailed or full Parliamentary scrutiny (owing to its origin in the Vienna Convention), and the reporting offence under s.330 of POCA 2002 had been imported across from amendments made to the Terrorism Act 2000 (made in the febrile atmosphere following 9/11—terrorism and money laundering for political reasons, having been frequently, and perhaps artificially, linked). In any event, Parliament has now deemed it expedient to legislate on the point under primary legislation. By s.37 of the Serious Crime Act 2015 (SCA 2015), amending s.338(4) of POCA 2002, it is now provided that:

> "where an authorised disclosure is made in good faith, no civil liability arises in respect of the disclosure on the part of the person on whose behalf it was made".

The first point to note is that the protection under SCA 2015 s.38 and POCA 2002 s.338(4) applies to "authorised" disclosures, that is to say, disclosures made under the "consent regime" in connection with ss.327–329 POCA 2002 (and related accessory and inchoate offences). Further, the drafting suffers from some residual ambiguity. It might be thought that if negligence was intended to be protected against, under ordinary rules of interpretation, the provision would say so in terms. Further, introducing the amendment at the Committee stage, Ms Karen Bradley MP said that financial institutions and others submitting SARs would continue to be liable for any negligent or malicious conduct.[234] That would appear to be wrong. The test for statutory protection seems to be discharging the burden (to the civil standard) of proving good faith. While the statutory amendment resolves the issue that was live in the *HSBC v Shah* litigation, banks and other reporters still have the evidential burden of having to establish the fact of

---

[234] Public Bill Committee debate, 13 January 2015.

suspicion (and its basis so as to satisfy the requirement of good faith). Further, a fanciful suspicion may not satisfy the requirement of good faith.[235]

Importantly, it should be noted that a bank that has made an SAR, where the NCA has not taken action within the moratorium period, will not be able to rely upon s.37 of SCA 2015 to continue to disregard client instructions after expiry of the moratorium period. That might arise where, for example, the bank is concerned about potential exposure to third party accessory liability to victims of fraud. In such circumstances the bank will have to bring its conduct within its contractual terms.[236]

Further, it is important to note that the protection only applies in relation to disclosures under the consent regime. Disclosures that are made pursuant to POCA 2002 s.330 (i.e. protected disclosures) while attracting protection from claims for breach of *confidence* (hence their name), do not enjoy similar protection. That having been said, since a disclosure under s.330 is unlikely to be transaction specific and does not trigger supervening illegality of the kind that underlies the consent regime, such a report is in any event much less likely to give rise to a claim for damages.

2.8 Civil Liability under the Money Laundering Regulations 2007

The 2007 Regulations regs 42–47 provided for civil as well as criminal penalties for breach. The civil penalties, unlike the criminal penalties, apply only to those relevant persons supervised by one of the designated authorities. While beyond

---

[235] For a discussion of the kind of suspicion that is necessary see, for example, *Parvizi v Barclays Bank plc* [2014] EWHC B2 (QB) (the claim was struck out because the bank was able to show grounded suspicion—albeit subject to criticism).

[236] I gratefully acknowledge Nicholas Medcroft, barrister, Wilberforce Chambers, as the source of this point, made by him in a Note in (2015) 5 J.I.B.F.L. referring to *Becker v Lloyds TSB Bank Plc* [2013] EWHC 3000 (Ch) as authority for the proposition.

the scope of this Chapter, the provisions in reg.36 are crucial to understanding the scope and limitations on the powers of the authorities. "Designated authority" for present purposes means the Authority, that is to say, the FCA (formerly FSA) and the Commissioners, namely HMRC. The OFT was previously a designated authority until its functions were transferred to the FCA and the Competition Markets Authority from 1 April 2014. The 2007 Regulations implement the EU Third Directive which, under Article 39, emphasised the approach required in relation to "administrative penalties" as distinct from criminal sanctions. Accordingly, regs 42–44 provide for civil penalties under enforcement powers of the designated authorities and related review and appeal procedures.

Regulation 42(1) provides that a designated authority may impose a penalty of such amount as it considers appropriate on a relevant person who fails to comply with any requirement under regs 7(1), (2), or (3); 8(1) or (3); 9(2); 10(1); 11(1); 14(1); 15(1) or (2); 16(1), (2), (3) or (4); 19(1), (4) or (6); 20(1), (4) or (5); 21; 26; 27(4) or 33 or a direction under reg.18. "Appropriate" means effective, proportionate and dissuasive.

There is a due diligence bar under reg.42(2) against imposing a civil penalty under Regulation 42(1):

> "The designated authority must not impose a penalty on a person under paragraph (1) where there are reasonable grounds for it to be satisfied that the person took all reasonable steps and exercised all due diligence to ensure that he requirement would be complied with."

Regulation 42(3) provides that in deciding whether a person has failed to comply with the 2007 Regulations, the designated authority must consider whether he followed any relevant guidance which was at the time issued by a supervisory authority or other appropriate body approved by the Treasury and published in a manner approved by the Treasury as suitable in their opinion to bring the guidance to the attention of the persons likely to be affected by it.

The procedure for challenging penalties imposed under reg.42 is provided for under regs 43 and 44.

It is likely that under the new Regulations that will implement the Fourth Directive, the scheme of sanctions and penalties will be substantially revised. It has been apparently recognised that an excessively sanctions-based regulatory regime imposed on the regulated financial sector has tended to engender a defensive (and sometimes negative) response from businesses rather than eliciting the co-operative engagement between regulated entities and law enforcement agencies that it is thought may operate more effectively (and efficiently) in denying the financial system to money launderers.

Chapter 3

International Considerations

Ben Hammond
Partner
Ashurst LLP

3.1 Introduction

Economic globalisation requires a financial infrastructure through which money can flow easily across international borders. That facilitates commerce, but it also facilitates money laundering. Money launderers are able to move money more quickly and easily than in the past, and money laundering thrives on exploiting differences in law and regulation; it tends to migrate to jurisdictions which offer the least resistance. The imposition of realistic and uniform anti-money laundering (AML) standards by the international community is therefore critical to tackling money laundering, as is efficient and effective co-operation.

Despite recognising the problem, international AML efforts have historically been fragmented. Various national and inter-governmental bodies have produced initiatives and standards, but there has been little cooperation or consultation. The situation has improved in recent years as the Financial Action Task Force (FATF) in particular has marshalled the international AML effort and has had considerable success in aligning international standards. Money laundering activity may remain high but the international community is beginning to present a united front.

Initially international action was galvanised by combatting the global drugs trade. More recently it is the global threat of terrorism which has given impetus to international action. The attacks on the US in September 2001 served to focus interest on the extent to which money laundering sustains and enables terrorism. The international community is now focused on a new paradigm of insurgency threat in the form of Islamic State in Iraq and the Levant (ISIL), but the fundamental objective of cutting off illicit money supplies remains the same.

3.2 The Financial Action Task Force

3.2.1 Background

When the heads of state and government of the G7 countries and the President of the European Commission convened in Paris in July 1989 for the fifteenth G7 summit, they met amid mounting alarm over the international drugs problem. There was widespread concern over the size of the threat posed by money laundering to financial institutions and the banking system. It was decided that firm action was needed at both national and international level to combat the problem.

As a result, the G7 attendees convened the FATF to assess the results of cooperation already underway to prevent money laundering, to examine current money laundering techniques and trends, and to establish measures for future implementation, including the adaptation as necessary of the statutory and regulatory systems of members to enhance multilateral assistance.

The founding members of the FATF were the G7 summit participants (the US, Japan, Germany, France, the UK, Italy, Canada and the European Commission). Eight other countries (Sweden, the Netherlands, Belgium, Luxembourg, Switzerland, Austria, Spain and Australia) were also invited to join in order to enlarge the expertise of the FATF and to reflect the views of other countries which were particularly concerned by, or which had particular expertise in, combatting money laundering.

The FATF was conceived as an inter-governmental policy-making body that would work to generate the political will to bring about national legislative and regulatory reforms necessary to combat money laundering. It was intended to be flexible, with no closely-drawn constitution, nor even an unlimited life-span. This flexibility remains: the FATF reviews its mission periodically and its current mandate, adopted in April 2012, will continue until 31 December 2020. Whether the FATF continues to exist beyond 2020 depends on whether its members agree that that remains necessary.[1]

The number of FATF members has now grown from the founding 16 to 36, including two regional organisations (the European Commission and the Gulf Co-operation Council (GCC)).[2] India is the most recent country to join the FATF as a member (in 2010) and, in June 2014, the FATF decided on a further limited expansion of membership. The criteria for membership require that a candidate country must be strategically important and must enhance the FATF's geographic balance. Malaysia (since October 2014) and Saudi Arabia (since June 2015) have held observer status as they work towards meeting the requirements for full membership.

The FATF is led by a President. This is a one-year position held by a high-level government official appointed from among the FATF members. A small Secretariat unit assists the President and services the FATF. Housed at the headquarters of the Organisation for Economic Co-operation and Development (the OECD) in Paris, the FATF nevertheless is an independent body and is not a part of the OECD.

The FATF members meet three times each year at plenary meetings in February, June and October. These meetings are

---

[1] FATF mandate (2012–20), available at *http://www.fatf-gafi.org/media/fatf/documents/FINAL%20FATF%20MANDATE%202012-2020.pdf* [Accessed 25 September 2015].

[2] The 36 current FATF members (34 jurisdictions and two regional organisations) are: Argentina, Australia, Austria, Belgium, Brazil, Canada, China, Denmark, European Commission, Finland, France, Germany, Greece, GCC, Hong Kong (China), Iceland, India, Ireland, Italy, Japan, Republic of Korea, Luxembourg, Mexico, the Netherlands, New Zealand, Norway, Portugal, Russian Federation, Singapore, South Africa, Spain, Sweden, Switzerland, Turkey, the UK and the US.

161

used to discuss policy direction and initiatives. Discussions typically encompass analyses of money laundering trends and counter-measures, the progress of implementation of AML measures within the FATF and the establishment of a world-wide AML network. A consensual decision-making process is employed, with decisions made by the FATF on the basis of papers prepared by the Secretariat or written or oral reports from delegations, with the FATF's main publication being its annual report, which records the FATF's work and activities over the preceding year.

Money laundering techniques are also examined each year at "typologies" meetings. These meetings provide a forum for law enforcement and regulatory experts from FATF member countries, together with certain international organisations and bodies, as well as representatives from other countries, to discuss the prevailing money laundering methods, the emerging threats, and any effective counter-measures that have been developed. The FATF releases typologies reports to promulgate the FATF's findings on trends, techniques and counter-measures in various areas.

Various geographic ad hoc groups are also convened to discuss issues that are relevant to particular regions of the world, with further ad hoc groups covering special topics that require more detailed analysis. Such groups have specific mandates and report to each plenary meeting regarding their work.

3.2.2 The 40 Recommendations

In April 1990, the FATF published a set of 40 recommendations (the Recommendations), which were intended to provide a comprehensive blueprint of the steps required to take forward the fight against money laundering.

The Recommendations were first revised in 1996 to take into account changes in money laundering trends and to anticipate potential future threats. The focus until 1996 had been on the creation of an offence of drug money laundering, but the principal amendment to the revised Recommendations was to extend the offence beyond drugs to serious crimes. Interpretive notes were also produced to clarify the application of specific Recommendations and to provide additional guidance.

The Recommendations were designed for universal application and as a complete set of counter-measures against money laundering, covering the criminal justice system and law enforcement, the financial system and its regulation, and international cooperation. It was, however, recognised that member countries had diverse legal and financial systems and so could not all adopt identical measures. The Recommendations were therefore framed as a set of principles for action rather than prescriptive rules which countries could then implement, with a measure of flexibility, according to their particular circumstances and constitutional frameworks.

The Recommendations were drafted to avoid being complex and not to compromise the freedom to engage in legitimate transactions or threaten economic development. In that, they (and their revisions, discussed below) appear to have been successful. They have since been recognised, endorsed or adopted by many international bodies and many countries have made a political commitment to combat money laundering by implementing them. The Recommendations are now commonly accepted internationally as the global policy benchmark for AML measures.

3.2.3 *The Special Recommendations*

Following the terrorist attacks in New York and Washington on 11 September 2001, at an extraordinary plenary meeting in October 2001, the FATF expanded its mission to include countering the financing of terrorism (CFT) and called on all countries to adopt and implement eight further "Special Recommendations" by June 2002.

The Special Recommendations were intended to be read and applied alongside the Recommendations and, together, to establish a basic framework for the detection and prevention of the financing of terrorism. They advocated:

163

(a) immediate steps to ratify and implement the 1999 UN International Convention for the Suppression of the Financing of Terrorism. Countries were also encouraged to implement immediately the UN resolutions relating to the prevention and suppression of the financing of terrorist acts;

(b) immediate steps to criminalise the financing of terrorism, terrorist acts and terrorist organisations and to designate those offences as money laundering predicate offences (i.e. offences from which the proceeds form the underlying resources for money laundering);

(c) measures to freeze funds or other assets of terrorists, those who finance terrorism and terrorist organisations, and to empower authorities to seize and confiscate property that is the proceeds of, or used in, or intended or allocated for use in, the financing of terrorism, terrorist acts or terrorist organisations;

(d) requirements for those, such as financial institutions, which are subject to AML obligations, to report promptly suspicions of funds linked to terrorism;

(e) the mutual provision by jurisdictions of assistance in connection with criminal or civil enforcement, investigations, inquiries and proceedings relating to the financing of terrorism and to ensure that jurisdictions do not provide safe havens for individuals charged with such offences;

(f) the licensing and registration of all persons or entities that provide a service for the transmission of money or value and for them to be subject to all of the Recommendations that apply to banks and non-bank financial institutions;

(g) requirements for financial institutions to include accurate and meaningful originator information on funds transfers and for the information to remain with the transfer throughout the payment chain; and

(h) reviews by countries of the adequacy of laws relating to entities that can be abused for the financing of terrorism, with non-profit organisations considered to be particularly vulnerable.

A ninth Special Recommendation relating to "cash couriers" was adopted in October 2004. The intention was to ensure that countries could detect the physical cross-border transportation of currency and bearer negotiable instruments and restrain the currency or instruments where suspected of a connection to terrorist financing.

3.2.4 *Revision of the Recommendations in 2003*

In 2001, developments in money laundering trends and techniques, and the identification of areas of weakness in the Recommendations, prompted the FATF to launch a review of the Recommendations. Following consultation, revised Recommendations were published on 20 June 2003.

This was a significant review, and the revised Recommendations incorporated many key additions and changes. However, the fundamental approach was left unchanged: the Recommendations continued to adopt a risk-based approach. That is to say, within limits, countries and institutions could determine the extent of the measures that must be taken by reference to the risk of money laundering or terrorist financing for the particular customer, type of transaction or product.

The Joint Forum of the Basel Committee on Banking Supervision, the International Organization of Securities Commissions and the International Association of Insurance Supervisors (the Joint Forum) issued a note in June 2003.[3] This note stated that measures and standards countering money laundering and terrorist financing must be reasonably consistent across the banking, insurance and securities sectors, to the extent that institutions in each sector offer the same services. There would otherwise be a tendency for criminal funds to flow to institutions in the sectors operating under less stringent standards. However, the Joint Forum also expressed a belief that these measures and standards must be tailored to the circumstances of each relationship between institution and customer. The note pointed out that the revision of the Recommendations provided an opportunity for standard-setting organisations in each sector to review their standards

---

[3] Available at *http://www.bis.org/publ/joint05.pdf* [Accessed 25 September 2015].

and guidance, with the aim of preventing inconsistencies between these standards and guidance where this is unwarranted from a risk-based approach.

3.2.5 Further review and consolidation

During 2010 and 2011, the FATF undertook further rounds of consultation, intended to ensure that the Recommendations and the Special Recommendations remained up-to-date and relevant. The review was focused on addressing deficiencies and loopholes whilst maintaining stability in the standards.

The review culminated in further revisions to the Recommendations, which were adopted on 16 February 2012. Building on the previous incarnations of the Recommendations, the revisions included strengthened requirements for higher risk situations, and allowed countries to take a more focused approach in areas where high risks remained or implementation could be enhanced.

Against a backdrop of growing concern over the threat of global terrorism, and recognising the overlap of AML and CFT, the Special Recommendations were absorbed into the Recommendations and the former ceased to comprise a standalone set of principles. Certain Recommendations were combined with equivalent Special Recommendations, such as Recommendation 20 (reporting of suspicious transactions), but new Recommendations unique to CFT were also introduced including: Recommendation 5 (the criminalisation of terrorist financing); Recommendation 6 (targeted financial sanctions related to terrorism & terrorist financing); Recommendation 8 (measures to prevent the misuse of non-profit organisations); and Recommendation 32 (cash couriers).

In 2008, the FATF's mandate was expanded to include dealing with the financing of proliferation of weapons of mass destruction. The FATF also adopted a new Recommendation following the 2012 review (Recommendation 7) aimed at ensuring consistent and effective implementation of targeted financial sanctions when they were called for by the UN Security Council.

3.2.6 The Current Recommendations

The Recommendations are split into the following seven subject areas, and comprise standards addressed variously to countries and to market participants:

(a) AML/CFT policies and coordination;
(b) money laundering and confiscation;
(c) terrorist financing and financing of proliferation;
(d) preventive measures;
(e) transparency and beneficial ownership of legal persons and arrangements;
(f) powers and responsibilities of competent authorities and other institutional measures; and
(g) international cooperation.

The Recommendations are accompanied by interpretive notes, which contain much of the detail.

3.2.6.1 AML/CFT policies and coordination (Recommendations 1 and 2)

Recommendation 1 articulates a risk-based approach to assessing risks for AML and CFT and, unlike previous Recommendations, applies this at a national level. Countries are required to identify, assess and understand the money laundering and terrorist financing risks they face, and to take action, including designating an authority or mechanism to coordinate actions to assess risks, and apply resources, aimed at ensuring the risks are mitigated effectively. On the basis of this "national risk assessment", countries are then required to ensure that their AML and CFT measures are commensurate with the risks identified.

Countries are required to maintain national AML/CFT policies, informed by the risks identified, which are regularly

167

reviewed, and which designate an authority or have a coordination or other mechanism responsible for policies (Recommendation 2).

3.2.6.2 *Money laundering and confiscation (Recommendations 3 and 4)*

Recommendation 3 requires the criminalisation of money laundering and that all serious offences be made "predicate" offences to the crime of money laundering. A list of designated predicate offences is set out in an interpretive note and, for the first time, this has been expanded to include tax crimes.

In the interpretive note to Recommendation 3, the FATF discusses the mental state required to prove the offence of money laundering, and specifies that it should be capable of being inferred from objective factual circumstances. The note also provides that liability should attach to legal as well as natural persons, and that there should be appropriate ancillary offences to the offence of money laundering, including participation in, association with or conspiracy to commit, attempt, aiding and abetting, facilitating, and counselling the commission, unless that is not permitted by fundamental principles of domestic law.

Recommendation 4 requires the adoption of measures for confiscation of laundered money, including powers of identification, freezing and seizing, and investigation.

3.2.6.3 *Terrorist financing and financing of proliferation (Recommendations 5–8)*

Mirroring Recommendation 3 in relation to AML, Recommendation 5 requires the criminalisation of terrorist financing. That includes the financing of terrorists and terrorist organisations, even in the absence of a link to a specific terrorist act or acts, and requires countries to ensure that those offences are money laundering predicate offences.

Recommendations 6 and 7 require implementation of financial sanctions regimes to comply with UN Security Council resolutions relating to the prevention and suppression of terrorism and terrorist financing and to the prevention, suppression and disruption of proliferation of weapons of mass destruction and its financing.

Recommendation 8 requires countries to review the adequacy of law and regulation relating to entities capable of abuse for the financing of terrorism, focusing (in line with what was previously Special Recommendation 8) on non-profit organisations. These are identified as particularly vulnerable to misuse by terrorist organisations: (a) to pose as legitimate entities; (b) as conduits for terrorist financing; and (c) to conceal or obscure the clandestine diversion of funds intended for legitimate purposes.

3.2.6.4   *Preventive measures (Recommendations 9–23)*

Recommendation 9 requires countries to ensure that secrecy laws applicable to financial institutions do not inhibit implementation of the Recommendations.

3.2.6.4.1   Customer due diligence and record keeping

Recommendation 10 stipulates that financial institutions should be prohibited from keeping anonymous accounts or accounts in obviously fictitious names and should implement measures to identify and verify the identity of customers and beneficial owners, and to conduct due diligence on an ongoing basis. The extent of those measures will depend on the risk inherent in the type of transaction or customer involved, i.e. again reflecting a risk-based approach.

Recommendation 11 specifies the maintenance, for at least five years, of records of both transactions carried out and identification data obtained, both of which should be available to comply with information requests from competent authorities.

3.2.6.4.2 Additional measures for specific customers and activities

In Recommendations 12 and 13, the FATF identifies the areas of politically exposed persons (PEPs) and correspondent banking as requiring additional due diligence measures owing to the particular risks of money laundering or terrorist financing.

Recommendation 14 focuses on an issue previously addressed in the sixth Special Recommendation: money or value transfer services (MVTS). It requires countries to ensure that natural or legal persons that provide MVTS are licensed or registered, and subject to effective systems for monitoring and ensuring FATF compliance, as well as steps to be taken for focusing on agents of the MVTS provider.

Recommendation 15 identifies the risks associated with new technologies and the particular risks that arise when: (a) developing new products and new business practices, including new delivery mechanisms; and (b) using new or developing technologies for both new and pre-existing products.

Recommendation 16 also derives from the Special Recommendations and focuses on wire transfers, monitoring such transfers, and ensuring that financial institutions include accurate originator information and beneficiary information on wire transfers and related messages, and that that information remains with the wire transfer or related message throughout the payment chain.

3.2.6.4.3 Reliance, Controls and Financial Groups

The FATF recognises that it is common for countries to allow financial institutions to rely on intermediaries or other third parties to perform customer due diligence. Accordingly, Recommendation 17 permits countries to allow institutions to rely on appropriately regulated and supervised third parties, provided certain conditions are met. Ultimate responsibility must, however, remain with the financial institution relying on the third party.

Financial institutions are recommended to develop AML programmes that include the development of internal policies and controls, an ongoing employee training programme and an audit function to test their systems (Recommendation 18).

Financial institutions are similarly directed, in Recommendation 19, to pay special attention to business relationships and transactions with persons, including financial institutions, from countries that do not apply the Recommendations, or countries which apply them insufficiently. Whenever transactions have no apparent economic or visible lawful purpose, their background and purpose should be examined, and the findings established in writing and made available to help competent authorities.

3.2.6.4.4   Reporting of suspicious transactions

The FATF has called for mandatory suspicious transaction reporting since 1996. This requirement is now reflected in Recommendation 20 and covers both the proceeds of criminal activity, and funds related to terrorist financing.

Persons reporting suspicious transactions should be legally protected from criminal or civil liability for breach of any restriction on disclosure of information. Disclosure of the fact that a suspicious transaction report has been made must be prohibited and Recommendation 21 also introduces specific prohibitions on tipping off and, conversely, requires protection from criminal and civil liability for breach of any restriction on disclosure of information imposed by contract or by any legislative, regulatory or administrative provision, if a report of suspicions is made in good faith.

3.2.6.4.5   Designated non-financial businesses and professions

Recommendations 22 and 23 extend the scope of customer due diligence and suspicious transaction reporting to: casinos; real estate agents; dealers in precious metals and dealers in precious stones; lawyers, notaries, other independent legal professionals and accountants (with some exemptions for professional secrecy and legal professional privilege); and trust and company service providers.

3.2.6.5 *Transparency and beneficial ownership of legal persons and arrangements (Recommendations 24 and 25)*

Recommendations 24 and 25 set out the FATF's aim of ensuring that adequate, accurate and timely information on the beneficial ownership and control of legal persons and arrangements such as trusts is obtainable or accessible. In particular, countries that permit companies to issue bearer shares must take appropriate measures to ensure that they are not misused for money laundering purposes.

3.2.6.6 *Powers and responsibilities of competent authorities and other institutional measures (Recommendations 26–35)*

3.2.6.6.1 Regulation and supervision

Recommendations 26 and 28 provide that:

(a) measures should be taken to ensure that financial institutions are not owned or managed by criminals or their associates;
(b) the regulatory and supervisory measures that apply to banks and insurance and securities firms for prudential purposes should also apply in respect of AML and CFT;
(c) other financial institutions must be regulated and subject to supervision or oversight, having regard to the risk of money laundering or terrorist financing;
(d) bureaux de change and money remittance businesses must, at a minimum, be registered or licensed, and monitored to ensure compliance;
(e) casinos must be licensed and supervised; and
(f) on a risk-sensitive basis, other businesses and professions must be subject to effective systems for monitoring and ensuring compliance, which could be by a government authority or a self-regulatory organisation.

Recommendation 27 provides that supervisors should have adequate powers to supervise or monitor, and ensure compliance by, financial institutions with requirements to combat money laundering and terrorist financing, including the authority to conduct inspections. They should be authorised to compel production of any information from financial institutions that is relevant to monitoring such compliance, and to impose sanctions for failure to comply with such requirements.

3.2.6.6.2 Operational and law enforcement

Recommendations 29 and 30 require countries to establish financial intelligence units (FIUs) to serve as national centres for receiving suspicious transaction reports and to designate law enforcement agencies for money laundering and financing of terrorism investigations. These authorities and financial supervisors are required by Recommendations 30 and 31 to have appropriate responsibilities and powers, sufficient resources, and effective mechanisms for cooperation and coordination. Countries are also directed to maintain statistics on the effectiveness and efficiency of their AML and CFT systems.

The specific requirements relating to cash couriers are now set out in Recommendation 32. Countries must have measures in place to detect the physical cross-border transportation of currency and bearer negotiable instruments, including through a declaration system and/or disclosure system, with competent authorities having the legal authority to stop or restrain currency or bearer negotiable instruments that are suspected to be related to terrorist financing, money laundering or predicate offences, or that are falsely declared or disclosed.

3.2.6.6.3 General Requirements

Countries are required to maintain comprehensive statistics on the effectiveness and efficiency of their AML/CFT systems, including statistics on suspicious transaction reports, on money laundering and terrorist financing investigations, prosecutions and convictions, on frozen, seized and confiscated

173

property, and on mutual legal assistance or other international requests for co-operation (Recommendation 33).

Competent authorities, supervisors and self-regulatory bodies must establish guidelines, and provide feedback, which will assist financial institutions and designated non-financial businesses and professions in applying national measures to combat money laundering and terrorist financing, and, in particular, in detecting and reporting suspicious transactions (Recommendation 34).

3.2.6.6.4 Sanctions

Recommendation 35 requires countries to ensure that there is a range of effective, proportionate and dissuasive sanctions, criminal, civil and administrative, available to deal with natural or legal persons who fail to comply with AML/CFT requirements.

3.2.6.7 *International co-operation (Recommendations 36–40)*

This final set of Recommendations aims to promote the widest possible international co-operation between countries' competent authorities, and the establishment of clear and effective gateways of information. Countries are urged to ratify and implement relevant UN and other international conventions on money laundering and terrorist financing and to establish procedures for mutual legal assistance. Countries should ensure that they are able to take prompt action to identify, freeze, seize and confiscate proceeds of crime. Extradition procedures should also be in place to deal with the movement of individuals involved in money laundering offences.

3.2.7 *FATF Reports*

The Recommendations continue to be supplemented by a range of other publications. As well as mutual evaluation reports in the context of monitoring implementation (discussed in the next section), the FATF publishes reports on typologies, guidance and best practice to assist jurisdictions in their implementation of the Recommendations, and guidance papers on the application of a risk-based approach in various business sectors and product-types (such as banking, virtual currencies, prepaid cards, mobile payments and internet-based payment services).

In February 2015, the FATF published a report, *Financing of the Terrorist Organisation Islamic State in Iraq and the Levant (ISIL)*.[4] The FATF also announced a programme of ongoing research into ISIL (which was subsequently discussed at its plenary in June 2015) and its plenary in October 2015 had CFT as a main theme.

In its report on ISIL, the FATF identified the emergence of a new form of terrorist organisation: one for which funding was central and critical to its activities. The report discussed ISIL's primary sources of revenue, mainly derived from illicit proceeds from its occupation of territory, but the report also identified other new and emerging typologies which had not yet been addressed by the FATF, such as the extortion of goods and cash transiting territory where ISIL operates, and ISIL's grass roots funding strategies which include crowd-funding through the internet and social media. The report observed that cutting off such revenue streams would be a challenge that would require increased international co-operation and the development of new counter-measures, but it would also be an opportunity for the global community to defeat ISIL.

3.2.8 Monitoring implementation

Member countries' progress in implementing the FATF's Recommendations is monitored by the FATF by way of a mutual evaluation procedure. The first round of mutual evaluations started in 1992 and the latest, the fourth round, began in 2014.

Under the mutual evaluation procedure, each member country is examined in turn by the FATF through a desk-based review

---

4   *http://www.fatf-gafi.org/media/fatf/documents/reports/Financing-of-the-terrorist-organisation-ISIL.pdf* [Accessed 25 September 2015].

(supported by information provided by the country and information drawn from a country's previous evaluation), followed by an on-site visit generally lasting about 10 days and conducted by a small team of experts from the legal, financial and law enforcement fields from other member governments. The team presents its conclusions in a mutual evaluation report (MER), drafts of which are discussed in plenary meetings and in further meetings with the country prior to the MER's finalisation and adoption. A summary of each MER is also contained in the year's FATF annual report.[5]

With the revision of the Recommendations in 2012, the FATF also introduced a new monitoring and assessment methodology for its latest round of mutual evaluations. Those procedures were published in 2013 and are substantially different in nature from previous assessments.[6] Previously the methodology had focused on technical compliance with the Recommendations. The FATF's focus has now shifted to considering both: (a) the extent to which a country is compliant with the standards (the technical compliance component); and (b) the effectiveness of its AML/CFT systems (the effectiveness component). Countries are required not only to demonstrate that they have the required AML/CFT systems and controls in place, but that those systems and controls are being effectively implemented at all levels: supervisors will need to demonstrate that they appropriately supervise financial institutions and designated non-financial businesses and professions for compliance with AML/CFT requirements commensurate with their risks.

Following the discussion and adoption of an MER, a country could be placed in either regular or enhanced follow up. The philosophy underpinning the FATF's approach is gradually to increase the peer pressure on non-compliant countries to take

---

[5] FATF, *Annual Report for 2013–2014*, published on 21 October 2014: *http://www.fatf-gafi.org/countries/n-r/russianfederation/documents/annual-report-2013-2014html.html* [Accessed 25 September 2015].

[6] *Methodology for assessing technical compliance with the FATF Recommendations and the effectiveness of AML/CFT systems*, published in February 2013: *http://www.fatf-gafi.org/media/fatf/documents/methodology/FATF%20Methodology%2022%20Feb%20 2013.pdf* [Accessed 25 September 2015].

action to tighten their money laundering regimes. Regular follow up is the default monitoring mechanism, and is based on a system of biennial reporting. Enhanced follow up is based on the FATF's policy for dealing with members with significant deficiencies (for technical compliance or effectiveness) in their AML/CFT systems, and involves a more intensive process of follow up. Under both regular and enhanced follow up, the country would also have a follow up assessment after five years. That is intended to be a targeted but more comprehensive report on the country's progress, with the main focus being on areas in which there have been changes, on high risk areas identified in the MER, or subsequently on the priority areas for action.

Where a country is found to be non-compliant, the FATF's policy is to start by requiring the country concerned to deliver a report at a plenary meeting. The FATF President can then send a letter or high-level mission to the non-compliant country. Other measures at the FATF's disposal are to apply Recommendation 19 requiring special attention to be given to relationships and transactions with persons from such a country, and to issue a statement requiring financial institutions in FATF member countries to comply with it. Ultimately, the FATF can also decide to suspend or terminate the membership of the country concerned.

The GCC is in the unique position of being a member of the FATF, but having non-FATF countries as members.[7] The GCC also evaluates the level of implementation and effectiveness of AML measures within GCC members. All six members of the GCC have undergone mutual evaluations.

---

[7] Bahrain, Kuwait, Oman, Qatar, Saudi Arabia and the United Arab Emirates. Saudi Arabia is, however, currently in the process of becoming a member of FATF in its own right.

3.2.9 Implementation by the UK

Whilst not yet formally scheduled, the UK is expected to undergo a mutual evaluation in March/April 2018.[8] The UK was most recently assessed under the mutual evaluation procedure in June 2007, with the report published on the FATF's website.[9] The report highlighted the threat posed by serious organised crime and money laundering to the UK. The total social and economic cost, including the cost of prevention, was estimated at more than £20 billion a year.

However, the report concluded that the UK has a comprehensive legal structure in place, with broad offences for money laundering and terrorist financing. The Proceeds of Crime Act 2002 was judged to have had a substantial impact on the country's ability to deal with the proceeds of organised crime, and the implementation of the Third EU Money Laundering Directive later in 2007 was expected to introduce consistency to the preventative measures in place for financial institutions.

3.2.10 Non-Co-operative Countries and Territories (NCCTs)

As part of its fight against money laundering, in 2000 the FATF began an initiative to identify NCCTs. The process aimed to ensure that all financial centres adopted and implemented AML measures meeting internationally recognised standards.

Following a plenary meeting in February 2000, the FATF published an initial report on NCCTs.[10] It set out 25 criteria to identify detrimental rules and practices that impede international cooperation in the fight against money laundering. The report also described a process designed to identify jurisdictions that have rules and practices which impede the fight against money laundering and to encourage these

---

[8] As reported in the FATF's Global Assessments Calendar: *http://www.fatf-gafi.org/ media/fatf/documents/assessments/Global-assessment-calendar.pdf* [Accessed 21 October 2015].

[9] *http://www.fatf-gafi.org/countries/u-z/unitedkingdom/* [Accessed 25 September 2015].

[10] FATF, *Report on Non-Co-operative Countries and Territories*, 14 February 2000, *http://www.fatf-gafi.org/media/fatf/documents/reports/Initial%20Report%20on%20 NCCTs%2002_2000.pdf* [Accessed 25 September 2015].

jurisdictions to implement international standards in the relevant area. Finally, the report contained a set of possible counter-measures that FATF members could use to protect their economies against the proceeds of crime.

The FATF's aim was to apply counter-measures in a gradual, proportionate and flexible manner, in the hope that the prospect of enhanced surveillance and reporting of financial transactions with the NCCTs would persuade them to intro-duce the required anti-money laundering measures.

Twenty-three jurisdictions were identified as NCCTs during the course of 2000 and 2001, but by October 2006 the last country had been removed from the list. The FATF's 2007–2008 Annual Report declared the NCCT process to have been a success, citing significant efforts amongst all of the, previously, NCCTs to improve AML and CFT systems.[11]

3.2.11   The International Co-operation Review Group (ICRG)

Since 2007, the FATF's ICRG has been responsible for analysing high-risk jurisdictions and recommending specific action to address money laundering and terrorist financing risks ema-nating from those jurisdictions. The FATF has issued a series of public statements expressing concerns about significant defi-ciencies in the AML/CFT regimes of a number of jurisdictions. For two jurisdictions, Iran and Democratic People's Republic of Korea, the FATF has, additionally, called on FATF members, and urged all other jurisdictions, to apply counter-measures to protect their financial sectors from money laundering and terrorist financing risks emanating from these countries. The FATF has re-iterated this call at subsequent plenary meetings.

In April 2009, the G20 called on the FATF to reinvigorate its process for assessing compliance with international AML/CFT standards and publicly identify high-risk jurisdictions by February 2010. In response, in June 2009, the FATF adopted a new set of procedures for the ICRG.

---

[11] FATF, *Annual Report 2007-2008*, 30 June 2008, *http://www.fatf-gafi.org/media/fatf/ documents/reports/2007-2008%20ENG.pdf* [Accessed 25 September 2015].

Under these, still current, procedures, initial referral to the ICRG is based primarily on the result of a jurisdiction's mutual evaluation. Jurisdictions whose mutual evaluation reveals a significant number of key deficiencies are referred to the ICRG for a preliminary review conducted by one of four ICRG regional review groups. This initial review includes outreach to the jurisdiction, including the opportunity to comment on the draft report. Based upon that report, the FATF then decides whether it should conduct a more in-depth review of the jurisdiction's deficiencies. Each reviewed jurisdiction has the opportunity to participate in face-to-face meetings to discuss the report, including developing an action plan to address deficiencies. The FATF specifically requests high-level political commitment from each reviewed jurisdiction to implement these action plans.

As of 2015, and on the basis of the ICRG's analysis, the FATF has identified Iran and the Democratic People's Republic of Korea as jurisdictions for which counter-measures are required to protect the international financial system from an on-going and substantial money laundering and terrorist financing risk.[12] Since February 2015, it is understood that the Democratic People's Republic of Korea has engaged with the FATF regarding deficiencies identified in its action plan. As yet, however, the FATF does not consider there has been sufficient progress.

In addition, Algeria and Myanmar are currently identified by the FATF as jurisdictions with strategic AML/CFT deficiencies which are judged not to have not made sufficient progress in addressing those deficiencies or have not committed to an action plan developed with the FATF to address the deficiencies. Accordingly, the FATF asks members specifically to consider the risks arising from specific deficiencies.[13]

---

[12] FATF Public Statement, 26 June 2015. *http://www.fatf-gafi.org/documents/documents/public-statement-june-2015.html* [Accessed 25 September 2015].

[13] FATF Public Statement, 26 June 2015.

3.2.12 FATF-style regional bodies and organisations (FSRBs)

Several regional or international bodies, either exclusively or as part of their work, perform similar functions to the FATF, and the FATF makes an active effort to support their development. Many of these groups (referred to as FSRBs) have observer status with the FATF and have similar form and functions to the FATF with some FATF members belonging to more than one body.

FSRBs now exist in the Caribbean, Europe, Asia, Asia/Pacific, Africa and South America. They include: the Asia/Pacific Group on Money Laundering (APG); the Caribbean Financial Action Task Force (CFATF); the Council of Europe Select Committee of Experts on the Evaluation of Anti-Money Laundering Measures (Moneyval); the Eastern and Southern Africa Anti-Money Laundering Group (ESAAMLG); the Latin America Anti-Money Laundering Group (GAFILAT); the West Africa Money Laundering Group (GIABA); the Middle East and North Africa Financial Action Task Force (MENAFATF); and the Eurasian group on combating money laundering and financing of terrorism (EAG). The Task Force on Money Laundering in Central Africa (GABAC) is currently in the process of becoming an FRSB.

The Channel Islands (Jersey and Guernsey) and the Isle of Man are not FATF members but, in October 2012, they, as Crown Dependencies of the UK, joined Moneyval.

The FATF also works with various international organisations to implement effective worldwide AML measures, some of which also have FATF observer status such as the Egmont Group of Financial Intelligence Units. As reflected in Recommendation 29, over the last 15 years, a number of countries have established specialised government agencies, or FIUs, as part of their response to money laundering activity. Since 1995, a number of FIUs have informally worked together as the Egmont Group.[14] They increasingly serve as a focal point for

---

[14] The definition of a "financial intelligence unit" as agreed by the Egmont Group is now widely accepted: "A central, national agency responsible for receiving (and,

AML programmes and allow rapid and effective co-operation between states. The UK is represented in the Egmont Group by the National Crime Agency.[15]

3.2.13 *Interaction with EU and UK law and regulation*

It is an indication of the importance attached to the FATF's work that its findings and recommendations are used as benchmarks, and in turn feed into, EU and UK legislation and the UK regulatory regime.

The FATF's Recommendations, as revised in 2003, were implemented in the EU through the incorporation of the Recommendations in the EU's Third Money Laundering Directive[16] (the Third Directive) and through its subsequent transposition into the national law of individual EU Member States.

The EU's Fourth Money Laundering Directive[17] (the Fourth Directive), which entered into force on 25 June 2015 and repeals and replaces the Third Directive, will, following the same approach, implement the revised 2012 Recommendations across the EU (although it also goes further than the revised Recommendations). The Fourth Directive requires EU member states to implement changes to national law, regulation and administration necessary to comply with it by 26 June 2017.

---

as permitted, requesting), analysing and disseminating to the competent authorities, disclosures of financial information (i) concerning suspected proceeds of crime, or (ii) required by national legislation or regulation, in order to counter money laundering".

[15] A list of members is available at *http://www.egmontgroup.org/membership/list-of-members* [Accessed 6 October 2015].

[16] Directive 2005/60/EC of the European Parliament and of the Council of 26 October 2005 on the prevention of the use of the financial system for the purpose of money laundering and terrorist financing [2005] OJ L309/15.

[17] Directive (EU) 2015/849 of the European Parliament and of the Council of 20 May 2015 on the prevention of the use of the financial system for the purposes of money laundering or terrorist financing, amending Regulation (EU) No 648/2012 of the European Parliament and of the Council, and repealing Directive 2005/60/EC of the European Parliament and of the Council and Commission Directive 2006/70/EC [2015] OJ L141/73.

In the UK, the Third Directive was implemented through the Money Laundering Regulations 2007 (the 2007 Regulations),[18] which repealed and replaced the previous Money Laundering Regulations 2003. The approach to implementing the Fourth Directive is, in due course, expected to be through further amendment of the 2007 Regulations.

The 2007 Regulations had a limited effect in the UK when they came into force. The UK regime already had in place many of the changes made by the Third Directive as the UK had gone further than was strictly necessary when it implemented the Second Money Laundering Directive. That, coupled with the fact that the 2006 version of the Joint Money Laundering Steering Group's (JMLSG) industry guidance incorporated a substantial number of the changes that would arise from the Third Directive, meant that only minor changes were needed to the financial crime regime.

The effect of the Fourth Directive is, again, unlikely to precipitate significant changes to the 2007 Regulations. The UK has continued to gold-plate the minimum requirements mandated in EU legislation, and the JMLSG guidance continues to reflect developments in the Recommendations notwithstanding the absence of specific EU requirements. Nevertheless, some adjustment will be required, for example, in relation to increasing the transparency of beneficial owners, enhanced due diligence required for domestic PEPs and new requirements for written risk assessments.

The 2007 Regulations already mandate a risk-based approach which, in practice, means a relatively non-prescriptive regime focused on increasing the effectiveness of existing systems and controls in place to deal with financial crime. However, it is significant that the 2007 Regulations give HM Treasury the power to direct any person who carries on relevant business not to enter a business relationship, carry out any one-off transaction or proceed any further with a business relationship or one-off transaction in relation to a person who is based or

---

[18] The Money Laundering Regulations 2007 (SI 2007/2157) came into force on 15 December 2007.

incorporated in a non-EEA state to which the FATF has decided to apply counter-measures. Failure to comply would render the person guilty of an offence and liable, on conviction on indictment, to imprisonment for a term not exceeding two years, to a fine or to both, and on summary conviction, to a fine up to the statutory maximum.

Alongside the Third Directive, the EU Commission instituted a new legal framework for wire transfer payments to implement what was then FATF's Special Recommendation 7. That framework was established by means of a Regulation on information on the payer accompanying transfers of funds (the Wire Transfer Regulation).[19] The Wire Transfer Regulation was adopted on 15 November 2006 and came into effect in EU member states on 1 January 2007.

To accompany the Fourth Directive package, and reflecting the integration of Special Recommendation 7 into the revised FATF Recommendations (Recommendation 16), the Wire Transfer Regulation is also being replaced by a revised regulation (WTR2),[20] which came into effect on 25 June 2015 and will apply from 26 June 2017.

Recommendation 16 states that countries should take measures to require financial institutions, including money remitters, to include accurate and meaningful originator information (name, address and account number) on funds transfers and related messages that are sent, and the information should remain with the transfer or related message through the payment chain. The WTR2 is designed to address areas where gaps in transparency currently exist, reflecting the increased level of information under Recommendation 16 compared to Special Recommendation 7.

Alongside legislative change, the FATF's findings and pronouncements are also integrated into the UK's regulatory

---

[19] Regulation (EC) No 1781/2006 of the European Parliament and of the Council on information on the payer accompanying transfers of funds [2006] OJ L345/1.

[20] Regulation (EU) 2015/847 of the European Parliament and of the Council of 20 May 2015 on information accompanying transfers of funds [2015] OJ L141/1.

regime in the form of both guidance and standard setting. Both the Financial Conduct Authority (FCA), which is the AML regulator of many of the firms subject to the 2007 Regulations, and the JMLSG refer to the FATF's findings in their guidance.

The FCA's stated aim is to ensure that international standards, including the FATF's Recommendations, assessment method-ologies, guidance and typologies papers, promote an effective, proportionate and risk-based approach to AML and CFT.[21]

The JMLSG's guidance uses the FATF as a key point of reference on procedure and counterparty risk assessment. For example, the guidance states that enhanced due diligence (EDD) is needed where the counterparty is situated in a non-FATF country, and money laundering reporting officers are instructed to ensure that the firm obtains, and makes appropriate use of, any government or FATF findings concern-ing the approach to money laundering prevention in particular countries or jurisdictions.[22]

3.2.14 Recognition by the United Nations

When the UN General Assembly adopted the UN's Political Declaration and Action Plan Against Money Laundering in June 1998, it reinforced the status of the FATF's Recommenda-tions in Resolution S-20/4 by explicitly citing them as the global benchmark for action by the international community in terms of AML measures.[23]

---

[21] As stated, for example, in para.5.6 of the FCA's AML annual report 2012/13 (*http://www.fca.org.uk/static/documents/anti-money-laundering-report.pdf*) [Accessed 25 September 2015].

[22] Part 1 of the JMLSG's 2014 Guidance para.3.25.

[23] UN Resolution S-20/4 *http://www.un.org/documents/ga/res/20sp/a20spr04.htm* [Accessed 25 September 2015].

3.3   The United Nations

3.3.1   *The Vienna Convention*

Even before the international community's concern about the drug problem had led to the creation of the FATF, the UN had become sufficiently concerned about the situation that, in December 1984, the UN General Assembly adopted a resolution that expressed the conviction that the wide scope of the illicit trade in drugs and its consequences made it necessary to prepare a convention.[24]

The result was the 1988 UN Convention against Illicit Traffic in Narcotic Drugs and Psychotropic Substances (the Vienna Convention). It was eventually adopted in Vienna in December 1988 and, while focusing on drug trafficking in general, it contained explicit provisions to deal with drug money laundering. It was the first inter-governmental initiative to address the issue of drug money laundering (although it does not cover criminal proceeds beyond this) and is a landmark in international money laundering control. The UK ratified it in 1991 and has since extended its application to jurisdictions for whose foreign affairs it is responsible, including Bermuda, the Cayman Islands and the British Virgin Islands.

The Vienna Convention created an obligation on states to criminalise the laundering of money derived from drug trafficking, including the acquisition, possession or use of property known at the time of receipt to derive from drug trafficking, together with conspiracy, aiding and abetting, and facilitating the commission of drug trafficking offences. It also encouraged the making of arrangements for extradition between signatory states applicable in money laundering cases and set out principles to facilitate cooperative administrative investigations as well as the principle that banking secrecy should not interfere with criminal investigations in the context of international cooperation.

---

[24] UN General Assembly resolution on International Campaign Against Traffic in Narcotic Drugs, UN Doc A/RES/39/141, available at *http://www.un.org/documents/ga/res/39/a39r141.htm* [Accessed 25 September 2015].

3.3.2 The Global Programme against Money Laundering

Since the adoption of the Vienna Convention, the UN has not lost interest in the subject and the UN Office on Drugs and Crime (UNODC) is responsible for the Global Programme against Money Laundering (the GPML) as its key instrument in its efforts to combat money laundering.[25] The UNODC's mandate was strengthened in 1998 by the UN General Assembly Special Session Political Declaration and Action Plan against Money Laundering Political Declaration, which broadened the scope of the mandate to cover all serious crime, not just drug-related offences.

Through the GPML, the UN helps member states to introduce AML legislation and develop and maintain the necessary mechanisms to enforce it. The programme encourages AML policy development, monitors and analyses problems and responses, raises public awareness about money laundering and acts as a coordinator of joint AML initiatives by the UN with other international organisations.

The GPML also coordinates the International Money Laundering Information Network website (IMoLIN) on behalf of the UN, the FATF, the Commonwealth Secretariat, the Council of Europe, Interpol, the Organisation of American States and the Asia/Pacific Group on Money Laundering. IMoLIN is an internet-based information network, providing a secure news forum, an electronic library, a database of laws and regulations (the AML Information Database, or AMLID) and a calendar of events to assist governments, organizations and individuals in their AML and CFT initiatives. IMoLIN is publicly accessible, but AMLID, which is a compendium of analyses of AML laws and regulations as well as information about national contacts and authorities, is a secure database and not available for public access.

---

[25] See UNODC's website *https://www.unodc.org/unodc/en/money-laundering/index.html* [Accessed 25 September 2015].

3.3.3 The Palermo Convention

Recognising that organised crime is a serious and growing problem in all countries, the UN adopted the Convention against Transnational Organized Crime (the Palermo Convention) in November 2000. That was the first comprehensive multilateral legal instrument in the fight against organised crime and entered into force on 29 September 2003. It aims to promote international co-operation in preventing and combating transnational organised crime, and it is also designed to provide greater co-ordination of national approaches to organised crime in the spheres of policy, legislation, administration and enforcement.

3.3.4 The Terrorist Financing Convention

As with the FATF, the UN has also been active in producing CFT measures. The International Convention for the Suppression of the Financing of Terrorism (the Terrorist Financing Convention) was adopted by the UN General Assembly in December 1999 and entered into force in April 2002.[26] Ratification and full implementation by its members is addressed in the FATF's Recommendation 36, as summarised above.

The Terrorist Financing Convention aims to suppress terrorist acts by depriving terrorists and terrorist organisations of their financing.[27] Parties are obliged to criminalise and take other measures to prevent the provision or collection of funds for the purpose of committing terrorist acts and to cooperate with other parties to the Convention in the prevention, detection, investigation and prosecution of terrorist financing, including in the freezing and confiscation of funds.

The terrorist attacks on the US in September 2001 demonstrated the extensive financial networks established by terrorist organisations and highlighted the fact that it was not possible

---

[26] UN Doc A/Res/54/109, available at *https://treaties.un.org/doc/Publication/MTDSG/Volume%20II/Chapter%20XVIII/XVIII-11.en.pdf* [Accessed 25 September 2015].

[27] This is implemented by the Terrorism Act 2000 in the United Kingdom.

for one country acting alone to close such networks down. In response to the attacks, the UN passed Security Council Resolution 1373 on 28 September 2001.[28] That reinforced the significance of the Terrorist Financing Convention by imposing international legal obligations on UN members, requiring them to take several of the measures provided for in the Convention and calling on states that had not already done so to ratify it.

Resolution 1373 provides the primary legal basis for requiring UN members to take action because, pursuant to Chapter VII of the UN Charter, a Security Council resolution taken in response to a threat to international peace and security is a decision that is legally binding on all members. Resolution 1373 also established a Security Council Counter-Terrorism Committee to oversee states' compliance with the Resolution.

3.4 The Council of Europe

The Council of Europe was established in 1949 with a focus on human rights. Today it covers all major issues facing European society other than defence, although it does not have the power to bind states as the EU does. Its primary significance is that, with 47 member states, its influence extends to many of the jurisdictions in Central and Eastern Europe in which dirty money is suspected to originate and which, for the time being at least, the EU does not have the power to influence directly.

When considering the UN's Vienna Convention, European Ministers of Justice considered that the growing problem of drug trafficking should also be tackled by the Council. This led to the 1990 Council of Europe Convention on Laundering, Search, Seizure and Confiscation of the Proceeds of Crime (the Strasbourg Convention).[29] The Strasbourg Convention

---

[28] S/RES/1373, available at *http://www.un.org/en/sc/ctc/specialmeetings/2012/docs/ United%20Nations%20Security%20Council%20Resolution%201373%20(2001).pdf* [Accessed 25 September 2015].

[29] Convention on Laundering, Search, Seizure and Confiscation of the Proceeds from Crime (Strasbourg, 1990) (1991) (CETS 141), available at *http://conventions. coe.int/Treaty/en/Treaties/Html/141.htm* [Accessed 25 September 2015].

required the extension of the criminalisation of money laundering to all crimes rather than just that of drug trafficking, thus surpassing the requirements of the Vienna Convention. This extrapolation was later reflected in the revised FATF Recommendations as published in June 1996 and discussed above.

The Strasbourg Convention provided that not only could laundered money be the product of all predicate offences but that the predicate offence did not even have to be committed within the jurisdiction of the state concerned. It has been widely ratified: to date, 49 states are party to this treaty, including all 47 Council of Europe Member States and two non-Member States (Australia and Kazakhstan). It was signed on behalf of the UK in November 1990 and ratified in September 1992.

In 2003, the Council updated and widened the Strasbourg Convention to take into account the fact that not only could terrorism be financed through money laundering from criminal activity, but also through legitimate activities. That process was completed in 2005 with the adoption on 3 May of the Convention on Laundering, Search, Seizure and Confiscation of the Proceeds from Crime and on the Financing of Terrorism (the Warsaw Convention).[30]

Alongside the Strasbourg and Warsaw Conventions, the Council has been active in providing conferences and seminars on AML measures for Central and Eastern Europe. In 1997, it established Moneyval (an FSRB, as discussed above) to conduct self-assessment and mutual evaluation exercises of the AML measures in place in Council of Europe Member States that are not in the FATF. Moneyval primarily consists of Central and Eastern European countries, but in recent years, it has been expanded to include Israel, in January 2006, the Holy See, in April 2011, (both of which are Observer States at the Council of Europe) and Russia, which is an FATF member, in

---

[30] Convention on Laundering, Search, Seizure and Confiscation of the Proceeds from Crime and on the Financing of Terrorism (Warsaw, 2005) (CETS 198), available at *http://conventions.coe.int/Treaty/EN/Treaties/Html/198.htm* [Accessed 25 September 2015].

2003. Moneyval's work methods mirror those used by the FATF, from which it also receives political and technical support. Moneyval became an Associate Member of the FATF in 2006.

3.5 The Basel Committee

The financial sector has not been a passive participant in the development of AML strategies. Prompted by the collapse of BCCI, and seeing for themselves that the financial system could unwittingly be targeted as a medium ripe for manipulation by criminals, in 1988 the Basel Committee on Banking Supervision (the Committee) published a Statement of Principles to which it expected the international banking community to adhere.[31]

The Committee considered that banking supervisors had a general role to encourage ethical standards of professional conduct among banks. The Statement of Principles encouraged the management of banks to put in place effective procedures to ensure that all persons conducting business with the institution concerned were properly identified, that transactions that did not appear legitimate were discouraged, and that effective cooperation with law enforcement agencies was achieved. Not restricting itself to the proceeds of drug trafficking as the Vienna Convention had done, the Committee, as the Council Convention was to do two years later, stated that the Statement of Principles was to apply to criminal activity more generally.

Several years later, in reviewing the findings of an internal survey of cross-border banking in 1999, the Committee identified deficiencies in the bank know-your-customer (KYC) policies of a large number of countries. It consequently asked the Working Group on Cross-Border Banking to examine the procedures then in place and to draw up recommended

---

[31] Publication No.137, *Prevention of Criminal Use of the Banking System for the Purpose of Money Laundering*, December 1988, (*http://www.bis.org/publ/bcbsc137.pdf*) [Accessed 25 September 2015].

standards applicable to banks in all countries. They were issued as a consultative document in January 2001. That resulted in the publication in October of that year of the Committee's *Customer due diligence for banks* report.[32] The Committee made clear its expectation that the report would become the benchmark for supervisors to establish national practices and for banks to design their own KYC programmes, although it noted that some jurisdictions already met or exceeded the standards set out in the report.

In publishing the report, the Committee stressed that it continued strongly to support the adoption and implementation of the FATF Recommendations and that its KYC principles were intended to be consistent with them. It also said that it would consider the adoption of any higher standards introduced by the FATF as a result of its current review of the Recommendations.

The Committee's view was that KYC safeguards should exceed simple account opening and record-keeping, and require banks to formulate customer acceptance policies, tiered customer identification programmes that involved more extensive due diligence for higher-risk accounts, and pro-active monitoring for suspicious activities. KYC should be a core feature of banks' risk management and control procedures and be complemented by regular compliance reviews and internal audit. The Committee advised that the intensity of KYC programmes beyond such essential elements should be tailored to the degree of risk.

In September 2012, the Committee reaffirmed its stance by publishing a revised version of its 1988 Statement of Principles, in which a dedicated principle (Principle 29) deals with the abuse of financial services. As a further step, in January 2014, the Committee issued a set of guidelines to describe how banks should include the management of risks related to money laundering and financing of terrorism within their overall risk

---

[32] Basel Committee on Banking Supervision, Publication No.85, *Customer due diligence for banks*, October 2001 (*http://www.bis.org/publ/bcbs85.pdf*) [Accessed 2 October 2015].

management framework.[33] Noting that prudent management of these risks, together with effective supervisory oversight, would be critical in protecting the safety and soundness of banks as well as the integrity of the financial system, the guidelines are intended to be consistent with the FATF's Recommendations and to supplement their goals and objectives. Indeed, the guidelines include cross-references to the Recommendations to help banks comply with national requirements based on those standards.

3.6 The Wolfsberg Standards

As the public sector reacted to the threat to the financial system posed by money laundering with a multiplicity of initiatives and bodies, the private sector was also taking steps to address its own needs in the area. In October 2000, 11 major international private banks,[34] known as the Wolfsberg Group, signed and unveiled a set of non-binding best practice guidelines. The Global AML Guidelines for Private Banking (known as the Wolfsberg Principles) govern the establishment and maintenance of relationships between private banks and clients. The Wolfsberg Principles provide guidelines on client acceptance and identify situations where additional due diligence should be carried out.

In May 2002 two new members joined the Wolfsberg Group[35] and, since 2000, the Wolfsberg Principles have been revised twice (in 2002 and in 2012) and other sets of AML principles and guidance addressed to specific types of business (such as trade finance, correspondent banking, prepaid and stored value cards, and mobile and internet payment services) and

---

[33] Publication No.275, *Sound management of risks related to money laundering and financing of terrorism*, January 2014 (*http://www.bis.org/publ/bcbs275.pdf*) [Accessed 25 September 2015].

[34] ABN AMRO Bank NV, Barclays Bank, Banco Santander Central Hispano, SA, The Chase Manhattan Private Bank, Citibank, NA, Credit Suisse Group, Deutsche Bank AG, HSBC, JP Morgan, Société Générale and UBS AG.

[35] The current members of the Wolfsberg Group are: Banco Santander, Bank of America, Bank of Tokyo-Mitsubishi UFJ, Barclays, Citigroup, Credit Suisse, Deutsche Bank, Goldman Sachs, HSBC, J.P. Morgan Chase, Société Générale, Standard Chartered Bank and UBS.

specific activities (such as the approach to screening, monitoring and searching[36]) have been developed. Together, these comprise the "Wolfsberg Standards".

3.6.1 The Wolfsberg Principles

The starting point of the Wolfsberg Principles is to identify, as the objectives of suitable AML policies and procedures, the prevention of the use of banks' worldwide operations for criminal purposes and to protect banks' reputations. It directs banks to design policies and procedures to mitigate the risk of money laundering and to cooperate with governments and their agencies in the detection of money laundering.

In keeping with growing regulatory emphasis on senior management responsibility within banks, the Wolfsberg Principles also state that banks should periodically assess the risk of its private banking business and the bank senior and executive Management must be made aware of these risks. They identify, as a responsibility of senior and executive management, the approval of written policies and procedures to address these risks, adopting a risk-based approach, and overseeing the implementation of these policies, procedures and relevant controls.

Banks must endeavour to accept only those clients whose source of wealth and funds can be reasonably established to be legitimate and principles, and minimum standards, for identifying and verifying clients' identities are set out. Thus banks are directed to take reasonable measures to establish the identity of all clients and beneficial owners and only to accept clients once this process has been completed.

Similarly, where accounts are held in the name of a client's intermediary (such as an asset manager) and a financial intermediary introduces a client, the bank should perform due diligence on the intermediary and establish that they have a similar process for their clients that is satisfactory to the bank.

---

[36] Wolfsberg Statement on AML Screening, Monitoring and Searching, 2009.

Verification of the identity of the holders of powers of attorney or authorised signatories over accounts, and understanding their relationship with the account holder, is also required.

Furthermore, banks are directed to consider whether walk-in clients or relationships initiated through electronic channels require a higher degree of due diligence prior to account opening and banks must have specific measures to establish and verify the identity of non-face-to-face customers.

Numbered or alternate name accounts should only be accepted if the bank has established the identity of the client and the beneficial owner. Heightened scrutiny should be applied to clients and beneficial owners resident in and funds sourced from countries identified by credible sources as having inadequate anti-money laundering standards as well as to individuals (and their families and close associates) who have or have had positions of public trust.

Applying a risk-based approach, banks are directed to corroborate information on the basis of documentary evidence or reliable sources and, unless other measures reasonably suffice to conduct the due diligence on a client (e.g. through references), clients should be met prior to account opening and identities verified on the basis of official identity documents. Finally, all terms of client acceptance, all new clients and new accounts should be approved by at least one person other than the private banker responsible for the matter.

Banks are directed to specify the categories of customers that it will not accept or maintain and to define categories of persons whose circumstances warrant enhanced due diligence, typically where the circumstances are likely to pose a higher than average risk to a bank. In that context, the Principles include a definition of "Politically Exposed Persons" (PEPs), referring to individuals who have or have had positions of public trust and who should be subjected to heightened scrutiny. Additional guidance has been published in a set of Frequently Asked Questions indicating that the term should be understood to include persons whose current or former position (the rule of thumb being that they would continue to be PEPs for one year after leaving office) could attract publicity beyond the borders of the country concerned and whose financial circumstances may be the subject of additional public interest.

The Wolfsberg Principles also provide that banks' internal policies should indicate whether senior management approval was required to enter into relationships with clients in any of the situations outlined as requiring additional due diligence, but that relationships with PEPs should only be entered into once the approval of senior management had been obtained, mirroring FATF Recommendation 12.

Other principles address the updating of client files, policies on the identification and following up of unusual or suspicious activities, monitoring and sanctions screening programmes, internal allocation of control responsibilities (including an independent audit function to test procedures), regular management reporting, record retention requirements and training programmes to educate employees how to identify and prevent money laundering.

3.6.2 Guidance on a Risk Based Approach for Managing Money Laundering Risks

Reflecting the approach adopted in the Wolfsberg Principles, in 2006, the Wolfsberg Group published *Guidance on a Risk Based Approach for Managing Money Laundering Risks* (the Guidance).[37] In the absence of a universally agreed and accepted methodology that prescribed the nature and extent of a risk-based approach, and recognised that the specifics of an institution's particular risk based process would need to be responsive to the institution's individual operations, the Guidance seeks to articulate considerations which institutions might find useful in developing a reasonably designed risk-based approach.

---

[37] Wolfsberg Group, *Guidance on a Risk Based Approach for Managing Money Laundering Risks* http://www.wolfsberg-principles.com/pdf/standards/Wolfsberg_RBA_Guidance_(2006).pdf [Accessed 25 September 2015].

The Guidance adopts the approach of measuring money laundering risks using various categories (the most commonly used of which it observes are: country risk, customer risk and services risk), which may then be modified by risk variables (such as the level of assets deposited by a customer, the size of jurisdiction, the level of regulation or other oversight to which a customer is subject, the regularity or duration of the customer relationship) and then weighted according to the institution.

3.7 Conclusion

In recent years, the threat of terrorism, the international drug problem and the growth of financial crime have been increasingly perceived as requiring an international response. Both the number of international initiatives and their scope have grown and the FATF's revised Recommendations, in particular, now provide a wide-ranging and comprehensive code. The Recommendations increasingly act as a stimulus to national legislation and thereby to a more consistent international framework of law and regulation to combat terrorism and money laundering.

Chapter 4

The Money Laundering Regulations 2007

Stephen Gentle
Partner

Cherie Spinks
Supervising Associate
Simmons & Simmons LLP

4.1   Background

The current AML legislation for the proceeds of crime is found in the Proceeds of Crime Act 2002[1] (POCA 2002) and the Money Laundering Regulations 2007[2] (the 2007 Regulations). Laundering the proceeds of terrorism is covered by the Terrorism Act 2000[3] (TA 2000).

The 2007 Regulations came into force on 15 December 2007. The 2007 Regulations implemented the Third EU Money Laundering Directive[4] (the Third Directive).[5]

The 2007 Regulations allow a risk-based and less prescriptive approach than was previously the case for AML legislation.

---

[1]   As amended by the Serious Organised Crime and Police Act 2005 and Serious Crime Act 2015.
[2]   Money Laundering Regulations 2007 (SI 2007/2157).
[3]   As amended by the Anti-Terrorism, Crime and Security Act 2001 and Crime (International Co-operation) Act 2008.
[4]   Directive 2005/60/EC of the European Parliament and of the Council of 26 October 2005 on the prevention of the use of the financial system for the purpose of money laundering and terrorist financing [2005] OJ L309/15.
[5]   2007 Regulations (SI 2007/2157) reg.5.

They were designed to be more efficient and to improve the availability of information to law enforcement agencies because they are:

- more flexible—recognising that the risk of money laundering can vary widely depending on the jurisdiction or business sector;
- more effective—they encourage regulated persons to prepare themselves so they are in a better position to assess, mitigate and control risk internally, rather than waiting until they are investigated by their regulator;
- more proportionate—they are based on a "common sense approach" which is preferable to a "one size fits all" tick-box approach; and
- more cost effective—they encourage regulated persons to focus their efforts and resources on areas that are necessary.

On 23 June 2015, the Government issued a "call for evidence" on the impact on businesses of the current AML and terrorist financing regime, and specifically on the role of supervisors in the regime[6]. The Government is also interested to receive evidence on how implementation of the risk-based approach might be improved. The review runs until 23 October 2015. Relevant findings are to be fed into the analysis of responses received through other forthcoming Government consultations, for example, the consultation due to be issued later in 2015 on the Fourth EU Money Laundering Directive[7] (the Fourth Directive) (see para.4.2 below).

This Chapter will consider the 2007 Regulations which require businesses to put compliance systems in place.

---

[6] See *https://cutting-red-tape.cabinetoffice.gov.uk/anti-money-laundering/* [Accessed 28 September 2015].

[7] Directive (EU) 2015/849 of the European Parliament and of the Council of 20 May 2015 on the prevention of the use of the financial system for the purposes of money laundering or terrorist financing, amending Regulation (EU) No 648/2012 of the European Parliament and of the Council, and repealing Directive 2005/60/EC of the European Parliament and of the Council and Commission Directive 2006/70/EC [2015] OJ L141/73.

4.2 The Third Directive and a new Fourth Directive

The Third Directive strengthened the existing EU regime which was based on previous directives.[8]

The Third Directive had three main objectives:

- To make clear the existence of a strong link between money laundering and terrorist financing. It is based on the presumption that in order to assist governments in combating terrorism, it is necessary to apply the AML compliance regime to the financing of terrorism, even in circumstances where the funds had actually been obtained legitimately;
- To clamp down on the use of offshore companies by criminals who use such mechanisms to conceal proceeds of crime from the enforcement authorities. The Third Directive introduced strict new requirements for the identification of the ultimate beneficial owners of firms (i.e. placing an obligation on professionals to find out the ultimate beneficial owner behind their client's organisation(s)); and
- To place a renewed emphasis on the importance of taking a risk-sensitive approach to AML compliance. The Third Directive acknowledges that risks may vary depending on the facts of a specific case. It requires a high standard of customer due diligence in high-risk situations—for example, where a transaction involves politically exposed persons, or where the beneficial owner is obscured, or in circumstances where there is a non-face-to-face business, but allows for simplified due diligence (SDD) in low-risk situations.

---

[8] Directive 2001/97/EC of the European Parliament and of the Council of 4 December 2001 amending Council Directive 91/308/EEC on prevention of the use of the financial system for the purpose of money laundering [2001] OJ L344/76; Council Directive 91/308/EEC of 10 June 1991 on prevention of the use of the financial system for the purpose of money laundering [1991] OJ L166/77.

The Fourth Directive came into force on 25 June 2015.[9] Its aims include providing for a more targeted and focussed risk based approach, the introduction of new rules on PEPs and to clarify provisions on customer due diligence. The Fourth Directive introduces a number of new requirements which will need to be transposed by member states into national law by 26 June 2017. The changes introduced by the Fourth Directive include the following:

- A requirement for companies, trusts and other entities to obtain and hold adequate, accurate and current information identifying their beneficial owners which is held in a central register by each member state or in a public register. For trusts, the requirement covers collating information about the settlor, the trustee(s), the protector (if there is one), the beneficiaries or class of beneficiaries and any other natural person exercising effective control over the trust. The information must be available for access by competent authorities and financial intelligence units, entities that must conduct customer due diligence under the Fourth Directive, and any person or organisation that can demonstrate a legitimate interest[10];
- The application of SDD measures must be justified on the basis that the business relationship or transaction presents a lower risk;
- The definition of a PEP has been broadened to include domestic PEPs;
- High value dealers trading in goods of a value of €10,000 or more in cash are now within scope. Under the Third Directive, the threshold was €15,000; and
- The definition of "criminal activity" is amended to specifically include tax crimes relating to direct and indirect taxes.

---

[9] See *http://eur-lex.europa.eu/legal-content/EN/TXT/HTML/?uri=OJ:JOL_2015_141_R_0003&from=EN* [Accessed 28 September 2015].

[10] The Small Business, Enterprise and Employment Act 2015, which will come into force in the UK in April 2016, will require companies to maintain a register of persons having significant control. However, the provisions of the Fourth Directive are wider than the provisions of the Act.

At the time of writing, HM Treasury has not yet issued a consultation on changes to the 2007 Regulations. Any changes are expected to be modest, but until the new provisions are implemented in the UK, the requirements in the 2007 Regulations remain current. It would, however, be prudent for firms to review their procedures in due course to consider whether changes will need to be made in order to comply with the new requirements.

4.3 The Money Laundering Regulations 2007

The 2007 Regulations implement in the UK the provisions required by the Third Directive as discussed above.

4.3.1 Application of the 2007 Regulations

Businesses need to consider whether they are "relevant persons" within the meaning of regs 3 and 4 to determine whether they are within the scope of the 2007 Regulations.

4.3.2 To whom do the 2007 Regulations apply?

The definition of "relevant persons" within the 2007 Regulations includes the following:

- almost all regulated banking and financial services businesses (including payment services firms and money services businesses;
- auditors, insolvency practitioners, external accountants, and tax advisers;
- lawyers;
- estate agents;
- trust or company service providers;
- casino operators; and
- dealers in high value goods (e.g. auctioneers) who deal in goods of any description where the activity involves accepting payment in cash of €15,000 or more (this is to be reduced to €10,000 or more under the Fourth Directive).

203

4.3.3 Registration and supervision under the 2007 Regulations

Relevant persons are required to be monitored for compliance under the 2007 Regulations by a supervisory authority. Those firms already regulated by the FCA or a professional body, such as the Law Society or the Institute of Chartered Accountants, will automatically be supervised by their existing regulator.

Those firms not already regulated, are required to register for supervision with the specified supervisory authorities as follows:

(a) HM Revenue & Customs (HMRC):
   • money services businesses (if not already supervised by the FCA);
   • high value dealers;
   • trust or company services providers (if not already supervised by the FCA or a professional body);
   • accountancy service providers (if not already supervised by a professional body); and
   • estate agency businesses.[11]
(b) FCA—firms carrying out the following activities:
   • lending (e.g. mortgage credit, factoring with or without recourse and financing of commercial transactions);
   • financial leasing;
   • provision of payment services;
   • issuing and administering other means of payment;
   • offering guarantees and commitments;
   • trading for own account or for account customers in: money market instruments, foreign exchange, financial futures and options, exchange and interest-rate instruments or transferrable securities;
   • safe custody services;
   • money broking;
   • portfolio management advice;

---

[11] See *https://www.gov.uk/guidance/money-laundering-regulations-who-needs-to-register* [Accessed 28 September 2015].

- safekeeping and administration of securities;
- participation in securities issues and providing services related to such issues; and
- advice to undertakings on capital structure, industrial strategy and related questions and advice as well as services relating to mergers and the purchase of undertakings.[12]

4.3.4 Obligations under the 2007 Regulations

If a firm falls within the definition of "relevant persons" it must:

- carry out customer due diligence measures (regs 5–18);
- establish and maintain internal policies and procedures, including record keeping, training of employees and reporting suspicions (regs 19–21); and
- consider whether it is required to register with a supervisory authority (regs 22–35).

4.4 Professional guidance

The Joint Money Laundering Steering Group (JMLSG) produces guidance notes for the regulated sector which have been approved by HM Treasury.[13] The JMLSG consists of organisations from the financial sector in the UK, including the British Bankers' Association. Its aim is to give practical assistance in interpreting the UK money laundering legislation for those working in the financial sector.

The Guidance Notes were first issued in 1990 and the latest revised version was published in 2014 (the JMLSG Guidance Notes). In determining both whether an offence has been committed contrary to the Proceeds of Crime Act 2002 (POCA

---

[12] See *http://www.fca.org.uk/about/what/enforcing/money-laundering/register* [Accessed 28 September 2015].

[13] Joint Money Laundering Steering Group, Prevention of Money Laundering/Combating Terrorist Financing, Guidance for the UK Financial Sector Pts I, II and III. See *http://www.jmlsg.org.uk/industry-guidance/article/jmlsg-guidance-current* [Accessed 28 September 2015].

2002) s.330 and the 2007 Regulations reg.45, a court must consider guidance provided by an appropriate body and approved by HM Treasury.[14]

HMRC issued guidance for those firms which it supervises for the purposes of the 2007 Regulations (see Section 4.8 below):

- money services businesses;
- high value dealers;
- trust or company services providers; and
- the accountancy sector.[15]

That guidance sets out practical help on implementing the requirements of the 2007 Regulations. HMRC has also published guidance providing advice to firms on whether they are required to register with HMRC for supervision. That includes guidance on supervision for estate agents who became subject to HMRC supervision in April 2014 when the Office of Fair Trading ceased to exist.

The Law Society issued its updated Practice Note on Money Laundering (the Practice Note) in October 2013.[16]

The Practice Note is designed to outline good practice on implementing legal requirements and for developing systems and controls to prevent solicitors being used to facilitate money laundering and terrorist funding. It is also intended that the Practice Note provide effective guidance on applying the risk-based approach to internal compliance.

Compliance with the Practice Note is not mandatory, but the Law Society makes clear that the SRA will take into account whether a solicitor has complied with it when undertaking its role as a "supervisor" under the 2007 Regulations.[17]

---

[14] POCA 2002 s.330(8); 2007 Regulations (SI 2007/2157) reg.45(2).
[15] See *https://www.gov.uk/government/collections/money-laundering-regulations-forms-and-guidance* [Accessed 28 September 2015].
[16] See *http://www.lawsociety.org.uk/support-services/advice/practice-notes/aml/* [Accessed 28 September 2015].
[17] Law Society AML Practice Note, para.1.5.

The Law Society received HM Treasury approval for the Practice Note under POCA 2002 s.330(8) and reg.45(2) of the 2007 Regulations. That means that a court will be required to consider compliance with the content of the Practice Note in assessing whether a solicitor has exercised all due diligence to avoid committing an offence.

The Consultative Committee of Accountancy Bodies (the CCAB) issued guidance for the accountancy profession in December 2007 which was updated following approval by HM Treasury in July 2008.[18] The courts must take it into account in deciding whether or not an offence has been committed under ss.330–331 POCA 2002, or the 2007 Regulations by an individual or business within its scope.

The Gambling Commission issued guidance for casinos on the prevention of money laundering and the combating of the financing of terrorism in December 2007 which was updated in July 2013.[19] That guidance has been approved by HM Treasury.

A number of other professional bodies have issued guidance for their members on the application of the 2007 Regulations, including the Electronic Money Association and the Royal Institute of Chartered Surveyors.

4.5   The risk-based approach

The risk-based approach and monitoring was recommended by the JMLSG and the Law Society in its earlier guidance in respect of the Money Laundering Regulations 2003[20] and was codified by the implementation of the Third Directive in the 2007 Regulations.

---

[18] See *http://www.ccab.org.uk/documents/20140217%20FINAL%202008%20CCAB%20 guidance%20amended%202014-2-17pdf.pdf* [Accessed 28 September 2015].

[19] See *http://www.gamblingcommission.gov.uk/pdf/Prevention%20of%20money%20 laundering%20and%20combating%20the%20financing%20of%20terrorism%20-%20 July%202013.pdf* [Accessed 28 September 2015].

[20] Money Laundering Regulations 2003 (SI 2003/3075).

The risk-based approach to customer due diligence measures and the conducting of ongoing monitoring are thus now legal requirements enshrined in the 2007 Regulations.

4.6 Customer due diligence measures (Regs 5–19)

4.6.1 Application of customer due diligence measures

4.6.1.1 Introduction

The requirement to conduct customer due diligence (CDD) under the 2007 Regulations is set out in reg.7. Customer due diligence includes the following concepts:

- adopting a risk-based approach when determining the extent of verification measures that are necessary;
- simplified due diligence (SDD);
- the introduction of enhanced due diligence (EDD) in certain circumstances; and
- a requirement to identify customers' beneficial owners.

4.6.1.2 When should due diligence be conducted?

The 2007 Regulations require that relevant persons carry out CDD whenever they[21]:

(a) establish a "business relationship" (defined as "a business, professional or commercial relationship between a relevant person and a customer, which is expected by the relevant person, at the time when contact is established, to have an element of duration")[22];
(b) carry out an "occasional transaction" (defined as "a transaction (carried out other than as part of a business relationship) amounting to €15,000 or more, whether the transaction is carried out in a single operation or several operations which appear to be linked")[23];

---

[21] 2007 Regulations (SI 2007/2157) reg.7(1).
[22] 2007 Regulations (SI 2007/2157) reg.2(1).
[23] 2007 Regulations (SI 2007/2157) reg.2(1).

(c) suspect money laundering or terrorist financing; or

(d) doubt the veracity or adequacy of any documents, data or information previously obtained for the purposes of verification or identification.

A relevant person must also apply CDD measures at other appropriate times to existing customers on a risk-sensitive basis.[24]

If a relevant person is unable to carry out CDD measures, he must not carry out a transaction with or for the customer through a bank account and the person must not establish a business relationship or enter into an occasional transaction with the customer. In addition, the person should terminate any existing business relationships with the customer and consider if he is required to make a disclosure under POCA 2002 or TA 2000.[25]

4.6.1.3   What is required?

Under reg.5 of the 2007 Regulations, CDD involves:

- identifying the customer and verifying the customer's identity on the basis of documents, data or information obtained from a reliable and independent source;
- identifying, where there is a beneficial owner who is not the customer, the beneficial owner and taking adequate measures, on a risk-sensitive basis, to verify his identity so that the relevant person is satisfied that he knows who the beneficial owner is, including, in the case of a legal person, trust or similar legal arrangement, measures to understand the ownership and control structure of the person, trust or arrangement; and
- obtaining information on the purpose and intended nature of the business relationship or transaction.

According to the JMLSG Guidance Notes, the types of evidence and how much information a person should request for the

---

[24] 2007 Regulations (SI 2007/2157) reg.7(2).
[25] 2007 Regulations (SI 2007/2157) reg.11(1).

purpose of verifying the identity of a customer is a matter of judgement for the firm, which should be exercised using a risk-based approach. In deciding what evidence to request from customers, relevant persons should take into account factors such as the nature of the product or service sought by the customer, any existing or previous relationship between the customer and the person, any assurances from other regulated persons that may be relied upon and whether the customer is physically present.[26]

4.6.2 Exceptions

The general rule is that verification of a customer's identity should be completed before the establishment of a business relationship or carrying out of an occasional transaction.[27] There are three exceptions to this general requirement, which arise under reg.9:

- Verification of the customer's identity may be completed during the establishment of a business relationship if:
  - this is necessary so as not to interrupt the normal conduct of business; and
  - there is little risk of money laundering or terrorist financing,

  provided the verification is completed as soon as possible after contact is first established.[28]
- Verification of the identity of a beneficiary under a life insurance policy may take place after the business relationship has been established, provided that the verification occurs at or before the time of payout under the policy, or at or before the time when the beneficiary exercises a right vested under the policy.[29]
- Verification of the identity of a bank account holder may take place after the bank account has been opened, provided that there are adequate safeguards to ensure that the account is not closed, and that transactions are not

---

[26] JMLSG Guidance para.5.3.29.
[27] 2007 Regulations (SI 2007/2157) reg.9(2).
[28] 2007 Regulations (SI 2007/2157) reg.9(3).
[29] 2007 Regulations (SI 2007/2157) reg.9(4).

carried out by or on behalf of the account holder, before verification has been completed.[30]

The 2007 Regulations also allow relevant persons to rely on due diligence carried out on their customers by third parties in some situations, as discussed at Section 4.6.7.

4.6.3 Simplified due diligence (SDD)

The 2007 Regulations state that a relevant person does not need to carry out CDD if he has reasonable grounds for believing that the customer, transaction or product related to such transaction is listed in reg.13(2)–(9).

Examples of customers on which SDD may be carried out include companies whose securities are listed on a regulated market and are subject to specific disclosure obligations, credit or financial institutions either subject to the requirements of the Third Directive or situated in non-EEA states which have equivalent requirements to the Third Directive, and public authorities situated in the UK.

The EU has issued a list of jurisdictions outside the EEA which are considered by the EU to have equivalent AML legislation to the Third Directive.[31] While this list may be useful when establishing whether SDD is appropriate, some commentators have suggested that certain countries which one would expect to be included are missing, and others which are behind the EU in AML regulation are featured. It may, therefore, be unsafe to place too much reliance on this list.

The types of products for which SDD may be carried out are those which carry a low risk of money laundering. These include certain life insurance contracts, pension and superannuation schemes and e-money products.

---

[30] 2007 Regulations (SI 2007/2157) reg.9(5).
[31] See   *http://ec.europa.eu/internal_market/company/docs/financial-crime/3rd-country-equivalence-list_en.pdf* [Accessed 28 September 2015].

Even if a customer or transaction is eligible for SDD, CDD measures must be conducted if the person suspects money laundering or terrorist financing.

4.6.4   Enhanced due diligence (EDD)

4.6.4.1   Requirement

Regulation 14 requires relevant persons to undertake an EDD process, on a risk-sensitive basis, in the following situations:

- where the customer has not been physically present for identification purposes;
- where a credit institution has or proposes to have a correspondent banking relationship with a respondent institution from a non-EEA state;
- where a relevant person proposes to establish a business relationship or enter into an occasional transaction with a politically exposed person; or
- in any other situation which by its nature can present a higher risk of money laundering or terrorist financing.

4.6.4.2   Customer not physically present[32]

If the customer is not physically present for identification purposes, a person should take specific and adequate measures to compensate for the higher risk, for example by applying at least one of the following measures:

- ensuring that the customer's identity is established by additional documents, data or information;
- taking supplementary measures to verify or certify the supplied documents or require their confirmatory certification by a credit or financial institution which is subject to the Third Directive; or
- ensuring that the first payment is carried out through an account opened in the customer's name with a credit institution.

---

[32]   2007 Regulations (SI 2007/2157) reg.14(2).

4.6.4.3   Correspondent banking relationship[33]

If a credit institution has, or proposes to have, a correspondent banking relationship with a respondent institution from a non-EEA state, it must:

- gather sufficient information about the respondent to understand fully the nature of its business;
- determine from publicly available information the reputation of the respondent and the quality of its supervision;
- assess the respondent's AML and anti-terrorist financing controls;
- obtain approval from senior management before establishing a new correspondent banking relationship;
- document the respective responsibilities of the respondent and correspondent; and
- be satisfied that, in respect of those of the respondent's customers who have direct access to accounts of the correspondent, the respondent:
  — has verified the identity of, and conducts ongoing monitoring in respect of, such customers; and
  — is able to provide to the correspondent, upon request, the documents, data or information obtained when applying CDD measures and ongoing monitoring.

4.6.4.4   Politically exposed persons (PEPs)[34]

The Third Directive introduced a new requirement for PEPs to reflect the need to conduct due diligence on persons who may be more susceptible to receiving bribes and corruption.

The 2007 Regulations define a PEP as any individual who has, at any time in the preceding year, been appointed to a prominent function by a state (other than the UK, although changes introduced by the Fourth Directive will mean that domestic PEPs will be included in the definition), a Community institution or another international body,[35] Schedule 2 to

---

[33] 2007 Regulations (SI 2007/2157) reg.14(3).
[34] 2007 Regulations (SI 2007/2157) reg.14(4).
[35] 2007 Regulations (SI 2007/2157) reg.14(5)(a).

the 2007 Regulations provides examples of those classified as PEPs, which include prominent figures such as heads of state or government, ministers, members of parliament, members of supreme courts and ambassadors.

The definition of PEP also covers the person's immediate family and known close associates. Immediate family members are the person's spouse, partner, children (and their spouses or partners) and parents.

The definition of "known close associate" is less clear although examples of known close associates are provided in Sch.2 to the 2007 Regulations. Those include

> "any individual who is known to have joint beneficial ownership of a legal entity or legal arrangement, or any other close business relations with a person referred to in Regulation 14(5)(a) and any individual who has sole beneficial ownership of a legal entity or legal arrangement which is known to have been set up for the benefit of a person referred to in Regulation 14(5)(a)".

A firm should look at the extent to which it needs to screen its customers, for the purpose of concluding whether they are PEPs, based on the nature and scope of the firm's business, and a risk-based approach should be taken.

Establishing whether individuals qualify as PEPs can present difficulties. However, firms need not go beyond the information available in the public domain. According to the JMLSG Guidance Notes, firms may be able to rely on an internet search engine for specific checks, or consult relevant reports and databases on corruption risk published by specialised organisations. If a firm's risk level is high and it needs to conduct more thorough checks, subscription to a specialist PEP database may be needed.[36] Although these types of database serve to assist in establishing whether a person is a PEP, there is currently no conclusive list of PEPs which can be fully relied upon in all situations.

---

[36] JMLSG Guidance Notes para.5.5.27.

If a firm proposes to establish a business relationship or enter into an occasional transaction with a PEP, a firm must also:

- have approval from senior management to establish a business relationship with the person;
- take adequate measures to establish the source of wealth and the source of funds which are involved in the proposed business relationship or occasional transaction; and
- where the business relationship is entered into, conduct enhanced ongoing monitoring of the relationship.[37]

4.6.5 Beneficial owners

4.6.5.1 Requirement

Regulation 5 requires that due diligence be carried out not only on the customer, but also on any beneficial owner of the customer.

A relevant person must take adequate measures to satisfy himself that he knows the identity of the customer's beneficial owner. That requirement includes, in the case of a legal person, trust or similar legal arrangement, taking measures to understand the ownership structure and control of the person, trust or arrangement. Although "adequate measures" are not defined in the 2007 Regulations, the JMLSG Guidance Notes state:

> "The obligation to verify the identity of a beneficial owner is for the firm to take risk-based and adequate measures so that it is satisfied that it knows who the beneficial owner is. It is up to each firm to consider whether it is appropriate, in light of the money laundering or terrorist financing risk associated with the business relationship, to make use of records of beneficial owners in the public domain (if any exist), ask their customers for relevant data, require evidence of the beneficial owner's identity on the

---

[37] 2007 Regulations (SI 2007/2157) reg.14(4).

basis of documents, data or information obtained from a reliable and independent source or obtain the information otherwise."[38]

The JMLSG Guidance Notes also suggest that, in a low-risk situation, it may be appropriate for a person to rely on either written or oral information provided by the customer regarding the identity of a beneficial owner. If oral evidence is provided then a record of that must be kept in writing by the firm.[39]

4.6.5.2   Meaning of beneficial ownership

"Beneficial owner" is defined by reg.6 of the 2007 Regulations.

A beneficial owner of a company is any individual who ultimately owns or controls more than 25 per cent of the shares or voting rights in that company, or any individual who exercises control over the management of the body.

In the case of a partnership, a beneficial owner is any individual who is ultimately entitled to or controls more than 25 per cent of the capital or profits of the partnership or more than 25 per cent of the voting rights in the partnership, or any individual who otherwise exercises control over the management of the partnership.

In the case of a trust, a beneficial owner is any individual entitled to a specified interest of at least 25 per cent in the capital of the trust property or the class of persons in whose main interest the trust is set up or operates, or any individual who has control over the trust.

In respect of trusts, "control" is defined as:

"a power under the trust instrument or by law to:

---

[38] JMLSG Guidance Notes, para.5.3.11.
[39] JMLSG Guidance Notes, para.5.3.12.

(a) dispose of, advance, lend, invest, pay or apply trust property;
(b) vary the trust;
(c) add or remove a person as a beneficiary or to form a class of beneficiaries;
(d) appoint or remove trustees;
(e) direct, withhold, consent to or veto the exercise of a power such as is mentioned in sub paragraph (a), (b), (c) or (d)."[40]

4.6.6 Ongoing monitoring

Firms must conduct ongoing monitoring of a business relationship[41] on a risk-sensitive basis. Ongoing monitoring involves:

(a) scrutiny of transactions undertaken throughout the course of the relationship (including, where necessary, the source of funds) to ensure that the transactions are consistent with the relevant person's knowledge of the customer, his business and risk profile; and
(b) keeping the documents, data or information obtained for the purpose of applying customer due diligence measures up-to-date.[42]

Monitoring should assist firms in identifying unusual activity which may involve money laundering or terrorist financing, assessing risk and, if warning signs arise, considering whether to make a disclosure to the National Crime Agency.

4.6.7 Third-party reliance

The 2007 Regulations provide that a relevant person may rely on third parties to apply customer due diligence measures provided that the other person consents to being relied upon.[43]

---

[40] 2007 Regulations (SI 2007/2157) reg.6(4).
[41] 2007 Regulations (SI 2007/2157) reg.8(1).
[42] 2007 Regulations (SI 2007/2157) reg.8(2).
[43] 2007 Regulations (SI 2007/2157) reg.17(1).

Prior to the 2007 Regulations, that was a practice that was adopted by regulated persons in some parts of the financial sector.

The relevant person will remain liable for any failure to apply such measures.[44] Those persons who may be relied upon are:

(a) a credit or financial institution which is authorised by the FCA;

(b) an auditor, insolvency practitioner, external accountant, tax adviser or independent legal professional (all of whom must be regulated by one of the professional bodies listed in Sch.3 to the 2007 Regulations);

(c) an auditor, insolvency practitioner, external accountant, tax adviser, credit or financial institution or independent legal professional, who conducts business in another EEA state if it is subject to mandatory professional regulations and is subject to the requirements laid down in the Third Directive; and

(d) an auditor, insolvency practitioner, external accountant, tax adviser, credit or financial institution or independent legal professional, who conducts business in a non-EEA state if it is subject to equivalent mandatory professional regulations and is subject to the requirements equivalent to those laid down in the Third Directive and is supervised for compliance with those requirements.[45]

A relevant person seeking to rely on a person outside the UK, particularly a person in a non-EEA state, must also be satisfied that the third party is a regulated person or entity and that the country in which it is based has equivalent money laundering requirements to those in the UK.[46] In June 2012, the EU published a Common Understanding setting out the latest list of jurisdictions which are considered to have equivalent anti-money laundering legislation to the Third Directive.[47] That list includes jurisdictions such as South Korea and India.

---

[44] 2007 Regulations (SI 2007/2157) reg.17(1)(b).
[45] 2007 Regulations (SI 2007/2157) reg.17(2).
[46] 2007 Regulations (SI 2007/2157) reg.17(2)(c) and (d).
[47] See *http://ec.europa.eu/internal_market/company/docs/financial-crime/3rd-country-equivalence-list_en.pdf* [Accessed 28 September 2015].

4.7 Internal policies and procedures (including record keeping, training of employees and reporting) (Regs 19–21)

4.7.1 Record keeping

Whilst a firm is required to establish and verify a client's identity, it must also keep the supporting records.[48] During the consultation on the 2007 Regulations, it was proposed that, in a relaxation of the rules existing at the time, firms be given the option to keep any references to evidence of customer identity that they had collected rather than keeping actual copies of the information and evidence. That proposal was broadly welcomed by respondents to the consultation and that change was reflected in the 2007 Regulations in reg.19(2)(a).

In addition to that, firms are required to keep original documents or copies as supporting records in respect of business relationships or occasional transactions which were the subject of CDD measures or ongoing monitoring.

Records must be kept for five years from the date on which the relevant business relationship ended. In the case of records relating to a particular one-off transaction, the records must be kept for five years from the date of completion of all activities taking place in the course of that transaction.

4.7.2 Professional training

Regulation 21 provides that a relevant person must take appropriate measures so that all relevant employees are made aware of the law relating to money laundering and terrorist financing. Employees must also be given regular training in how to recognise and deal with transactions and other activities which may be related to money laundering and terrorist financing.

---

[48] 2007 Regulations (SI 2007/2157) reg.19(2)(b).

Section 330(7) of POCA 2002 gives an employee a defence to failing to report money laundering if he has not received sufficient training.

4.7.3 Reporting

A "relevant person" must establish and maintain appropriate and risk-sensitive policies and procedures relating to reporting for the purpose of preventing activities related to money laundering and terrorist financing. For this purpose, a nominated officer (known as the Money Laundering Reporting Officer (MLRO)) must be identified.[49] That is the person within the company to whom a report is to be made of any information or other matter which comes to the attention of a person in the course of a business in the regulated sector and which gives rise to a knowledge or suspicion that another is engaged in money laundering.

It is the role of the MLRO to consider any internal reports of a suspicion or knowledge that another is engaged in money laundering. The MLRO must consider the internal report with reference to any relevant information and decide whether or not the facts reported internally give rise to such a knowledge or suspicion. If the MLRO decides that the report does give rise to a knowledge or suspicion of money laundering, he is required to report that suspicion. In practice, that report will be to the National Crime Agency.

An exception to the obligation to report will apply in circumstances where the information on which the knowledge or suspicion is based comes to a professional legal adviser (or other relevant professional adviser) in "privileged circumstances".[50] That exception does not apply however if the information is communicated with a view to furthering a criminal purpose.[51] Under s.330(10) POCA 2002, information or other matters come to a professional legal adviser in privileged circumstances if it is communicated or given to him:

---

[49] 2007 Regulations (SI 2007/2157) reg.20(2)(d).
[50] The term "privileged circumstances" is defined by POCA 2002 s.330(10).
[51] POCA 2002 s.330(11).

(a) by (or by a representative of) a client of his in connection with the giving by the adviser of legal advice to the client;
(b) by (or by a representative of) a person seeking legal advice from the adviser; or
(c) by a person in connection with legal proceedings or contemplated legal proceedings.[52]

The Law Society Practice Note provides helpful guidance on privileged circumstances.[53]

Guidance produced by the CCAB suggests that a careful record should be maintained of the surrounding circumstances where a decision is taken so that a report need not be made on the basis of the privilege reporting exemption. That is because a "relevant professional adviser" may find himself working for a client in both privileged and non-privileged circumstances.

4.8 Consequences of breaching the 2007 Regulations

Failure to comply with the 2007 Regulations may result in both civil penalties imposed by the relevant supervising authority and criminal sanctions of a term of prison not exceeding two years, a fine or both.[54]

Where a company or partnership has committed an offence under the 2007 Regulations, it is possible that an offence may also have been committed by one or more individuals with management responsibilities (e.g. a director of a company or a partner of a partnership).

At the time of writing, no prosecutions of firms for breaching the 2007 Regulations have been brought.

---

[52] POCA 2002 s.330(10).
[53] Law Society AML Practice Note para.6.5.
[54] 2007 Regulations (SI 2007/2157), Pt 5.

4.9 Casinos

Regulation 10 provides that casinos must establish and verify the identity of any customer:

(a) before allowing that person to use the casino's gaming facilities or, where the facilities are for remote gaming, before access is given to the facilities; or

(b) who, in the course of a 24-hour period, purchases or exchanges chips worth €2,000 or more, pays €2,000 or more for the use of gambling machines, or pays €2,000 or more in connection with remote gaming facilities (if the conditions specified in reg.10(2) are met).

4.10 Money service businesses and high value dealers

A register of money service businesses and high-value dealers must be maintained by HMRC.[55] A high-value dealer is someone whose business activity involves dealing in goods of any description by way of business (including auctioneers) whenever a transaction involves accepting a total cash payment of €15,000 or more (to be reduced to €10,000 or more under the Fourth Directive).[56] A money service business is an undertaking which, by way of business, operates a currency exchange office, transmits money or cashes cheques.[57]

A money service business or high-value dealer must register with HMRC unless already subject to supervision by the FCA. In order to consider an application for registration, HMRC may require that the following information be provided[58]:

(a) the person's name and (if different) address of the business;

(b) the nature of the business;

---

[55] 2007 Regulations (SI 2007/2157) reg.25(1).
[56] 2007 Regulations (SI 2007/2157) reg.3(12).
[57] 2007 Regulations (SI 2007/2157) reg.2(1).
[58] 2007 Regulations (SI 2007/2157) reg.27(2).

(c) the name of the nominated officer; and
(d) in the case of a money service business, the name of any person who effectively directs or will direct the business and any beneficial owner of the business.

Registration with HMRC is subject to the applicant satisfying the "fit and proper test" provided by reg.28(1). The criteria which must be met in order to be considered a fit and proper person are set out in reg.28(2). If any of the following persons do not meet those criteria, the applicant may not be registered:

(a) the applicant;
(b) the person who effectively directs the applicant;
(c) a beneficial owner of the applicant; or
(d) the nominated officer of the applicant.

HMRC can request additional information that it reasonably considers necessary to assist in a determination of the application.[59] A fee will be charged to an applicant on registration and annually following registration.

HMRC must notify the applicant of its decision whether or not to register the applicant within 45 days from receiving the application or, if applicable, from the date on which any requested additional information is received.[60]

HMRC has the power to cancel an existing registration if it is satisfied that the applicant is not a fit and proper person or information provided with the application was false or misleading. HMRC may also cancel a registration if it subsequently becomes apparent that HMRC would have had grounds to refuse registration in the first instance. Any decision to cancel a registration must be given in writing, providing the date from which registration is cancelled, the reason for the decision, the procedure for review and the right to appeal to a tribunal.[61]

---

[59] 2007 Regulations (SI 2007/2157) reg.27(3).
[60] 2007 Regulations (SI 2007/2157) reg.29(2).
[61] 2007 Regulations (SI 2007/2157) reg.30.

4.11   Trust or company service providers

The 2007 Regulations introduced a new requirement for trust or company service providers to register with HMRC.[62] A trust or company service provider is a firm or sole practitioner who, by way of business, provides any of the following services to other persons[63]:

(a)   forming companies or other legal persons;
(b)   acting, or arranging for another person to act:
    (i)   as a director or secretary of a company;
    (ii) as a partner of a partnership; or
    (iii) in a similar position in relation to other legal persons;
(c)   providing a registered office, business address, correspondence or administrative address or other related services for a company, partnership or any other legal person or arrangement; or
(d)   acting, or arranging for another person to act, as:
    (i)   a trustee of an express trust or similar legal arrangement; or
    (ii) a nominee shareholder for a person other than a company whose securities are listed on a regulated market, when providing such services.

The requirements for registration with HMRC are the same as for high-value dealers and money service businesses, as discussed at Section 4.11 above.

4.12   Powers of investigation and enforcement

The FCA, HMRC and the Department of Enterprise, Trade and Investment in Northern Ireland (the Authorities) and their officers have been provided with a range of powers to enforce the 2007 Regulations.[64]

---

[62]   2007 Regulations (SI 2007/2157) reg.25(1)(c).
[63]   2007 Regulations (SI 2007/2157) reg.3(10).
[64]   2007 Regulations (SI 2007/2157) Pt 5.

4.12.1 Entry and inspection without a warrant[65]

If an officer of an authority has reasonable cause to believe that any premises are being used by a relevant person in connection with his business or professional activities, the officer may, on producing evidence of his authority, at any reasonable time, enter and inspect the premises. The officer may inspect any information or currencies found on the premises and observe the carrying on of the business or professional activities. The officer may require any person to provide an explanation of any recorded information or to state where recorded information may be found, and may take copies of or make extracts from any of the recorded information found on the premises.

4.12.2 Power to require information from, and the attendance of, a relevant or connected person[66]

Under reg.37(1), an officer of the relevant authority may serve a notice on a relevant person (or person connected with a relevant person), requiring the relevant person to:

(a) provide information specified in the notice;
(b) produce recorded information; or
(c) attend a meeting with the officer at a specified time and place to answer questions.

Schedule 4 to the 2007 Regulations defines "connected persons". For a body corporate, connected persons are defined as any officer, manager or agent of that body corporate or its parent company and any employee of that body corporate. For partnerships, any member, manager, employee or agent of the partnership will be a connected person. Employees or agents of an individual will be considered connected persons.

---

[65] 2007 Regulations (SI 2007/2157) reg.38.
[66] 2007 Regulations (SI 2007/2157) reg.37.

4.12.3 *Power to obtain a court order for access to recorded information*[67]

If a person fails to comply with a notice issued in accordance with reg.37(1), the relevant authority[68] may apply to the court to obtain an order requiring that person to comply with the original notice and remedy the consequences of its failure to comply.

If a body corporate, partnership or other unincorporated association has failed to comply with a notice, the court order may require any officer of the body corporate, partnership or unincorporated association, who is partly or wholly responsible for the failure, to meet the costs of the application as specified in the court order.

4.12.4 *Entry and inspection under a warrant*[69]

A court may issue a warrant for entry and inspection of premises if the judge is satisfied that, following evidence given on oath, there are reasonable grounds for suspecting that an offence is being, has been or is about to be committed by a relevant person under the 2007 Regulations. The judge must also be satisfied that there are reasonable grounds to believe that relevant recorded information is on the premises which, if requested, either would not be provided or would be removed or destroyed. The warrant would authorise the officer to:

(a) enter the premises;
(b) inspect the premises and take possession of or preserve the recorded information specified in the warrant;
(c) take copies of or extracts from the recorded information; and
(d) require any person on the premises to explain the recorded information specified in the warrant or state where it may be found.

---

[67] 2007 Regulations (SI 2007/2157) reg.40.
[68] Defined in reg.36.
[69] 2007 Regulations (SI 2007/2157) reg.39.

Force may be used to gain entry to the premises if necessary.

4.12.5   *Financial penalties*

The relevant supervising authority has the power to impose a financial penalty, starting at £5,000, on a relevant person that it supervises.[70] That power arises in respect of breaches of obligations under the 2007 Regulations, including failure to conduct customer due diligence measures and properly to comply with registration requirements.

It would be a defence to show that all reasonable steps had been taken to comply with the relevant regulatory requirement.

---

[70]   2007 Regulations (SI 2007/2157) reg.42.

Chapter 5

The Joint Money Laundering Steering Group: Guidance Notes for the Financial Sector[1]

Stephen Gentle
Partner

Cherie Spinks
Supervising Associate
Simmons & Simmons LLP

5.1 The Joint Money Laundering Steering Group

The Joint Money Laundering Steering Group (JMLSG) was created in 1989 to assist and update those working in the regulated sector with regard to their obligations under developing AML legislation. The JMLSG consists of the following organisations from the UK financial sector:

- Asset Based Finance Association;
- Association of British Credit Unions Ltd;
- Association of British Insurers;
- Association of Foreign Banks;
- Association of Friendly Societies;
- Association of Financial Mutuals;
- Association for Financial Markets in Europe;
- Association of Professional Financial Advisers;
- British Bankers' Association;
- British Venture Capital Association;

---

[1] Joint Money Laundering Steering Group, *Prevention of Money Laundering/ Combating Terrorist Financing: Guidance Notes for the UK Financial Sector*, December 2007.

- Building Societies Association;
- Council of Mortgage Lenders;
- Electronic Money Association;
- Finance and Leasing Association;
- Futures and Options Association;
- Tax Incentivised Savings Association;
- The Investment Association;
- The Wealth Management Association; and
- Wholesale Market Brokers' Association.

The JMLSG's stated aim is to "promulgate good practice in countering money laundering and to give practical assistance"[2] in interpreting the UK money laundering legislation for those working in the financial sector.

The JMLSG first issued Guidance Notes for the UK financial sector (the Guidance Notes) in 1990. They were regularly updated to take account of the Money Laundering Regulations of 1993, 2001 and 2003 and the implementation of the Proceeds of Crime Act 2002 (POCA 2002). The Guidance Notes were substantially revised in 2006, with a new focus being placed on a risk-based approach and senior management accountability. That edition was divided into two parts with general guidance being set out in Pt I and sector specific guidance set out in Pt II. A further version was published in December 2007 to take account of the Money Laundering Regulations 2007 (the 2007 Regulations), which came into force on 15 December 2007. That version has been updated a number of times, most recently in November 2014. Part III has been added to the Guidance Notes (revised in November 2013) which provides specialist guidance on how firms may approach compliance with specified general legislative and regulatory obligations or on determining the "equivalence" of particular overseas jurisdictions or markets.

---

2   The JMLSG website, see *http://www.jmlsg.org.uk/what-is-jmlsg* [Accessed 28 September 2015].

5.2   Purpose of the Guidance Notes

The purpose of the Guidance Notes is to:

- outline the legal and regulatory framework for AML/counter-terrorist financing (CTF) requirements and systems across the financial services sector;
- interpret the requirements of the relevant law and regulations, and how they may be implemented in practice;
- indicate good industry practice through a proportionate, risk-based approach; and
- assist firms to design and implement systems and controls necessary to mitigate the risks of the firm being used in connection with money laundering and the financing of terrorism.[3]

5.2.1   To whom are the Guidance Notes aimed?

The Guidance Notes cover firms, such as banks, building societies, and financial advisers who are in the industry sectors represented by members of the JMLSG and other firms regulated by the FCA. The JMLSG also encourages other financial sector firms to have regard to the Guidance Notes and it considers them as industry good practice.

Firms outside the financial sector may also find the Guidance Notes useful.[4] For example, the Law Society's AML Practice Note issued in October 2013 refers solicitors to the Guidance Notes as a useful source of information.[5] The sets of money laundering guidance issued by the Consultative Committee of Accountancy Bodies[6] and HM Revenue and Customs (HMRC)[7] both refer to the Guidance Notes.

---

[3]   See the Preface to Pt I of the Guidance Notes.
[4]   See para.15 of the Preface to Pt.I of the Guidance Notes.
[5]   See *http://www.lawsociety.org.uk/support-services/advice/practice-notes/aml/* [Accessed 28 September 2015].
[6]   AML Guidance for the Accountancy Sector, see *http://www.ccab.org.uk/PDFs/070612%20CCAB%20Guidance%20Clean.pdf* [Accessed 28 September 2015].
[7]   *https://www.gov.uk/guidance/money-laundering-regulations-introduction* [Accessed 28 September 2015].

5.2.2 The importance of the JMLSG

The JMLSG was a member of the panel which advised the FSA in its consultation[8] about the FSA's new role relating to AML legislation and on the drafting of the FSA's money laundering requirements. When the FSA replaced its *Money Laundering Sourcebook* in 2006 with high-level provisions in its *Senior Management Arrangements, Systems and Controls Sourcebook* (SYSC), it worked closely with the JMLSG to ensure that its requirements were appropriate.

A representative of the JMLSG also participated in the HM Treasury's Money Laundering Advisory Committee which oversaw the implementation of the Second[9] and Third[10] EU Money Laundering Directives in the UK by the 2003[11] and 2007[12] Regulations.

5.3 The Guidance Notes

5.3.1 Are the Guidance Notes mandatory?

The Guidance Notes are not mandatory and failure to comply with their provisions does not mean that a financial sector firm has automatically breached the 2007 Regulations or the FCA's money laundering provisions. The preface to the Guidance Notes states, however, that:

> "It is not intended that the guidance be applied unthinkingly, as a checklist of the steps to take. Firms should encourage their staff to 'think risk' as they carry out their

---

[8] FSA, Consultation Paper 46, *Money Laundering: the FSA's New Role*, April 2000.

[9] Directive 2001/97/EC of the European Parliament and of the Council of 4 December 2001 amending Council Directive 91/308/EEC on prevention of the use of the financial system for the purpose of money laundering [2001] OJ L344/76.

[10] Directive 2005/60/EC of the European Parliament and of the Council of 26 October 2005 on the prevention of the use of the financial system for the purpose of money laundering and terrorist financing [2005] OJ L309/15.

[11] Money Laundering Regulations 2003 (SI 2003/3075).

[12] Money Laundering Regulations 2007 (SI 2007/2157).

duties within the legal and regulatory framework govern-ing AML/CTF. The FCA has made clear its expectation that FCA-regulated firms address their management of risk in a thoughtful and considered way, and establish and maintain systems and procedures that are appropriate, and proportionate to the risks identified. This guidance assists firms to do this.

The guidance ... provides a sound basis for firms to meet their legislative and regulatory obligations when tailored by firms to their particular business risk profile. Depar-tures from this guidance, and the rationale for so doing, should be documented, and firms will have to stand prepared to justify departures, for example to the FSA."[13]

5.3.2 *Treasury approval*

The Proceeds of Crime Act 2002 (POCA 2002) s.330(8) provides that a court must take into account any guidance issued by a supervisory authority or appropriate body which has been approved by HM Treasury when considering whether a person has committed an offence of failing to disclose knowledge or suspicion or reasonable grounds for knowledge or suspicion of money laundering. Under POCA 2002, an "appropriate body" is any body which regulates or is representative of any trade, profession, business or employment carried on by the alleged offender.[14] The JMLSG is an appropriate body for financial sector firms for the purposes of the Act. Regulations 42 and 45 of the 2007 Regulations create a similar guideline for a designated authority when considering whether to impose a civil penalty or for a court considering whether a person has committed an offence.[15] The current edition of the Guidance Notes has received HM Treasury approval with the exception of certain sections of Pt III in which there was no expectation that they would be approved.

---

[13] The Preface to Pt I of the Guidance Notes, paras 18 and 29.
[14] POCA 2002 s.330(13).
[15] 2007 Regulations regs 42(3) and 45(2).

5.3.3 The FCA's approach to compliance with the Guidance Notes

"The FCA, when considering whether a breach of its rules on systems and controls against money laundering has occurred, will have regard to whether a firm has followed relevant provisions in the guidance for the United Kingdom financial sector issued by the Joint Money Laundering Steering Group."[16]

The FCA and its predecessor, the FSA, has consistently looked at the level of compliance with the Guidance Notes when assessing whether its money laundering provisions have been breached. On 17 December 2002, the Royal Bank of Scotland (RBS) was fined £750,000 by the FSA, in what was the first investigation by the FSA to result in a fine levied upon a regulated body for breaches of the rules then contained in the Money Laundering Sourcebook.[17] In the Final Notice served upon RBS, the FSA relied upon the fact that the JMLSG has provided advice on best practice in AML controls since 1990.[18] RBS was found to be in breach of then Rule 3.1.3 on obtaining client identification and then Rule 7.3.2 which required records of client identity to be retained. The Final Notice stated that "each account file was examined, having regard to the identification criteria set out in the Guidance Notes to determine whether there was sufficient evidence to show that the client was who he had claimed to be".[19]

More recently, in January 2014, the FCA fined Standard Bank PLC £7.6 million for failings relating to its anti-money laundering policies and procedures for corporate clients.[20] In particular, the FCA found serious weaknesses in relation to due

---

[16] SYSC 6.3.5G.

[17] See "FSA Fines Royal Bank of Scotland Plc £750,000 for Money Laundering Control Failings", FA/PN/123/2002, 17 December 2002, *http://webarchive. nationalarchives.gov.uk/20130301170532/http://www.fsa.gov.uk/pages/library/ communication/pr/2002/123.shtml* [Accessed 28 September 2015].

[18] Para.3.6 of the Final Notice *http://www.fca.org.uk/static/pubs/final/rbs_12dec02.pdf* [Accessed 28 September 2015].

[19] Para.3.18 of the Final Notice.

[20] See *http://www.fca.org.uk/news/standard-bank-plc-fined-for-failures-in-its-antimoney- laundering-controls#* [Accessed 28 September 2015].

diligence carried out in respect of politically exposed persons. That was considered to be particularly serious by the FCA since Standard Bank provided services to customers who emanated from, or operated in, jurisdictions which posed a higher money laundering risk. The Decision Notice issued in respect of the matter stated that the FCA "has had regard to whether Standard Bank followed the relevant provisions of the JMLSG Guidance when considering whether to take action in respect a failure to comply with the ML Regulations."[21] This case is also the first AML case decided under the FCA's new penalty system and is an example of a significant fine being imposed.

5.3.4   The 2014 Guidance Notes

Part I of the Guidance Notes sets out guidance on the following subjects:

- senior management responsibility;
- internal controls;
- nominated officer/MLRO;
- risk-based approach;
- customer due diligence;
- suspicious activities, reporting and data protection;
- staff awareness, training and alertness; and
- record keeping.

Part II of the Guidance Notes includes guidance for specific sectors, such as financial advisers, corporate finance and wholesale markets. The guidance in Pt II is designed to be read in conjunction with Pt I.

Part III of the Guidance Notes provides special guidance on the following subjects:

- Transparency in electronic payments (wire transfers);
- Equivalent jurisdictions;
- Equivalent markets;

---

[21] See   *http://www.fca.org.uk/static/documents/decision-notices/standard-bank-plc.pdf* [Accessed 28 September 2015].

- Compliance with the UK financial sanctions regime; and
- Directions under the Counter-Terrorism Act 2008 Sch.7.

The above guidance is also intended to be read within the context of Pt I.

5.3.4.1   Risk-based approach

Chapter 4 of Pt I sets out guidance on applying the risk-based approach, taking account of the 2007 Regulations which enshrine the risk-based approach in law. The JMLSG advises that in identifying its money laundering risk, a firm should consider a range of factors, including its customer, product and activity profiles, and the complexity and volume of its transactions.[22]

5.3.4.2   Customer due diligence (CDD)

That includes guidance on ongoing monitoring, which was a new concept introduced by the 2007 Regulations. Guidance is also given on the timing of verification of identity.

Commentary is also included on simplified due diligence (SDD) and enhanced due diligence (EDD). Under the 2007 Regulations, EDD must be carried out on, among others, politically exposed persons (PEPs). The JMLSG advises that:

> "Although under the definition of a PEP an individual ceases to be so regarded after he has left office for one year, firms are encouraged to apply a risk-based approach in determining whether they should cease carrying out appropriately enhanced monitoring of his transactions or activity at the end of this period. In many cases, a longer period might be appropriate, in order to ensure that the higher risks associated with the individual's previous position have adequately abated."[23]

---

[22] JMLSG Guidance Notes para.4.19.
[23] JMLSG Guidance Notes para.5.5.20.

The Guidance Notes continue to give guidance on how to establish whether an individual is a PEP.[24]

5.4   Part III: Equivalent jurisdictions

Regulation 13 of the 2007 Regulations provides that firms may apply SDD where the customer is itself a credit or financial institution which is subject to the requirements of the Third Directive, or is situated in a jurisdiction which imposes requirements equivalent to those laid down in the Third Directive.

Regulation 17 also provides that firms may rely on others to undertake customer due diligence on their behalf, but if the firm is from a non-EEA state, it must also be subject to requirements equivalent to those of the Third Directive.

The JMLSG published guidance on "Equivalent Jurisdictions" on 8 August 2008. This guidance now forms a chapter in Pt III. The guidance advises that firms document their decisions on whether a particular jurisdiction is equivalent. The guidance divides countries into a number of categories:

- EU/EEA Member States;
- countries designated as equivalent by the EU;
- Financial Action Task Force members and Gulf Co-operation Council countries; and
- other jurisdictions.

Firms are entitled to make a presumption of equivalence for EU/EEA Member States through their implementation of the Third Directive. However, firms should be aware that significant variations may exist in the way in which the Third Directive has been transposed into national law in each EU jurisdiction. The EU issued a Common Understanding on third country equivalence in June 2010.[25] As at the date of writing,

---

[24] JMLSG Guidance Notes para.5.5.27.
[25] *http://ec.europa.eu/internal_market/company/docs/financial-crime/3rd-country-equivalence-list_en.pdf* [Accessed 28 September 2015].

the following jurisdictions are listed as having equivalent money laundering provisions to the EU:

- Australia;
- Brazil;
- Canada;
- Hong Kong;
- India;
- Japan;
- Mexico;
- Singapore;
- South Africa;
- Switzerland; and
- The US.

French and Dutch overseas territories and UK Crown Dependencies may also be considered as equivalent.

5.5 Part III: Equivalent markets

Regulation 13 of the 2007 Regulations also provides that firms may apply SDD to customers whose securities are listed on a regulated market that is subject to specified disclosure obligations. The JMLSG describes such markets as "equivalent markets". The JMLSG issued guidance on the meaning of equivalent markets on 21 January 2009. This guidance now forms a chapter in Pt III. As with equivalent jurisdictions, the JMLSG advises that decisions on equivalent markets should be documented at the time the decision is made.

The guidance states that the principal markets in the EU/EEA Member States are likely to be equivalent under the 2007 Regulations. However, that will only include regulated markets within the meaning of the Markets in Financial Instruments Directive.[26] Markets outside the EEA will be equivalent

---

[26] Directive 2004/39/EC of the European Parliament and of the Council of 21 April 2004 on markets in financial instruments amending Council Directives 85/611/EEC and 93/6/EEC and Directive 2000/12/EC of the European Parliament and of the Council and repealing Council Directive 93/22/EEC [2004] OJ L145/1.

if they subject companies whose securities are admitted to trading to disclosure obligations which are set out in international standards and are equivalent to the specified disclosure obligations.[27]

Other markets cannot be presumed to be equivalent and the JMLSG sets out factors to be taken into account when assessing other markets:

* Do the obligations in the particular market meet the specified disclosure obligations?

Other relevant matters to consider:

* membership of an international or regional group;
* contextual factors—political stability, level of (endemic) corruption etc;
* evidence of relevant (public) criticism of a market;
* independent and public assessment of the market's overall disclosure and transparency standards;
* need for any assessment to be recent; and
* implementation standards (including quality and effectiveness of supervision).

5.6 Part III: Compliance with the UK financial sanctions regime

Part III of the Guidance Notes also includes guidance on complying with financial sanctions and asset freezes. The Guidance Notes acknowledge the challenging nature of the sanctions regime and the fact that firms are likely to focus on implementing appropriate systems and controls to identify persons who are subject to financial sanctions based on an assessment of the likelihood of dealing with such parties.[28] The JMLSG recommends that a firm takes into account a range of

---

[27] 2007 Regulations (SI 2007/2157) reg.2(1), definition of "regulated market".
[28] Pt III para.4.4.

factors when conducting its assessment, including its customer, product and activity profiles, and the geographic risk of where it does business.[29]

The JMLSG also provides guidance on screening customers and making reports to HM Treasury.

5.7 Conclusion

Firms operating in the financial sector must have knowledge of the Guidance Notes and should be aware of any updates placed on the JMLSG website. It is clear that the FCA gives much value and consideration to whether a firm has complied with the Guidance Notes when investigating breaches of its Rules and deciding on the appropriate form of any action to take. The importance of following the JMLSG's guidance must not be underestimated.

---

[29] Pt III para.4.23.

Chapter 6

FCA Regulation of the UK Money Laundering Regime

Ben Kingsley
Partner
Slaughter and May

6.1 Regulatory context

The Financial Conduct Authority (FCA), like the Financial Services Authority (FSA) before it, regards weak financial crime controls as a key area of focus for supervisory and enforcement activity. It is therefore no surprise to find that AML controls, as a central element of financial crime controls, has been a feature of the FCA's enforcement agenda.

While none of the FSA or FCA's enforcement actions have yet rivalled the AML penalties imposed by US authorities (and most notably of those, the $1.9 billion AML fine paid by HSBC to US authorities in 2012), there has nevertheless been a notable streak of AML-related penalties for otherwise well-respected institutions, arising principally out of system and control weaknesses rather than the identification of money laundering in fact having taken place. These have included:

(a) The January 2014 fine of £7.6 million imposed on Standard Bank Plc for failings relating to its AML policies and procedures for corporate customers connected to politically exposed persons (PEPs). That was the first AML case that the FCA had brought that focused on commercial banking activity;

(b)   The April 2013 fine of £4.2 million imposed on EFG Private Bank for weaknesses in AML controls relating to high risk and PEP customers; and

(c)   The March 2012 fine of £8.75 million imposed on Coutts & Co, also for weaknesses in AML controls relating to high risk and PEP customers.

6.2   Background to the FCA's rules

The FCA's interest in financial crime is, perhaps predictably, not merely altruistic. Under the Financial Services and Markets Act 2000 (FSMA 2000), the Financial Conduct Authority has been given a strategic objective (ensuring that the relevant markets function well) and three operational objectives (the protection of consumers; protecting and enhancing the integrity of the UK financial system; and promoting effective competition). In addition, FSMA 2000 requires that when discharging its regulatory functions, the FCA must have regard to "the importance of taking action intended to minimise the extent to which it is possible" for a business carried on by an regulated firm (or a firm that ought to be regulated) to be used for a purpose connected with financial crime.[1]

Financial crime for those purposes is stated to include any offence involving[2]:

(a)   fraud or dishonesty;
(b)   misconduct in, or misuse of information relating to, a financial market;
(c)   handling the proceeds of crime; or
(d)   the financing of terrorism.

For the purpose of those provisions, a "regulated firm" means any authorised person and any recognised investment exchange. That is, all banks, investment firms (including

---

[1]   FSMA 2000 s.1B(5).
[2]   FSMA 2000 s.1H(3).

investment advisers, investment managers, stockbrokers, corporate finance firms and others involved in providing professional services in relation to investments), insurance and reinsurance firms including intermediaries, mortgage and consumer credit providers, whose activities require authorisation by the FCA pursuant to the requirements of FSMA 2000 and therefore fall within the FCA's jurisdiction.[3]

Most, if not quite all, of these institutions will, of course, be regarded as carrying on relevant business for the purposes of the Money Laundering Regulations 2007 (the 2007 Regulations, see Ch.4), and will therefore be required to comply with the requirements of those Regulations (and would have been required to comply with the requirements of the previous Money Laundering Regulations of 1994 and 2003).

As originally adopted, FSMA 2000 gave the FSA power to make rules specifically in relation to the prevention and detection of money laundering.[4]

The FSA used that power to create a specific *Money Laundering Sourcebook* under which a "parallel but separate" regime for the prevention and detection of money laundering was developed alongside the existing statutory regulatory regime created by the Money Laundering Regulations.

During the consultation process for those specialised rules, questions were raised as to whether the FCA's approach (i.e. writing its own set of rules to exist alongside the Money Laundering Regulations) was in fact the right one, given the complexity of the law in the area and a doubt as to whether the imposition of a new set of regulatory requirements would add proportionately to the effectiveness of the regime as a whole. Notwithstanding those doubts, the FSA stuck to its original approach, and the *Money Laundering Sourcebook* came into

---

[3] The FCA's jurisdiction, and thus the application of its AML requirements, was extended with effect from October 2004 to cover mortgage lenders and brokers; with effect from January 2005, to cover general insurance brokers; and with effect from 1 April 2014 to cover consumer credit providers previously licensed by the Office of Fair Trading.

[4] FSMA 2000 s.146.

being as an additional layer of AML regulation for the financial sector, covering much of the same ground as the Money Laundering Regulations but with some differences of detail, and bringing with it a separate set of regulatory sanctions.

The *Money Laundering Sourcebook* contained eight separate chapters dealing, in quite specific terms, with matters such as client identification (including detailed provisions reflecting the Government's concerns about financial exclusion), the reporting of suspicious transactions (including provisions requiring a firm to give its Money Laundering Reporting Officer (MLRO) access to "know your business" information which might be relevant to a decision as to whether a transaction was indeed suspicious), the use of national and international findings of material deficiency in the AML arrangements in any other state or jurisdiction, staff awareness and training and the appointment and role of the MLRO (including requirements as to his level of seniority within the organisation and the resources available to him to perform his functions effectively).

It was recognised at the time that, in addition to the specific provisions of the *Money Laundering Sourcebook*, it was also necessary for firms to bear in mind that failure to operate appropriate AML procedures might result in breaches of provisions elsewhere in the FSA Handbook. The Principles for Businesses, which were then, and remain, part of the High Level Standards block of the Rulebook (and which constitute Rules, the breach of which can give rise to disciplinary proceedings notwithstanding the high-level and generalised way in which they are expressed) require a firm to take reasonable care to organise and control its affairs responsibly and effectively, with adequate risk management systems.[5]

This requirement is developed in more detail in the *Senior Management, Systems and Controls Sourcebook* (SYSC) which provides, for example, that a firm must take reasonable care to establish and maintain such systems and controls as are

---

[5]   PRIN 2.1.1R, Principle 3.

"appropriate to its business",[6] and that a firm must take reasonable care to establish and maintain effective systems and controls for compliance with applicable requirements and standards under the regulatory system and for countering the risk that the firm might be used to further financial crime.[7]

With effect from 1 March 2006, however, the FSA took the decision to delete its specialist *Money Laundering Sourcebook* in its entirety and instead looked only to the higher level framework rules of SYSC as the basis for its financial crime (including AML) risk management requirements. That, it was said at the time, would better reflect the FSA's focus on risk management and systems and controls as well as its desire to encourage a more flexible, risk-based approach to AML safeguards in firms and a clearer focus on the oversight responsibility of senior management.[8]

6.3 The SYSC rules and guidance on money laundering

The SYSC rules and guidance encourage firms to adopt a risk-based approach to AML risk, by actively identifying and then managing the particular money laundering risks to which they are exposed, rather than simply attempting to meet a series of formal regulatory obligations.

That focus on outcomes rather than on detailed processes was intended by the FSA to give a degree of flexibility, allowing firms to tailor their approach to their particular circumstances, and also placing a greater emphasis on the responsibility of senior management to establish and maintain effective systems and controls, and it remains consistent with the FCA's approach to senior management responsibility and reliance on higher level principles as much as granular rules.

---

[6] SYSC 3.1.1R.
[7] SYSC 3.2.6R and SYSC 6.1.1R.
[8] FSA CP 05/10, Ch.2.

The AML aspects of the SYSC rules and guidance are addressed in the following sections.

6.3.1 SYSC 1—application and purpose

The SYSC rules and guidance relating to AML risk management apply to all authorised firms other than those whose only regulated activities consist of certain types of insurance business (essentially, general insurance, broking in relation to general insurance and pure protection, long-term insurance business falling outside the Consolidated Life Directive[9] collective insurance, insurance relating to certain Lloyd's business and mortgage broking and administration) or mortgage broking and administration.[10]

The rules also apply to UK branches of passporting EEA firms to the extent that they cover matters for which responsibility is not reserved to the relevant home state regulator. As, under the single market directives, prudential matters are reserved to home state regulators, in practice that means that the rules (with the express exception, in the case of firms subject to the Markets in Financial Instruments Directive (MiFID),[11] of the SYSC record-keeping requirements) do not apply to UK branches of EEA firms. EEA firms which are operating on a services-only basis in the UK are not required to comply with the relevant parts of SYSC.

By virtue of SYSC 1 Annex 1, the rules are modified in their application to sole traders, Undertakings for Collective Investment in Transferable Securities (UCITS) qualifiers (operators, trustees or depositaries of recognised collective investment schemes authorised under FSMA 2000 Sch.5), Alternative Investment Fund Managers (AIFM), authorised Alternative

---

[9] Directive 2002/83/EC of the European Parliament and of the Council of 5 November 2002 concerning life assurance [2002] OJ L345/1.

[10] SYSC 1 Annex 1.

[11] Directive 2004/39/EC of the European Parliament and of the Council of 21 April 2004 on markets in financial instruments amending Council Directives 85/611/EEC and 93/6/EEC and Directive 2000/12/EC of the European Parliament and of the Council and repealing Council Directive 93/22/EEC [2004] OJ L145/1.

Investment Funds (AIF), authorised professional firms and certain other more esoteric categories of firm.

The exclusion of certain types of insurance business, which mirrors similar exclusions previously set out in the *Money Laundering Sourcebook*, stems from a mismatch between the scope of FSMA 2000 and the scope of the Money Laundering Regulations. The latter apply to most financial institutions, but not to companies conducting insurance business of a type referred to in SYSC 1.1.3AR. At the time when the exclusion in respect of these companies was made, the FCA took the view that its Rules should not apply more widely than the Money Laundering Regulations. It did, however, issue a warning that it would reconsider the position if that seemed necessary, and might at the same time ask the Treasury to consider extending the scope of the Money Laundering Regulations (then the 2003 Regulations) to cover general insurance so as to maintain the connection between the two sets of requirements.[12] However, the 2007 Regulations similarly do not apply to insurance companies other than insurance companies which are duly authorised in accordance with the Consolidated Life Directive when they carry out activities covered by that Directive, and insurance intermediaries acting in respect of long-term contracts of insurance.[13]

It is to be noted, however, that there are other mismatches which are outside the power of the FCA to remedy. For example, bureaux de change activities are not regulated under FSMA 2000, with the result that the SYSC rules do not apply to them, but they are subject to the 2007 Regulations and as a result to the parallel regulatory regime overseen by HMRC. In that connection, when activity of that type is carried on by an authorised person or by a subsidiary of an authorised person, the FCA will regard that activity as relevant to the performance of the FCA's authorisation and supervision functions in relation to the authorised person because of the reputational, managerial, financial or other exposure which could arise from carrying on those activities even though the FCA will not have

---

[12] Consultation Paper 46 para.4.10.
[13] 2007 Regulations (SI 2007/2157) reg.3(3)(b) and (c).

formal supervisory powers in respect of those activities. Under the 2007 Regulations, any authorised person proposing to carry on (or cease to carry on) bureaux de change business must first inform the FCA.

In general, SYSC applies only in relation to activities carried on from an establishment in the UK. The FCA has, however, noted that where a UK-authorised firm is able to exercise control over business carried on outside the UK (e.g. through an overseas branch or subsidiary), it will look at how that control is exercised in the prevention and detection of money laundering in the non-UK business. Once again, it cites reputational, managerial, financial or other exposure of the relevant firm as the justification for this broad approach. It is not clear whether the FCA regards compliance with host state rules as sufficient in these circumstances.

Three of the stated purposes of SYSC, which pre-date the introduction of the high-level rules on money laundering, are:

(a) "to encourage firms' directors and senior managers to take appropriate practical responsibility for their firms' arrangements on matters likely to be of interest to the FCA";

(b) to increase certainty by amplifying Principle 3 under which a firm must "take reasonable care to organise and control its affairs responsibly and effectively, with adequate risk management systems"; and

(c) "to encourage firms to vest responsibility for effective and responsible organisation in specific directors and senior managers".[14]

With the implementation of MiFID in November 2007, SYSC underwent some restructuring. In particular, SYSC 4–18 were inserted to implement the MiFID requirements in respect of the organisation and management of relevant firms. Those sections initially applied only to "common platform firms" (i.e. firms

---

[14] SYSC 1.2.1G.

which are subject either to MiFID or to the Capital Requirements Directive).[15] For those firms, SYSC 6.3 set out the
requirements relevant to AML procedures in terms which were
essentially identical to the equivalent provisions of SYSC
3.2.6R, which then applied to all other regulated firms subject
to the exclusions set out above.

With effect from 1 April 2009, however, SYSC was amended
further so that the "common platform" requirements (including SYSC 6) apply to all firms other than insurers, managing
agents and Lloyd's, with some modifications for firms which
are not common platform firms.[16] This Chapter refers in most
cases primarily to the requirements of SYSC 6.3, since these
have been (with effect from 1 April 2009) the provisions which
apply to most regulated firms; reference is nevertheless made
to the equivalent provisions of SYSC 3.2.6R, which remain
relevant for insurers, managing agents and Lloyd's.

6.3.2 SYSC 3.2.6R/SYSC 6.1.1R

SYSC 3.2.6R is the cornerstone of the rules and guidance which
replaced the FSA's *Money Laundering Sourcebook*. It requires a
regulated firm to take reasonable care to establish and maintain
effective systems and controls for compliance with applicable
requirements and standards under the regulatory system and
for countering the risk that the firm will be used to further
financial crime. The rules and guidance at SYSC 3.2.6AR–
3.2.6JG are essentially an amplification of that cornerstone rule.

SYSC 6.1.1R is the equivalent provision in the post-MiFID
regime. It is expressed as an absolute obligation (rather than a
"reasonable care" obligation) on firms to establish, implement
and maintain adequate practices and procedures sufficient to

---

15 Directive 2013/36/EU of the European Parliament and of the Council of 26 June
  2013 on access to the activity of credit institutions and the prudential supervision
  of credit institutions and investment firms, amending Directive 2002/87/EC and
  repealing Directives 2006/48/EC and 2006/49/EC [2013] OJ L208/73.
16 Senior Management Arrangements, Systems and Controls (Extension of Common Platform Provisions) Instrument 2008 (FCA 2008/40).

ensure compliance under the regulatory system and for containing the risk that the firm might be used to further financial crime.

It should be noted that SYSC 6.1.1R, as with SYSC 3.2.6R in its original form, does apply to general insurance and mortgage intermediary firms. Accordingly, even though they are not obliged to comply with the 2007 Regulations, those firms must have appropriate systems and controls in place to comply with the regulatory system and to counter the risk that they will be used to further financial crime.

6.3.3 SYSC 6.3.1R/SYSC 3.2.6AR—adequacy of systems and controls

This rule requires a firm to ensure that the systems and controls established and maintained under SYSC 6.1.1R/SYSC 3.2.6R enable it to identify, assess, monitor and manage money laundering risk. The systems and controls must be comprehensive and proportionate to the nature, scale and complexity of the firm's activities.

This rule aims to encourage firms to adopt a risk-based approach, and is discussed in slightly more detail in the guidance contained in SYSC 6.3.6G/SYSC 3.2.6FG. However, the interpretation of the rule must necessarily rely upon the detailed provisions of the JMLSG Guidance Notes, which describe the steps a firm should take in order to follow a risk-based approach.[17] A firm should:

(a) identify the money laundering and terrorist financing risks that are relevant to the firm;
(b) assess the risks posed by the firm's particular customers, products, delivery channels, geographical areas of operation;
(c) design and implement controls to manage and mitigate these assessed risks, in the context of the firm's risk appetite;

---

[17] JMLSG Guidance Ch.4 para.4.12.

(d) monitor and improve the effective operation of these controls; and

(e) record appropriately what has been done and why.

6.3.4   *SYSC 6.3.2G/SYSC 3.2.6BG—definition of "money laundering risk"*

This guidance defines "money laundering risk" as the risk that a firm may be used to further money laundering, and notes that a failure to manage this risk effectively will increase the risk to society of crime and terrorism.

From a technical point of view, this definition indicates a distinction between the rules and guidance in SYSC and the JMLSG Guidance Notes. Although SYSC 6.1.1R/SYSC 3.2.6R requires firms to establish systems and controls to counter the risk that they will be used to further financial crime, the further rules and guidance in SYSC, strictly speaking, only deal with the risk of money laundering. According to the FCA Glossary, "financial crime" is defined widely and encompasses any kind of criminal conduct relating to money or to financial services or markets. "Money laundering", on the other hand, relates only to the offences in the Proceeds of Crime Act 2002 (POCA 2002) and the money laundering offence in the Terrorism Act 2000 (TA 2000) s.18.

The result is that the bulk of the rules and guidance in SYSC deal only with money laundering. By contrast, the JMLSG Guidance Notes deal also with terrorist financing, and indeed the title of those materials is *Prevention of money laundering/ combating terrorist financing—guidance for the UK financial sector*.

The difference is, however, unlikely to be important in practice, given that the general obligation in SYSC 6.1.1R/SYSC 3.2.6R requires that a firm's systems and controls counter the risk that a firm is used to further financial crime, which would include terrorist financing.

6.3.5   SYSC 6.3.3R/SYSC 3.2.6CR—*regular assessment*

This rule requires a firm to carry out regular assessments of the adequacy of its systems and controls to ensure continued compliance with SYSC 6.3.1R/SYSC 3.2.6AR. This requirement is similar to the recommendation that firms monitor the effective operation of their controls set out in the JMLSG Guidance Notes.[18]

6.3.6   SYSC 6.3.4G/SYSC 3.2.6DG—*other legal obligations*

This guidance states that a firm may have separate obligations to comply with relevant legal requirements, including TA 2000, POCA 2002 and the 2007 Regulations. It also states that the new rules and guidance in SYSC are not relevant guidance for the purposes of POCA 2002 s.330(8), TA 2000 s.21A(6) or reg.3(3) of the 2003 Regulations, which has been replaced by the equivalent regs 42(3) and 45(2) of the 2007 Regulations.

This maintains the relationship between the FCA rules and guidance and the JMLSG Guidance Notes. The JMLSG Guidance Notes are "relevant guidance", having been approved by HM Treasury in relation to this primary and secondary legislation.

6.3.7   SYSC 6.3.5G/SYSC 3.2.6EG—*relationship with the Guidance Notes*

SYSC 6.3.5G/SYSC 3.2.6EG states that, when considering whether a firm has breached the FCA's rules on systems and controls in relation to money laundering, the FCA will have regard to whether the firm has followed the JMLSG Guidance Notes.

---

[18] JMLSG Guidance Ch.3 para.3.28.

6.3.8 *SYSC 6.3.6G/SYSC 3.2.6FG—identifying money laundering risk*

This guidance recommends that, in identifying money laundering risk and in establishing the nature of the systems and controls required, a firm should consider a range of factors, including:

(a) its customer, product and activity profiles;
(b) its distribution channels;
(c) the complexity and volume of its transactions;
(d) its processes and systems; and
(e) its operating environment.

This guidance provides slightly more detail to support the requirement in SYSC 6.3.1R/SYSC 3.2.6AR to identify money laundering risk. Although the guidance remains high level, the JMLSG Guidance Notes cover the topic in more detail.[19]

However, neither the FCA rules and guidance nor the JMLSG Guidance Notes explain what is meant by the "operating environment". In the absence of further explanation from the FCA, firms may choose to define this term widely.

6.3.9 *SYSC 6.3.7G/SYSC 3.2.6GG—nature of systems and controls*

The guidance in SYSC 6.3.7G/SYSC 3.2.6GG covers five different components of the required systems and controls:

(1) A firm should ensure that the systems and controls include appropriate training for that firm's employees in relation to money laundering.
   This single sentence effectively replaces all of the detailed rules that had originally been set out in the specialist *Money Laundering Sourcebook* in respect of training. It is more broadly targeted than those earlier detailed rules and is aligned more closely with statutory requirements. For

---

[19] JMLSG Guidance Ch.4 paras 4.27–4.41.

example, the *Money Laundering Sourcebook* referred to awareness and training specifically for staff who handle, or who are managerially responsible for, transactions which may involve money laundering, whereas the offence of failing to report in POCA 2002 s.330 applies to all persons who come into contact with relevant information in the course of their business in the regulated sector, and makes no reference to whether or not these staff handle or are managerially responsible for such transactions. Given that a person who fails to report has a defence if he has not been provided with training by his employer,[20] the deletion of the reference to training for particular staff helps to avoid the risk of a mismatch between the FCA rules and legislation.

The JMLSG Guidance Notes deal with staff awareness, training and alertness, providing additional detail on this topic.[21]

(2) A firm should ensure that the systems and controls include appropriate provision of information to that firm's governing body and senior management, including a report at least annually by that firm's MLRO on the operation and effectiveness of those systems and controls.

This guidance aims to ensure that senior management are given adequate information in order to perform their function in line with the FCA's increased focus on senior management responsibility. The content of the MLRO's annual report is briefly elaborated in the JMLSG Guidance Notes.[22]

(3) A firm should ensure that its systems and controls include appropriate documentation of its risk management policies and risk profile in relation to money laundering, including documentation of its application of those policies (SYSC 9/SYSC 3.2.20R to SYSC 3.2.22G).

This guidance clearly demonstrates the FCA's risk-based approach to money laundering. The terms "risk management policy" and "risk profile" are not defined in that context.

---

[20] POCA 2002 s.330(7)(b).
[21] JMLSG Guidance Ch.7.
[22] JMLSG Guidance paras 3.31–3.39.

Guidance refers to the high-level record-keeping requirements in SYSC 9/SYSC 3.2. According to those requirements, a firm must take reasonable care to make and retain
adequate records of matters and dealings (including
accounting records) which are the subject of requirements
and standards under the regulatory system. In general,
and subject to other Handbook requirements, all records
must be capable of being reproduced in English on paper.
However, if a firm's records relate to business carried on
from an establishment in a country or territory outside the
UK, an official language of that country or territory may
be used instead of English.[23]

Furthermore, guidance in SYSC 9/SYSC 3.2 indicates that
a firm should have appropriate systems and controls in
place to fulfil its regulatory and statutory obligations with
respect to the adequacy of the records, access to such
records, the periods of retention for the records and their
security. The general principle is that records should be
kept for as long as is relevant for the purposes for which
they were made.[24] The guidance also refers to the detailed
record-keeping requirements for different types of firm,
which are located in Sch.1 to each module of the
Handbook.[25]

(4) A firm should ensure that the systems and controls include
appropriate measures to ensure that money laundering
risk is taken into account in its day-to-day operation,
including in relation to:
   (a) the development of new products;
   (b) the taking on of new customers; and
   (c) changes in its business profile.

This guidance elaborates the requirement in SYSC 6.3.1R/
SYSC 3.2.6AR to identify money laundering risk by
ensuring that it is considered on a day-to-day basis.

(5) A firm should ensure that the systems and controls include
appropriate measures to ensure that procedures for
identification of new customers do not unreasonably deny

---

[23] SYSC 9.1.4G/SYSC 3.2.20R.
[24] SYSC 9.1.5G/SYSC 3.2.21G.
[25] SYSC 9.1.6G/SYSC 3.2.22G.

access to its services to potential customers who cannot reasonably be expected to produce detailed evidence of identity.

This guidance effectively replaces a set of much more detailed guidance in relation to financial exclusion that had originally been set out in the specialist *Money Laundering Sourcebook*. The JMLSG Guidance Notes detail alternative identification procedures for individuals without access to the normal documentation required.[26]

6.3.10 SYSC 6.3.8R/SYSC 3.2.6HR—senior management responsibility

This rule requires a firm to allocate to a director or senior manager the overall responsibility within the firm for the establishment and maintenance of effective anti-money laundering systems and controls.

6.3.11 SYSC 6.3.9R/SYSC 3.2.6I—the Money Laundering Reporting Officer

This rule requires a firm to appoint an MLRO with responsibility for the oversight of its compliance with the FCA's rules on systems and controls against money laundering. The firm also has to ensure that its MLRO has a level of authority and independence within the firm and access to resources and information sufficient to enable him to carry out that responsibility.

6.3.12 SYSC 6.3.10G/SYSC 3.2.6JG—the role of the Money Laundering Reporting Officer

This guidance aims to explain the nature of the MLRO's role, stating that his job is to act as "the focal point for all activity in the firm relating to money laundering". It adds that it is expected that a firm's MLRO will be based in the UK.

---

[26] JMLSG Guidance Pt I paras 5.3.88–5.3.105; Pt II paras 1.38–1.41 and Annex to Ch.1.

The description of the MLRO highlights a possible confusion over the nature of his role in relation to the role of the director or senior manager responsible for money laundering. Often they will be one and the same person, but not necessarily so.

Chapter 3 of the JMLSG Guidance Notes deals extensively with the role and duties of the MLRO, and at para.1.31 in the 2014 edition contains the following statement:

"The relationship between the MLRO and the director/ senior manager allocated overall responsibility for the establishment and maintenance of the firm's AML/CTF systems (where they are not the same person) is one of the keys to a successful AML/CTF regime. It is important that this relationship is clearly defined and documented, so that each knows the extent of his, and the other's, role and day to day responsibilities."

6.3.13   SYSC 6.3.11G/SYSC 3.2.6KG—the FCA's Financial Crime: A guide for firms

In June 2011, the FSA launched a consultation on new regulatory guidance to help firms address the risk of financial crime. Based on the FSA's previously published thematic work, *Financial Crime: A guide for firms* (the Guide) is designed to help firms assess and improve their anti-financial crime systems and controls. The Guide was published in December 2011 after receiving considerable support from consultation respondents.

Part 1 of the Guide provides guidance on financial crime systems and controls, both generally and in relation to specific risks such as money laundering, bribery and corruption and fraud. Part 2 provides summaries of, and links to, FSA and FCA thematic reviews of various financial crime risks and sets out the full examples of good and poor practice that were included with the reviews' findings.

Although the material in the Guide does not form part of the Handbook, it provides guidance on Handbook rules and principles, particularly:

- SYSC 3.2.6R and SYSC 6.1.1R (establishing effective systems and controls to prevent the risk of furthering financial crime);
- Principles 1 (integrity), 2 (skill, care and diligence), 3 (management and control) and 11 (relations with regulators) of the Principles for Businesses in PRIN 2.1.1R; and
- the Statements of Principle for Approved Persons set out in APER 2.1.2P.

Updates to the Guide are periodically announced by the FCA. For example, amendments were made in April 2015 to incorporate examples of good practice from FCA thematic reviews of small banks' AML and sanctions procedures, and small commercial brokers' anti-bribery and corruption procedures.

The Guide is not mandatory: it does not impose rules or new requirements, and departure from the guidance is not presumed to indicate a breach of FCA rules. The Guide should not be viewed as exhaustive nor thought of as a comprehensive checklist but the FCA nevertheless encourages firms to apply its guidance in a risk-based, proportionate way and reminds firms to consult all available industry guidance, particularly "relevant guidance", as designated by applicable statutes and regulations.

Despite those disclaimers, the guidance, self-assessment questions and examples of good and poor practice provided by the Guide have become valuable tools for firms when evaluating compliance with their legal and regulatory obligations in relation to financial crime.

6.4 Conclusion

The FCA continues to regard financial crime, including money laundering, as one of the major threats to confidence in the UK markets and has demonstrated, and will continue to demonstrate, its willingness to take action against firms that have not adequately responded to the risks to which financial services business increasingly face in this regard.

Against that background, it is clear that firms in the regulated sector must expect to continue to devote significant financial and managerial resources to ensuring that they both implement and observe the procedures, and also the culture, necessary to ensure compliance in that area.

Chapter 7

The Role of the Financial Conduct Authority

Elizabeth Richards
Consultant, Policy and Risk Team, Specialist Supervision Division

James London
Manager, Policy and Risk Team, Specialist Supervision Division

7.1 Introduction

This Chapter explains the role of the Financial Conduct Authority (FCA) in the UK's collective efforts to combat money laundering and the financing of terrorism. Money laundering (which, for the purposes of this Chapter, includes the financing of terrorism) is a crime with many victims. As with other ostensibly "financial" crimes, it can facilitate and fund much darker offences. As such, in addition to prohibiting money laundering, the law also provides for various steps to be taken by the financial services sector to detect and prevent money laundering. The FCA has been charged with overseeing that. If successful, the financial industry's efforts will make crime less attractive, and, it is to be hoped, reduce both its incidence, and the damage it does to society.

7.2 The Financial Conduct Authority

The FCA was established in 2013 to regulate how financial firms in the UK conduct their business. It is responsible for supervising a wide range of financial firms, including banks, building societies, credit unions, financial and investment advisors, general and life insurers and insurance intermediaries, mortgage providers and brokers and a range of market participants. Over 90 per cent of the firms that the FCA supervises are solely based in the UK.

The Prudential Regulation Authority (PRA) is charged with overseeing the financial soundness of financial firms like banks, building societies and insurance companies; the PRA has not been assigned a role in relation to money laundering supervision. Both the FCA and the PRA are successor bodies to the Financial Services Authority.

Countering money laundering is a key aspect of the FCA's remit, but how does the FCA achieve this aim? The FCA pursues its objectives relating to money laundering chiefly through its ability to influence the behaviour of the financial sector, including imposing rules, supervising firms' compliance with these rules and other requirements, making statements and taking enforcement action. The FCA can also undertake a criminal prosecution for breaches of the Money Laundering Regulations 2007[1] (the 2007 Regulations).

The FCA is a non-governmental body that funds itself by charging fees to the firms it regulates. In 2013/14, the FCA's operating costs were £434.5 million. It is not possible to say what amount of that sum was spent specifically on anti-money laundering (AML) supervision, although the FCA does run a dedicated department staffed by specialists charged with reviewing firms' efforts to tackle financial crime, including money laundering.

7.3 Legal context

7.3.1 *What the law requires of the FCA*

The FCA was given statutory powers by the Financial Services and Markets Act 2000 (FSMA 2000), which also sets out the organisation's duties. The FCA's strategic objective is ensuring

---

[1] Money Laundering Regulations 2007 (SI 2007/2157).

that the relevant markets function well. The FCA also has three operational objectives. They are:

- securing an appropriate degree of protection for consumers;
- protecting and enhancing the integrity of the UK financial systems; and
- promoting effective competition in the interests of consumers in specified markets.

FSMA 2000 confirms that the integrity of the UK financial systems includes misuse for a purpose connected with "financial crime", which is defined to include "handling the proceeds of crime" (in other words, money laundering). FSMA 2000 further requires that the FCA must, when discharging its general functions, have regard to the importance of taking action intended to minimise the extent to which it is possible for businesses which are or should be authorised by the FCA to be used for a purpose connected with financial crime.

In addition, the FCA is charged with overseeing financial firms' compliance with the 2007 Regulations. The FCA is the AML supervisor for all credit and financial firms which are subject to the 2007 Regulations, including about 350 "Annex I financial firms"[2]. From 1 April 2014, the FCA also became the AML (and general) supervisor for consumer credit firms; these had previously been overseen by the Office of Fair Trading before its dissolution.

The FCA also derives responsibilities related to AML from different legislative sources:

---

[2]   Annex I financial firms are firms which do not carry out "regulated activities" as defined by FSMA 2000 and are therefore not otherwise authorised by the FCA or subject to mainstream FCA supervision, but which carry out certain of the activities specified in Annex 1 of the Capital Requirements Directive (Directive 2013/36/EU of the European Parliament and of the Council of 26 June 2013 on access to the activity of credit institutions and the prudential supervision of credit institutions and investment firms, amending Directive 2002/87/EC and repealing Directives 2006/48/EC and 2006/49/EC [2013] OJ L176/338); for example, commercial lenders or non-bank providers of safe deposit boxes.

- The FCA may apply for confiscation and restraint of the proceeds of crime under the Proceeds of Crime Act 2002 (POCA 2002);
- The Transfer of Funds (Information on the Payer) Regulations 2007[3] enable the FCA to enforce EU Regulation 1781/2006[4];
- The FCA also has investigation and enforcement powers under Sch.7 to the Counter-Terrorism Act 2008;
- The FCA is the AML supervisory authority for e-money firms pursuant to the Electronic Money Regulations 2011[5];
- Under the Payment Services Regulations 2009[6], the FCA is the general conduct supervisor for payment firms, although HM Revenue and Customs supervises payment firms' compliance with the 2007 Regulations;
- The FCA also has supervisory responsibility for many consumer credit firms under the Consumer Credit Act 1974; and
- The Immigration Act 2014 contains a provision that prohibits banks and building societies from opening current accounts for certain people.[7] The FCA has a duty to monitor and enforce compliance with this prohibition.

Box 1: The UK framework in an international context

The UK's AML regime reflects international legal and regulatory standards. The FCA feeds into domestic and international policy debates about the development of these standards.

Two important stakeholders are:

The *Financial Action Task Force* (FATF) is an international body. Its purpose is the development and promotion of recommendations designed to help Member States combat money laundering and terrorist financing.

---

[3] Transfer of Funds (Information on the Payer) Regulations 2007 (SI 2007/3298).
[4] Regulation (EC) No 1781/2006 of the European Parliament and of the Council of 15 November 2006 on information on the payer accompanying transfers of funds [2006] OJ L345/1.
[5] Electronic Money Regulations 2011 (SI 2011/99).
[6] Payment Services Regulations 2009 (SI 2009/209).
[7] For full details, see: *https://www.fca.org.uk/firms/being-regulated/meeting your-obligations/firm-guides/immigration-act-2014* [Accessed 23 September 2015].

Box 1: The UK framework in an international context

The *European Union* has translated FATF's recommendations into directives and regulations that Member States must transpose into domestic law. The Fourth Directive[8] is a recent example. The directive will be transposed into UK law by 2017 through updating the 2007 Regulations.

7.3.2   *What the law requires of financial firms*

This topic is covered more fully in other chapters of this book, although a brief summary is provided here. The firms regulated by the FCA are subject to many legal obligations relating to financial crime in general, and money laundering in particular. The FCA must ensure that firms meet these requirements.

Box 2: Two key laws

Proceeds of Crime Act 2002 (POCA 2002)

Criminalises all forms of money laundering, and creates other offences such as tipping off and failing to report knowledge or suspicion of money laundering.

Terrorism Act 2000 (TA 2000)

Establishes a series of offences related to involvement in the funding of terrorism, and creates other offences such as tipping off and failing to report knowledge or suspicion of terrorist financing.

All firms authorised and regulated by the FCA (apart from general insurance firms and mortgage intermediaries) are subject to the MLR which require that firms take specified steps to detect and prevent money laundering: more detail is in Box 3.

---

[8]   Directive (EU) 2015/849 of the European Parliament and of the Council of 20 May 2015 on the prevention of the use of the financial system for the purposes of money laundering or terrorist financing, amending Regulation (EU) No 648/2012 of the European Parliament and of the Council, and repealing Directive 2005/60/EC of the European Parliament and of the Council and Commission Directive 2006/70/EC [2015] OJ L141/73.

Box 3: Key requirements of the 2007 Regulations

- The 2007 Regulations require that firms establish *appropriate* and *risk-sensitive* policies and procedures relating to:
- customer due diligence checks;
- *ongoing monitoring* of business relationships;
- *reporting of suspicions*, both within the firm, and to the NCA via suspicious activity reports;
- assessment of money laundering risks and the application of *enhanced measures* in higher risk situations (e.g. politically exposed persons);
- record keeping;
- monitoring compliance with procedures;
- internal *communication* of policies and procedures; and
- *staff awareness and training* on money laundering matters.

7.4 The FCA's approach to combatting money laundering

The FCA has an extensive range of supervisory powers to support its financial crime responsibilities and take action for breaches. Much of the legislation outlined in 7.3.1 gives the FCA powers to obtain information and documents, impose civil penalties and prosecute criminal offences. However one of the principles of good regulation[9] is that of proportionality: a burden that is imposed on an institution by the FCA should be proportionate to the benefits which are expected to result. The FCA must also have regard to the need to be economic and efficient in its use of resources.

As such, when it pursues its responsibilities, the FCA seeks to adopt a "risk-based" approach to its work, including its efforts to tackle money laundering. That means that, given the many possible claims on its resources, the FCA aims to concentrate its efforts where the risks are greatest. It also expects financial firms to follow the same principle when designing and

---

[9] See *https://www.fca.org.uk/about/operate/principles* [Accessed 23 September 2015].

implementing their own AML measures. As a consequence, firms—and their boards and senior management—have a responsibility to identify, assess, mitigate and monitor their money laundering risks on a considered and continuing basis.

To be successful in applying a risk-based approach to combating money laundering, it is first necessary to form a view of where the money laundering risks lie, and for that assessment to be based on good information. With an up-to-date risk assessment in place, it is then possible to ask: "how should we allocate the resource we have?" or "do we have sufficient resource, given the risks?" If successful, a risk-based approach can help to ensure that measures (whether taken by an institution or a regulator):

(a)   are proportionate to the risks;
(b)   can adapt as risks evolve; and
(c)   do not impose undue burdens on the law-abiding public.

The use of a risk-based approach means that the FCA will not routinely inspect all firms' AML controls. Instead, visits and reviews will be targeted towards firms about which the FCA has concerns, or the most systemically important firms. In the case of a thematic review considering how the industry handles a specific risk, the FCA will review a discrete sample of firms. Meanwhile, an institution that takes a risk-based approach may, for example, choose to tailor its due diligence checks to the type of customer, so that those buying a higher-risk product are asked to provide fuller evidence of their identity than customers buying lower-risk products. Clearly, the risk-based approach does have limits: a bank in the UK cannot take a risk-based judgment to, for example, open anonymous accounts, because that is explicitly outlawed.

7.5 What is required of financial firms by the FCA?

All firms authorised by the FCA, including general insurance firms and mortgage intermediaries, are subject to a high-level regulatory requirement relating to financial crime.

This requirement sits in the Systems and Controls Chapter of the FCA's *Handbook of Rules and Guidance* and states:

> "An institution must establish, implement and maintain adequate policies and procedures sufficient to ensure compliance ... with its obligations under the regulatory system and for countering the risk that the institution might be used to further financial crime." (SYSC 6.1.1R. See also SYSC 3.2.6R)

There are specific money laundering systems and controls requirements (see SYSC 6.3 or SYSC 3.2.6A–3.2.6J) that apply to all firms, except mortgage intermediaries and general insurance firms (see below). Financial crime, including money laundering, is relevant to other parts of the Handbook. For example, financial crime has a bearing on the *Principles for Businesses* which, among other things, require an institution to take reasonable care to organise and control its affairs responsibly and effectively. *Approved persons* are under similar obligations under the *Statements of Principle for Approved Persons*.[10] Financial crime considerations can also affect the FCA's judgments of an institution's continued ability to satisfy the *threshold conditions*, particularly regarding assessments of fitness and propriety.

The FCA is concerned that some banks are no longer offering financial services to whole categories of customers or potential customers, in particular money transmitters, charities, FinTech

---

[10] Note that deposit-takers, insurers and investment firms designated by the PRA will, from March 2016, be subject to a new Senior Managers Regime and Senior Insurance Managers Regime that requires them to assign "prescribed responsibilities"—including a responsibility for overseeing a firm's arrangement for tackling financial crime—to senior members of staff.

companies. That is incompatible with the risk-based approach unless the individual business relationship has been risk assessed.[11]

7.5.1 Financial crime: a guide for firms

In 2011, the Financial Services Authority consulted on a new body of non-binding guidance for firms it regulated. The FCA has retained and updated its guidance *Financial crime: a guide for firms*.[12] This guidance provides practical assistance and information for firms of all sizes and across all FCA-supervised sectors. It sets out self-assessment questions and examples of good and poor practice that can help firms to prepare effective systems and controls to counter financial crime, and is periodically updated to reflect the findings of thematic reviews undertaken by the FCA.

7.5.2 The Joint Money Laundering Steering Group's guidance

Detailed practical guidance on the steps that firms regulated by the FCA can take to meet their obligations under the 2007 Regulations, and other relevant laws, is available from the Joint Money Laundering Steering Group (JMLSG), a body made up of trade associations from across the industry.[13]

As well as being comprehensive and practical, the JMLSG guidance is noteworthy for the unique way it is drafted. It is prepared by practitioners with an appreciation of the operational issues, and includes material tailored to the different sectors of the financial industry. That helps to ensure that its recommendations are consistent with prevalent AML standards. It does that by subjecting the draft text to challenge from law enforcement agencies and interested government departments.

---

[11] Derisking: Banks' management of money-laundering risk-FCA expectations, *https://www.fca.org.uk/about/what/enforcing/money-laundering/derisking* [Accessed 23 September 2015].

[12] It is available free of charge at *https://fshandbook.info/FS/html/FCA/FC/link/PDF* [Accessed 23 September 2015].

[13] The guidance is available free of charge at *www.jmlsg.org.uk* [Accessed 23 September 2015].

The status of the guidance is further enhanced because it is formally approved by HM Treasury for the purposes of POCA 2002, which means that a court must take JMLSG guidance into account when deciding if an individual in the regulated sector has committed a failure to report offence.

The FCA is required by the 2007 Regulations to take account of whether an institution followed JMLSG guidance.[14] The FCA has also committed to "have regard to whether an institution has followed relevant provisions in the guidance for the UK financial sector issued by the Joint Money Laundering Steering Group" when "considering whether a breach of its rules on systems and controls against money laundering has occurred" (SYSC 6.3.5G). On the other hand, firms should not feel bound by the JMLSG's recommendations—it is recognised that firms can take alternative routes to the same destination—but they should be able to justify why they chose to take an alternative approach.

7.5.3 Mortgage intermediaries and general insurance firms

As noted above, mortgage intermediaries and general insurance firms are not subject to the 2007 Regulations, or the provisions of SYSC that specifically relate to money laundering. That, for example, means that those firms are under no obligation to appoint a Money Laundering Reporting Officer. However, those firms are subject to the high-level regulatory requirement to counter financial crime (SYSC 3.2.6R). As such, general insurance firms and mortgage intermediaries must take reasonable care to counter the risk that they may be used to further financial crime, including money laundering. So, although these firms are under no specific obligation to, say, perform customer due diligence checks on their client, it is wrong to conclude that they have no obligations in this area. Firms may be expected to collect information from the customer for a range of reasons (e.g. customer service, fraud

---

[14] Money Laundering Regulations 2007 (SI 2007/2157) reg.42(3).

control, sanctions compliance, and assessing creditworthiness) some of which are consistent with the high-level requirement in SYSC 3.2.6R.

7.5.4 Senior Managers Regime

The Senior Managers Regime will come into effect in March 2016. Responsibility for oversight of the adequacy of the firm's financial crime controls, including over money laundering, must be assigned to a specific member of a firm's board or executive committee. The FCA expects this will have an implicit effect in improving the overall quality of information senior managers receive so they can better understand the risks to which their banks are exposed; the management of which they will be accountable for.

7.6 Conclusion

The FCA plays a multifaceted role in the fight against money laundering. Both the regulatory regime and industry practice have moved forward substantially since the FCA was established. Complacency should be avoided, however: new challenges such as derisking are constantly emerging.

Chapter 8

Practical Systems and Controls

Debbie Ward
Partner, Financial Crime Team

Colin Pickard
Director, Financial Crime Team

Gabriela Grosicka
Manager, Financial Crime Team
Ernst & Young LLP

8.1 Introduction

Anti-money laundering and sanctions, terrorist financing (AML/STF) controls to deter, prevent and detect potential offences facilitating financial crime are increasingly considered to be part of the essential core risk-management structure of financial institutions. Some financial institutions also include other financial crime risks and their risk management structure such as fraud and market abuse. Strong regulatory action in many countries, including substantial fines levied on a series of banks, have contributed to the momentum for establishing comprehensive arrangements for ensuring compliance with economic sanctions, AML and terrorist financing as critical business processes for managing material operational risk. Hence, inclusion in an overall risk management framework has become essential.

Governments have deliberately increased focus on financial institutions as a mechanism to combat crime, partly by providing intelligence, and partly through effective controls leading to prevention and disruption of criminal and terrorist activities. This is also an effective tool to mobilise the international community for non-violent international pressure on recalcitrant governments through imposition of economic sanctions. That has led to a continuing change in the expected standard of compliance with standards driven by regulatory guidance and intervention and, in the case of economic sanctions, increasing complexity of rules for implementation, currently demonstrated by Russian and Ukrainian economic sanctions.

In 2012, the Financial Action Task Force (FATF) published revised recommendations on combating money laundering and terrorist financing. That review of international standards influenced the EU to revise its money laundering legislation, and indirectly, the laws in Member States. The Fourth Money Laundering Directive[1] (the Fourth Directive) will require Member States to bring their domestic AML regulation in line with those new standards.

UK regulators and industry groups have taken further actions to ensure standards of due diligence, monitoring and record keeping in the UK have evolved to keep pace with changing international standards in attempts to prevent and detect money laundering and terrorist financing and the increasing complexity of economic sanctions. Examples of this include the Joint Money Laundering Steering Group (JMLSG) review and update of the benchmark JMLSG Guidance and the Wolfsberg Group revisions on Correspondent Banking.

Financial institutions must adapt to continuously developing risk management standards. The Small Business, Enterprise and Employment Act 2015, approved in March 2015, supported the new FATF and Fourth Directive requirements on transparency of ownership by requiring the UK companies to maintain a register with people with significant control over the company and abolish bearer shares.

---

[1] Directive (EU) 2015/849 of the European Parliament and of the Council of 20 May 2015 on the prevention of the use of the financial system for the purposes of money laundering or terrorist financing, amending Regulation (EU) No 648/2012 of the European Parliament and of the Council, and repealing Directive 2005/60/EC of the European Parliament and of the Council and Commission Directive 2006/70/EC [2015] OJ L141/73.

Further legislation is anticipated, creating potential corporate offences around facilitating tax evasion which may lead to additional liabilities and obligations on financial institutions.

The evolution in risk management and consideration of the impact of financial crime on wider society have increased the profile of AML, and have led to the advancement of risk-based approaches to strengthen controls over more risky business activities, allocating resources in a more cost-effective fashion, which accords with the overall risk-management framework of an institution.

The Financial Conduct Authority (FCA) has actively supported a risk-based approach to AML and counter-terrorist financing controls. However, it is left to institutions to understand the inherent financial crime risk exposure of the institution and develop the appropriate controls to manage those particular risks. Working groups, established by industry bodies such as the British Bankers' Association, often bring peer institutions together to develop robust and compliant methodologies for organisations to adapt and implement as necessary.

Tightening standards have also coincided with an increased focus on the responsibility of senior management to establish appropriate controls to manage risk, including financial crime risk, and to oversee the effective operation of controls around money laundering, terrorist financing and compliance with economic sanctions. Senior managers are increasingly being asked to formally attest to the completeness and effectiveness of controls in place.

Notwithstanding the focus on senior managers within the risk-based regulatory environment, it is important to note that the FCA continues to place emphasis on the competence of staff at all levels, as well as senior management and those performing controlled functions, such as the Money Laundering Reporting Officer (MLRO). Notably, the FCA's enforcement actions for money laundering control failings are becoming more focussed on the culpability of such individuals within institutions as well as the institutions themselves[2]. That in itself presents additional challenges to any firm attempting to implement effective systems and controls, because although the FCA does not suggest a "zero tolerance" approach, it does expect firms to be able to manage their own affairs competently. Increasing focus on personal liability can be expected to lead to more risk-averse behaviour. In some instances, "de-risking" may move the test applied beyond the purpose and intention of the regulation.[3]

Developing a coherent and effective framework within which to identify and manage financial crime risks starts with the identification of risk, setting of risk appetite and consideration of the appropriate controls to deter, prevent and detect potentially criminal behaviour. That approach is founded on the premise that the business accepts responsibility for managing risk, and that that process should be monitored and evidenced through appropriate governance arrangements.

8.2 The Financial Crime Control Framework (FCC Framework)

An FCC Framework will include the key components required and reference the end-to-end processes, associated escalation and decision paths required to manage relevant financial crime risk exposure. In developing and implementing an FCC framework, firms must fully engage all business areas, ensuring involvement and adequate training of staff at all levels.

An example of a simple FCC framework is shown at the end of this Chapter.

---

[2] FCA Consultation Paper P15/22, *Strengthening accountability in banking: Final rules and consultation on extending the Certification Regime to wholesale market activities*, July 2015.

[3] BBC Magazine "Why did HSBC shut down bank accounts?", 28 July 2015, *http://www.bbc.com/news/magazine-33677946* [Accessed 24 September 2015].

8.2.1   Establish governance and control environment

The UK regulators imposed a set of principles and fundamental rules that financial institutions must adhere to. FCA Principle 3 directly applies to the governance and control environment:

> "A firm must take reasonable care to organise and control its affairs responsibly and effectively, with adequate risk management systems."[4]

Although financial institutions are expected to establish systems and controls on a risk-sensitive basis, the Financial Services Authority, and its successor the Financial Conduct Authority (FCA), have made significant efforts to provide firms with practical guidance highlighting examples of good and bad practice.

Published material includes *The FCA Financial Crime Guide*, thematic reviews, enforcement actions and consultation papers. The array of practical examples identified across various sectors of financial services is a constructive guide to practitioners.

A firm's governance structures will naturally take into account the nature, scale and complexity of the business and must take account of the risk appetite.[5] Directors and senior managers of the firm will establish a firm's strategy and risk appetite and articulate these to the rest of the business. Communication of a firm's compliance culture and risk approach need to be driven by the appropriate "tone from the top" to convey not just the content and expectation, but also make clear the position of senior management.

Delivering the strategy into adequate and effective systems and controls is the essence of a firm's successful anti-financial crime controls. Those systems and controls must be applied in

---

4   FCA Handbook PRIN 2.1.1R.
5   FCA, *How small banks manage money laundering and sanctions risk*, November 2014.

an appropriate way to mitigate the inherent financial crime risks identified by the business.

The FCA's *Senior Management Arrangements, Systems and Controls* Sourcebook (SYSC) provides guidance on systems and controls that a financial institution should consider when designing its anti-financial crime governance framework. SYSC guidelines address the following components of the systems and controls framework[6]:

8.2.1.1   AML/STF training

Appropriate training, including scenarios tailored to respective areas of the business, must be provided to staff at all levels, emphasising that it is the staff's clear personal responsibility to report any suspicion of financial crime. That will enable individuals to identify suspicious activity and report any suspicion to the MLRO.

8.2.1.2   MLRO report (at least annually)

A firm must appoint a senior manager with an overall responsibility for establishing, maintaining and monitoring the financial crime processes and controls.[7]

Senior management must remain informed on the key financial crime risks the firm is facing, how they have changed or are changing since the last report and the effectiveness of the FCC framework in preventing individual and systemic failures. Depending on the size and nature of the firm, compliance, including financial crime measures, is usually a standing agenda item for the Board. Larger firms also operate compliance committees, attended by Board members and senior compliance managers, which may consider both the report and associated material.

The senior manager, the MLRO, is accountable to the Board and the Regulator. On an annual basis, the MLRO will provide

---

[6]   FCA Handbook, SYSC 3.2.6GG.
[7]   FCA Handbook, SYSC 3.2.6HR.

the Board with a report on the effectiveness of the firm's financial crime systems and controls.

8.2.1.3   Risk management policies and risk profile

Firms are required to establish and document their risk-based approach to financial crime and associated risk management policies and procedures. These documents need to be updated on a regular basis to address, where appropriate, changes in internal risk profiles, legislation, regulatory expectations and any changes in the operation of the business that impact the financial crime risk.

8.2.1.4   Measures to ensure money laundering risk is taken into account in day-to-day operation

AML/STF risk assessment is clearly not a one-off exercise. One aspect of this is to identify changes in clients' circumstances on an ongoing basis. Triggers may indicate changes in a risk profile, and may therefore require further consideration of risk and controls to mitigate risk, such as additional or enhanced due diligence. Those triggers may involve additional products or changes in business profile.

8.2.1.5   Procedures to identify new customers that do not unreasonably deny access to potential customers

Some people may struggle to comply with the identification process. Firms must develop a process by which they can consider how to allow potential customers to use the financial services system without the need to produce certain types of documentary evidence which they may not have.

8.2.2   Develop and manage people

The requirement for regulated firms to provide relevant employees with adequate AML/STF awareness and training has continued to retain its importance through the implementation of the Proceeds of Crime Act 2002 (POCA 2002), the

Money Laundering Regulations 2007[8] (the 2007 Regulations) and the revised JMLSG Guidance. Associated requirements under the Bribery Act 2010 highlighted the importance of training and awareness and extended it by creating potential corporate offences where management have not taken sufficient action to train and equip staff to prevent financial crimes.

Although financial institutions must employ staff with relevant skills, knowledge and expertise,[9] regular AML/STF training is required to educate staff on existing money laundering and terrorist financing laws and enable them to identify suspicious activity.[10] It is also important that core training incorporates not only the wider legal requirements, but also the individual firm's own standards and procedures, including those contained in the firm's AML policy or relevant sections of the compliance manual.

The rationale for defining training needs, ensuring its delivery, and measuring its effectiveness needs to be included in a firm's assessment of its own individual money laundering and terrorist financing risks. For most firms, it is unlikely that delivery of the same training with the same frequency to all employees will be an adequate response to its money laundering and terrorist financing risk.

In assessing what action firms should be taking in that area, it is first necessary to differentiate between legal and regulatory requirements and an individual firm's in-house procedures. Whilst training should incorporate both elements, it is important that firms make employees sufficiently aware of their responsibilities under the relevant legislation and regulatory rules (including POCA 2002 and the Terrorism Act 2000) as well as the possible individual sanctions that exist in the event of a conviction or breach. Staff must be made aware of the

---

8   Money Laundering Regulations 2007 (SI 2007/2157).
9   FCA Handbook SYSC 5.1.1R.
10 2007 Regulations (SI 2007/2157) reg.21(a) and (b).

name of the firm's nominated officer, internal processes for the reporting of any suspicions as well as obligations under the "tipping off" provisions.[11]

Training can be provided in a manner suitable to the firm: smaller firms may provide face-to-face training while larger institutions may offer online training, often provided by vendors recognised in the market. AML/STF training should be tailored to specific business areas and staff functions. However, a minimum (or standard) level training should usually be provided to all staff from the Chief Executive all the way through to administration and secretarial staff. On a risk-based approach, this would be prudent and it would ensure that all relevant staff receive an appropriate level of training.

All individuals have a responsibility to remain informed about the financial crime risks and internal controls of their firm. This is amplified at senior levels with the Board being ultimately responsible. The relevant FCA thematic reviews have focused on money laundering controls and have highlighted concerns over the level of knowledge and engagement among the senior members of firms. For example, senior management of one firm were unable to discuss the key risks or red flags identified internally,[12] indicating that any training provided was not sufficiently rooted in the risk profile of the firm itself.

To keep training fresh and relevant to employees, it is important that the approach incorporates feedback and learning from events and experiences at the firm. For instance, repeated failings or systemic errors identified in account opening documentation standards (possibly through internal audit or compliance monitoring) should be addressed through remedial training. Similarly, if the MLRO considers the historical number of internal suspicion reports to be lower than should reasonably be expected from any part of the business, then that situation could be addressed through providing

---

[11] POCA 2002 s.333.
[12] FCA, *How small banks manage money laundering and sanctions risk*, November 2014.

further clarity on the type of activity which may be unusual, as well as on the suspicion reporting process.

Additionally, by utilising in-house or "real world" examples of money laundering and terrorist financing, senior management should actively seek to raise awareness of money laundering risk to improve employees' recognition of suspicious activity.

It is common practice for AML training to be delivered upon the commencement of employment at a particular firm and then repeated (in many cases using the same material) at regular ongoing intervals. In the current regulatory climate, with both legislation and market practice evolving almost constantly, it is imperative that training material is reviewed and updated regularly to keep pace with developments.

Legislation and regulation define a schedule for ongoing training as "regularly". Many institutions choose to provide formal training annually, at least to staff in higher risk roles, incorporating changes brought in by updated regulations and relevant guidance, as well as developments in the increasingly high-profile area of terrorist financing. Whatever approach is taken for the ongoing training of employees, it is important that the rationale for that approach be documented and agreed by senior management. The basic principle to be applied when considering the training strategy is that employees most likely to identify suspicious activity, or who are otherwise engaged in key AML roles, such as relationship managers, receive more in-depth training more often than those with less exposure to these issues, such as secretarial staff.

Training, especially for frontline staff, should also include testing of understanding with escalation for staff unable to successfully attain a set pass mark. Records of training given and test scores are needed to ensure the firm is able to demonstrate that the staff have the required knowledge to discharge their obligations under financial crime legislation.

The "objective test" for the failure to report offences and the "inadequate training" defence available to staff have prompted many firms to continually monitor and review the content, delivery method and frequency of the AML and terrorist financing training provided to staff.

In addition to scheduled training, firms should seek to proactively raise awareness of financial crime. Dissemination of more immediate issues, such as changes in policies or procedures, the imposition of sanctions against individuals, organisations or materially deficient jurisdictions through the issue of staff e-mails, memos or via their intranet is one way to achieve that.

8.3 A risk-based approach to inherent FC business risk assessment

An inherent FC business risk assessment should be at the core of a firm's AML/STF efforts.[13] Firms must identify and consider their exposure to money laundering and terrorist financing risks, posed by whatever material risk factors are present for the organisation such as their customers, products, business lines, geographical location and delivery channels. An FC inherent risk assessment will determine the nature of exposure the firm faces, and therefore aid the development of effective controls to be applied in all those areas to appropriately mitigate the risks identified. For example, appropriate identification of customer risk at the on-boarding stage will determine information and documentary evidence requirements, as well as the scope and frequency of any ongoing monitoring appropriate to be confident that a specific customer is not committing a financial crime.

Firms are encouraged to use standards recommended by various domestic and international bodies but must be able to apply those standards to the firm's own risk appetite and strategy. Transparency International, FATF and JMLSG are only some of the sources commonly used by financial institutions

---

[13] FCA, *Financial crime: a guide for firms, Pt.1: a firm's guide to preventing financial crime*, April 2015.

alongside proprietary information vendors in the risk assessment process. Regulatory authorities commend others, such as the JMLSG Guidance, to the industry.

The 2007 Regulations underpin the obligation for risk assessments. Under reg.20, financial institutions are required to develop risk-sensitive policies and procedures relating to:

(a) customer due diligence measures and ongoing monitoring;
(b) reporting;
(c) record-keeping;
(d) internal control;
(e) risk assessment and management; and
(f) the monitoring and management of compliance with, and the internal communication of, such policies and procedures.[14]

Ongoing monitoring and quality assurance will therefore determine the effectiveness of a firm's systems and controls in these areas.

Those obligations are reinforced by the FCA SYSC rules, which require systems and controls in particular to:

> "identify, assess, monitor and manage money laundering risk and be comprehensive and proportionate to the nature, scale and complexity of a firm's activities".[15]

In the UK, a risk-based approach was introduced by the FSA, as part of a conscious decision to move from a rules-based to principles-based approach.[16] This requires firms to implement systems and controls on a risk-sensitive basis—driven by the actual financial crime risks manifesting and based on the nature and scope of their business activities.

---

[14] 2007 Regulations (SI 2007/2157) reg.20(1)(a)-(f).
[15] FCA Handbook SYSC 6.3.1R.
[16] FSA, *Principles-based regulation, focusing on the outcomes that matter*, April 2007.

The regulator supervises that area through visits and thematic reviews, and certain outcomes are published for guidance. Adequate assessment of money laundering risk and firms' implementation of effective controls remain key focus areas for the regulator, as demonstrated through recent enforcement action.

It is important to acknowledge that an inherent FC business risk assessment is not a one-off exercise. Changes in global standards, worldwide events or a firm's business model will affect risk profiles, and therefore financial crime risks and the associated controls required. Financial sanctions are a good example where firms must remain informed of relevant triggers and update their financial crime risk framework accordingly. Firms must also carry out internal monitoring, identifying changes in customers' profiles and assessing appropriate risk ratings on an ongoing basis.

Within the risk-based approach, the breadth and depth of customer due diligence a firm should conduct has to be aligned with the firm's assessment of the risk posed by the customer. However, the risk assessment should take into account three broad categories of due diligence provided for by legislation:

- *simplified due diligence (SDD)*—for certain specified lower-risk customers (e.g. an EEA-regulated financial institution) or lower-risk products (e.g. a child trust fund);
- *customer due diligence (CDD)*—the "standard", expected for customers that exhibit neither lower nor higher-risk characteristics; and
- *enhanced due diligence (EDD)*— for higher-risk customers, including certain specified categories of customer (e.g. politically exposed persons (PEPs) and correspondent relationships).

Although legislation and guidance help to establish which of the different levels of due diligence is appropriate for broad categories of customers, it is the responsibility of the firm to decide how it fulfils its obligations and what measures it will undertake within its own due diligence programme. That gives the firm the flexibility to tailor its processes and implement them to its risk appetite, its customers' expectations, its own particular products and delivery channels, as well as its own particular operating style. This presents the firm with the opportunity to enhance the customer experience, and reduce, or at least manage, compliance costs for low-risk customers while focusing relatively greater resources on higher-risk customers; it also presents a challenge in that the firm needs to operate risk-appropriate controls, the rationale for which the firm can demonstrate it has considered and documented.

8.3.1 Conduct client due diligence and risk monitoring

The CDD process has become the cornerstone of most institutions' AML strategies. Whereas customer identification may once have been a one-off event, CDD expands the concept of "knowing your customer" and "knowing your customer's business" into being an ongoing process that lasts throughout the life of the customer relationship.

An effective CDD programme includes risk assessment of the customer, the initial "take-on" decision, account-opening procedures, and maintaining up-to-date customer information. A firm therefore needs to have processes in place to perform each of the key elements of CDD:

- identifying the customer, verifying the customer's identity, along with any relevant beneficial owners, and where necessary verifying their identity (KYC); and
- establishing the intended nature and purpose of the customer's relationship with the firm (KYB).[17]

As noted above, a firm's CDD procedures will be aligned to, and will depend upon, an adequate risk assessment. The JMLSG Guidance goes some way to assist firms in determining the acceptable evidence required to establish and verify customer identity. It covers a wide range of customer types, and effectively establishes a benchmark by which identity can

---

[17] 2007 Regulations (SI 2007/2157) reg.5(a), (b) and (c).

be appropriately determined. Although that is useful for all firms, the specific types of evidence acceptable to an organisation and the amount of verification required need to be defined and justified in its own risk-based approach to cover CDD, SDD and EDD.

In practice, this means that as part of the due diligence process, a firm needs to have an effective means of categorising its customers according to risk. These procedures may need to vary across an institution, particularly one that operates across jurisdictions, to take account of the specific circumstances of different locations and types of product. As a minimum, a firm's CDD programme must allow for more detailed identity checks and verification for higher-risk customers. The rationale for differing levels of due diligence must be transparent and clearly articulated.

Firms must determine the factors indicating a higher risk of money laundering over and above specified risks such as PEP and correspondent relationships, and develop appropriate procedures as to when and how to apply EDD measures to any customer relationship. EDD checks will depend on the nature of a particular customer and the specific risks identified but, in any case, will involve more detailed enquiries into the source of both the customer's wealth and the origin of funds for the account.

Typically, higher-risk indicators include complex ownership structures, offshore intermediaries, political exposure, businesses that generate a high volume of cash-based transactions and opaque ownership or control (e.g. nominee shareholders or directors). It is important to acknowledge that higher-risk factors associated with a prospective relationship do not necessarily indicate that the customer is involved in financial crime, but if the inherent risks are material, due diligence will need to be significantly detailed to be confident that any risk identified is appropriately understood. The reasons for a specific ownership structure or more unusual activity may be perfectly legitimate, but firms must be able to establish the specific levels of financial crime risk associated with a customer and decide whether the relationship falls within risk appetite. Firms must also satisfy themselves that any new relationship and associated account will be able to be appropriately monitored on an ongoing basis to ensure that any financial crime risks are mitigated.

A firm's due diligence procedures also need to take account of the requirement to identify any beneficial owners behind the customer. Information required to establish the identity of a beneficial owner can be the same as that required for the customer and can therefore follow the JMLSG Guidance. It is for firms to decide in what circumstances they will *verify* the beneficial owner's identity.

Identification and verification of beneficial owners can become increasingly complex when the beneficial owner is a legal person with a further layer of beneficial owners, as can often be the case with corporate or trust structures. In addition to deciding and defining when and how beneficial owners will be verified, firms need to consider how the results of that verification will influence the risk categorisation of the actual customer.

Whenever a firm is required to verify the identity of a customer or beneficial owner, the objective is the same—to obtain confirmation from independent and reliable sources that the customer is who or what it claims to be.

Traditionally, for "face-to-face" businesses, this has been completed by reviewing and copying documents such as state-issued identity documents, utility bills, company registration documents, etc. However, an increase in the availability and apparent authenticity of false documents, a rise in the incidence of identity theft, and the growth of "non-face-to-face" businesses has meant that firms are now expected to have a more varied and flexible approach to verification. Their approach has to be aligned to their own assessment of the risk posed by the customer or beneficial owner. For example, the 2007 Regulations highlight the increased risk of false identities arising in "non-face-to-face" business and require measures to compensate for this additional risk by, for example, requesting additional documents, data or information on the customer's identity.

Under some circumstances firms can meet their verification requirements using electronic evidence or "e-verification"[18]. The use of commercial databases to confirm an entity's identity can be attractive, as it has minimum customer impact, can access multiple data sources (positive and negative), and can be conducted quickly at a low unit cost. Firms must consider whether their data provider meets the minimum criteria suggested in the JMLSG Guidance, particularly in its ability to provide the firm with a transparent record of what checks have been completed: the provision of only a "pass/fail" rating or a percentage score without a detailed understanding of what information has been confirmed should not be considered adequate. The need to establish how identity was verified lies with the firm and not with the data provider, so firms must ensure that their data provider is meeting their regulatory as well as operational business requirements. Firms must also take care not to allow such automated processes to effectively lead to financial exclusion for any potential clients.

Verification of identity for entities in overseas jurisdictions can be more difficult. Local knowledge can be helpful, both with translation of relevant documents and knowing what equivalent documents can and should be available. Possible address verification methods might involve the use of local offices to provide the necessary information, or personal visits to organisations and individuals to physically confirm an address. The requirement is for verification of an actual address, so provision, for example, of PO Box information is unlikely to be acceptable.

The appropriateness of CDD for correspondent and agency-type relationships has also attracted significant attention and many financial institutions are re-visiting how to mitigate the specific financial crime risks of correspondent relationships. Whilst in EEA jurisdictions, proof of regulated status may be

---

[18] JMLSG 5.3.34–5.3.39.

the core account opening check, clients in non-EEA jurisdictions or jurisdictions with AML legislation and controls identified as being non-equivalent or materially deficient have to be subjected to additional checks. This may include an assessment of the individual institution's AML controls, or the need to perform full CDD checks on the correspondent's customers. Maintaining correspondent relationships has been an area of focus, particularly with respect to "nested relationships" and their involvement in sanctions violations. It is increasingly an issue, in respect of the US Foreign Account Tax Compliance Act 2010 and a broader international drive for tax transparency, that banks are required to understand whether customers of their correspondents are potentially evading lawful taxes.

As part of the identification and verification process, the firm should ensure that their customers, and where appropriate, the beneficial owners, are acceptable according to the legislation to which the firm is subject and within the firm's own risk appetite. Commonly, this requires some form of screening to identify customers or beneficial owners that fall into one or more of the following categories:

- those with whom the firm is legally prohibited from doing business (e.g. government-sanctioned entities);
- those who can only be accepted by the firm subject to special conditions (e.g. politically exposed persons (PEPs) who require senior management approval and EDD); or
- those who are otherwise outside the firm's risk appetite. That may include those operating in certain business sectors (e.g. weapons production; those operating in high-risk countries; or those who may be subject to other countries' sanction regimes).

Commonly, all customers and parties associated with them are screened. In addition to considering who to screen, firms must also decide and define what information sources they will screen against, and how they will react to the results of that screening. Firms should include their rationale for screening customers, beneficial owners and controllers in the documentation supporting their overall risk-based approach. Their operating procedures should include processes for obtaining sanctions/PEP lists; re-screening existing customers when lists are updated; investigating and validating potential matches; risk-rating actual matches (e.g. current PEPs as opposed to former PEPs or their family); approving or declining customers; documenting decision and rationale and monitoring the ongoing risk exposure.

8.3.2 The nature and purpose of the relationship

The CDD process goes beyond KYC—identification and verification of customers, owners and controllers. Firms are also required to establish why the customer wants the relationship and the sort of business that the relationship will include. More than ever, it is about really starting to "know your customer's business" (KYB). Getting to know your customer at take-on is essential to the ongoing maintenance of the relationship from a commercial as well as a financial crime risk perspective. The requirement to monitor the customer's activity within the relationship is recognised as vital in the fight against financial crime as this is often where money laundering is identified. For monitoring to be a success and to identify unusual activity, institutions must understand what "normal" activity should look like. The account opening process should be the first significant step in building the customer profile, and information such as source of funds, source of wealth and the expected types and levels of transactions gathered at this stage will help to establish a picture of what "normal" activity for that customer is expected to be.

Retail savings and investment institutions have historically been much better at obtaining this broader information than others. Historically, they have completed "fact finds" on their customers, often not primarily for AML purposes, but in order to establish, among other things, the level of credit risk they are willing to take, suitable products for the customer and marketing strategies for the future. A significant by-product of those fact finds, where details were appropriately recorded and archived, was valuable customer information that could be used to help in CDD. To some extent, for affected firms, the Markets in Financial Instruments Directive[19] has presented a similar opportunity, where the information gathered to assess customer type under the directive can also be useful for AML purposes.

The key challenge to any institution is having the information that it holds about the customer available in a format, sometimes in a single place that can be used to assist in establishing what the customer's normal activity looks like. This is especially the case given the increasing complexity of customer relationships, where a customer may hold multiple products, or operate across numerous jurisdictions or across different parts of the same business. Effective management of customer information, even given the constraints of privacy and data protection laws, can be a formidable tool in helping to establish the full picture of a customer's relationship with the firm.

8.3.3 Reliance on third parties

The responsibility and associated liability for ensuring that the legislative and regulatory CDD requirements have been complied with always rests with the firm itself. However, for business efficiency, and in order to prevent a customer from having to present the same information to a number of firms or different parts of the same financial group, institutions are permitted to rely on some or all of the CDD measures carried out by a third party. The circumstances under which such reliance is acceptable are defined in the 2007 Regulations reg.17, and include, for example, where the third party is an EEA financial institution subject to equivalent AML require-ments which has consented to be relied upon by the firm.[20] The

---

[19] Directive 2004/39/EC of the European Parliament and of the Council of 21 April 2004 on markets in financial instruments amending Council Directives 85/611/EEC and 93/6/EEC and Directive 2000/12/EC of the European Parliament and of the Council and repealing Council Directive 93/22/EEC [2004] OJ L145/1.

[20] 2007 Regulations (SI 2007/2157) reg.17(2)(c).

reliance provisions in the 2007 Regulations may change once the UK Government legislates to effect changes set out in the Fourth Directive.

Although a firm *may* rely on the customer verification completed by a third party, the decision as to whether or not to do so will be based on a risk assessment of that third party, its AML programme and the risk appetite of the institution placing reliance. If the third party is within the same group as the firm, then the risk assessment should be relatively straightforward. However, if the third party operates in another jurisdiction, provides a completely different product in terms of money-laundering risk, or is known to have previously had compliance failings, the risk assessment will be more complex.

The practicalities of adequately risk-assessing third parties and their procedures are such that many institutions do not rely solely on third parties to perform their CDD. The rapidity of change in the risk landscape of the financial services sector, recent collapses of previously "safe" institutions, and the regulators' increased focus on fighting financial crime mean that in most cases, firms prefer to rely on their own verification processes rather than those of others.

Even where firms do rely on a third party's due diligence procedures, the responsibility for legal and regulatory compliance ultimately rests with the firm itself. It is imperative that institutions are able to demonstrate how they ensure that the customer's (and any beneficial owner's) identity has been verified, and that the third party understands its obligation to provide copies of the verification material on request. In addition, they need to know what level of due diligence has been carried out for each customer, as reliance on another firm's simplified due diligence will not meet the verification requirements for "standard" CDD.

Where customers are introduced between different parts of the same group, the JMLSG Guidance offers a pragmatic alternative to acquiring customers' primary documentation, by means of a certificate confirming customer identification and verification (Group Introduction Certificate). This is primarily of use for certain customer groups where it is deemed unreasonable to require identification and verification with every firm within a group, particularly where the customers are transacting on an intra-group basis, especially within the same country. Similarly, a confirmation certificate can be used between firms not in the same group. This goes some way to evidencing the third party's understanding of their obligations, and their consent to be relied upon for CDD purposes.

An alternative to the Group Introduction Certificate is for copy documentation to be passed between legal entities, divisions or departments within a group, or for different parts of a group to have access to all group customer information. However, secrecy laws and data protection issues will often mean that documentation and information cannot be passed between companies or particularly across borders. Institutions need to consider carefully how they manage the occasionally conflicting requirements of AML and data protection legislation where CDD information is shared.

8.4 Provide ongoing advice

Firms must take necessary actions to remain abreast of current and future AML/STF risks. Regulatory bodies and industry associations offer numerous publications, courses and workshops during a typical year to keep firms updated on the current and anticipated issues and events applicable to the industry. It is highly recommended for financial institutions to actively seek and maintain relationship with industry peers to share best practices and discuss the latest developments. In recent years, representatives of firms in various financial sectors have arranged regular sessions to discuss the latest updates to the regulatory approach or legislation. Not only does this help firms identify potential areas for improvements, it also ensures consistency in approach across financial sectors. Representatives of financial institutions are expected to attend and contribute to various fora and conferences to demonstrate a firm's involvement and support for such initiatives.

Firms are also encouraged to formally document this approach to demonstrate their involvement and ongoing effort to identify and implement best practices. Firms should also demonstrate how their internal systems and controls are developed as a result of participation in such sessions.

8.5 Disclosures and production orders

Suspicious activity reporting has also been in the regulatory spotlight in recent years, as there has been increased pressure on banks and others in the regulated sector to report any transactions or activity deemed suspicious. Although the pressure has increased in terms of both frequency and quality of reporting, the essentials of the system have remained the same: actual knowledge of money laundering or terrorist financing must be reported, as must activity giving reasonable grounds to suspect money laundering or terrorist financing. In addition, if a firm has prior knowledge of a transaction that gives rise to a Suspicious Activity Report (SAR) it must seek prior consent from the National Crime Agency (NCA) to conduct that transaction.

Firms covered by the 2007 Regulations must appoint a Nominated Officer (NO) who is the individual within the firm responsible for SAR investigations and deciding whether suspicious activity warrants external disclosure. In most cases, the MLRO will also be the NO. Firms are now increasing resources in that area and for larger firms, creating whole teams dedicated to investigating potential suspicious activity and the associated reporting processes. This is to encourage internal reporting, review of these reports, expedite external reporting, manage consent issues, respond to production and other orders and liaise with NCA and other law enforcement agencies.

All staff engaged in initiating, investigating and deciding on the outcome of such reports need to be conscious of "tipping off" offences and the need to minimise the risk of any leakage of information about the suspicion back to the customers. It is advisable that SARs and records relating to investigations are kept securely by the MLRO.

8.5.1 Internal reports

Identification of suspicious activity depends on the effectiveness of AML/STF procedures at all stages of a firm's control process—in particular, the adequacy of CDD information to understand what constitutes a "normal" transaction, the quality of transaction monitoring and the level and extent of training provided to staff involved in the process.

Any unusual activity or initial suspicions, identified as a result of account opening or transaction monitoring, should be recorded and investigated. In most instances, the first level of investigation will be by staff directly involved in the transaction or account opening process. It is important that direct reporting to the NO be always available, and the reporting process should be defined, documented and communicated to all staff. It remains an individual employee's responsibility to report their suspicion. It is then the responsibility of the NO to further investigate the case and determine whether to raise an external report to the NCA. It is crucial that at each stage of the process the reviews are properly documented, such that the decision to report or not to report has full rationale and is transparent for the necessary departments and/or authorities (e.g. internal audit, compliance, FCA).

It is important that the NO remains involved throughout the whole suspicious activity reporting process. However, the ability of the NO to be personally involved in the reporting of decisions becomes more difficult as the number of reports increase. Despite the potential difficulties incurred, the requirements remain unchanged and a practical way of maintaining the NO's involvement must be found.

If possible, the process could be improved if each stage were made visible to the NO, who would then have the ability to remotely interrogate each investigation, review its status and the conclusions reached. In addition, automatic feeds could be made available from the individual investigators to the NO, by way of e-mail, for questions, follow up and approval.

Detailed performance metrics, such as areas of the business which are issuing reports and the number of those which would lead to external reports, should be monitored to improve efficiency, ensure the correct allocation of resources and to enable the NO to keep senior management aware of the issues being reported. This information is also central to compiling the MLRO's annual report. At the very least, the NO should always review a sample of internal reports to assess the appropriateness of these and identify any training requirements that arise, for example, where reported cases are not actually suspicious and the actions of staff suggest fundamental misunderstandings of AML requirements.

8.5.2 External disclosures

The NO will ultimately decide whether suspicions raised in the SAR must be escalated to the NCA.

Transactions requiring consent from the NCA pose a continuing challenge to many institutions, having the potential to raise the risks of criminal prosecution through the "tipping off" offence, civil litigation for breach of contract, and ongoing customer management concerns. Stopping or delaying a customer's transaction can be problematic, potentially bringing the NO into conflict with the business, the customer and law enforcement.

This has been highlighted by the landmark case of *Shah v HSBC*[21], in which Mr Shah claimed for damages against the bank. In September 2006, HSBC filed a SAR, resulting in a delayed transaction, whilst HSBC were waiting for consent to

---

[21] *Shah v HSBC Private Bank (UK) Ltd* [2012] EWHC 1283 (QB); [2013] Bus. L.R. D38.

proceed from the Serious Organised Crime Agency. Mr Shah's account was frozen and this resulted in an alleged loss of over US $300 million. Mr Shah sued to recover the loss. In May 2012 the court dismissed his claim. This means that banks are correct to not proceed with transactions if there is reasonable suspicion of a financial crime. Where a pending consent request is subsequently given, this does not create a liability for the original decision not to proceed.

All relevant staff within an institution must be made aware of the consent regime, and the importance of escalating internal reports which may require consent at the earliest opportunity. The NO therefore needs to ensure that the facilities for accessing and submitting internal reports are accessible and comprehensible to relevant staff, and that there are means of identifying and prioritising internal reports which may result in considerations of consent. That emphasises the importance of firms in providing detailed tailored training for staff as noted in 9.2.2, which is undertaken on a regular basis and embeds the understanding of the risks and procedures for escalating suspicions.

The NCA operates according to the statutory deadlines conferred in POCA 2002. The response can be expected after seven working days from when the SAR is filed. The NCA can allow a further 31 calendar days to investigate should the consent be declined and further investigation required. The NO must track the NCA's response to the consent request as well as record the action taken in blocking the transaction and subsequently acting on the NCA's response. This is an area where an effective case handling system, whether electronic or manual, is essential.

The NCA commented on the quality of SARs and delays to consent requests caused by missing, often basic, information. As a result, from 1 October 2014 the NCA reserved the right to reject consent requests should the standard information not be provided.[22]

---

[22] NCA, *Closure of cases requesting consent*, September 2014.

It is important that all processes are handled in a consistent way across the business which can significantly reduce the risks of committing the offences of "tipping off" or prejudicing an investigation that could otherwise arise from inexperienced staff dealing with SARs and consent requests on an infrequent basis.

8.5.3 Production orders

Law enforcement agencies can obtain and use a production order requesting access to information required to investigate a criminal activity. Production orders are often granted as part of a confiscation, money laundering or civil recovery investigation.

A production order requires firms to give specified material (or access to that material) to investigating officers.

Investigating officers can retain the necessary information provided for as long as required, or (if the material is needed for legal proceedings and would otherwise be unavailable) until those proceedings are concluded. Typically production orders are applied without notice.

A production order may be used in conjunction with an order to grant entry under POCA 2002 s.347.

Firms must comply with production orders within the specified timeframe, normally seven days, but the order granted can be varied to either a longer or shorter period for compliance.

8.6 Develop financial crime intelligence

The increased threat to security in the constantly evolving "borderless" global environment pressures firms to respond to the approach taken by suspected money launderers they are attempting to detect. Increasing the sharing of information globally and encouraging cross-border co-operation whilst observing varying data protection and bank secrecy provisions may be a significant aid in this area. The increasing importance of tax transparency and the expectation that banks will assist governments also makes this a developing area.

A greater awareness of the global financial crime environment, including any immediate changes to the financial crime environment which can have a great impact on the firm, is important. Examples of relatively short notice and complex changes include economic sanctions applied in respect of Russia and Ukraine.

To manage both operational and financial crime risk, firms need to have a greater understanding of potential change and subsequent impact, and where possible anticipate events. To enable the ease and speed of communication, it is important that infrastructure and technology are "fit for purpose" and updated on a regular basis. This will also assist firms in taking the necessary steps to effectively manage financial crime risk and keep pace with evolving regulatory expectations. Currently, some firms' systems are less efficient in managing the financial crime risk environment. However, recent investment in staffing levels may increase the focus on technology as a method to reduce the apparently inexorable rise in financial crime compliance costs.

8.6.1 Financial Crime Intelligence Unit (FCIU)

FCIU is the part of the financial institution which ensures that information held by the bank and information from external sources is used effectively and efficiently to detect and mitigate financial crime. It would usually include the "horizon scanning" to ensure banks' policies and procedures remain in line with evolving regulatory expectations. A core purpose of an FCIU is to ensure that information flow within an organisation and from external sources is adequate and appropriate to support a FCC framework, and that staff charged with investigating potential financial crime have the necessary information available to enable an investigation to proceed swiftly and definitively.

To develop a strong FCIU team and ensure they have a solid foundation for training, understanding and growth, a clear definition of AML/STF intelligence is important. This would provide a base that could then be incorporated into the strategy for the function, the business and the broader risk management decision-making process. In addition, clear intelligence gathering and dissemination processes enable decision-makers to effectively and appropriately incorporate it in to the firms risk assessment for efficient decisions.

The FCIU role includes remaining current with regulatory changes or enforcements and changing typologies identified in use by financial criminals. To that end, it is important to have ongoing and proactive research, incorporating varied industry sources with well documented outputs. This should be performed by members of staff that have undertaken specialised training and have the necessary skills and technical knowledge.

Once the information has been gathered, analysis should be performed in the context of data and information already known to the firm. If appropriate technology is available, this can include a level of automation. Where possible, analysis should lead to effective insight to better understand known risks and identify both emerging trends and horizon issues.

The real value of information gathered and insights obtained within an FCIU research team is only revealed when in the hands of staff able to use it to prevent, detect, deter or investigate potential financial crime. It is therefore essential that the FCIU external communication and information distribution plans are well known and trusted by all parts of the enterprise. The sharing of intelligence should help tighten controls across the wider financial crime risk management framework. Furthermore, if information can be shared between peer institutions, relevant industry groups and, potentially, intelligence agencies, it will add to the overall drive in society to limit such activities.

The FCIU and the outputs generated can also make a valuable contribution to understanding the current inherent financial crime risk facing a business area and therefore aid in focussing often scarce resources to strengthen and enhance controls in the areas of the business where they can have the greatest impact in fighting financial crime.

The level and nature of communication between financial services firms and law enforcement can also be improved by an effective FCIU. SARs can be completed with adequate reference information and clearly labelled with the nature of suspicion and the evidence to support the suspicion. Production order responses can be made with as much contextual information as bank secrecy restrictions and client confidentiality permit. It is important that firms learn to communicate as openly as possible and work more closely with both domestic and international law enforcement agencies. Transparency in that area and a willingness to work together will provide an effective tool in the fight against financial crime.

Firms, where possible, should aim to perform regular thorough investigations and forensic deep dives and have this undertaken by specialised teams that have had the necessary training to ensure any crucial factors that could increase potential risk are detected and flagged immediately.

Overall, the sharing of information gathered and the openness in which intelligence is communicated globally is still seen as a challenge for firms. This will look to improve the quality of information, the depth and speed it is able to be analysed and interpreted and enable a more effective and global mechanism in the deterrence prevention and detection of financial crime.

8.7 Report and manage information

Management information is essential for managers to be able to understand and control financial crime risk in terms of both measuring exposure and monitoring the effectiveness of controls in place to mitigate identified risks.

Among other things, it can be used for trend analysis, forecasting and as an input to shaping a firm's financial crime risk profile to ensure adherence to their risk appetite.

> "[Management information] should provide senior management with sufficient information to understand the financial crime risks to which their firm is exposed."[23]

Typical AML related management information collected by a financial institution includes:

- the number of SARs;
- money laundering incidents;
- present and emerging financial crime risks;
- regulatory developments;
- an overview of the effectiveness of a firm's financial crime systems and controls; and
- the number and nature of business relationships deemed to be higher risk.[24]

Management information collation in large institutions should be through an automated process where possible and produced on a regular basis. Reporting should be targeted and trends should be proactively identified and investigated. Some firms may consider a risk-based approach, where certain services are monitored more closely in instances involving riskier products or solutions.

In large, established financial institutions, with comprehensive controls dashboard reports, management information is commonly produced on a daily basis and there is a process to ensure all stakeholders receive the reports as required. Furthermore, the MI reported to different governance committees is defined for the purpose of the forum within an overall programme. Individual committees with clear roles and responsibilities to monitor the progress of any significant

---

[23] FCA, *Financial crime: a guide for firms, Pt 1: A firm's guide to preventing financial crime*, April 2015.

[24] FCA, *Financial crime: a guide for firms, Pt 1: A firm's guide to preventing financial crime*, April 2015.

remedial programmes are reported to senior management and the deficiencies are proactively addressed. However, these processes should be appropriate for the type of business.

The MLRO report on the operation and effectiveness of the firm's systems and controls to combat money laundering on an annual basis should explain what MI is used in the FC Framework.[25] It should contain consistent key management information and Key Performance Indicators (KPIs) to allow senior management to track changes in the performance of AML/STF controls, and monitor for change in the inherent financial crime risks that the customer base poses to the firm.

8.7.1 Record keeping

The compilation and maintenance of adequate records is a key feature in the development of a comprehensive FC framework of AML/STF systems and controls.

> "Firms must keep copies or references to evidence the customer's identity for five years after the business relationship ends; and transactional documents for five years from the completion of the transaction. In circumstances where a firm is relied on by others to perform due diligence checks, it must keep its records *of those checks for five years from the date it was relied on. Firms must also keep records sufficient to demonstrate to us that their Customer Due Diligence (CDD) measures are appropriate in view of the risk of money laundering and terrorist financing.*"[26]

Record-keeping requirements tend to place greatest importance on account opening and CDD information. A firm's records should cover customer information, transactions, internal and external suspicion reports, MLRO reports, information not acted upon, training, compliance monitoring and

---

[25] FCA Handbook SYSC 6.3.7G.
[26] FCA, *Financial crime: a guide for firms, Pt 1: A firm's guide to preventing financial crime,*
April 2015.

information about the effectiveness of training.[27] Many firms find it useful to incorporate the random sampling of information and records as part of an internal audit or compliance monitoring programme.

Firms typically use various means, both electronic and paper-based, to verify the identity of their clients. Whatever the method used, it is important that the documentation can be produced in the required format and in the required time period for review by the firm or an external authority. Indeed, as well as verifying the content and quality of information, firms should also monitor the time taken to produce such information against the requirements contained in POCA 2002 (e.g. seven days in the case of a production order). This may be a particular issue where firms outsource document storage, or information is contained on remote or inaccessible servers. Records must be kept in a medium that allows the storage of information to be accessible for future reference by the appropriate regulator[28] so that the regulator can access them readily and reconstitute each key stage of processing of each transaction. Furthermore, it must be possible for any corrections/ amendments to be easily ascertained and it must not be possible to manipulate or alter the records.

8.8 Conduct assurance and monitoring activities

One of the key elements of the risk-based approach involves institutions checking that the controls they have put in place are actually operating effectively and addressing their money laundering and terrorist financing risks. Most firms operate a three-tier level of oversight for their AML/STF programmes: the business is responsible for day-to-day monitoring and quality control; the MLRO and/or compliance oversees these operations, driving consistency across the business while carrying out their own compliance testing or reviews; and finally, internal and external audit carry out focused testing

---

[27] JMLSG 8.6.

[28] FCA Handbook, *https://www.handbook.fca.org.uk/?definition=G2972* [Accessed 6 October 2015].

over both the operational level and the MLRO, including his/her oversight responsibilities.

In large financial institutions, Internal Audit should carry out a periodic review of AML/STF processes with comprehensive and regular testing on all aspects of the AML/STF compliance function. Systems should also regularly be tested for effectiveness and monitoring programmes should include thematic reviews across the firm focusing on defined controls related to AML/STF.

The assurance process will normally involve a mixture of management information reporting and risk-based process testing. All monitoring and assurance work has one main goal—to inform the MLRO and senior management of the operational effectiveness of the AML/STF controls in place, hence it is vital that the results of all such work be adequately recorded and appropriately escalated. Whilst in smaller firms, an annual MLRO report may suffice, most firms operate some form of AML compliance reporting on at least a quarterly if not a monthly basis.

Data feed assurance should be performed on a periodic basis to ensure all relevant data is being passed to screening systems. Client systems should also be monitored to identify changes which may be leveraged to enhance the screening systems.

Institutions should avoid using compliance staff to undertake what should be operational roles at the expense of them fulfilling a compliance oversight role. For example, if compliance staff complete or finalise the CDD process, there needs to be some additional independent oversight of their work, as they cannot impartially monitor or assure their own work. Additionally, as the compliance and internal audit functions should play an important role in making sure that appropriate AML procedures are in place and operating effectively, their ability to fulfil this requirement is coming under increased regulatory scrutiny. Many firms have recruited AML specialists into those areas, or created specialised audit teams to fulfil those roles, generally improving their effectiveness and demonstrating a high degree of rigour in their monitoring and testing functions.

Where monitoring and assurance identifies weaknesses or deficiencies, firms should have appropriate means of recording and tracking the remediation of those issues through to resolution. Once an issue has been identified, the FCA would expect to see a documented plan to close the issue and take any other remedial action, and this is a key area where senior management should be involved. Larger firms often operate an "AML oversight" forum where issues can be discussed, problems shared and solutions devised, but that is not always practical for smaller firms where there is not an internal AML network to draw on for advice. In those circumstances, AML professionals in smaller firms have found some of the industry-wide trade associations and specialist AML forums to be a useful means of sharing and developing best practice.

> "The MLRO should report on the outcome of any relevant quality assurance or internal audit reviews of the firm's AML/STF processes, as well as the outcome of any review of the firm's risk assessment procedures."[29]

8.9 Make continuous improvement

The process for obtaining AML advice should be fully documented and understood by all staff. Representatives of the financial institution should actively seek this advice to aid in the development and enhancement of industry standards. Representatives of the firm should also actively engage with key industry bodies to ensure cohesive and constructive dialogue with other industry peers.

Change projects are typically initiated in response to identified risks, changes in policy or regulation and observations of opportunities for improvement. A number of financial institutions have also recently initiated change management projects

---

[29] JMLSG 3.35.

and risk mitigation programmes following regulatory failings, usually under the direction of the relevant Regulator. Under the Financial Services and Markets Act 2000 s.166:

> "The appropriate regulator (FCA/PRA) may, by giving a written notice, itself appoint a skilled person to provide it with a report, or require any of the following persons to provide it with a report by a skilled person."[30]

Those projects should have a strategic aspiration, target end state and work breakdown structure at the programme level. At a project level, workstreams should be established with appropriate planning and budgetary documentation. Milestones should be tracked appropriately, with programme assurance management underpinning this to assure delivery and strong outcomes.

To ensure that the change projects are effective, there is often a dedicated change team made up from skilled resources, to manage changes through to implementation with the larger changes managed through formal programmes of work. The changes should be fully documented and assessed for the impact on governance, people, process and technology components in line with prescribed governance and change implementation methodologies.

8.10 Conclusion

The FC Control Framework should be a comprehensive structure to enable transparent governance of all aspects of the operation of a financial institution to prevent, detect, deter financial crime activity and where such activity is suspected, escalate, investigate and resolve the suspicion.

Clarity around the framework puts the financial institution on a solid footing to understand FC risk, apply proportionate

---

[30] FCA Handbook, SUP 5.2.1G.

controls and handle events that give rise to suspicion that an account or transaction may represent a potential financial crime.

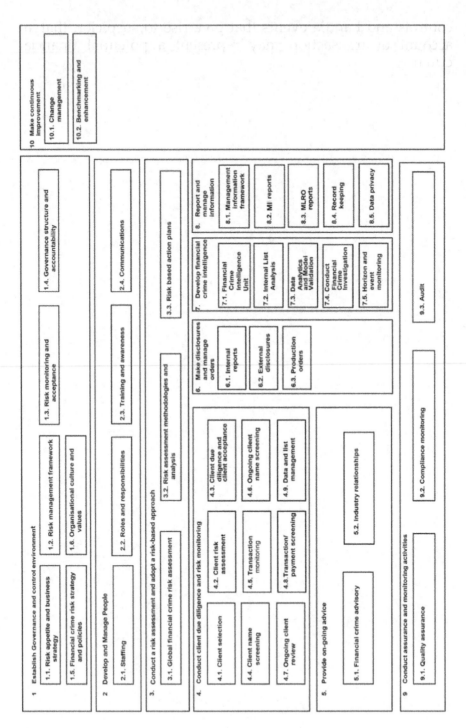

Figure: Sample Financial Crime Control Framework

Chapter 9

The Application of the AML Legislation to International Transactions

Paul Marshall

Richard Jones QC

What have we here? Darkness and mud. Aristophanes

This Chapter provides an outline of the international dimension that is characteristic of money laundering and its context, and then a brief further discussion of some important aspects, including: (i) the application of UK regulatory requirements to subsidiaries and related entities where these are located outside the UK. There is a short discussion of the vexed issue under English law of the criminal liability of corporations and unincorporated associations. (ii) The approach adopted by the courts of the UK to the interpretation of extra-territorial provisions under POCA 2002, the significant difficulty that these have presented, and the difference between the substantive money laundering offences and the interpretative provisions under POCA 2002 s.340. This includes a recent instance where the Court of Appeal has discovered a seemingly novel, but potentially important, approach to extra-territorial criminal jurisdiction over acts carried out outside the UK. (iii) Some conceptual problems in "transposition", related to the idea of "single criminality" (the legal hypothesis that predicate conduct under POCA 2002 is treated as though it took place in the UK, when that is in fact not the case, for determining whether it would have constituted an offence had it done so) and (subject to minor qualification), whether the relevant facts would disclose an offence under the laws of the place where the act in question actually occurred.

There must be a degree of sympathy for the legislature in providing, as it had to, for the complexities of an international dimension in the AML regime. Equally, the courts have had to balance competing policy interests and resolve inevitable tensions when applying those provisions, which are by no means straightforward. Nonetheless, it is the practitioners in this field who have to do their best to interpret the legislation and to make sense of the decided cases, neither of which is a simple task.

9.1   Introduction

Possibly the greatest single driver of the rapid development of money laundering law, and the remarkable convergence of international domestic criminal legislation as well as representing a triumph of so-called "soft law", is the work of the FATF in its 40 Recommendations. Recommendation 3 (formerly 1) provides that

> "Countries should criminalise money laundering on the basis of the Vienna Convention and the Palermo Convention. Countries should apply the crime of money laundering to all serious offences, with a view to including the widest range of predicate offences."[1]

The February 2012 40 Recommendations were accepted by the EU Commission and are the basis for the Fourth EU Directive (the Fourth Directive).[2] The Interpretative Note to Recommendation 3 provides that:

---

[1]   The qualification having been from time to time lost sight of—see, for example, *Dare v CPS* [2012] EWHC 2074 Admin; [2013] Crim. L.R. 413, in which Bean J rightly dismissed a misconceived attempt to use POCA 2002 s.328 as a sort of "catch-all"—which concerned the taking of a motor vehicle!

[2]   Directive (EU) 2015/849 of the European Parliament and of the Council of 20 May 2015 on the prevention of the use of the financial system for the purposes of money laundering or terrorist financing, amending Regulation (EU) No 648/2012 of the European Parliament and of the Council, and repealing Directive

" 1.   Countries should apply the crime of money launder-
        ing to all serious offences, with a view to including
        the widest range of predicate offences. Predicate
        offences may be described by reference to all offences;
        or to a threshold linked either to a category of serious
        offences; or to the penalty of imprisonment applicable
        to the predicate offence (threshold approach); or to a
        list of predicate offences; or a combination of these
        approaches.

   2.   Where countries apply a threshold approach, predi-
        cate offences should, at a minimum, comprise all
        offences that fall within the category of serious
        offences under their national law, or should include
        offences that are punishable by a maximum penalty of
        more than one year's imprisonment, or, for those
        countries that have a minimum threshold for offences
        in their legal system, predicate offences should
        comprise all offences that are punished by a minimum
        penalty of more than six months imprisonment.

   3.   Whichever approach is adopted, each country should,
        at a minimum, include a range of offences within each
        of the designated categories of offences. The offence of
        money laundering should extend to any type of
        property, regardless of its value, that directly or
        indirectly represents the proceeds of crime. When
        proving that property is the proceeds of crime, it
        should not be necessary that a person be convicted of
        a predicate offence.

   4.   Predicate offences for money laundering should
        extend to conduct that occurred in another country,
        which constitutes an offence in that country, and
        which would have constituted a predicate offence had
        it occurred domestically. Countries may provide that
        the only prerequisite is that the conduct would have
        constituted a predicate offence, had it occurred
        domestically.[3]

2005/60/EC of the European Parliament and of the Council and Commission
Directive 2006/70/EC [2015] OJ L141/73.

[3] i.e. the test adopted by the UK, namely "single" as distinct from "double"
criminality (see further below for the difficulty this presents in "transposition").

5. Countries may provide that the offence of money laundering does not apply to persons who committed the predicate offence, where this is required by fundamental principles of their domestic law."

Possibly the most intractable issue arising from the internationalising of money laundering law has been how to criminalise conduct that relates to property derived from the original (predicate) criminal conduct (criminal offence) where that conduct took place outside the jurisdiction over which, *ex hypothesi*, the domestic courts have no jurisdiction. (More recently, the Court of Appeal has developed a novel and doubtful jurisdiction in connection with the place where the money laundering offence itself occurs—see *R. v Rogers*[4] below.) As will be seen, the problem presents conceptual, substantive and evidential difficulties—quite apart from problems of statutory interpretation that have eluded unanimity even at the level of the Supreme Court. The reason for this, in grossly oversimplified terms, is that the criminal jurisdiction is typically concerned with domestic conduct and, outside public international law, historically has not engaged with conduct beyond the boundaries of the state.

To illustrate the problem to which money laundering law is addressed, following the overthrow of President Bakiyev in April 2010, it appeared that Kyrgyzstan's Asia Universal Bank (AUB) had been used for large scale money laundering carried out through corporate entities that included companies registered in the UK. One such company had a Russian shareholder who, it much later emerged, had died some years before the company was incorporated. Around US $700 million appeared to have flowed through the company's bank accounts at AUB. It had no discernible business in the UK and failed to file any statutory accounts. (Typically, around half a million companies are removed from the register of companies annually and a significant proportion of these have never filed accounts.) Reports suggested that several UK registered companies that had bank accounts with AUB, shared nominee directors in the

---

[4] *R. v Rogers (Bradley David)* [2014] EWCA Crim 1680; [2015] 1 W.L.R. 1017; [2014] 2 Cr. App. R. 32 (p.516).

Seychelles and had Russian owners who purported to have held annual company meetings in London, on the same day at the same location, despite one of them being dead. Some US $1.2 billion flowed through the accounts of just three of those companies before being dissolved. None filed statutory accounts.[5] This illustrates the fundamental point, long ago emphasised by the Organisation for Economic Co-operation and Development (OECD), that most money laundering is carried out through corporate entities where the nominal (legal) and actual (beneficial) interests are divided, often by jurisdiction and typically through secrecy jurisdictions, and disguised. It remains curious that English company law has been particularly well-suited to separating and disguising corporate ownership and control, and the same has been true of English trust law. Disguise is fundamental to the money laundering process. It is no accident that the first two of the substantive offences under POCA 2002 s.327 are those of *concealing* and *disguising* criminal property. In principle, the greater the complexity and opacity of transactions, the more difficult it is for laundering to be detected, let alone successfully prosecuted.

The intractable problem that AUB and its interconnectedness with other financial institutions represented was a recognised structural difficulty that was addressed by the Financial Action Task Force (FATF) under its 2012 Recommendations 24 and 25 which provide:

> **"24. Transparency and beneficial ownership of legal persons**
>
> Countries should take measures to prevent the misuse of legal persons for money laundering or terrorist financing. Countries should ensure that there is adequate, accurate and timely information on the beneficial ownership and control of legal persons that can be obtained or accessed in a timely fashion by competent authorities. In particular, countries that have legal persons that are able to issue

---

[5] A more detailed analysis is to be found at: *https://www.globalwitness.org/sites/ default/files/library/GraveSecrecy_singlepagefinal.pdf* [Accessed 29 September 2015].

bearer shares or bearer share warrants, or which allow nominee shareholders or nominee directors, should take effective measures to ensure that they are not misused for money laundering or terrorist financing. Countries should consider measures to facilitate access to beneficial ownership and control information by financial institutions and DNFBPs [Designated Non-Financial Businesses and Professions] undertaking the requirements set out in Recommendations 10 and 22.

25. Transparency and beneficial ownership of legal arrangements

Countries should take measures to prevent the misuse of legal arrangements for money laundering or terrorist financing. In particular, countries should ensure that there is adequate, accurate and timely information on express trusts, including information on the settlor, trustee and beneficiaries that can be obtained or accessed in a timely fashion by competent authorities. Countries should consider measures to facilitate access to beneficial ownership and control information by financial institutions and DNFBPs undertaking the requirements set out in Recommendations 10 and 22."

Those recommendations were enthusiastically endorsed by the UK at the G8 Summit at Loch Erne in June 2013 and have now been given effect by the EU under the Fourth Directive. Their implementation will represent a significant hardening of the UK's AML regime so far as abuse of UK corporate legal structures and trusts have long caused it to be, paradoxically, a money laundering jurisdiction of choice. The framework for how that is to be done is provided by the Fourth Directive which is required to be implemented in the UK by 26 June 2017. Those requirements represent major and far-reaching changes in company and trust law. For example, historically, English company legislation has been wholly indifferent to beneficial ownership: the Companies Act 2006 (like its predecessors) is almost exclusively concerned with (registered) legal ownership (the legal holder of shares). Part of the rationale is that beneficial ownership has been easy to transfer (because an oral agreement will be effective to create a beneficial interest) and not easy to identify. The range and complexity of the changes that will be effected by implementation of the Fourth Directive are already to be seen, hidden within the depths of the Small Business, Enterprise and Employment Act 2015 and the Deregulation Act 2015, both enacted in March 2015, which together run to in excess of 900 pages of new legislation. It can be said with some confidence that company and trust law in the United Kingdom will be substantially changed by the Fourth Directive.

Money laundering is characteristically an international phenomenon and activity, with the flow of illicit funds across borders according to some estimates ranking third after foreign exchange and oil revenues. Typically, the criminal act from which property is derived will have occurred in a different jurisdiction from the eventual location of that (tainted) property. It is therefore unfortunate, to say the least, that the legislative measures taken to address the extra-territorial dimension of money laundering, though robust, have been so ill-drafted and the Parliamentary intention so poorly and opaquely expressed. The historical explanation for this is that when POCA 2002 was introduced in February 2003, it was treated substantially as merely a consolidating statute—albeit an important one. But the legislation that it consolidated was new, all of it dating from later than 1980,[6] and came from two separate sources, on the one hand, domestic criminal statutes that had been the subject of meticulous consideration by the Law Commission over more than 20 years, and on the other, provisions that gave effect to international obligations including under EU law and treaty obligations (notably the Vienna Convention). Both impacted, in different ways, on long-established common law principles, notably that the territorial scope of the criminal law, subject to notable exceptions such as piracy, was traditionally domestic in its ambit (that also being a principle of international law and comity). So while it is true to say that POCA 2002 was a consolidating statute, the legislation

---

[6] The entire corpus of money laundering law in the United Kingdom post-dates the House of Lords' decision in *R. v Cuthbertson* [1981] A.C. 470 HL at 485.

that it consolidated in many instances had received insufficient scrutiny, with far-reaching consequences.

Should that proposition require support, it is strikingly illustrated by contrasting views and understanding of Parliamentary intention expressed at the highest level of the judiciary by justices of the Supreme Court. The important decision in *Serious Organised Crime Agency v Perry*[7] reversed the unanimous decision of the Court of Appeal (Hooper, Tomlinson and Maurice Kay LJJ).[8] In a judgment of a nine-judge court, Lord Phillips PSC, having reviewed the structure of POCA 2002 Pt 5 (Civil Recovery), held:

> "In summary, apart from the definition of property in Section 316(4) and the enigmatic section 286, there is nothing in Part 5, from first to last, that suggests that its application extends to property outside England and Wales, Scotland and Northern Ireland[9] ... Had Parliament, or those responsible for drafting POCA [2002], intended Part 5 confiscation to extend to property outside the United Kingdom they would surely have included provisions parallel to section 74. The fact that they did not do so strongly suggests that there was no intention that Part 5 should have extra territorial effect."[10]

Six other Justices of the Supreme Court agreed. However, in a dissenting minority joint speech, Lord Judge CJ and Lord Clarke of Stone-cum-Ebony, a former Master of the Rolls, said that, while POCA 2002 is "poorly drafted", its objective is clear.[11] They expressed the view that: "[t]here is in our opinion nothing in the scheme or language of the Act which supports the conclusion that Part 5 is limited to property within the

---

[7] *Serious Organised Crime Agency v Perry* [2012] UKSC 35; [2013] 1 A.C. 182; [2013] 1 Cr. App. R. 6 (p.61).

[8] Upholding the judgment of Foskett J who declined to set aside orders made by HH Judge Kay QC (sitting as a judge of the High Court). The ineluctable conclusion from the Supreme Court's decision is that five judges, three in the Court of Appeal and two in the High Court, had incorrectly interpreted the territorial effect of Pt 5 of POCA 2002.

[9] *Perry* [2012] UKSC 35 at [50].

[10] *Perry* [2012] UKSC 35 at [56].

[11] *Perry* [2012] UKSC 35 at [160].

jurisdiction …". That is not an isolated instance of the Supreme Court reversing the Court of Appeal on the meaning and effect of POCA 2002. Similarly, as recently as April 2015, the Supreme Court reversed the decision of the Court of Appeal[12] in *R. v GH*[13] explaining that for the purposes of POCA 2002 s.328 (arrangements) "criminal property" meant property that *already had the quality of being criminal property* as defined by s.340 by reason of conduct distinct[14] from the conduct alleged to constitute the actus reus of the money laundering offence itself. It is troubling that 12 years after the introduction of POCA 2002, the meaning of a fundamental provision needed to be explained by the Supreme Court—reversing the unanimous opposite conclusion reached by the Court of Appeal. The propensity to collapse the distinction between the predicate and money laundering offences continues to cause problems as discussed further below. If the most senior judges in the land find it difficult to agree on the meaning and effect of central statutory provisions under POCA 2002, it is no surprise that those subject to its complex and onerous provisions, required to implement it as "gatekeepers" to the financial system, have found its meaning and effect as a guide to action difficult and at times intractable.

While the object of POCA 2002 may be clear enough, it is elementary natural law, and also in human rights law under the ECHR and in EU jurisprudence, that law which exposes the individual to criminal penalties is required to be clear and certain (see further below). POCA 2002 falls short. It is worth noting that the Supreme Court's decision in *Perry* was not welcomed by Parliament, and the effect of the decision was reversed by the Crime and Courts Act 2013 s.48[15]—a provision that, exceptionally, was provided with retrospective effect. The approach of the Supreme Court in *Perry* nevertheless remains illuminating because it reveals how the court will (or should) approach the question of the extra-territorial criminal reach of POCA 2002. It is no comfort that yet further uncertainty (and

---

[12] *R. v G* [2013] EWCA Crim 2237 (Lloyd Jones LJ, Irwin and Green JJ).
[13] *R. v GH* [2015] UKSC 24; [2015] 1 W.L.R. 2126; [2015] 2 Cr. App. R. 12 (p.195).
[14] i.e. the "predicate conduct".
[15] Which among other things replaced SOCA by the NCA.

indeed risk) has recently been introduced by the Court of Appeal decision in *R. v Rogers*[16] in 2014. That decision may be doubted as to its correctness, but it has wide-ranging implications and effects as referred to in a little more detail below. While the discussion is aimed at those in the regulated sector grappling with the consequences of international transactions, inevitably there is some overlap with the principles applicable to purely domestic transactions. That said, it will be evident from this Chapter that the problems of applying the relevant rules and statutory provisions cause particular problems for those with an international dimension to their practices.

Some of the discussion focuses on the criminal consequences which can flow from breach of the duties imposed by POCA 2002. That is not to underestimate other consequences which may follow, whether these are reputational, regulatory or client relations. Even if an adviser decides that there is no obligation to make a SAR in respect of a particular transaction, because of the application of the evidential rule of privileged communication, it does not always follow that the adviser would or should continue to act in the same transaction.

Problems caused by the extra-territorial aspects of POCA 2002 have given rise to considerable debate and commentary. Further guidance may be obtained, in particular, on the websites maintained by the Joint Money Laundering Steering Group (JMLSG) that provides guidance to the BBA[17] by the Law Society[18] (updated in October 2013 following creation of the NCA and recently updated in June 2015 to include a policy update following the introduction of the Fourth Directive) and by the Institute of Chartered Accountants of England and Wales.[19] The JMLSG Guidance originally received Treasury approval on 18 December 2007. In its revised form, it was published on 20 November 2013 and updated in November

---

[16] *R. v Rogers (Bradley David)* [2014] EWCA Crim 1680; [2015] 1 W.L.R. 1017; [2014] Cr. App. R. 32 (p.516).

[17] See the JMLSG website *http://www.jmlsg.org.uk* [Accessed 29 September 2015].

[18] *http://www.lawsociety.org.uk/support-services/advice/practice-notes/aml/* [Accessed 29 September 2015].

[19] *http://www.icaew.com/en/technical/legal-and-regulatory/money-laundering/uk-law-and-guidance* [Accessed 29 September 2015].

2014. The guidance is some 359 pages long and, like the other guidance provided by the Law Society and ICAEW, is of particular importance under Pt 7 of POCA 2002[20] and the 2007 Regulations.[21] An important question for practitioners is whether a particular jurisdiction can be considered to have equivalent AML and CFT measures in place. A note was originally published by the JMLSG on 8 August 2008 dealing with jurisdictions considered to be equivalent and not equivalent and that was updated under Pt III section 2 of the updated guidance in 2014. The JMLSG equivalence list refers to the list that was published by the EU Commission in June 2012.[22] The JMLSG guidance provides that:

> "Although firms may initially presume equivalence, significant variations may exist in the precise measures (and in the timing of their introduction) that have been taken to transpose the money laundering directive (and its predecessors) into national laws and regulations. Moreover, the standards of compliance monitoring in respect of credit and financial institutions will also vary. Where firms have substantive information which indicates that a presumption of equivalence cannot be sustained, either in general or for particular products, they will need to consider whether their procedures should be enhanced to take account of this information."[23]

Detailed consideration of the JMLSG Guidance Notes and other available guidance is beyond the scope of the present discussion. In summer 2014, the FCA published a list of countries considered to represent a heightened risk of money laundering and financial crime. The list was later withdrawn in response to representations to the FCA including on the methodology adopted, and it seems that there is no intention on the part of the FCA to publish a revised list. The list of

---

[20] POCA 2002 s.330 in particular.
[21] Money Laundering Regulations 2007 (SI 2007/2157) reg.41(2).
[22] *http://ec.europa.eu/internal_market/company/docs/financial-crime/3rd-country-equivalence-list_en.pdf* [Accessed 29 September 2015].
[23] *Equivalent jurisdictions*, section 2.2, *www.jmlsg.org.uk/download/8201* [Accessed 29 September 2015].

countries identified by the FCA as representing a significant risk of financial crime is set out in the footnote below.[24]

9.2 Application of POCA 2002 and relevant regulations to overseas branches, offices and subsidiaries of UK entities

Two issues are considered here: the general principles of law so far as they concern the application of domestic legislation to those outside the jurisdiction, both UK nationals and non-nationals; second, the money laundering legislation as representing a significant statutory derogation from those principles.

With certain limited exceptions, English criminal law is local in its effect and is not concerned with crimes committed abroad. That broad proposition was restated in *Ex p. Pinochet (No.3).*[25] Accordingly, insofar as POCA 2002 creates criminal offences in accordance with normal principles, those offences can be committed only by those within the jurisdiction of the courts of the UK. However, as discussed at section 10.4, extra-territorial acts are clearly relevant to criminal liability under POCA 2002 for offences relating to money laundering.

Legislation does not occur in a legal vacuum, but depends upon the more general legal structure in which the enactment

---

[24] The following countries were categorised by the FCA as high risk: Afghanistan, Algeria, Angola, Argentina, Azerbaijan, Bahrain, Bangladesh, Belarus, Benin, Bolivia, Bosnia and Herzegovina, Brazil, Bulgaria, Burundi, Cambodia, Cayman Islands, China, Colombia, Republic of the Congo, Democratic Republic of Congo, Cuba, Djibouti, Dominican Republic, Ecuador, Egypt, Equatorial Guinea, Eritrea, Ethiopia, Fiji, Gabon, Guatemala, Guinea, Guinea-Bissau, Haiti, Honduras, India, Indonesia, Iran, Iraq, Israel, Ivory Coast (Cote d'Ivoire), Jamaica, Kazakhstan, Kenya, Korea (North), Kosovo, Kuwait, Kyrgyzstan, Laos, Latvia, Lebanon, Liberia, Libya, Malaysia, Mali, Mexico, Montenegro , Morocco, Myanmar, Nauru, Nepal, Nicaragua, Niger, Nigeria, Pakistan, Palestine, Panama, Romania, Russia, Saudi Arabia, Serbia, Seychelles, Sierra Leone, Somalia, South Africa, Sri Lanka, Sudan (North), Sudan (South), Suriname, Swaziland, Syria, Tajikistan, Tanzania, Thailand, Tunisia, Turkey, Turkmenistan, UAE, Ukraine, Uzbekistan, Vatican City, Venezuela, Yemen, Zambia, Zimbabwe.

[25] *R. v Bow Street Metropolitan Stipendiary Magistrate Ex p. Pinochet Ugarte (No.3)* [2000] 1 A.C. 147; [1999] 2 W.L.R. 827 HL.

takes place. There is a presumption in English law that, unless otherwise expressly provided for by the statute, the general rules of private international law that prevail will in turn apply to that legislation. Thus, it is presumed that an Act of Parliament is intended to comply with conflicts of laws rules so far as these constitute part of domestic law. One such rule is that, ordinarily, the criminal jurisdiction does not extend to conduct which occurs abroad, in particular, where the conduct concerns foreign nationals. This is a reflection of the traditional view that the criminal jurisdiction is an incident of state sovereignty and thus closely identified with the territory of the state in question.

Further, it is well established, that unless the contrary intention appears, subject to the general rules of private international law, an enactment of Parliament is not intended to apply to Britons (including corporations), outside the territory of the UK. In its extreme form, the proposition is that of Viscount Simonds in *Cox v Army Council*[26]:

> "apart from those exceptional cases in which specific provision is made in regard to acts committed abroad, the whole body of the criminal law of England deals only with acts committed in England".

The principle applies a fortiori to legislation with a penal element. In *BBC Enterprises Ltd v Hi-Tech Xtravision*,[27] Staughton LJ said that Parliament is not assumed, in a criminal enactment, to regulate conduct outside this country. As is further discussed below, the "exceptional cases" referred to by Viscount Simonds are much less exceptional now than previously. That is, in part, a consequence of broad recognition and acceptance that international financial crime is incapable of being satisfactorily combated by a criminal jurisdiction based upon the narrow territorial principle.[28]

---

[26] *Cox v Army Council* [1963] A.C. 48 HL at 67.

[27] *BBC Enterprises Ltd v Hi-Tech Xtravision Ltd* [1990] 2 W.L.R. 1123 CA at 1127.

[28] For an extended discussion of the present inadequacy of "territoriality" as the primary governing principle for jurisdiction in criminal law, see Michael Hirst, *Jurisdiction and the Ambit of the Criminal Law*, (Oxford: Oxford University Press, 2003).

Prior to the relatively recent international concern about the effects of international economically motivated crime, there existed a number of long-established exceptions to the narrow territorial principle of criminal jurisdiction. The most important of those was the jurisdiction based on so-called "active nationality". It is under that doctrine that the criminal courts of England and Wales have jurisdiction over murder and manslaughter committed abroad. High Treason is justifiable on the same basis under the Treason Act 1351. The rationale for that jurisdiction is based upon the active nationality principle and the gravity of the crimes in question. A yet more extensive exception to the narrow territorial jurisdiction is the principle of "universality" where jurisdiction is taken regardless of the place where the crime was committed or the nationality of the accused or the victim. The origin of the universal jurisdiction is rooted in piracy and owes its origin to the joint interest of states in combating crime that affected all. The modern development of that jurisdiction is based not upon joint interest, but upon upholding universal values. This concern is commonly, though not exclusively, a concern of public, rather than private, international law.

As to the position of foreign persons outside the UK, in the absence of a clearly expressed intention to do so, Parliament is not to be taken to intend to legislate for non-nationals outside the UK. The reason for this is that the protective principle of the criminal law jurisdiction provides that subjection to law involves protection by the law in return, which those outside the jurisdiction are not in a position to receive. Lord Hoffmann, in *Société Eram Shipping Co Ltd v Cie International de Navigation*[29] said:

> "It is a general principle of international law that one sovereign state should not trespass upon the authority of another, by attempting to seize assets situated within the jurisdiction of the foreign state or compelling its citizens to do acts within its boundaries."

---

[29] *Société Eram Shipping Co Ltd v Compagnie International de Navigation* [2003] UKHL 30; [2004] 1 A.C. 260; [2003] 1 C.L.C. 1163 at [54].

Similarly, in *Arab Bank Plc v Mercantile Holdings Ltd,*[30] Millett J was invited to give a literal construction to the prohibition on financial assistance under Companies Act 1985 s.151 as having application to a foreign subsidiary of an English parent company. He declined to do so, observing:

> "[t]here is a presumption that, in the absence of a contrary intention express or implied, United Kingdom legislation does not apply to foreign persons or corporations outside the United Kingdom whose acts are performed outside the United Kingdom".

An important example of an express intention to regulate the conduct of those abroad is to be found under s.89 of the Financial Services Act 2012.[31] Section 89(2) makes it an offence (subject to prescribed defences under s.89(3)) for a person to make a materially false or misleading statement, knowingly or recklessly, or dishonestly to conceal material facts for the purpose of inducing another person (a) to enter into or refrain from entering into a relevant agreement or (b) to exercise or refrain from exercising any rights conferred by a relevant investment. The basis of extra-territorial jurisdiction conferred by the provision under s.89(4), which makes it an offence even though the relevant act may occur outside the (territorial) jurisdiction, is that there are substantial effects within the jurisdiction. Section 89(4) provides that no offence will be committed unless:

(a) the statement is made in or from, or the facts are concealed in or from, the United Kingdom or arrangements are made in or from the United Kingdom for the statement to be made or the facts to be concealed;
(b) the person on whom the inducement is intended to or may have effect is in the United Kingdom; or
(c) the agreement is or would be entered into or the rights are or would be exercised in the United Kingdom.

---

[30] *Arab Bank Plc v Mercantile Holdings Ltd* [1994] Ch. 71 Ch.D at 80–81.
[31] Superseding similar provisions under s.397 of FSMA 2000.

Nevertheless, Parliament has also been willing to take jurisdiction over acts taking place abroad where there are no significant effects in the UK. The most notable example is under the Criminal Justice Act 1993 (CJA 1993), part of which was the culmination of more than 23 years of work by the Law Commission and others, on the question of how the courts of the UK might deal with the threat posed to the integrity of the financial markets by international financial crime and the risk that such crime presented to the reputation of the UK as the leading centre for such services. Section 5 of CJA 1993 introduced a greatly extended extra-territorial criminal jurisdiction for the so-called "inchoate" offences of conspiracy and incitement, subject to the requirement that the offence must have some connection with the UK. Significantly, the legislation here adopted the recommendation of the Law Commission and imposes a test of double-criminality for these offences. That is to say, the conduct in question must be an offence both under domestic law *and also* an offence under the law of the place where it in fact occurs.

From the above it will be seen that ordinarily, in the absence of a clearly expressed intention to do so, legislation is not intended to regulate the conduct of persons (including corporations) which takes place outside the UK. While it continues to be the case that individuals will not be subject to the criminal jurisdiction of the courts of the UK under the provisions of POCA 2002 unless they are present within the jurisdiction, POCA 2002 nevertheless has important extra-territorial consequences for conduct which takes place abroad and which is *deemed*, under the definitional provisions under POCA 2002 s.340, to be "criminal conduct" and from which "criminal property" is derived. The significance of those provisions is that a person may be liable to prosecution in the UK for acts which take place abroad and from which criminal property is derived, but which have no effects in the UK. Likewise, a person in the "regulated sector" may be criminally liable where they have, or ought to have, knowledge or suspicion of such acts and fail to disclose them. Potentially, that is a very wide basis for the imposition of criminal liability.

On the other hand, so far as the position of UK companies abroad is concerned, on ordinary territorial jurisdictional principles, UK entities, their branches, offices or subsidiaries, where these are located overseas, are subject to the local criminal jurisdiction and ordinarily will be subject to regulation by the relevant overseas (that is to say, domestic and local) regulatory authority.[32] Similarly, branches of UK entities operating pursuant to passport rights within the EEA are subject to the host state regulator's applicable provisions as notified.[33] Within the EEA, the position should present no real difficulty given the requirement for harmonisation under the Directives. Where material differences exist between a host-state regulatory regime and those provided for under the UK money laundering regulations, it is a matter of judgment as to what procedures to adopt. The JMLSG Guidance provides that:

> "The UK legal and regulatory regime is primarily concerned with preventing money laundering which is connected with the UK. Where a UK financial institution has overseas branches, subsidiaries or associates, where control can be exercised over business carried on outside the United Kingdom, or where elements of its UK business have been outsourced to offshore locations ... the firm must put in place a group AML/CTF strategy."[34]

Prudence and common sense may well suggest that if the domestic standard is lower than that provided for under the 2007 Regulations, the Regulations will be followed rather than the lower, local, standard. In reality, circumstances and choices will rarely be so clear-cut. But for credit and financial institutions with branches or subsidiaries in non-EEA states, the position in relation to customer due diligence, monitoring and record keeping is regulated by statute. The 2007 Regulations reg.15 provides that:

---

[32] The expression "overseas regulatory authority" is a defined term under Companies Act 1989 s.82(2). See also JMLSG Guidance at Pt 1 para.2.11.

[33] FSMA 2000 Sch.3 Pt 3.

[34] JMLSG Guidance Notes Pt 1 at para.1.46.

"15. Branches and subsidiaries

(1) A credit or financial institution must require its branches and subsidiary undertakings which are located in a non-EEA state to apply, to the extent permitted by the law of that state, measures at least equivalent to those set out in these Regulations with regard to customer due diligence measures, ongoing monitoring and record-keeping.

(2) Where the law of a non-EEA state does not permit the application of such equivalent measures by the branch or subsidiary undertaking located in that state, the credit or financial institution must—

    (a) inform its supervisory authority accordingly; and

    (b) take additional measures to handle effectively the risk of money laundering and terrorist financing.
..."

The JMLSG Guidance, at Pt 1 paras 2.8 and 2.9, emphasises that the responsibility of FCA regulated firms which outsource activities and functions remains with the regulated, delegating, entity:

"2.8 Many firms outsource some of their systems and controls and/or processing to elsewhere within the UK and to other jurisdictions, and/or to other group companies. Involving other entities in the operation of a firm's systems brings an additional dimension to the risks that the firm faces, and this risk must be actively managed. It is in the interests of the firm to ensure that outsourcing does not result in reduced standards or requirements being applied. In all cases, the firm should have regard to the FCA's guidance on out-sourcing.

2.9 FCA-regulated firms cannot contract out of their regulatory responsibilities, and therefore remain responsible for systems and controls in relation to the activities outsourced, whether within the UK or to another jurisdiction. In all instances of outsourcing it

is the delegating firm that bears the ultimate responsibility for the duties undertaken in its name."

It may be noted that, in addition to the regulatory structure
relating to money laundering under the 2007 Regulations, the
FCA has issued its own Money Laundering Guidance in its
Financial Crime Guide (see further, Chapter 3). The FCA has said
that where a UK-authorised firm is able to exercise control over
business conducted outside the UK through a branch or
subsidiary, it will look into the way in which such control is
exercised in the prevention and detection of money laundering
in the non-UK business. The justification for that position is the
reputational, managerial and financial exposure of the firm in
question in the context of the regulatory objectives, which
include promoting market confidence and reducing financial
crime. It is clear that the FCA will not necessarily consider
compliance with host state rules as sufficient.

9.3 Application of POCA 2002 and relevant money laundering regulations to overseas entities carrying on business in the UK

In the discussion which follows, it is useful to bear in mind that
the 2007 Regulations and the money laundering provisions
under Pt 7 POCA 2002, though of course closely connected by
reason of their common subject matter, have different objects.

Money laundering regulations are made by HM Treasury
under the European Communities Act 1972. The Money
Laundering Regulations 1993 were one of the principal means
by which the First EU Money Laundering Directive[35] was
implemented in the UK. The 2007 Regulations, in force from 15
December 2007, are made pursuant to the Third EU Money
Laundering Directive[36] and, additionally, were made in order

---

[35] Council Directive 91/308/EEC of 10 June 1991 on prevention of the use of the
financial system for the purpose of money laundering [1991] OJ L166/77.
[36] Directive 2005/60/EC of the European Parliament and of the Council of 26
October 2005 on the prevention of the use of the financial system for the purpose
of money laundering and terrorist financing [2005] OJ L309/15.

to give effect to FSMA 2000. The Money Laundering Regulations are concerned with what may be described as "preventive" money laundering rules intended to deny the use of the financial system to would-be money launderers,[37] and, as their name suggests, are "regulatory" in their purpose.

The substantive money laundering provisions under Pt 7 of POCA 2002, on the other hand, are a consolidation and extension of previous criminal legislation[38] concerned with imposing criminal liability upon those actually engaged in money laundering. In that respect, POCA 2002 is "suppressive", rather than preventive or regulatory, in its primary object. Nevertheless, Pt 7 includes, under s.330, extensive reporting obligations on those in the "regulated sector" to disclose to the criminal investigation and enforcement agencies material that gives rise to suspicion of money laundering.[39] In so far as the purpose of those provisions is to assist in denying the use of the financial system to would-be launderers, they may be seen to be preventive and regulatory in their primary object. Apart from a limited obligation under the Drug Trafficking Act 1994 s.52, which imposed a duty to report actual knowledge or suspicion of drug trafficking, the general reporting obligation under POCA 2002 s.330 when introduced in February 2003 was wholly new.[40]

POCA 2002 and the 2007 Regulations impose criminal liability quite differently. The key distinction is whether the person in question is an individual, corporation or a partnership.

If overseas entities carry on business in the UK through a local presence, then plainly the resident entities are subject to UK regulation and to UK laws. On ordinary territorial principles,

---

[37] See recitals to 91/308/EEC.

[38] Primarily the Criminal Justice Act 1988 and the Drug Trafficking Act 1994.

[39] The POCA 2002 provisions being foreshadowed by the disclosure requirements under s.21A Anti-Terrorism Crime and Security Act 2001 in relation to suspicion of laundering of terrorist property.

[40] The obligation to report suspicion of defined criminal conduct, such as drug trafficking, gives rise to no real difficulty. The problem occurs where there is generic labelling of "criminal conduct" together with a duty to report suspicion of such conduct.

all UK resident staff of overseas undertakings are subject to the provisions of POCA 2002. That includes, whether or not the undertaking carries on business in the "regulated sector" under Sch.9, the money laundering provisions under ss.327, 328 and 329 (the substantive money laundering offences), together with the inchoate offences such as conspiracy. In addition, if the relevant business is within the definition of the "regulated sector", individuals carrying on the relevant business in the UK will additionally be subject to the obligations under s.330 and related provisions, together with the penalties for failure promptly to disclose actual or constructive knowledge or suspicion of money laundering.[41]

9.4 Criminal liability for money laundering of persons other than individuals

The criminal liability under POCA 2002 of persons other than individuals, that is to say, corporate persons, partnerships and unincorporated associations, perhaps surprisingly, is an issue that remains of some difficulty and uncertainty. It is clear that the FATF recommend that criminal sanctions should apply to both natural and legal persons. That was previously clear under Recommendation 2(b) that has now been moved in the 2012 Revised Recommendations to the Interpretative Note to Recommendation 3. In terms that (by the penultimate sentence of (c) below) could scarcely be clearer as to the FATF intention, the Interpretative Note provides that:

> "...
>
> (b) Effective, proportionate and dissuasive criminal sanctions should apply to natural persons convicted of money laundering.
> (c) Criminal liability and sanctions, and, where that is not possible (due to fundamental principles of domestic law), civil or administrative liability and sanctions, should apply to legal persons. This should not

---

[41] That includes, of course, EEA entities exercising their passport rights under Sch.3 FSMA 2000, subject to terms as provided by para.15.

> preclude parallel criminal, civil or administrative proceedings with respect to legal persons in countries in which more than one form of liability is available. *Such measures should be without prejudice to the criminal liability of natural persons.*[42] All sanctions should be effective, proportionate and dissuasive."

It is striking that POCA 2002 does not adopt a structure that reflects or gives effect to the FATF guidance under (c) above in its penultimate sentence (even though the guidance itself is not, as noted, new).

Corporate criminal liability is an issue that continues to cause difficulty for English courts. Sometimes statutory provisions provide a clear steer. For example, it is reasonably clear under reg.7 of the 2007 Regulations, which requires *a relevant person* in the course of business carried on by *him* to apply customer due diligence measures in prescribed circumstances, that the expression "person" here is to be given its usual primary meaning of a natural person or individual. But liability for offences by infringement of the 2007 Regulations is not confined to individuals as natural persons. Criminal liability is also imposed upon corporations, partnerships and unincorporated associations.[43] As to their criminal liability, the Regulations provide a detailed scheme:

"47. Offences by bodies corporate etc.

(1) If an offence under regulation 45[44] committed by a body corporate is shown—
   (a) to have been committed with the consent or the connivance of an officer of the body corporate; or
   (b) to be attributable to any neglect on his part,
   the officer *as well as the body corporate*[45] is guilty of an offence and liable to be proceeded against and punished accordingly.

---

[42] Emphasis supplied.
[43] See reg.27 of the 2003 Regulations (SI 2003/3075) for offences by bodies corporate and partnerships.
[44] That enumerates all the various offences under the Regulations.
[45] Emphasis added.

(2) If an offence under regulation 45 committed by a partnership is shown—
    (a) to have been committed with the consent or the connivance of a partner; or
    (b) to be attributable to any neglect on his part,
the partner *as well as the partnership*[46] is guilty of an offence and liable to be proceeded against and punished accordingly.

(3) If an offence under regulation 45 committed by an unincorporated association (other than a partnership) is shown—
    (a) to have been committed with the consent or the connivance of an officer of the association; or
    (b) to be attributable to any neglect on his part,
that officer *as well as the association*[47] is guilty of an offence and liable to be proceeded against and punished accordingly.

(4) If the affairs of a body corporate are managed by its members, paragraph (1) applies in relation to the acts and defaults of a member in connection with his functions of management as if he were a director of the body."

The approach is broadly replicated under the Bribery Act 2010 that provides in s.14:

"14. Offences under sections 1, 2 and 6 by bodies corporate etc.

This section has no associated Explanatory Notes

(1) This section applies if an offence under section 1, 2 or 6 is committed by a body corporate or a Scottish partnership.

(2) If the offence is proved to have been committed with the consent or connivance of—
    (a) a senior officer of the body corporate or Scottish partnership, or

---

[46] Emphasis as before.
[47] Emphasis as before.

> (b) a person purporting to act in such a capacity,
> the senior officer or person (as well as the body
> corporate or partnership) is guilty of the offence and
> liable to be proceeded against and punished accord-
> ingly ..."

Both the 2007 Regulations and the Bribery Act 2010 clearly
show that it is the intention that both corporations and
unincorporated associations shall be subject to criminal liability where the relevant facts are established. It is a very
surprising peculiarity that by design or otherwise there are no
such express provisions within Pt 7, and it is left to the courts
to apply the traditional tests to determine corporate liability. In
the absence of express statutory provisions providing for the
criminal liability of abstract legal persons and unincorporated
associations, despite the continuous refinement of company
law, there exists no consensus as to the general jurisprudential
nature or purpose of corporate criminal liability beyond strict
liability offences, that is to say, offences that require mens rea
or a guilty mind.[48] The unresolved difficulty remains as to in
what circumstances, and how, is the act and state of mind of an
individual to be attributed to an abstract legal person. In
summary, there are two views. One is the "identification
principle", explained by Lord Reid in *Tesco Supermarkets Ltd. v.
Nattrass*,[49] by which the acts and state of mind of the
controllers of a company are treated *as the acts and state of mind
of the company*. A different, and arguably somewhat wider and
more flexible basis for attribution is provided in *Meridian v
Global Funds Management Ltd v Securities Commission*.[50] Lord
Hoffmann, in contrast with what may be seen as inappropriate
anthropomorphism under the identification approach, emphasised that the requirement in every case was *to identify the
applicable rule of attribution and the policy* to which the statute

---

[48] For an illuminating discussion see Professor Eilis Ferran, "Corporate attribution
and the directing mind and will" (2011) 127 L.Q.R. 239.

[49] *Tesco Supermarkets Ltd v Nattrass* [1972] A.C. 153 HL at 170: a company "must act
through living persons, though not always one or the same person. Then the
person who acts is not speaking or acting for the company. He is acting *as the
company and his mind which directs his acts is the mind of the company.*"

[50] *Meridian Global Funds Management Asia Ltd v Securities Commission* [1995] 2 A.C.
500; [1995] 3 W.L.R. 413; [1995] B.C.C. 942 PC(NZ).

gives effect. Liability under that approach need not attach only to controllers if the applicable rule and policy indicate otherwise. The *Meridian* approach was expected to cause a sea change but that has not happened.[51] The difficulty in securing a conviction and judicial conservatism under the identification principle is well known. The Director of Public Prosecutions described it as "almost impossible" to prosecute successfully under that (i.e. the identification) principle.[52] Partly in recognition of that, the Law Commission has recently advocated that a context-based, more interpretative approach to crimes created by statute should have a greater influence than it does at present,[53] that is to say, an approach more in line with *Meridian*.

The "identification principle" under *Tesco v Nattrass* is rather less obviously applicable to partnerships than to corporations. An alternative analysis is nevertheless available, by analogy with the approach to attribution of individual acts to companies that Lord Hoffmann explained in *Meridian Global Funds Management Ltd v Securities Commission*.[54] The case concerned the circumstances in which an individual's knowledge can be attributed to a corporation even though the relevant unauthorised acts were carried out behind the company's back (a circumstance that bears analogy with the issue of liability under POCA 2002—including where by extension applied to the relevant suspicion (necessarily entertained by an individual) in connection with the substantive offences or for the purposes the reporting offence). His Lordship said:

> "It is worth pausing at this stage to make what may seem an obvious point. Any statement about what a company has or has not done, or can or cannot do, is necessarily a reference to the rules of attribution (primary and general) as they apply to that company. Judges sometimes say that a company "as such" cannot do anything; it must act by

---

[51] The Court of Appeal has even suggested that *Meridian* represents an *affirmation* of the identification principle: Rose LJ in *Attorney-General's Reference (No.2 of 1999)* [2000] Q.B. 796; [2000] 3 W.L.R. 195; [2000] 2 Cr. App. R. 207 CA.

[52] HMSO 2009 HL Paper No.115 para.17.

[53] Law Commission, *Criminal Liability in Regulatory Contexts* (HMSO, 2010) Commission Paper 195.

[54] *Meridian* [1995] 2 A.C. 500; [1995] 3 W.L.R. 413; [1995] B.C.C. 942 PC(NZ).

servants or agents. This may seem an unexceptionable, even banal remark. And of course the meaning is usually perfectly clear. But a reference to a company "as such" might suggest that there is something out there called the company of which one can meaningfully say that it can or cannot do something. There is in fact no such thing as the company as such, no *ding an sich*, only the applicable rules. To say that a company cannot do something means only that there is no one whose doing of that act would, under the applicable rules of attribution, count as an act of the company."[55]

He went to say:

"It is a question of construction in each case as to whether the particular rule requires that knowledge that an act has been done, or the state of mind with which it was done, should be attributed to the company."[56]

Following illustrations of attribution and a counter-example of non-attribution, he concluded with the observation:

"There is no inconsistency [between the examples]: each is an example of an attribution rule for a particular purpose, tailored as it always must be to the terms and policies of the substantive rule."[57]

The analysis is compelling, both as a matter of logic and principle, and there is no reason why the approach should not be applied to the question of attribution of a partner's (or other person's) state of mind to a partnership. If that approach is adopted, the terms of the policy and the substantive rule require to be identified, by which liability is imposed on a company by POCA 2002 ss.327-329 and/or by s.330. Neither the policy, nor any applicable substantive rule of attribution, may be discerned in POCA 2002 itself or otherwise beyond the provision under s.5 of the Interpretation Act 1978. It is

---

[55] *Meridian* [1995] 2 A.C. 500 PC(NZ) at 506.
[56] *Meridian* [1995] 2 A.C. 500 PC(NZ) at 511.
[57] *Meridian* [1995] 2 A.C. 500 PC(NZ) at 511.

suggested that this is an inadequate foundation for criminal liability for a serious offence. The position may be contrasted with the position under s.14 of the Bribery Act 2010 previously referred to.

In practice, it seems very improbable that judges will be enthusiastic to look for rules of attribution beyond the confines of the statute, where to do so is to enter upon wholly uncharted waters. If, as Professor Ferran has observed, "the courts have been reluctant to impose the stigma of a serious criminal conviction on a company in the absence of a very clear steer from Parliament that this was actually intended and have struggled to find such a steer in criminal offences not formulated with the position of companies specifically in mind",[58] even greater reluctance may be expected in relation to unincorporated associations such as "old style partnerships" where the sole basis for imposing liability would appear to rest on the terms of s.5 of the Interpretation Act 1978.

It is of interest, in the context of the foregoing discussion, that during the House of Lords' debates on the Proceeds of Crime Bill, the Attorney General expressed his view that there was no reason why "lifestyle" provisions[59] should not apply to corporate defendants. Recommendations that would have had the effect of making this explicit under the legislation were however rejected.[60]

At the time of writing, there appears to have been no reported instance of a company being convicted of an offence under ss.327-329 or s.330. That is not to say that there is no criminal liability under POCA 2002 other than individual liability. Where the essence of any offence (the necessary mens rea) is perforce the knowledge or suspicion of an individual, and the legislation itself provides no explicit assistance or guidance, it may be that the prosecution of persons *other than individuals* for money laundering presents an unnecessary and avoidable legal difficulty. But, as with issues of corporate and trust

---

[58] Professor Ferran, (2011) 127 L.Q.R. 239 at 247.
[59] Now POCA 2002 s.223.
[60] HL debates 25 June 2002 col.1216 and 11 July 2002 col.840 respectively.

transparency that have long been of concern to FATF, but until recently disregarded and not been given effect by legislation, it may be that in the future, criminal liability of corporations and unincorporated persons will rise up the FATF agenda. The important subject of US extra-territoriality is addressed in Chapter 10.

9.5   Extra-territorial issues arising out of the legislative drafting of POCA 2002

As discussed in outline above, Parliament can, and does, legislate for criminal jurisdiction over conduct which takes place abroad. It has done so under POCA 2002. It should occasion no surprise that POCA 2002 should have an extra-territorial dimension. Indeed, given the objectives of the AML provisions and the commonly international character of the laundering of criminal proceeds, it is absolutely essential. Nevertheless, the ways in which such a dimension was originally introduced under POCA 2002 caused a degree of understandable surprise and concern to practitioners and the recent amending provisions intended to address some of those concerns are complex. The relevant provisions will be examined in detail below.

There are three important, separate but related, aspects of extra-territoriality to be considered: the first is the definition of "criminal conduct" under POCA s.340(3); second, the definition of "money laundering" itself under POCA 2002 s.340(11); and third, the defences to money laundering offences and failure to notify the NCA of money laundering activity. The latter are inserted into the relevant provisions of POCA 2002 by the Serious Organised Crime and Police Act 2005 s.102 (SOCPA 2005).

"Criminal conduct" is an essential element in the definition of "criminal property". Criminal property is property that:

(i)   constitutes, or represents, a person's benefit from criminal conduct; and

(ii) the alleged offender knows or suspects that it constitutes such a benefit.

A critical consideration is whether any particular property in question is "criminal" and when it became so. In *R. v Geary*,[61] Moore-Bick LJ said:

> "In our view the natural and ordinary meaning of s 328(1) was that the arrangement to which it referred had to be one which related to property which was criminal property at the time when the arrangement began to operate on it. To say that it extended to property which was originally legitimate but became criminal only as a result of carrying out the arrangement was to stretch the language of the section beyond its proper limits."

The Court of Appeal applied that reasoning in the bribery case *Kensington International Ltd v Republic of Congo*,[62] and more recently in *Akhtar*,[63] the last in a series of appeals that concerned the ambit of s.328 and the necessity for the *property to be criminal in an independent freestanding sense*, as opposed to becoming criminal property by the arrangement itself.

Criminal property is, in turn, an essential element for each of the substantive offences under POCA 2002 ss.327, 328 and 329. The incorporation of an extra-territorial element in the definition of criminal conduct is therefore a critical part of the definition of any of the substantive offences.

The key definition of "criminal conduct" introduces extra-territoriality. Section 340(2)(b) provides:

> "Criminal conduct is conduct which –
>
> (a) constitutes an offence in any part of the United Kingdom, or

---

[61] *R. v Geary (Michael)* [2010] EWCA Crim 1925; [2011] 1 W.L.R. 1634; [2011] 1 Cr. App. R. 8 (p.73) at [19].

[62] *Kensington International Ltd v Republic of Congo (formerly People's Republic of Congo)* [2007] EWCA Civ 1128; [2008] 1 W.L.R. 1144; [2008] C.P. Rep. 6.

[63] *R. v Akhtar (Urfan)* [2011] EWCA Crim 146; [2011] 1 Cr. App. R. 37 (p.464).

(b)   would constitute an offence in any part of the United Kingdom if it occurred there."

Thus, criminal conduct includes not only conduct which amounts to a criminal offence in any part of the UK, but also conduct that takes place abroad and that would constitute an offence in any part of the UK, *had it* occurred here.[64] Subject to the new statutory defence provided by SOCPA 2005, dealt with below, whether the conduct infringes the criminal code of the place where it in fact occurs appears to be irrelevant if the strict words of the statute are construed in the normal way. That gives rise to a whole series of questions for those with international dimensions to their operations, as is further considered below. In the discussion which follows, it should be borne in mind that the classification of predicate conduct[65] as "criminal conduct" is not for the purpose of conferring jurisdiction upon the domestic courts over *that conduct*, but as an essential ingredient of the (substantive) laundering offence. It is not meaningful to speak of the laundering of property derived from lawful conduct.

It is important, in construing the meaning of "criminal conduct" for the purposes of POCA 2002 Pt 7, to note that the "Civil Recovery" jurisdiction under POCA 2002 Pt 5 is concerned with the recovery of property obtained through "unlawful conduct" without the prior requirement for prosecution and conviction of an offence. There is in fact no material difference between property that is derived from "unlawful conduct" under Pt 5 and that which is derived from criminal conduct under Pt 7. Part 5, like Pt 7, defines property by reference to its derivation from criminal offences. However, there is a critical distinction, in that, under Pt 5, conduct is

---

[64] That issue is itself by no means necessarily straightforward. See, for example, Lord Keith's comments in *Tarling v Singapore* (1980) 70 Cr. App. R. 77 HL at 136 (a case relating to fraud and dishonesty of a group of companies in the Far East and issues relating to extradition): "In considering the jurisdiction aspect it is necessary to suppose that England is substituted for Singapore as regards all the circumstances of the case connected with the latter country, and to examine the question whether upon that hypothesis and upon the evidence adduced the English courts would have jurisdiction to try the offences charged."

[65] That is, the conduct which generates the property that is the subject of the laundering activities.

"unlawful conduct" where the predicate conduct is unlawful *both* under the criminal law of the country where it actually occurred, and would also be an offence in the UK had it occurred here. That is the conventional application of a test of double criminality that is conspicuously absent under Pt 7 and which, accordingly, has wider extra-territorial implications.

The other definition which gives rise to extra-territorial implications is the definition of money laundering itself. The importance and relevance of that definition is that the disclosure provisions under POCA s.330, and all the consequential requirements together with the defences, apply to all money laundering offences as these are defined. Money laundering is defined in traditional terms as one of the substantive offences. It also embraces such related "inchoate" offences as incitement to commit any of the substantive offences, and aiding and abetting the substantive offences. However, at the end of the definition of money laundering under s.340(11)(d), an important extended meaning is given to money laundering. That sub-section provides that money laundering is an offence that *would* constitute an offence under ss.327, 328 and 329 (or the inchoate offences) *if done in the UK*. So whatever act may give rise to a substantive offence (e.g. concealing or disguising criminal proceeds) has, if it occurred outside the UK, to be transposed to the UK *as if it had occurred here*. The full consequences of the disclosure requirements then appear to apply to such acts, even though they occurred outside the UK, subject to the defence now provided by SOCPA 2005 (see below).

This brief summary is intended to highlight the extra-territorial provisions which are now considered in more detail. It is essential, in any given set of circumstances, to analyse the application of the definition of "criminal conduct" before assessing whether the defences provided under SOCPA 2005 are engaged. Although there is a new defence related to whether or not criminal conduct took place in a jurisdiction where the relevant activity did not constitute a criminal offence, it is important to bear in mind that the definition of "criminal conduct" was not directly amended by SOCPA 2005.

9.6 The courts' approach to statutory extra-territoriality

While much of the commentary on the extra-territorial provisions under POCA 2002 in the previous edition of this Chapter continues to present difficulty in analysis and interpretation, the position has been clarified by the decision of the Supreme Court in *SOCA v Perry*,[66] which despite it having been reversed as to its effect by new primary legislation under the Crime and Courts Act 2013 s.48 (below), remains instructive as to the (welcome) conservative approach (see fn.140 below) that the Supreme Court requires to be adopted in construing provisions that require consideration to be given to apparent extra-territorial effect. The decision is a salutary reminder of the importance of careful drafting and a reminder of the traditional (liberal) approach of the court, namely, construing criminal statutes narrowly where expediency (and the understandable desire to serve the objectives of POCA 2002) invites a looser and broader approach (namely, that favoured by Lords Judge and Clarke JJSC). That Parliament legislated to reverse[67] *Perry* within a few months of the decision merely underlines that to give extra-territorial effect, clear expression of that parliamentary intention is necessary. Paradoxically, a much more difficult, and, it is submitted, unsatisfactory reading of the extra-territorial effects of POCA 2002 is to be found in *R. v Rogers*,[68] a decision of the Court of Appeal (Treacy LJ, Lang J and HH Judge Bevan QC) of August 2014, the effect of which must and should give rise to give considerable concern.

---

[66] *Serious Organised Crime Agency v Perry* [2012] UKSC 35; [2013] 1 A.C. 182; [2013] 1 Cr. App. R. 6 (p.61).

[67] A word used advisedly—see the judgment of Lloyd LJ in *Serious Organised Crime Agency v Azam* [2013] EWCA Civ 970; [2013] 1 W.L.R 3800; [2013] C.P. Rep. 47 at [20].

[68] *R. v Rogers (Bradley David)* [2014] EWCA Crim 1680; [2015] 1 W.L.R. 1017; [2014] 2 Cr. App. R. 32 (p.516).

9.6.1 Property and Property Freezing Orders—SOCA v Perry[69]

In October 2007, Mr Perry was convicted in Israel of fraud. He was sentenced to 12 years in prison and fined approximately £3 million, which he subsequently paid. In August 2008, SOCA obtained a disclosure order from the High Court. Notices were served by SOCA on Mr Perry and his daughters by letter to an address in Mayfair which Mr Perry was known to keep, despite SOCA being aware that they did not reside in the UK and that they were out of the jurisdiction.

In October 2009, an order was granted under POCA 2002 s.245A for a worldwide property freezing order (PFO) against Mr Perry and those associated with him, including his immediate family. The PFO included the usual requirements for the defendants to disclose their assets worldwide. Mr Perry, with the other appellants, challenged both the disclosure order and the PFO. At first instance, and at the Court of Appeal (Criminal Division), the challenges were dismissed on the grounds that, despite a presumption against giving statutes extra-territorial effect, the language of the relevant provisions of POCA 2002 clearly applied to property outside of England and Wales, the defendants had sufficient presence within the jurisdiction and a valid information notice could be served on a person outside the jurisdiction by posting it to an address within the jurisdiction.

Lord Phillips PSC, giving the principal[70] judgment of the Supreme Court, having explained the relevant statutory structure for civil recovery under POCA 2002 Pt 5, went on to emphasise issues of reciprocity and a "coherent scheme that accords with international law". On the issue of reciprocity, Lord Phillips explained that Pt 5 is intended to comply with the Strasbourg Convention. The reasoning of Lord Phillips is clear

---

[69] *Serious Organised Crime Agency v Perry* [2012] UKSC 35; [2013] 1 A.C. 182; [2013] 1 Cr. App. R. 6 (p.61).

[70] The other substantive judgments being by Lord Reed JSC, touching on Scottish law issues, and Sir Anthony Hughes.

and explains how POCA 2002 fits in with the Strasbourg scheme and it merits citation despite length:

> "One obvious explanation for the provisions of Part 5 is that they were intended to comply with the obligations of the United Kingdom in respect of incoming requests under the Strasbourg Convention, and to afford similar assistance to states not party to that convention. Section 444(1) provides for the making of an Order in Council to make provision for a prohibition on dealing with property which is the subject of an external request and for the realisation of property for the purpose of giving effect to an external order. Section 444(2) provides that such an Order may include provision which (subject to any specified modification) corresponds to any provision of Part 2, 3, 4 or 5, excluding Chapter 3, which deals with cash seizure. Section 447 defines an 'external request' and an 'external order' as follows:
>
> (1) An external request is a request by an overseas authority to prohibit dealing with relevant property which is identified in the request …
> (2) An external order is an order which … (a) is made by an overseas court where property is found or believed to have been obtained as a result of or in connection with criminal conduct, and (b) is for the recovery of specified property or a specified sum of money.
>
> Thus, where a foreign court makes a finding that property has been, or is believed to have been, obtained as a result of or in connection with criminal conduct and orders the recovery of specified property or a specified sum of money, section 444 provides for an Order in Council that permits realisation of property to give effect to the order of the foreign court. Section 444 addresses both forms of confiscation order referred to in the Explanatory Report to the Strasbourg Convention: see para 28 above. Section 444 does not provide in terms that the property to be realised should be within the United Kingdom.

The power conferred by section 444 was exercised by the making of the Order. The Order enables the powers conferred by Parts 2, 3, 4 and 5 of POCA to be exercised for the purpose of giving effect to external requests and external orders, so that the provisions of the Order mirror the provisions of POCA. Part 2 of the Order provides for the Secretary of State to refer an external request in connection with criminal investigation or proceedings, or an external order arising from a criminal conviction, to, among others in England and Wales, the Director of Public Prosecutions. He will then apply to the Crown Court for the exercise of the powers conferred by Part 2. Parts 3 and 4 of the Order make equivalent provisions in respect of Scotland and Northern Ireland. Parts 2, 3 and 4 provide for measures to secure and realise 'relevant property'. Section 447(7) of POCA states that property is 'relevant property' if there are reasonable grounds to believe that it may be needed to satisfy an external order which has been or may be made. Part 2 of the Order is headed 'Giving Effect in England and Wales to External Requests in Connection with Criminal Investigations or Proceedings and to External Orders Arising from Such Proceedings' Parts 3 and 4 have equivalent headings. Parts 2, 3 and 4 of the Order expressly provide that the external request or order must relate to property in, respectively, England and Wales, Scotland and Northern Ireland. In *King v Director of the Serious Fraud Office*[71] the House of Lords held that the provisions of Part 2 of the Order only permitted a restraint order to be made in respect of property within England and Wales and that the same territorial restriction applied in respect of seizure and enforcement provisions.

Why do Parts 2, 3 and 4 of the Order expressly limit the assistance that can be sought by the foreign state to assistance in respect of property within England and Wales, Scotland and Northern Ireland? The answer must be that which I gave in *King v Director of the Serious Fraud Office* at para 31:

---

[71] *King v Director of the Serious Fraud Office* [2009] UKHL 17; [2009] 1 W.L.R. 718; [2009] 2 Cr. App. R. 2 (p.43).

'If a country wishes assistance from other countries in preserving or recovering property that is related to criminal activity, it makes sense for its request to each of those other countries to be restricted to the provision of assistance in relation to property located within its own jurisdiction. If each country were requested to take steps to procure the preservation or recovery of property on a worldwide basis, this would lead to a confusing, and possibly conflicting, overlap of international requests for assistance. Not only would such multiplication of activity be confusing, it would involve significant and unnecessary multiplication of effort and expense ...'

This reasoning underlies the scheme for assistance laid down in the Strasbourg Convention."[72]

Under the heading "A coherent scheme that accords with international law", Lord Phillips said that Pt 5 proceedings in respect of property outside the jurisdiction would involve the assertion of an exorbitant jurisdiction in personam without any basis in international law. He went on to criticise the reasoning and conclusion of the Court of Appeal in the following terms:

"At para 14 of his judgment Hooper LJ cited the following description by the appellants of the effect of SOCA's submissions:

'Parliament has conferred authority on the enforcement authorities to bring proceedings to vest in a trustee for civil recovery property situated abroad which derives entirely from unlawful conduct abroad where neither the holder of the property, nor any intermediate holders of the property, or property from which the holder's property is derived, have ever been domiciled, resident or present within the jurisdiction; in other words, where there is no connection with the jurisdiction whatsoever.'

---

[72] *Perry* [2012] UKSC 35 at [58]–[61].

Hooper LJ accepted that this result was startling. He was right to do so. Asserting in personam jurisdiction over the holder of such property, or of associated property, has, as I have said, no precedent in international law. It would not be reasonable to expect the holder of the property, or any person holding associated property or claiming to own the property, to submit to the jurisdiction of a United Kingdom court when neither they nor the property had any connection with that jurisdiction. Any order made would be likely to be made unopposed.

In these circumstances the exorbitant confiscation proceedings that had resulted in an unopposed recovery order would be unlikely to bear fruit. Hooper LJ stated on a number of occasions that the recovery order would operate in personam so as to give the trustee for civil recovery a right against the holder of the property. Such a right would, however, be likely to be nugatory, for there would be no basis upon which the trustee for civil recovery could found jurisdiction in the United Kingdom over the holder of the property or any associated property so long as they remained outside the jurisdiction. The fact that they had been served in the Part 5 proceedings would not confer jurisdiction in relation to a claim by the trustee. It was common ground that if in such circumstances the trustee sought to bring a civil claim in respect of the property in the state where it was located, his title would not be likely to be recognised.

Hooper LJ advanced the following practical justification for according Part 5 extraterritorial effect. He held, at para.15, that if the appellants were correct:

'a court in this jurisdiction would be unable to make a civil recovery order in respect of land or other property in Spain bought with the proceeds of crimes committed here by a person resident here. Unable to obtain a civil recovery order, the enforcement authority could not take any steps here to require the person to hand over the property in Spain. Nor (so it appears)

> could the United Kingdom take enforcement action in
> Spain pursuant to [the Strasbourg Convention] (to
> which I return below) because there would be no
> order of the court to enforce: see paragraph 81 below.'
>
> This reasoning is not compelling. The appropriate course
> in the circumstances envisaged by Hooper LJ would be to
> obtain a confiscation order under Part 2, 3 or 4 and to
> make a request for assistance via the Secretary of State in
> accordance with section 74.
>
> I can see no compelling reason why Parliament should
> have wished to confer on SOCA a right to seek a civil
> recovery order in respect of the proceeds of a crime that
> was not committed within the United Kingdom where
> those proceeds are not within the United Kingdom."[73]

Lord Phillips concluded that the High Court of England and
Wales had no jurisdiction under Pt 5 to make a recovery order
in relation to property outside England and Wales and it
followed that the court had no jurisdiction to make the
worldwide PFO. The PFO appeal was allowed. As to the
disclosure order, Lord Phillips said that

> "[t]he point is a very short one. No authority is required
> under English law for a person to request information
> from another person anywhere in the world. But Section
> 357 authorises orders for requests for information with
> which the recipient is obliged to comply, subject to penal
> sanction. Subject to limited exceptions, it is contrary to
> international law for country A to purport to make
> criminal conduct in country B committed by persons who
> are not citizens of country A. Section 357, read with section
> 359, does not simply make proscribed conduct a criminal
> offence. It confers on a United Kingdom public authority
> the power to impose on persons positive obligations to
> provide information subject to criminal sanction in the
> event of non-compliance. To confer such authority in
> respect of persons outside the jurisdiction would be a

---

[73] *Perry* [2012] UKSC 35 at [70]-[73].

particularly startling breach of international law. For this reason alone I consider it implicit that the authority given under section 357 can only be exercised in respect of persons who are within the jurisdiction."[74]

Baroness Hale, Lord Kerr, Lord Wilson, Lord Reed, Sir Anthony Hughes and Lord Brown concurred.

Regardless of the true statutory interpretation of the extra-territorial effects of Pt 5, it seems that the conclusion reached did not reflect what Parliament had intended and legislation followed (surprisingly quickly).

The decision is of great importance, despite it being reversed by primary legislation as to its effect. Amongst other things it demonstrates that POCA 2002 is to be read in the light of international agreements (specifically for Pt 5 of the Strasbourg Convention) and that the temptation to latch on to isolated statutory provisions and then to give them broad effect should be resisted.

Of importance for the interpretation of Pt 7 and the definition of criminal property, Lord Phillips said this:

"Section 316(4) has a definition of property (the definition) that applies in Part 5: 'Property is all property wherever situated and includes—(i) money, (ii) all forms of property, real or personal, heritable or moveable, (c) things in action and other intangible or incorporeal property.' Mitting J and the Court of Appeal were impressed by the natural meaning of the words 'wherever situated' and concluded that those words should be applied, without restriction, to property in respect of which a recovery order could be made. Thus a recovery order could be made in respect of any form of property, whether real, personal or a chose in action, and wherever in the world that property was situated. The words 'wherever situated' do not describe the type of property to which Pt 5 applies. Rather they indicate the location of the property to which the

---

[74] *Perry* [2012] UKSC 35 at [94].

provisions of Pt 5 can apply. The definition is repeated no less than eight times in POCA 2002: ss.84(1), 150(1), 232(1), 316(4), 326(9), 340(9), 414(1) and 447(4). POCA is peppered with references to 'property'. All fall within the definition. But the definition cannot be applied so as to add to the words 'property', wherever it appears, the words 'wherever situated'."[75]

He concluded (the first of the numbered conclusions under [12] of the judgment) that "[t]he courts below placed undue weight on the definition of 'property' in POCA".

On 25 April 2013, the Crime and Courts Act 2013 was passed, which by s.48 provides for a new POCA 2002 s.282A:

"**282A Scope of powers**

(1) An order under this Chapter may be made by the High Court in England and Wales or the Court of Session—
  (a) in respect of property wherever situated, and
  (b) in respect of a person wherever domiciled, resident or present,
  subject to subsection (2).
(2) Such an order may not be made by the High Court in England and Wales or the Court of Session in respect of—
  (a) property that is outside the United Kingdom, or
  (b) property that is in the United Kingdom but outside the relevant part of the United Kingdom,
  unless there is or has been a connection between the case and the relevant part of the United Kingdom ...[76]
(3) The circumstances in which there is or has been such a connection include those described in Schedule 7A.
  ..."

The new Sch.7A provides that:

---

[75] *Perry* [2012] UKSC 35 at [13]–[14].
[76] Omitted text.

"Unlawful conduct

1   There is a connection where the unlawful conduct occurred entirely or partly in the relevant part of the United Kingdom."

Property

2   There has been a connection where the property in question has been in the relevant part of the United Kingdom, but only if it was recoverable property in relation to the unlawful conduct for some or all of the time it was there.

3   There is a connection where there is other property in the relevant part of the United Kingdom that is recoverable property in relation to the unlawful conduct.

4   There has been a connection where, at any time, there has been other property in the relevant part of the United Kingdom that, at the time, was recoverable property in relation to the unlawful conduct.

Person

5(1) There is or has been a connection where a person described in sub-paragraph (2)—
    (a)   is linked to the relevant part of the United Kingdom,
    (b)   was linked to that part of the United Kingdom at a time when the unlawful conduct, or some of the unlawful conduct, was taking place, or
    (c)   has been linked to that part of the United Kingdom at any time since that conduct took place.

(2)   Those persons are—
    (a)   a person whose conduct was, or was part of, the unlawful conduct;
    (b)   a person who was deprived of property by the unlawful conduct;

(c) a person who holds the property in question;

(d) a person who has held the property in question, but only if it was recoverable property in relation to the unlawful conduct at the time;

(e) a person who holds other property that is recoverable property in relation to the unlawful conduct;

(f) a person who, at any time, has held other property that was recoverable property in relation to the unlawful conduct at the time.

(3) A person is linked to the relevant part of the United Kingdom if the person is—

(a) a British citizen, a British overseas territories citizen, a British National (Overseas) or a British Overseas citizen,

(b) a person who, under the British Nationality Act 1981, is a British subject,

(c) a British protected person within the meaning of that Act,

(d) a body incorporated or constituted under the law of any part of the United Kingdom, or

(e) a person domiciled, resident or present in the relevant part of the United Kingdom.[77]

9.7 Jurisdiction over money laundering offences committed abroad: *R. v Rogers*[78]

On 19 June 2013 in the Crown Court, Mr Rogers was convicted of converting criminal property under s.327(1)(c) of POCA 2002. It is of importance that while he was originally charged with an offence under s.327(1)(e) in relation to the removal of the proceeds of the fraud from the UK, the prosecution amended the indictment when it became clear that the offence under that subsection could not be made out (he did not do the relevant acts in the UK). The indictment provided that

---

[77] Other text omitted.

[78] *R. v Rogers (Bradley David)* [2014] EWCA Crim 1680; [2015] 1 W.L.R. 1017; [2014] 2 Cr. App. R. 32 (p.516).

"between 23 October 2007 and 1 September [he] converted the sum of £715,000 being criminal property obtained by fraud from England and Wales by permitting the receipt of money into his personal bank accounts in Spain and allowing the subsequent withdrawal of the money."

The offence related to advance fee scams operated by Rogers' co-accused. Call centres based in Spain or Turkey employed UK nationals and, in exchange for the (relevant advance) fee, offered false promises that included, variously, debt elimination and escort services. Callers made payment to UK bank accounts of bogus UK companies. Around £5.7 million in total was received. Rogers in Spain provided Spanish bank accounts into which some of the proceeds were transferred. Approximately £715,000 was received in this way.

On appeal, Mr Rogers contended that UK courts had no jurisdiction to deal with the offence because all the acts alleged against Rogers took place in Spain by a non-resident of the UK in relation to a Spanish bank account. It was argued the judge was wrong to conclude that the offence of laundering of criminal property, obtained by fraud that occurred in the UK, where the person accused lived and worked in Spain and merely permitted money to be received into his Spanish bank account and withdrawn by others, was justiciable in England. It was further contended UK consumers who paid money into the UK bank accounts suffered a loss at this point. Mr Rogers was not involved in the transfer of those monies and could not, accordingly, commit the s.327(1)(e) offence. The *subsequent* receipt and withdrawal of money from the Spanish bank account did not represent any additional loss to the UK consumer—that is to say, the acts in Spain had caused no distinct identifiable loss to the victims of the fraud, nor were they acts within the UK. Thus, by this argument, anything done by Mr Rogers was outside the jurisdiction of the English court and outside of the scope of s.327(1)(c) on conventional jurisdictional grounds. The prosecution submitted that POCA 2002 *did* provide the necessary jurisdiction and that the modern approach was to be found in the decision of the Court of

Appeal in *R. v Smith (Wallace Duncan) (No.4)*[79]. That decision was, in essence, that where a substantial measure of the activities constituting a crime takes place within the jurisdiction, the courts of England and Wales have jurisdiction to try the offence, save where it can seriously be argued that the acts alleged should be tried in another jurisdiction on grounds of comity. Put another way, rules of comity, it was said, do not require more than that a state should refrain from punishing persons for conduct within the territory of another state where the relevant conduct had no harmful consequences for the state imposing punishment. The difficulty, it is suggested, is that there is an inevitable tendency to elide the conduct that is relevant for the offence of laundering with the conduct for the predicate offence that gives rise to the criminal property as defined by POCA 2002. The place of the relevant acts in *Rogers* was different.

The Court of Appeal held that ss.327(2A) and 340(2)(b), together with the definitions of criminal property under POCA 2002 s.340(3) and (9), strongly indicated that money laundering abroad was potentially within the reach of the UK courts and that Parliament had intended for POCA 2002 to have extraterritorial reach. Further, s.340(11) provides that money laundering is an act which "(a) constitutes an offence under Section 327, 328 or 329, ... (d) would constitute an offence specified in paragraph (a), (b) or (c) if done in the United Kingdom ...". That appeared to the Court of Appeal to admit of no other construction than that Parliament intended extraterritorial effect to be given to POCA 2002. That view was fortified in the court's view by the provision of s.327(2A) (where an offence, in circumstances specified by statutory instrument, would constitute merely a regulatory offence in the UK). The court further held that the conduct was within the jurisdiction of the UK courts by virtue of *R. v Smith (Wallace Duncan) (No.4)* because the criminal acts took place within and impacted upon victims in the UK. The court considered that the Spanish courts would not be concerned with the acts and offences alleged.

---

[79] *R. v Smith (Wallace Duncan) (No.4)* [2004] EWCA Crim 631; [2004] Q.B. 1418; [2004] 2 Cr. App. R. 17 (p.269).

It will be immediately obvious from the foregoing, necessarily brief, summary of the facts and the approach of the Court of Appeal that the decision has potentially wide-ranging effects. The conventional understanding of POCA 2002 is that it renders it an offence to launder criminal property (as laundering is defined by ss.327–329) in the UK where the predicate offence is committed outside the jurisdiction. *Rogers* postulates jurisdiction in the reverse scenario, namely where the predicate offence occurs in the jurisdiction and the criminal property is laundered (as that concept is understood by reference to ss.327–329 etc.) outside the jurisdiction. Put another way, the money laundering regime is directed towards making it an offence to (broadly) deal with property in the jurisdiction that is derived from an offence that occurred elsewhere (i.e. outside the jurisdiction). POCA 2002 makes it an offence to deal with property (i.e. the actus reus) in the jurisdiction where the property is derived from predicate criminal conduct that occurs elsewhere. In doing so, it gives effect to the intent of the 1991 First EU Money Laundering Directive[80]. The offence is the handling of the property under ss.327–329 in the jurisdiction irrespective of where the predicate offence took place. The criticism to which the decision in *R. v Rogers* is open is that it treats the rules on the *location of the predicate offence* and the immateriality of the location of the acts that constitute the relevant predicate conduct as indifferently applicable to the acts which constitute the offence of laundering. The result in *Rogers* is that the court has jurisdiction over *those* acts (namely, of money laundering) even though they are not acts that took place within the jurisdiction.

There is no statutory provision that appears to warrant that approach and the statutory provision for the first, in the absence of clear words, is not a basis for the second, reverse, position. That is a novel approach, given that the place where the actus reus of an offence took place remains of cardinal importance for conferring the criminal jurisdiction unless otherwise provided for (as, for example, under s.89 of the Financial Services Act 2012 referred to above). To take the

---

[80] Council Directive 91/308/EEC of 10 June 1991 on prevention of the use of the financial system for the purpose of money laundering [1991] OJ L166/77.

Court of Appeal's decision to its logical conclusion, it would follow that the court would have jurisdiction to try an offence alleged where both the predicate conduct and the laundering occurred other than within the jurisdiction. The practical issue of whether a prosecutor would be remotely interested in bringing a prosecution in that circumstance is not of course relevant to the formal issue of jurisdiction itself.

Full discussion is beyond the scope of this Chapter, but it can be seen that s.327(c) makes it an offence to convert criminal property. The only definitional concepts necessary are the definition of criminal property, namely, what criminal property is for the purposes of the subsection/offence. that is provided by ss 340(2) and (3). By s. 340(3), property is "criminal property" if "(a) it constitutes a person's benefit from criminal conduct or it represents such a benefit (in whole or part and whether directly or indirectly), and (b) the alleged offender knows or suspects that it constitutes or represents such a benefit". Section 340(2) provides the well known single criminality test for predicate conduct abroad. Criminal conduct "is conduct which (a) constitutes an offence in any part of the United Kingdom, or (b) would constitute an offence in any part of the United Kingdom if it occurred there". In contrast with the substantive money laundering offences, the concept of "money laundering", not an expression used under ss.327-329, is used in the (difficult and complicated) reporting offences for suspicion of money laundering under ss.330–332. The actus reus of those offences is having (relevant) suspicion of money laundering and not reporting it. Thus the suspected act is defined by s.340(11)(a)-(c) as the substantive offences under ss.327–329 and the inchoate and accessory offences. Section 340(11)(d) provides that acts under subsection (11)(a)–(c) would constitute an offence had those acts occurred in the United Kingdom. So what that provision does is explain that it is an offence to entertain suspicion of money laundering where *the suspected laundering* itself occurs outside the jurisdiction. There is a difference, it is suggested, between a definitional provision necessary for the purpose of interpreting ss.330–332 (which use the expression "money laundering") and establishing the actus reus of the reporting offences (crudely, the objectionable turning a "blind eye" to money laundering), and using that definition essential for the suspecting offences as a basis for conferring extra-territorial jurisdiction over the acts under ss.327–329. To adopt by analogy, Lord Phillips's reasoning in *Perry*,[81] if Parliament's intention was to confer extra-territorial jurisdiction under ss.327–329, it might have been expected to do so expressly, which would render s.340(11)(d) unnecessary for explanation of the meaning of the reporting suspicion offences under ss.330-332. The fact that Parliament found it necessary to explain that, *for the purpose of the reporting offences*, it does not matter where the suspected laundering occurs, supports the reverse conclusion from that reached by the Court of Appeal, namely that for the offences under ss.327–329, the relevant acts (actus reus) must occur in this jurisdiction. Put another way, the Court of Appeal in *Rogers* took the proposition that the *locus* of the predicate (namely, underlying criminal) conduct was irrelevant for jurisdiction for money laundering offences as the basis for taking jurisdiction over the laundering offence, despite the relevant acts for the (derivative) laundering offence occurring *outside* the jurisdiction.

While the conclusion may be doubted, the decision has potentially far-reaching effects on those who provide services abroad, including most obviously, handling funds and asset management services. The decision in *Rogers* has the consequence that persons outside the UK dealing with criminal property in any of the circumstances provided for under ss.327–329 are exposed to criminal liability. Whether that is confined to UK nationals or not is not clear. But if not, it is another major (and insufficiently explained) departure from

---

[81] *Perry* [2012] UKSC 35 at [36]: "Had Parliament ... intended Part 5 to extend to property outside the United Kingdom they would surely have included provisions parallel to section 74. The fact that they did not do so strongly suggests that there was no intention that Part 5 should have extra-territorial effect." Similarly, in *Perry*, Lord Phillips criticised the courts below for an overemphasis and a contextual reliance on the definition of "property". At [11]: "The courts below placed undue weight on the definition of property in POCA". In *Rogers*, the court said at [46] that "[t]he definition of criminal property in section 340(3) taken together with the provision in section 340(9) that 'Property is all property wherever situated...', is a further indication of the extra-territorial reach intended by Parliament."

the basic principle of construction that, if any construction is otherwise possible, an Act will not be construed as applying to foreigners in respect of acts done by them outside the dominions of the sovereign power enacting.[82] If the jurisdiction under *Rogers* is confined to UK nationals, that would seem to be a curious result—but the alternative would be quite extraordinary. While the result in *Rogers* is to be doubted, it is of course the law until reviewed and reversed on the point by the Supreme Court.

9.7.1 Money laundering under POCA 2002

The importance of money laundering as a discrete offence is that it is concerned with those involved, in a variety of ways, in the transmission of tangible or intangible property that is derived from a criminal offence for the purpose of disguising or concealing its criminal origin. The requirement for under-lying, predicate, criminal conduct from which property is derived is thus an essential element of the laundering offence. There are thus, generally, two offences:

- the underlying offence from which the property is derived, commonly referred to as the "predicate" offence; and
- the laundering offence.

Where the predicate offence occurs within the territorial jurisdiction, that commonly presents no difficulty. The key attribute of money laundering as a discrete offence, separate from the predicate offence,[83] is that it establishes a legal basis for judicial authorities to take action (whether by seizure or confiscation) in respect of *proceeds* from a foreign offence and over which the authorities otherwise have no jurisdiction under ordinary territorial principles. The jurisdiction is derived from the "deeming" provision under s.340(2)(b) which trans-poses the predicate conduct to the UK and then applies domestic criminal law to it to determine whether it is criminal.

---

[82] *R. v Jameson* [1896] 2 Q.B. 425 QBD per Lord Russell of Killowen CJ.
[83] But which (predicate) offence is nonetheless an essential element of the substantive laundering offence.

The starting point is the definition of money laundering under s.340(11) POCA 2002:

> "(11) Money laundering is an act which –
>
> (a) constitutes an offence under section 327, 328 or 329,
> (b) constitutes an attempt, conspiracy or incitement to commit an offence specified in paragraph (a),
> (c) constitutes aiding, abetting, counselling or procuring the commission of an offence specified in paragraph (a), or
> (d) would constitute an offence specified in paragraph (a), (b) or (c) if done in the United Kingdom."

The definition is the same under POCA 2002 and under the 2007 Regulations. Under the previous primary legislation (principally the Criminal Justice Act 1988[84] and the Drug Trafficking Act 1994)[85], "money laundering" as such was not a defined independent offence. Further, under the Money Laundering Regulations 1993, there was an important qualification to the meaning of money laundering under the Criminal Justice Act 1988 so far as those subject to the Regulations were concerned and which is considered further below.

Thus, the primary substantive money laundering offences are by s.340 defined as the three offences under ss.327–329. These are discussed in more detail in Ch.1 at section 1.3.1. The primary elements of those offences are worth citing because each is an offence which relates to dealing with "criminal property"—a concept which, together with the concept of "criminal conduct", is central to the money laundering regime created under Pt 7 of POCA 2002:

> "327 Concealing etc
>
> (1) A person commits an offence if he –
>   (a) conceals criminal property;
>   (b) disguises criminal property;

---

[84] As amended by the Criminal Justice Act 1993.
[85] Consolidating the Drug Trafficking Offences Act 1986.

>   (c)   converts criminal property;
>   (d)   transfers criminal property;
>   (e)   removes criminal property from England and Wales or from Scotland or from Northern Ireland.

> ### 328 Arrangements
>
> (1) A person commits an offence if he enters into or becomes concerned in an arrangement which he knows or suspects facilitates (by whatever means) the acquisition, retention, use or control of criminal property by or on behalf of another person. ...

> ### 329 Acquisition, use and possession
>
> (1) A person commits an offence if he –
>   (a)   acquires criminal property;
>   (b)   uses criminal property;
>   (c)   has possession of criminal property. ..."

The offences of (broadly): (i) concealing and transferring criminal property; (ii) entering into or becoming concerned with an arrangement that a person knows facilitates the acquisition (etc.) of criminal property by or on behalf of another; and (iii) acquiring or having possession of criminal property together constitute a well-established structure in which the offences may be seen as concentric circles surrounding the original predicate criminal conduct and each being further removed from it. The general structure of the money laundering offences is derived from the wording of the Vienna Convention of 1988 and the First EU Money Laundering Directive of 1991 (the First Directive), though s.328, in particular, goes further than either art.3(1)(b) of the Convention or art.1 of the Directive. That was the view of the Court of Appeal in *Bowman v Fels*.[86]

The expression "becomes concerned in an arrangement" under s.328, the provision of most concern and greatest risk to

---

[86] *Bowman v Fels* [2005] EWCA Civ 226; [2005] 1 WLR 3083; [2005] 2 Cr. App. R. 19 (p.243) at [51].

professionals, is an expression that appears to be intentionally wide in its scope. Some assistance is to be derived from the 2007 Regulations in connection with the definition of an independent legal practitioner under reg.3(9) as a person who by way of business provides legal services when "participating in" a real property or financial transaction. Regulation 3(9) provides that: "For these purposes a person *participates in a transaction* by assisting in the planning or execution of the transaction or otherwise acting for or on behalf of a client in the transaction" (emphasis supplied).[87]

It is not necessary that the person under s.328 was involved from the start of the arrangement or transaction. It is sufficient that he becomes concerned in the relevant arrangement at some stage. But the assistance must be known or suspected by the person P to facilitate retention or control of the criminal property by or on behalf of A, whether by concealment, removal from the jurisdiction, transfer to third persons, or otherwise or else to enable A to have access to his criminal property or be used by him for his benefit to acquire other property.

To establish criminal liability for the offence under POCA 2002 s.328, it must be proved that the defendant who was involved in the arrangement by doing the prohibited act:

- knew or suspected that the arrangement related to any person's proceeds of criminal conduct;
- knew or suspected that by the arrangement, the defendant was facilitating the retention or control by A or access to or use by, or for the benefit of A;
- did not make an authorized disclosure to NCA as soon as practicable about the arrangement and has no reasonable excuse for not doing so; or
- if a disclosure (i.e. SAR) was made, he did the prohibited act without first having obtained the requisite consent: s.328(2)(a).

---

[87] See further, *R. v Afolabi (Aminat Adedoyin)* [2009] EWCA Crim 2879 which concerned a conveyancing solicitor.

"Criminal property" is defined by s.340(3):

> "(3) Property is criminal property if
>   (a) it constitutes a person's benefit from criminal conduct or it represents such a benefit (in whole or part and whether directly or indirectly), and
>   (b) the alleged offender knows or suspects that it constitutes or represents such a benefit."

"Criminal conduct" is defined by s.340(2) (for convenience here repeated):

> "(2) Criminal conduct is conduct which –
>   (a) constitutes an offence in any part of the United Kingdom, or
>   (b) would constitute an offence in any part of the United Kingdom if it occurred there."

As to the benefit being direct or indirect, in whole or in part, see *R. v Loizou*.[88] The leading case on the means by which the Crown can establish that property is derived from criminal conduct is *R. v Anwoir*.[89]

That definition is of critical importance to the structure of the money laundering provisions and is noteworthy not least because: (1) *any* offence is sufficient to support money laundering, subject to the requirement that there be property that constitutes or represents a benefit from the offence in question; (2) the test for criminality is a legal hypothesis that determines whether the conduct constitutes a criminal offence by the application of domestic criminal law to the predicate facts. That means that where the relevant (predicate) conduct takes place abroad, whether or not it is criminal conduct is determined *solely* by reference to UK criminal law. Conventionally, that is referred to as a "single-criminality" test, in contradistinction to a test of "double-criminality" which

---

[88] *R. v Loizou (Lisa)* [2005] EWCA Crim 1579; [2005] 2 Cr. App. R. 37 (p.618); [2005] Crim. L.R. 885.

[89] *R. v Anwoir (Ilham)* [2008] EWCA Crim 1354; [2009] 1 W.L.R. 980; [2008] 2 Cr. App. R. 36 (p.532).

requires consideration to be given to whether the (predicate) conduct supporting the laundering offence infringed the criminal code of the jurisdiction where it actually occurred. The single-criminality test under s.340(2)(b) is a remarkable, though not new, circumstance.

The First Directive provided that "money laundering shall be regarded as such even where the activities which generated the property to be laundered were perpetrated in the territory of another Member State or in that of a third country". The Criminal Justice Act 1993 (that introduced a new s.93A(7) to the Criminal Justice Act 1988) gave effect to this and provided:

> "(7) In this Part of this Act 'criminal conduct' means conduct which constitutes an offence to which this Part of this Act applies or would constitute such an offence if it had occurred in England and Wales or (as the case may be) Scotland."

Thus, the definition of criminal conduct under s.340(2)(b) POCA 2002 is essentially the same as that established for the first time in 1993. The material difference is that under the CJA 1988 (as amended), it was necessary that the conduct in question constitute (effectively) an indictable offence rather than one that could be tried summarily before a magistrates' court.

The effect of the provision under s.340(2)(b) means that, at least theoretically, prior to the application of the defences under SOCPA 2005, a person may be liable to prosecution in the UK for money laundering offences where the predicate conduct that occurred abroad may in fact not have infringed the criminal code of the place where it took place. For example, were bullfighting to occur in the UK, those involved would undoubtedly commit a variety of offences. But bullfighting is not an offence in Spain, but, on the contrary, a cherished part of national culture. The effect of s.340(2)(b) and 340(3) is that a person who, for example, receives in the UK the proceeds from bullfighting will be exposed to prosecution for money laundering (subject, of course, to the requirement that it be recognised (known or suspected)[90] by the person who benefits from the proceeds, that bullfighting would constitute an offence in the UK). It was this perceived unfairness in particular which gave rise to the limited defences provided by SOCPA 2005.

That represented a very significant extension of the criminal jurisdiction that gave rise to substantial criticism. It is certainly a jurisdiction that is difficult to reconcile with the principles outlined at the beginning of this Chapter. That the scope of the definition of criminal conduct is intentionally so wide is put beyond serious question by the fact that the new jurisdiction for "Civil Recovery" under Pt 5 POCA 2002 (namely, provisions concerned with the recovery of criminally derived assets without the prior requirement for prosecution and conviction of a criminal offence) adopts a double-criminality test under s.241.

The fact that the single-criminality test was introduced to the CJA 1988 by the CJA 1993 is the more remarkable because the same legislation for the first time conferred jurisdiction on English courts for serious inchoate offences such as conspiracy under the Theft Act 1968 where the intended criminal act was intended to take place abroad. At the time, that was considered to be an important derogation from the well-established narrow conception of the territorial jurisdiction.[91] The Law Commission had baulked at recommending a single-criminality test in relation to those offences under the proposed new (extra-territorial) jurisdiction notwithstanding the compelling argument that almost all jurisdictions would be likely to treat acts of theft and fraud as criminal. The Law Commission, in its 1989 Report,[92] commenting upon the possibility of a single-criminality test for the extended jurisdiction, stated that: "we are unwilling to countenance the introduction of a rule

---

[90] That is, for the purposes of s.340(3)(b).
[91] The criminal act itself would not occur in the UK and there would be no effects in the UK.
[92] Law Commission, *Jurisdiction over Offences of Fraud and Dishonesty with a Foreign Element* (HMSO, 1989).

that would penalize the preparation of plans to do what would not amount to an offence in the place where they were to be implemented".[93]

The jurisdiction which is conferred by s.340(2)(b) is properly characterised as "extra-territorial" so far as that expression is conventionally used to refer to jurisdiction that is not founded upon the territorial jurisdiction. As is clear from ss.327–329, the only requirement to found jurisdiction of the criminal courts to try a person for an offence is that they are within the jurisdiction. The "criminal property" under s.340(3) is itself not required to be within the jurisdiction because s.340(9) provides:

> "(9) Property is all property *wherever situated*[94] and includes
> (a) money;
> (b) all forms of property, real or personal, heritable or moveable;
> (c) things in action and other intangible or incorporeal property."

It will be apparent that the aspect of extra-territoriality discussed above gives rise to serious implications and difficult practical problems for those with any non-domestic dealings. Although it is easy to overstate such practical difficulties, transposing extra-territorial acts to the UK on a hypothetical basis is not always straightforward. What level of investigation is required as to the source and nature of any funds or other assets which are transferred? To what extent does any foreign transaction have to be investigated and understood? Plainly caution is required and the level of enquiry will need to be tailored with care to the surrounding circumstances of the transaction. Those issues are considered in further detail below.

One other point which has troubled practitioners is when an activity, which would require (for example) FCA approval in the UK but does not require regulatory approval in the foreign jurisdiction where it occurs, causes (by way of example) funds

---

[93] *Jurisdiction over Offences of Fraud and Dishonesty with a Foreign Element* at para.5.24.
[94] Emphasis added.

to be remitted to the UK. Is it really the case that by carrying out the hypothetical exercise of transposing the unauthorised activity to the UK, such "lawful" activity is rendered unlawful because it would be unlawful *had* that activity occurred in the UK? That appears to be the result from a strict construction.[95]Although it is likely that the courts will have to rule upon the interpretation of those principles in a criminal context where a level of certainty is undoubtedly required, until such time as there is further, much needed, clarification in this area, the prudent approach has to be to adopt a cautious attitude to any such activity.

It will be readily apparent that the extra-territorial impact of the POCA 2002 provisions created a number of practical problems. To meet those problems, and the many criticisms which were made, SOCPA 2005 provided for a new range of defences to offences created by ss.327–329 POCA 2002. As pointed out above, it would have been possible to re-define the concept of "criminal conduct" but that route was not adopted. Instead, for each of the three offences a separate (but identical) defence was legislated for.

Section 102 of SOCPA 2005 amended POCA 2002 by the addition of s.327(2A) and (2B), s.328(3) and (4), and s.329(2A) and (2B). It is a defence to any offence under those sections if (1) a person knows, or believes on reasonable grounds, that the relevant criminal conduct occurred in a particular country or territory outside the UK; and (2) the relevant criminal conduct was not, at the time it occurred, unlawful under the criminal law then applying in that country or territory; and (3) the relevant criminal conduct was not of a description prescribed by an order made by the Secretary of State. In each instance, the "relevant criminal conduct" is the criminal conduct by reference to which the property concerned is criminal property.

Accordingly, it is necessary to establish that there is a potential criminal liability, having applied the relevant provisions of ss.327–329. To do so necessarily requires an assessment as to

---

[95] A strict construction is difficult to avoid by necessary implication in the light of the definition of "unlawful conduct" under s.241.

whether or not there is criminal property. By applying POCA 2002 s.340(2) and (3), it is necessary to identify the criminal conduct by transposing it (if it occurred outside the UK) to the UK. If there is such criminal conduct, then the property must not only constitute a person's benefit from that conduct, but there must be the requisite knowledge or suspicion on the part of the alleged offender that the property constitutes or represents such a benefit. Having conducted that exercise, it is necessary to apply the defences (if appropriate). Does the relevant person know or believe on reasonable grounds that the relevant criminal conduct occurred in a particular country or territory outside the UK? The answer to this question in the circumstances is likely to be "yes". That is the first gateway of the defence.

If, however, the relevant criminal conduct was *not*, at the time it occurred, unlawful under the criminal law, then that is the second gateway of the defence. It is then necessary to pass the third gateway. This is that the relevant criminal conduct was *not* of a description prescribed by an order made by the Secretary of State. The order made by the Secretary of State was the Proceeds of Crime Act 2002 (Money Laundering: Exceptions to Overseas Conduct Defence) Order 2006.

That Order prescribes conduct which would constitute an offence punishable by imprisonment for a maximum term in excess of 12 months in any part of the UK if it occurred there other than an offence under the Gaming Act 1968, an offence under the Lotteries and Amusements Act 1976 or an offence under ss.23 or 25 FSMA 2000. Section 23 of FSMA 2000 addresses restrictions on financial promotion, and s.25 is concerned with contravention of the general prohibition. The latter provisions in particular caused much concern for financial institutions when they transposed conduct to the UK.

It will also be apparent that the question of the maximum sentence for an offence is one of the critical factors for the operation of the defences described above. It hardly needs to be said that, save in the most serious and obvious cases, that element will not be a matter of common knowledge, and imposes a new area which will require research and clarification.

While the analytical steps required under those provisions are not straightforward, the net result does remove some of the unfairness of the unamended POCA 2002. It remains the case that careful thought will have to be given to, and investigations made into, the underlying facts in order to ensure there is sufficient cogent material to make good the defence. In each instance of review, the "relevant criminal conduct" for investigation is the criminal conduct by reference to which the property concerned is (at least at an early stage of the analysis) criminal property.

9.8 The disclosure obligation

A number of the principles discussed in this section are of equal relevance to domestic transactions. But when considering the application of the disclosure obligations imposed under POCA 2002, so far as those apply to international transactions, it is appropriate to place the obligation in context. If one considers the trade in financial assets as a sub-class of intangible assets, the volume of cross-border trade is enormous, by many orders (perhaps as much as 30 times) exceeding trade in goods. While at the time of the second edition of this book in 2009 the global financial system appeared to be exceptionally fragile, Philip Wood[96] observed that in 2005, seven banks had balance sheets of about 10 per cent of the US GDP and that, globally, payment systems turn over US $1,500 trillion per year, that is to say, a sum equivalent to world GDP every fortnight. Thus, in the context of the volume of international financial transactions, it is to be expected, as inevitable, that circumstances giving rise to suspicion so as to trigger a report to the NCA are themselves going to be exceptional. To September 2014 there were 354,186 SARs. (that may be compared with fewer than 20,000 in 2000).

---

[96] Philip R. Wood, *The Law and Practice of International Finance*, (London: Sweet & Maxwell, 2008).

Of those, only 14,155 were "consent" SARs, that is to say "authorised disclosures". The overwhelming majority (82 per cent) of reports were made by banks. Retail banks continue to be the major contributor of SARs, with submissions from this sector alone (291,055) exceeding the total number of SARs received by the UK Finance Intelligence Unit for the reporting period of 2011/12 (278,665). It is also an increase of 15.80 per cent on the 2012/13 submissions by the sector (251,336)[97].

The policy objective underlying the reporting regime under POCA 2002 is the acquisition of data by the NCA and other law enforcement agencies that is the product of the disclosure obligations (the ELMER (i.e. SARs) database now holds more than a million SARs and it is an explicit law enforcement priority that this information be more widely disseminated and better utilised). That data is the product of the consent regime established by: (a) the disclosure provisions under s.338 (an "authorised disclosure"), which provides that the acts under POCA 2002 ss.327–329 are not offences where before the relevant (and otherwise "prohibited" money laundering) act is done, either the "appropriate" or deemed consent to the act is given; and (b) the disclosure provisions under POCA 2002 s.330(4) (by s.337 a "protected disclosure"—but protection only against a claim for breach of confidence analogous to the existing common law protection). Broadly, s.330 requires a person (A), who in the course of their business in the regulated sector knows or suspects, or has grounds for knowing or suspecting, that another (B) is engaged in money laundering, to report that knowledge or suspicion to the NCA as soon as practicable after the relevant information comes to them failing which an offence is committed. The robustness of the consent regime is clear from, on the one hand, the legal and practical consequences of making the relevant disclosure, and on the other, the penalties for failing to make a disclosure where disclosure is necessary to avoid criminal liability—penalties which, somewhat surprisingly, are similar to those for being engaged in the financing of terrorism.

---

[97] SARs Report, NCA, 2014, *http://www.nationalcrimeagency.gov.uk/publications/464-2014-sars-annual-report/file* [Accessed 30 September 2015].

The substantive money laundering offence (as distinct from the failure to disclosure offence under s.330), that arguably presents greatest risk to those engaged in the regulated sector, is under s.328 where the offence of money laundering is committed where a person either enters into or (more vaguely) becomes "concerned in" an arrangement that they know or suspect facilitates the acquisition, retention, use or control of criminal property by or on behalf of another. Both "entering into" or "becoming concerned in" are acts (s.340(11)) that occur at a point in time and no offence will be committed at any intermediate step that does not involve the acquisition, retention, use or control of criminal property.[98] Once a disclosure is made under s.338 in connection with an arrangement that facilitates any of the things specified under s.328, the legal effect of a SAR to the NCA is to *frustrate* by illegality the transaction following disclosure and pending consent. As a result, each party is relieved of further obligation to perform until the "appropriate consent" is given. That effect may be for a period of up to 40 days without restraint order (although it is to be noted that in practice consent is given to the majority of reported transactions within a few days). No private law remedy is available, either by way of injunction or for damage sustained as the result of delay. The sole, and very limited, remedy is judicial review. In *Squirrell Ltd v Natwest*,[99] Laddie J observed that that effect, leaving a party who may well be entirely innocent without apparent redress and without obligation on SOCA (now the NCA) to disclose the fact or nature of any investigation, is a potential "grave injustice". In *R. (on the application of UMBS Online Ltd) v SOCA*,[100] the Court of Appeal expressed serious concern about the ambit and effect of the provisions[101] and Sedley LJ was moved to comment that "in setting up the SOCA, the state has set out to create an *Alsatia*—a region of executive action free of judicial oversight".[102]

---

[98] *Bowman v Fels* at [67]–[69].

[99] *Squirrell Ltd v National Westminster Bank Plc* [2005] EWHC 664 (Ch); [2006] 1 W.L.R. 637.

[100] *R. (on the application of UMBS Online Ltd) v Serious Organised Crime Agency* [2007] EWCA Civ 406; [2007] Bus. L.R. 1317.

[101] See the judgment of Ward LJ.

[102] *UMBS Online* at [58].

Two threshold conditions need to be satisfied for liability under s.328. The first is entering into or becoming concerned with a transaction that is known or suspected to facilitate the acquisition retention (and so on) of criminal property. The second is having the relevant knowledge or suspicion. The concept of entering into a transaction is one that is fairly clear. Becoming "concerned in" a transaction is a much vaguer concept[103] and consequently a source of real uncertainty and thus legal risk. That has particularly been the case for lawyers engaged in giving advice on international transactions. Following the introduction of POCA 2002, it was widely thought that POCA 2002 represented a wide-ranging incursion into areas that had hitherto been protected by legal privilege, which privilege it was thought might be abrogated by the merest suspicion. The consequence, it was apprehended, might be, for example, that whenever a lawyer advising on an international transaction entertained misgivings about the provenance of funds, he was thereby, without more, exposed to criminal liability under s.328 with the attendant disclosure obligation outlined above. That would quite obviously represent a potentially massive legislative interference with commerce. While the issue has not been judicially considered, in the light of decisions since the introduction of POCA 2002, it appears strongly arguable that s.328 will not ordinarily be engaged where a person is giving or receiving legal advice in circumstances where legal professional privilege attaches (that is to say where the lawyer is retained in an advisory, not ministerial capacity). That conclusion is suggested by para.63 of the judgment in *Bowman v Fels* (above) where Brooke LJ, giving a purposive construction to POCA 2002 as a statute that gives effect to European legislation, said:

> "To our mind, it is as improbable that Parliament, being the UK legislator, had the ordinary conduct of legal proceedings to judgment in mind under Section 328 (or indeed under Sections 327 and 329) as it is to suppose that the European legislator had them in mind in article 7. If the European legislator did not intend article 7, and the

---

[103] *Bowman v Fels* [2005] EWCA Civ 226; [2005] 1 W.L.R. 3083; [2005] 2 Cr. App. R. 19 (p.243) at [67].

UK legislator did not intend Sections 327–329, to cover the ordinary conduct of legal proceedings or the ordinary giving of legal advice in circumstances not making the legal adviser a co-conspirator or accessory to any other offence, it was unnecessary—and would indeed have been inappropriate—to have introduced into either article 7 or into Sections 327–329 any equivalent exceptions to those provided, respectively, by article 6 and Section 330(6)(b), (10) and (11). Support for our conclusions is provided by linguistic and policy considerations."

Bowman was specifically concerned with litigation privilege rather than legal professional (or advice) privilege. However, one of the central issues in the decision was whether it was the Parliamentary intention that POCA 2002 should abrogate privilege save where privilege is specifically preserved under s.330(6)(b) and (10). The Court of Appeal followed the principle identified by the House of Lords in *Morgan Grenfell*[104] that because of the central importance of legal privilege in the administration of justice (an importance recognised in all Member States as reflected in the Money Laundering Directives), legal privilege is not intended to be abrogated by statute save by the clearest words. That principle applies equally to litigation and advice privilege. Thus, where a lawyer advising on a transaction has knowledge or suspicion for the purposes of s.328 derived from his role as adviser, the protection against disclosure afforded to the information received by legal privilege is not thereby lost so that, *without more*, the lawyer is exposed to criminal liability in the absence of making an authorised disclosure under s.338. That the giving of legal advice is not apt to engage the disclosure obligation under s.328 POCA 2002 is lent further support by the decision in the House of Lords in *Three Rivers District Council v Governor and Company of the Bank of England (No.6)*.[105] All communications between a solicitor and his client relating to a transaction in which the solicitor has been instructed for the purpose of

---

[104] *R. (on the application of Morgan Grenfell & Co Ltd) v Special Commissioners of Income Tax* [2002] UKHL 21; [2003] 1 A.C. 563; [2002] H.R.L.R. 42.

[105] *Three Rivers District Council v Governor and Company of the Bank of England (No.6)* [2004] UKHL 48; [2005] 1 A.C. 610; [2004] 3 W.L.R. 1274, affirming *Minter v Priest* [1929] 1 K.B. 655 CA.

obtaining legal advice will be privileged, notwithstanding that they do not contain advice on matters of law or construction, provided that they are directly related to the performance by the solicitor of his professional duty as legal adviser of his client. Nevertheless, it is to be remembered that the protection afforded by legal professional privilege is limited and only covers communications between lawyer and client as this relationship has been restrictively—and it is widely thought unsatisfactorily—interpreted by the Court of Appeal in the much criticised decision in *Three Rivers District Council v Governor and Company of the Bank of England (No.5).*[106]

The discussion above is subject to the important qualification, commonly but wrongly described as the "crime-fraud" exception to privilege. At common law there is no privilege *in communications made in furtherance of a criminal purpose*: *R. v Cox.*[107] There are two grounds upon which the privilege from compulsory disclosure that will ordinarily apply to communications between a client and his lawyer will not apply where the purpose of the communication is criminal: first, at a high level of abstraction, the public interest in protecting communications between lawyers and their clients is public interest in the administration of justice. That public interest itself is removed or abrogated and otherwise has no application where the purpose of the communication is crime and necessarily contrary to the public good. Secondly, it cannot be said that receipt by a lawyer of a communication made in furtherance of a criminal purpose is received by the lawyer in the ordinary conduct of their professional business—an essential condition for privilege.[108] It is important to note that the relevant criminal purpose is a *future* purpose. There can be no objection to consulting a lawyer or communicating information where an

---

[106] *Three Rivers District Council v Governor and Company of the Bank of England (No.5)* [2003] EWCA Civ 474; [2003] Q.B. 1556; [2003] 3 W.L.R. 667.

[107] *R. v Cox (Richard Cobden)* (1884) 14 Q.B.D. 153. The same applies in relation to civil fraud: *R. v Central Criminal Court Ex p. Francis & Francis (A Firm)* [1989] A.C. 346; [1988] 3 W.L.R. 989; (1989) 88 Cr. App. R. 213 HL.

[108] *R. v Cox* (1884) 14 Q.B.D. 153 at 167, restated in *Banque Keyser Ullman SA v Skandia (UK) Insurance Co* [1986] 1 Lloyd's Rep. 336 CA.

offence has already been committed—as explained by Lord Sumner in *O'Rourke v Darbishire*.[109]

At common law, it is irrelevant whether or not the lawyer to whom the communication is made is aware of the criminal purpose. Indeed, the purpose may be the purpose of a third party.[110] The effect of the common law rule is that privilege never exists at all in connection with the communication (it is therefore not, in reality, an exception to privilege—though that is the way it is usually referred to). Nevertheless, there is nothing to suggest that it is any part of the legislative intention that s.328 should have the effect of creating a strict liability offence for solicitors in circumstances where they believed, albeit incorrectly, that privilege obtained. Such a result would be contrary to ordinary principles of statutory construction in which there is a presumption against the imposition of strict liability in the absence of unambiguous statutory language[111]

9.9 Suspicion

Particularly in international transactions, the real problem confronting a person is what, in any particular circumstances, constitutes "suspicion" as a trigger for the obligation to make a report to the NCA, whether in the context of s.328 or, more commonly, s.330. Suspicion is not easy to define and was memorably described by Lord Devlin as no more than conjecture or surmise. The difficulty with the entire money laundering regime as applied to professionals is that it rests on an unsatisfactory foundation, namely mere suspicion. The existence of suspicion, as Longmore LJ has observed, is a subjective fact. There is no qualifying requirement that the relevant suspicion be reasonable. This can be contrasted with, for example, Criminal Justice Act 1988 s.93C(2), considered in

---

[109] *O'Rourke v Darbishire*; sub nom. *Re Whitworth* [1920] A.C. 581 HL at 613. This matter was expressly adverted to under the 2001 Money Laundering Directive.

[110] *R. v Central Criminal Court Ex p. Francis & Francis (A Firm)* [1989] A.C. 346 at 397 per Lord Goff.

[111] *Gammon (Hong Kong) Ltd v Attorney-General of Hong Kong* [1985] A.C. 1; [1984] 3 W.L.R. 437; (1985) 80 Cr. App. R. 194 PC(HK) per Lord Scarman.

some detail by Lord Hope in *R. v Saik*.[112] His Lordship suggested that the requirement for reasonable suspicion was introduced "in the interests of fairness" (at [52]). One unsatisfactory consequence of that is that for all practical purposes, the fact of suspicion is incapable of being effectively challenged by its object.[113]

In principle, the criteria that need to be satisfied to constitute the (non) disclosure offence (as distinct from the substantive money laundering offences which also require suspicion as a key element of the offence) are straightforward. But that is belied by the language of s.330, as repeatedly and frequently amended by other primary and secondary legislation (that for convenience is identified in the notes). POCA 2002 s.330 provides that:

330 Failure to disclose: regulated sector

(1) A person commits an offence if [the conditions in subsections (2) to (4) are satisfied][114]

(2) The first condition is that he –
    (a) knows or suspects, or
    (b) has reasonable grounds for knowing or suspecting,
    that another person is engaged in money laundering.

(3) The second condition is that the information or other matter –
    (a) on which his knowledge or suspicion is based, or
    (b) which gives reasonable grounds for such knowledge or suspicion,
    came to him in the course of a business in the regulated sector.

(3A) The third condition is[115]–

---

[112] *R. v Saik (Abdulrahman)* [2006] UKHL 18; [2007] 1 A.C. 18; [2006] 2 Cr. App. R. 26 (p.368) at [51]–[53].

[113] *K Ltd v National Westminster Bank Plc* [2006] EWCA Civ 1039; [2007] 1 W.L.R. 311; [2007] Bus. L.R. 26 at [19] [20].

[114] Amended by Serious Organised Crime and Police Act 2005 s.104(2) (1 July 2005).

[115] Section 330(3A)–(6) substituted for s.330(4)–(6) (subject to SI 2005/1521 art.3(4)) by Serious Organised Crime and Police Act 2005 (July 1, 2005).

      (a) that he can identify the other person mentioned in subsection (2) or the whereabouts of any of the laundered property, or

      (b) that he believes, or it is reasonable to expect him to believe, that the information or other matter mentioned in subsection (3) will or may assist in identifying that other person or the whereabouts of any of the laundered property.

(4) The fourth condition is that he does not make the required disclosure to –

      (a) a nominated officer, or

      (b) a person authorised for the purposes of this Part by the Director General of the Director General of the National Crime Agency.[116]

as soon as is practicable after the information or other matter mentioned in subsection (3) comes to him.

(5) The required disclosure is a disclosure of –

      (a) the identity of the other person mentioned in subsection (2), if he knows it,

      (b) the whereabouts of the laundered property, so far as he knows it, and

      (c) the information or other matter mentioned in subsection (3).

(5A) The laundered property is the property forming the subject-matter of the money laundering that he knows or suspects, or has reasonable grounds for knowing or suspecting, that other person to be engaged in.

(6) But he does not commit an offence under this section if—

      (a) he has a reasonable excuse for not making the required disclosure,

      (b) he is a professional legal adviser or[117] relevant professional adviser [118] and—

---

[116] Crime and Courts Act 2013 Sch.8(2) para.129 (October 7, 2013: SI 2013/1682 subject to savings and transitional provisions specified in 2013 c.22 s.15 and Sch.8).

[117] Word repealed by Terrorism Act 2000 and Proceeds of Crime Act 2002 (Amendment) Regulations 2007/3398 Sch.2 para.2 (December 26, 2007).

[118] Proceeds of Crime Act 2002 and Money Laundering Regulations 2003 (Amendment) Order 2006/308 art.(2) (February 21, 2006).

(i)   if he knows either of the things mentioned in subsection (5)(a) and (b), he knows the thing because of information or other matter that came to him in privileged circumstances, or

(ii) the information or other matter mentioned in subsection (3) came to him in privileged circumstances, or

(c) subsection (7) [or (7B)][119] applies to him.

(7) This subsection applies to a person if—

(a) he does not know or suspect that another person is engaged in money laundering, and

(b) he has not been provided by his employer with such training as is specified by the Secretary of State by order for the purposes of this section.

(7A) Nor does a person commit an offence under this section if—[120]

(a) he knows, or believes on reasonable grounds, that the money laundering is occurring in a particular country or territory outside the United Kingdom, and

(b) the money laundering—

(i)   is not unlawful under the criminal law applying in that country or territory, and

(ii) is not of a description prescribed in an order made by the Secretary of State.

(7B) This subsection applies to a person if—[121]

(a) he is employed by, or is in partnership with, a professional legal adviser or a relevant professional adviser to provide the adviser with assistance or support,

(b) the information or other matter mentioned in subsection (3) comes to the person in connection with the provision of such assistance or support, and

---

[119] Words inserted by Proceeds of Crime Act 2002 and Money Laundering Regulations 2003 (Amendment) Order 2006/308 art.2(3) (February 21, 2006).

[120] Section 7A inserted by Serious Organised Crime and Police Act 2005 s.102(5) (May 15, 2006).

[121] Section 7B inserted by the Proceeds of Crime Act 2002 and Money Laundering Regulations 2003 (Amendment) Order 2006/308 art.2(4) (February 21, 2006).

      (c) the information or other matter came to the adviser in privileged circumstances.

(8) In deciding whether a person committed an offence under this section the court must consider whether he followed any relevant guidance which was at the time concerned—

      (a) issued by a supervisory authority or any other appropriate body,

      (b) approved by the Treasury, and

      (c) published in a manner it approved as appropriate in its opinion to bring the guidance to the attention of persons likely to be affected by it.

(9) A disclosure to a nominated officer is a disclosure which—

      (a) is made to a person nominated by the alleged offender's employer to receive disclosures under this section, and

      (b) is made in the course of the alleged offender's employment.[122]

(9A) But a disclosure which satisfies paragraphs (a) and (b) of subsection (9) is not to be taken as a disclosure to a nominated officer if the person making the disclosure—[123]

      (a) is a professional legal adviser or relevant professional adviser][124],

      (b) makes it for the purpose of obtaining advice about making a disclosure under this section, and

      (c) does not intend it to be a disclosure under this section.

(10) Information or other matter comes to a professional legal adviser or relevant professional adviser[125] in privileged circumstances if it is communicated or given to him—

---

[122] Serious Organised Crime and Police Act 2005 Sch.17(2) para.1 (July 1, 2005 as SI 2005/1521).

[123] Section 9A inserted by the Serious Organised Crime and Police Act 2005 s.106(2) (July 1, 2005).

[124] See note to subsection (6)(b).

[125] See note to subsection (6)(b).

(a) by (or by a representative of) a client of his in connection with the giving by the adviser of legal advice to the client,

(b) by (or by a representative of) a person seeking legal advice from the adviser, or

(c) by a person in connection with legal proceedings or contemplated legal proceedings.

(11) But subsection (10) does not apply to information or other matter which is communicated or given with the intention of furthering a criminal purpose.

(12) Schedule 9 has effect for the purpose of determining what is—

(a) a business in the regulated sector;

(b) a supervisory authority.

(13) An appropriate body is any body which regulates or is representative of any trade, profession, business or employment carried on by the alleged offender.

(14) A relevant professional adviser is an accountant, auditor or tax adviser who is a member of a professional body which is established for accountants, auditors or tax advisers (as the case may be) and which makes provision for—[126]

(a) testing the competence of those seeking admission to membership of such a body as a condition for such admission; and

(b) imposing and maintaining professional and ethical standards for its members, as well as imposing sanctions for non-compliance with those standards.

In *K Ltd*, where the issue under consideration was the meaning of the word "suspicion" under s.93A Criminal Justice Act 1988,[127] Longmore LJ said:

"What then does the word 'suspecting' mean in its particular context in the 1988 Act? It seems to us that the essential element in the word 'suspect' and its affiliates, in

---

[126] Section 14 inserted by Proceeds of Crime Act 2002 and Money Laundering Regulations 2003 (Amendment) Order 2006/308 art.2(5) (February 21, 2006).

[127] The precursor to POCA 2002 s.328.

this context, is that *the defendant must think that there is a possibility, which is more than fanciful, that the relevant facts exist. A vague feeling of unease would not suffice.*[128] But the statute does not require the suspicion to be 'clear' or 'firmly grounded and targeted on specific facts', or based upon 'reasonable grounds'. To require the prosecution to satisfy such criteria as to the strength of the suspicion would, in our view, be putting a gloss on the section. We consider therefore that, for the purpose of a conviction under Section 93A(1)(a) of the 1988 Act, the prosecution must prove that the defendant's acts of facilitating another person's retention or control of the proceeds of criminal conduct were done by a defendant who thought that there was a possibility, which was more than fanciful, that the other person was or had been engaged in or had benefited from criminal conduct."

In *R. v Da Silva*,[129] the Court of Appeal acceded to the request that guidance be given by the court for the future as to the meaning of "suspect" in a civil, rather than criminal, context. The Court of Appeal said that the italicised passage above was the relevant test. In so doing, the court rejected the submission that any inkling or fleeting thought that the property might be criminal property would suffice. Longmore LJ said that in an appropriate case the test may be subject to a further requirement that the suspicion be of a "settled nature".

The issue thus becomes the fairly narrow consideration as to what is meant by the suspicion by a person (A) that another person (B) may be engaged in money laundering. It is clear from ss.327–328 that money laundering is *an act* that, as Brooke LJ observed in *Bowman v Fels*, occurs at a point in time. Further, it is axiomatic that the act be in connection with property, and specifically *criminal property* as this is defined. It is notorious that ordinarily a thing is not of itself criminal and thus it was necessary to provide a statutory definition so as to make, for the purposes of the legislation, property "criminal property".

---

[128] Emphasis provided.
[129] *R. v Da Silva (Hilda Gondwe)* [2006] EWCA Crim 1654; [2007] 1 W.L.R. 303; [2006] 2 Cr. App. R. 35 (p.517).

That is done by s.340. The definition of criminal property is a key concept of crucial importance in the understanding of the entire AML regime. Section 340, which provides the interpretation provisions for the money laundering provisions under Pt 7, here set out for ease of reference, provides:

" [Omitted text]

    (2) Criminal conduct is conduct which –
       (a) constitutes an offence in any part of the United Kingdom, or
       (b) would constitute an offence in any part of the United Kingdom if it occurred there.
    (3) Property is criminal property if –
       (a) it constitutes a person's benefit from criminal conduct or it represents such a benefit (in whole or part and whether directly or indirectly), and
       (b) the alleged offender knows or suspects that it constitutes or represents such a benefit.
    (4) It is immaterial –
       (a) who carried out the conduct;
       (b) who benefited from it;
       (c) whether the conduct occurred before or after the passing of this Act.
    (5) A person benefits from conduct if he obtains property as a result of or in connection with the conduct.
    (6) If a person obtains a pecuniary advantage as a result of or in connection with conduct, he is to be taken to obtain as a result of or in connection with the conduct a sum of money equal to the value of the pecuniary advantage.
    (7) References to property or a pecuniary advantage obtained in connection with conduct include references to property or a pecuniary advantage obtained in both that connection and some other.
    (8) If a person benefits from conduct his benefit is the property obtained as a result of or in connection with the conduct.
    (9) Property is all property wherever situated and includes –

     (a) money;

     (b) all forms of property, real or personal, heritable or moveable;

     (c) things in action and other intangible or incorporeal property.

(10) The following rules apply in relation to property –

     (a) property is obtained by a person if he obtains an interest in it;

     (b) references to an interest, in relation to land in England and Wales or Northern Ireland, are to any legal estate or equitable interest or power;

     (c) references to an interest, in relation to land in Scotland, are to any estate, interest, servitude or other heritable right in or over land, including a heritable security;

     (d) references to an interest, in relation to property other than land, include references to a right (including a right to possession).[omitted text]."

Section 340(4) makes it immaterial who carried out the *conduct* that is the relevant conduct under s.340(2). That is an essential element of all AML legislation which in every case separates the underlying conduct (the "predicate conduct" or "predicate offence") from the laundering, which is an entirely derivative offence connected with the predicate conduct only by the property derived from it.

9.9.1   Benefit from criminal conduct

In order for property to be deemed criminal property within the definition under s.340(3)(b), it is necessary that the offender (for the purposes of ss.327–329—disregarding the inchoate and accessory offences) "knows or suspects" (or ought to do so) that the property constitutes or represents a benefit from criminal conduct (whether as to the whole or part). This is the essential mental element (mens rea) for any money laundering offence. Further, it is necessary that the property in question *in fact* be the proceeds of criminal conduct. (The contrary was argued before the House of Lords in *R. v Montila*.[130]) A person is not guilty of money laundering where he deals with property suspecting that the property represents the proceeds of crime when *in actual fact* the property is the product of a legitimate windfall such as, for example, a lottery win.[131]

It follows from the foregoing that the knowledge or suspicion under s.330 is knowledge or suspicion of A (engaged in business in the regulated sector), whether such suspicion be subjective (i.e. did know or suspect) or objective (ought to have known or suspected) that another person B is engaged in an act within ss.327–329 in connection with property that B himself knows or suspects constitutes or represents a person's benefit from criminal conduct. It is obvious that such a test is apt to give rise to difficulty in practical application in circumstances where the underlying conduct occurs overseas.

All legislation is territorial and confined to the UK unless the contrary is the clear statutory purpose. The difficulty confronting the draftsman is that money laundering is notoriously an international offence for the obvious reason that severing the jurisdictional connection between the underlying criminal act and the location of the property derived from it is commonly an effective device in disguising its origin—the ultimate objective of laundering. As has been noted, the way in which this problem is addressed is by the "deeming provision" under s.340(2) which provides that criminal conduct is either conduct which is an offence in any part of the UK or else *would constitute an offence if the conduct in question occurred in the United Kingdom*. The meaning and application of the latter, "deeming", provision (i.e. statutory hypothesis or, less

---

[130] *R. v Montila (Steven William)* [2004] UKHL 50; [2004] 1 W.L.R. 3141; [2005] 1 Cr. App. R. 26 (p.425), in particular [27]–[29]. The appeal actually concerned the precursor provision under s.93C(2) CJA 1988, but the House of Lords considered the similar position under POCA 2002 and the same requirement (See James Richardson QC (ed), *Archbold on Criminal Pleading Evidence & Practice*, (London: Sweet and Maxwell, 2015). The same point was made in relation to the charge of criminal conspiracy by the Court of Criminal Appeal in *R. v Ali (Liaquat)* [2005] EWCA Crim 87; [2006] 2 W.L.R. 316; [2006] 1 Cr. App. R. 8 (p.143).

[131] The rather obvious point is that suspicion itself, though necessary, is not a sufficient condition for liability.

elegantly, legal fiction) is the crucial issue in circumstances where the conduct occurs overseas.

While the policy reasons for POCA 2002's artificial transposing of actions are reasonably clear, the legal consequences are unsatisfactory. The difficulty with s.340(2)(b) and the statutory fiction that criminal conduct is conduct which, if it occurred within the UK, would constitute an offence here is that acts are infinitely variable and the nature of wrongdoing in any particular case may be more or less connected with and tied to the place in which such wrongdoing takes place. Extreme examples include murder or piracy on the one hand, in which locality is almost entirely irrelevant and, at the other extreme, regulatory offences. Most regulatory offences are closely tied to the jurisdiction where they occur. Thus, the consideration of whether conduct in a particular jurisdiction would constitute an offence were it to occur in the UK may quickly give rise to conceptual difficulties, possible artificiality, and consequent uncertainty. This is very important because a fundamental requirement of the criminal law is that it be certain. In *Cox v Army Council*,[132] Lord Radcliffe observed that there must be some acts or omissions punishable if done in England which cannot be reproduced by any equivalent occurrence taking place outside this country, and there must be some acts or omissions occurring outside England which are so much identified with their locality that they cannot be translated into any equivalent offence. Lord Radcliffe went on to describe translations of conduct in one place to hypothetical conduct in another:

> "the problem is to find a fair and proper equivalent, since there cannot be literal reproduction. Secondly, the occurrence that is said to constitute the offence is always the actual occurrence itself as it took place outside England and that means importing into the hypothetical English

---

[132] *Cox v Army Council* [1963] A.C. 48 HL at 71–72. This case concerned an appeal that considered s.70 Army Act 1955 which makes it an offence for (in summary) a soldier (subject to military law) serving abroad to do any (civil) act which would constitute an offence if done in England and Wales. The offence tried was driving without due care and attention (contrary to Section 3(1) RTA 1960) on a German Road and was tried by Court Martial.

occurrence *the circumstances and conditions that prevailed at the place where and the time when the thing that is complained of was done or omitted.*[133] The difficult question, as I see it, is to decide in any particular case how far those circumstances and conditions are an essential element of the act which it is said would have constituted an offence if committed in England, and how far the English offence is capable of being applied to the non-English occurrence."

There are two issues which are related and combine to give rise to cumulative difficulty in analysis: the first is whether the act in respect of which suspicion may be entertained is an act which, had it occurred here, would have constituted an offence in any part of the UK; the second requirement is that for any person to be engaged in money laundering, as has previously been noted, it is necessary that the person in question (i.e. the alleged offender) knows or suspects that the property in question represents a person's benefit from criminal conduct and if they do not do so the mens rea for the offence does not exist.

The way in which Pt 7 gives rise to what may be thought to be insuperable difficulties in transposition can be illustrated by an example. Where a person in the regulated sector entertains suspicion that a person dealing with securities on a non-UK regulated exchange (proceeds of which might flow into domestic bank accounts) has price-sensitive information such that, if the relevant securities were traded on a UK exchange the provisions that make insider dealing an offence under s.52 CJA 1993 might be engaged, is there an obligation to report the circumstances to the NCA? It will be immediately obvious that property derived from insider dealing in principle will readily constitute criminal property for the purposes of s.340 POCA. The much more difficult question is whether the conduct in question is capable, in any meaningful sense, of constituting "criminal conduct" for the purposes of s.340(2). Of critical importance in the present circumstances is that the territorial scope of the insider dealing provisions under Pt 5 of CJA 1993 is both specific and limited. Section 62 requires that there be a

---

[133] Emphasis supplied.

link between the activities complained of and the UK. Accordingly a person will not be guilty of the "dealing offence" unless: (a) they were within the UK when they did any act constituting or forming part of the dealing; (b) the dealing took place on a market, which by order made by HM Treasury is identified as being (for the purposes of Pt 5) regulated by the UK (effectively all markets operated by UK-recognised investment exchanges); and (c) the professional intermediary concerned was within the UK when he did any act forming part of the dealing. An individual will not be guilty of either the encouraging offence or the disclosure offence unless he was within the UK at the time of the disclosure/ encouragement or the recipient of the disclosure/ encouragement was within the UK.[134]

In order to make the statutory hypothesis under s.340(2) POCA 2002 work in those circumstances, where the conduct in fact takes place overseas and the securities are traded on a non-UK regulated exchange, all the facts require to be severed from their actual context and hypothetically transposed to the UK in order to answer the question "had the conduct occurred here would it have constituted an offence"? The result is one of striking artificiality. That is without even getting to the central issue of the price sensitivity of the information in question and which ordinarily is the subject of expert evidence. The law can deem anything to be the case, however unreal. The law brings itself into disrepute however if it dignifies with legal significance a wholly artificial hypothesis.[135] The illustration serves but to show that the exercise of transposition under s.340(2)(b) is one that will frequently be complex and frequently will not be possible to undertake at all in a meaningful way for the purpose of analysing whether the conduct in question, where this occurs overseas, constitutes criminal conduct from which criminal property is derived.

Drawing some of these strands together, there are some grounds for the view that, in practice, it will frequently be the

---

[134] CJA 1993 s.62(2)(a).
[135] Francis Bennion, *Bennion on Statutory Interpretation*, 5th edn (London: LexisNexis, 2007), p.1003.

case that the application of the deeming provision under Section 340(2)(b) will give rise to insuperable conceptual difficulties in transposition and these will be the greater if the connection between the predicate conduct and the place where it occurred is more proximate. Such a high level of connectedness will typically be true of regulatory, or to give another example, environmental offences. Further, it may often be possible to take a moderately sanguine view of the nature of the risk presented of committing an offence where s.340(2)(b) is engaged, particularly where engaged in conjunction with disclosure obligations triggered by suspicion, under for example s.330, because of the very uncertainty to which the statutory drafting gives rise. It is in the interests of neither law enforcement nor commerce that fear of exposure to criminal penalties should give rise to reflex defensive reporting and it is unfortunate that the legislation has tended to have this effect with a disproportionate amount of reporting being of no or negligible utility. As is discussed in the final section of this Chapter, a fundamental requirement for the imposition of criminal liability is certainty in the law—a requirement that appears to remain unsatisfied by some of the provisions under Pt 7 POCA 2002. Nevertheless, it may be expected that, where the risk attendant on deciding not to make a disclosure is material, the taking of appropriate (legal) advice will provide the best protection.

9.9.2 The extended money laundering offences – POCA Section 340(11)

Money laundering is not exhaustively defined under ss.327–329. In addition there are the offences of attempt, conspiracy or incitement to commit those offences under s.340(11)(b) and aiding, abetting, counselling or procuring those offences under s.340(11)(c) where the relevant act either occurs in the UK or where it would constitute those offences if done in the UK. Thus it is necessary, as a matter of completeness, for any person in the regulated sector not only to consider whether the primary liability money laundering offences might be committed directly but whether, in continuing to act, one of the indirect offences might be committed whether or not the conduct in question occurs here.

The necessary mental element of the offence of conspiracy to commit money laundering offences (POCA s.340(11)(b)) was an issue considered by the House of Lords in *R. v Saik*.[136] The effect of the definition of conspiracy under the Criminal Law Act 1977 s.7 was that in order for there to be liability for conspiring to commit one of the offences under ss.327–329, it would be necessary, where the property had not yet been identified at the time of the relevant agreement, that the laundered property was *intended to be* "criminal property" (as to which see further the statement of Lord Hope at [67]) or, where the property had been identified, it was *known to be* criminal property. *Saik* is authority for the proposition that mere suspicion that property is "criminal property" is insufficient for the offence of conspiracy. Although conspiracy is the most common "roll-up" offence in criminal prosecutions for money laundering, it would appear only to have application for purposes of the present discussion where a person has a shared criminal purpose and where, additionally, there is the requisite agreement.

Subject to one qualification (below) it may be that the area of risk that may be of more general application is in connection with the offence of "aiding or abetting" the commission of one of the offences under ss.327–329.[137] The law of accessory criminal liability has recently been clarified by the Court of Criminal Appeal in *R. v Bryce*.[138] It is clear that for accessory liability, it is not necessary that at the time of any assistance, the principal should have formed a settled intention to commit the crime: all that is necessary is that at the time of the act of

---

[136] *R. v Saik (Abdulrahman)* [2006] UKHL 18; [2007] 1 A.C. 18; [2006] 2 Cr. App. R. 26 (p.368). The actual issue in the appeal was conspiring to contravene s.93C(2) of the CJA 1988.

[137] As this expression is further amplified by s.8 Accessories and Abettors Act 1861, as amended by s.1 Criminal Law Act 1977: "Whosoever shall aid, abet, counsel or procure the commission of any indictable offence whether the same be an offence at common law or by virtue of any act passed or to be passed, shall be liable to be tried, indicted and punished as the principal offender."

[138] *R. v Bryce (Craig Brian)* [2004] EWCA Crim 1231; [2004] 2 Cr. App. R. 35 (p.592).

assistance the defendant foresaw *a real possibility that the principal would commit the crime.* Where the act of assistance was done in advance of the crime, which was committed in the defendant's absence, the court gave the following guidance for the mental elements necessary to prove the offence of aiding and abetting. The prosecution must prove an act done by D which in fact assisted the later commission of the offence; that D did the act deliberately realising that it was capable of assisting the offence; that D at the time of doing the act contemplated the commission of the offence by A, that is, he foresaw it as a real or "substantial risk" or "real possibility"; and that D, when doing the act, intended to assist A in what he was doing.

The risk of aiding and abetting for a person engaged in the regulated sector in transactional business might appear to be greatest under s.327 POCA 2002 rather than s.328 and, in particular, under s.327(1)(d) (transferring criminal property). The nature of the offence has some similarities to liability in civil law for dishonest assistance in breach of trust—though with the notable distinction that dishonesty is not a necessary ingredient for the offence whereas it is essential for accessory liability in breach of trust. It appears unlikely, as a matter of construction, that Parliament intended that the bona fide giving of legal advice should fall within the primary money laundering offences so that the act of giving advice itself should constitute "money laundering". It is less clear that the giving of advice, in circumstances where it is contemplated that the giving of legal advice, recognised by the adviser as *capable of assisting in the commission of a substantive offence* where suspicion exists for the purposes of s.330, should not, in principle, itself be capable of amounting to aiding the commission of a substantive money laundering offence for the purposes of s.340(11)(c).

There are, however, arguments against the mere giving of legal advice in connection with a transaction being capable of constituting "aiding" the committing of an offence. The most powerful of those appears to be that if you cannot become liable as a secondary party for the commission of the offence of conspiracy (which requires *positive agreement* in the joint enterprise) without either *knowing or intending* that the property in question be criminal property (*Saik*), it would seem an extraordinary conclusion that you can be nevertheless liable for aiding the commission of a laundering offence where the relevant mens rea would, in effect, be mere suspicion under s.330 that the subject property was itself known or suspected by another person to be "criminal property"—that is to say, "suspicion of suspicion". That of course raises the question as to what, in the present circumstances, foreseeing a "substantial risk" or "real possibility" under *Bryce* means. It may very well be the case that mere suspicion of the kind entertained for the purposes of s.330 would be insufficient. On the other hand, acting disregarding properly founded suspicion is a course that conventionally properly carries significant downside risk. It is not possible to answer the question with confidence. The possibility of exposure to liability represents a not insignificant area of risk and, as always, where criminal liability is in issue, prudence suggests and commends caution.

The acts of counselling or procuring appear to require that it is necessary to prove that the defendant intended that the offence, or an offence of the same type, be committed (*Ferguson v Weaving*).[139] The mental element therefore is similar to that required for conspiracy. Furthermore, "counsel" in this context means *"advise that"* the offence in question be carried out.

9.10 The construction of criminal statutes and legal certainty

It is very well established in English law that any offence-creating provision should be construed narrowly.[140] It is a principle of legal policy that a person should not be penalised

---

[139] *Ferguson v Weaving* [1951] 1 K.B. 814 DC at 819.
[140] Francis Bennion, *Bennion on Statutory Interpretation*, 5th edn (London: LexisNexis, 2007), section 271 (p.825), a policy explained under the heading "Principle against penalization under doubtful law".

except under clear law.[141] If law is not certain, it is to that extent not known. Unless men know what the rule of conduct is, they cannot regulate their actions to conform to it. The rule fails in its primary function as a rule.[142] In *Fothergill v Monarch Airlines Ltd*,[143] Lord Diplock made the point in this way:

> "Elementary justice, or, to use the concept often cited by the European Court, the need for legal certainty demands that the rules by which the citizen is to be bound should be ascertainable by him (or more realistically by a competent lawyer advising him) by reference to identifiable sources that are publicly available."

A similar point was made by Lord Cohen, who in *Fawcett Properties Ltd v Buckingham County Council*[144] said that the principle was that:

> "a man is not to be put in peril upon an uncertainty ... if a statutory provision is ambiguous, the court should adopt any reasonable interpretation which would avoid the penalty".

Lord Bingham more recently restated the general effect of the common law in this way in *R. v Rimmington*[145]:

> "There are two guiding principles: no one should be punished under a law unless it is sufficiently clear and certain to enable him to know what conduct is forbidden before he does it; and no one should be punished for any act which was not clearly and ascertainably punishable when the act was done."

---

[141] *Bennion* at p.826, cited (and there recorded as cited) by Lord Bingham in *R. v Z*; sub nom. *Re Z (Attorney-General for Northern Ireland's Reference)* [2005] UKHL 35; [2005] 2 A.C. 645; [2005] Crim. L.R. 985.

[142] Lord Diplock, cited in *Bennion*.

[143] *Fothergill v Monarch Airlines Ltd* [1981] A.C. 251 HL at 279.

[144] *Fawcett Properties Ltd v Buckinghamshire CC* [1961] A.C. 636 HL at 662.

[145] *R. v Rimmington (Anthony)* [2005] UKHL 63; [2006] 1 A.C. 459; [2006] 1 Cr. App. R. 17 (p.257) at [33].

The test then adopted by the House of Lords, of great importance in the present discussion, was: (a) was the offence clear, precise, adequately defined and based on discernible rational principle; and (b) would a legal adviser asked to give his opinion in advance be able to do so with confidence. It is worthy of note that the Bank of England's Financial Markets Law Committee, in its October 2004 paper, "Issue 69" observed that the single-criminality provision under s.340(2)(b) POCA 2002 gave rise to substantial uncertainty and legal risk and raised compatibility issues under EU law and arguably infringed fundamental freedoms.[146] There have been no statutory amendments that meet those important and weighty criticisms head-on.

9.10.1 EU law

Legal certainty is also a core principle of EU law.

> "The [ECJ] has consistently held … that the principles of legal certainty and the protection of individuals require, in areas covered by [EU] law, that the Member States' legal rules should be worded unequivocally so as to give the persons concerned a clear and precise understanding of their rights and obligations and enable national courts to ensure that those rights and obligations are observed."[147]

It is a well-settled principle of EU law that "a penalty, even of a non-criminal nature, cannot be imposed unless it rests on a clear and unambiguous legal basis."[148] This requires certainty in any domestic legislation governed by EU law:

> "According to established case law, in areas covered by Community law, national rules should be worded unequivocally so as to give persons concerned a clear and precise understanding of their rights and obligations and

---

[146] See also Paul Marshall, "Risk and uncertainty under the Proceeds of Crime Act 2002—the result of legislative oversight", *The Company Lawyer*, Vol.25, No.12.

[147] *Commission v Italy (C257/86)* [1988] E.C.R. 3249; [1990] 3 C.M.L.R. 718 at [12].

[148] *Karl Konecke & Co. KG v Bundesanstalt fur Landwirtschaftliche Marktordnung (C117/83)* [1985] 3 C.M.L.R. 451 at [11].

enable national courts to ensure that those rights and obligations are observed ... A requirement to which the case law attaches particular importance is that rights flowing from directives must be unequivocally stated so that citizens have a clear and precise understanding of them."[149]

Similarly, in the context of the Convention on Human Rights, in *Kokkinakis v Greece*,[150] the ECHR stated that: "an offence must be clearly defined in law. This condition is satisfied where the individual can know from the wording of the relevant provision and, if need be, with the assistance of the courts' interpretation of it, what acts or omissions [constitute an offence]." Likewise, in *Sunday Times v UK (No.1)*,[151] the ECHR held that a norm cannot be regarded as a law unless it is formulated with sufficient precision to enable the citizen to regulate his conduct.

While it is undoubtedly the case that the potential penalties under Pt 7 are extreme and intended to operate *in terrorem* of those in the regulated sector for the purpose of their delivering information and data to law enforcement agencies, the very uncertainty of interpretation and application of some of those provisions, particularly in the context of cross-border transactions, may paradoxically render enforcement by prosecution extraordinarily difficult save in the most straightforward circumstances. The foregoing discussion may provide some comfort to the person who conscientiously and honestly seeks to perform his obligations under Pt 7 but who goes in fear of the consequences of failing to make a report when, with the cold clarity of hindsight, that may subsequently be found to have been required. That circumstance typically gives rise to

---

[149] Takis Tridimas, *The General Principles of EU Law*, 2nd edn, (Oxford: Oxford University Press) at p.246 citing *Commission v Germany (29/84)* [1985] E.C.R. 1661; [1986] 3 C.M.L.R. 579 ECJ; *Commission v Denmark (C143/83)*; sub nom. *Re Equal Pay Concepts* [1985] E.C.R. 427; [1986] 1 C.M.L.R. 44; *Commission v Italy (363/85)* [1987] E.C.R. 1733 ECJ; *Commission v Italy (C-120/88)* [1991] E.C.R. I-621; [1993] 1 C.M.L.R. 41; *Commission v Italy (C-119/92)* [1994] E.C.R. I-393; [1994] 3 C.M.L.R. 774.
[150] *Kokkinakis v Greece (A/260-A)* (1994) 17 E.H.R.R. 397 ECHR at [52].
[151] *Sunday Times v United Kingdom (A/30)* (1979-80) 2 E.H.R.R. 245 ECHR.

defensive reporting. Under the Fourth Directive, the emphasis, so far as the "regulated sector" is concerned, will increasingly be on improving the effectiveness of the AML regime under the 2007 Regulations and, in particular, the KYC and due diligence requirements (including, especially, corporate and trust transparency in ownership and control) and improving collaboration between the regulated sector and law enforcement,[152] rather than, save in the most obvious and egregious cases, by bringing prosecutions under the provisions of Pt 7 of POCA 2002. Such a development is undoubtedly to be welcomed.

The effectiveness of the reporting regime, compared with the burdens imposed, has been the subject of sustained and detailed criticism. Any policy must ultimately be tested against its stated objectives and on cost-benefit. Between 2005 and 2006, a mere £95 million was recovered from criminals by court orders (Home Office information 2007). In its 2014 SARS Report,[153] the NCA provided data on, among other things, the impact of the reporting regime (that is to say "authorised disclosures"). The number of consent requests remained very similar to previous years with 14,155 submitted in 2014, compared to 14,103 in 2012-2013. The total sum restrained in this period was £141,517,652 which represented a significant increase on the figure for the previous year, which was £20,104,214. But five significant cases were responsible for this shift. Four of the five cases involved restraint on behalf of overseas law enforcement agencies in the amounts of £44 million, £23 million, £22 million and £12 million. The fifth case protected creditors of a UK company seeking liquidation in the amount of £18 million. Cash seizure as a result of refused consent remains very low and for 2014 at £107,951 was lower than £173,374 the previous year. The amount of some £309,260 seized as a result of consent requests that were *granted* in 2014 more than doubled to from £148,374 in 2012–2013. The amount restrained as a result of granted consent requests was reported

---

[152] Sir Stephen Lander, *Review of the Suspicious Activity Reports Regime (The SARs Review)*, March 2006, commonly referred to as the Lander Report, at para.99: *http://www.betterregulation.com/external/SOCAtheSARsReview_FINAL_Web.pdf* [Accessed 1 October 2015].

[153] NCA, *SARS Annual Report 2014*, *http://www.nationalcrimeagency.gov.uk/publications/464-2014-sars-annual-report/file* [Accessed 1 October 2015].

as £339,540 in 2014, significantly higher than £217,081 the previous year. The NCA has said that taken together, the total figure of assets denied to criminals as a result of consent requests (refused and granted) during the reporting period is £141,934,863. The figures are distorted by the fact that there is no requirement for law enforcement agencies to inform the UKFIU of restraint, cash seizure or arrest figures as a result of granting consent (only refusal), and the figures provided by the NCA may be taken to be conservative. The refusal rate for refused consents has risen slightly, from 9.18 per cent in 2012–2013 to 11.5 per cent. About half of all consent SARs are resolved in slightly over four days from the date of the report. Perhaps the most startling statistic of all is that of all the refused consents, there were a mere 35 cases in which arrests were made and only 47 actual arrests recorded.

That compares with UK money laundering and CFT set-up costs of about £252 million (the KPMG SARs Report), an estimated market in illegal drugs in the UK worth some £10.7 billion per annum and fraud of all kinds worth some £9.9 billion per annum (Home Office estimates in October 2013). The KPMG Report (that in part contributed to the adoption by the UK of the "risk-based" approach, now to be adopted throughout the EU under the Fourth Directive) concluded that the proportion of AML requirements to GDP was almost one-quarter higher in the UK than in the US, over double that in Germany and almost three times that of France and Italy. In 2006, Sir Stephen Lander concluded his report by observing that "I judge the room for improvement in the overall operation of the regime is so large that my proposals have a good chance, over time, in making a real difference to the success of the UK's AML and CFT arrangements." The sums restrained and recovered as a result of the consent regime are slowly increasing, but are dwarfed by the value of illicit funds in circulation. It must be hoped that, despite the criticisms that readily may be made of it, the "risk-based" approach to money laundering introduced under the 2007 Regulations and now EU-wide under the Fourth Directive, together with increased corporate and trust transparency in ownership and control, will serve to reduce the perceived burden imposed on businesses, assist in promoting collaboration between the participants in the regime, and improve the effectiveness in the allocation of law enforcement resources. Nevertheless, at the heart of the money laundering regime lies the continuing conundrum of how effectively honest citizens can police financial crime—where, overwhelmingly, business is ordinarily conducted on an assumed basis of honesty, if not trust.

Chapter 10

The Extra-Territorial Effects of US Anti-Money Laundering Law

Denis J. McInerney
Partner

James L. Kerr
Counsel

Michael J. Russano
Counsel

Sarah Breslow
Associate
Davis Polk & Wardwell LLP[1]

The 11 September 2001 terrorist attacks on the US triggered a significant expansion of US law designed to combat money laundering. Before the attacks, US anti-money laundering (AML) law focused primarily on narcotics trafficking and activity inside the US, and relied on US banking laws to require record-keeping and reporting of transactions for AML and other domestic-oriented purposes.[2] The 11 September attacks prompted the US Congress to enact a series of measures designed to deny foreign terrorists the "financial fuel" which makes their activity possible. These AML provisions, which

---

[1] The authors would like to thank their summer colleagues, Kyle Holter, Ian Kerr, Louis Labriola, and Zachary Shapiro, for their assistance in preparing this Chapter.

[2] See President's Commission on Organized Crime, "The Cash Connection: Organized Crime, Financial Institutions, and Money Laundering" 7–8 (1984); Lani Cosette, Note, "New Long-Arm Authority over Foreign Banks Raises Due Process Concerns but Remains a Viable Tool to Prevent Money Launderers from Abusing the US Financial System", (2003) 71 Geo. Wash. L. Rev. 272 at 282–284.

have significant extra-territorial effect,[3] were adopted as part of the Uniting and Strengthening America by Providing Appropriate Tools Required to Intercept and Obstruct Terrorism Act of 2001 (the PATRIOT Act or the Act), signed into law less than two months after the 11 September attacks.[4] Fourteen years later, US AML law remains in a state of evolution and expansion, both in terms of its geographical reach and the numbers and categories of institutions subject to its regulations.[5] This Chapter will outline the basic structure of US AML law and discuss in detail the provisions of the PATRIOT Act that have extra-territorial effect, as well as recent developments in US AML law that may have an impact on the application of those provisions.

---

[3] Joseph J. Norton and Heba Shams, "Money laundering law and terrorist financing: post-September 11 responses—let us step back and take a deep breath?" (2002) 36 Int'l Lawyer 103 at 116 and 119–120.

[4] Pub. L. No. 107–56, 115 Stat. 272 (2001).

[5] For example, in an expansion well beyond the traditional regulation of banks, the categories of "covered financial institution[s]" that the PATRIOT Act regulates include insured banks (as defined in the Federal Deposit Insurance Act, 12 USC § 1813(h)), commercial banks or trust companies, branches of foreign banks in the US, credit unions, mutual funds, insurance companies, currency exchangers, and brokers or dealers registered with the Securities and Exchange Commission under the Securities Exchange Act of 1934. See 31 CFR § 1010.605(e) (2011). However, at the time the PATRIOT Act was passed, the Treasury Department determined that "foreign branches of insured banks should *not* be included within the definition of 'covered financial institution'" and that "correspondent accounts of foreign banks that are clearly established, maintained, administered, or managed only at foreign branches should not be subject" to the Act's regulation. Anti-Money Laundering Requirements—Correspondent Accounts for Foreign Shell Banks; Recordkeeping and Termination of Correspondent Accounts for Foreign Banks, 67 Fed. Reg. 60 at 562 and 565 (26 September 2002) (emphasis added). As discussed in greater detail in this Chapter, expansive judicial interpretation and aggressive prosecution of the law has resulted in the expansion of the reach of US AML law to include, among other things, the regulation of digital currency and internet gambling.

10.1   Basic structure of US AML law

10.1.1   Statutory scheme

On 27 October 1986, as part of a larger assault on drug trafficking, the US became the first nation to designate money laundering a criminal offence by enacting the Money Laundering Control Act (the MLCA).[6] Section 1956(a)(1) of the MLCA, directed towards "transaction offenses", prohibits conducting or attempting to conduct a financial transaction involving the proceeds of "specified unlawful activity"[7] with the intent to promote the unlawful activity, or with the knowledge that the transaction is designed to conceal the proceeds of the unlawful activity or to avoid transaction reporting requirements. The second subdivision of s.1956(a) is designed to prohibit extra-territorial "transportation offenses", and criminalises the transportation, transmission, or transfer of a monetary instrument or funds into or out of the US with the intent to promote some "specified unlawful activity", or with knowledge that such transportation represents the proceeds of some form of unlawful activity and that it is designed either to conceal the proceeds of "specified unlawful activity" or to avoid a reporting requirement.[8]

Section 1957, itself a "transaction offense" statute, prohibits knowingly engaging in a monetary transaction involving "criminally derived property that is of a value greater than US

---

[6]   See The Money Laundering Control Act of 1986, Subtitle H of Title I of the Anti-Drug Abuse Act of 1986, Pub. L. No. 99-570, §§ 1351–1367, 100 Stat. 3207, 3218-3239 (1986) (codified as amended in scattered sections of 12, 18, and 31 USC); see generally 1 John K. Villa, *Banking Crimes: Fraud, Money Laundering, and Embezzlement* § 8:1 (West: 2014).

[7]   18 USC § 1956(a)(1) (2012). "Specified unlawful activity", as defined in s.1956(c)(7), "refers to over 200 different US crimes", including most financially motivated federal crimes, "ranging from narcotics trafficking[,] through various kinds of fraud and counterfeiting[,] to kidnapping". Doug Hopton, *Money Laundering: A Concise Guide for All Business* 33, 2nd edn, (Gower Publishing Co: 2009). The definition also includes specified international crimes, such as crimes involving narcotics, bribery and embezzlement, certain violent crimes, and crimes against foreign financial institutions.

[8]   See 18 USC § 1956(a)(2) (2012).

$10,000 and is derived from specified unlawful activity".[9] Unlike s.1956, which covers all proceeds of "specified unlawful activity", s.1957 applies only to criminally derived property from "specified unlawful activity" exceeding $10,000.

Congress did not initially define "proceeds" as used in ss.1956 and 1957, and "for years it was unclear whether the term referred to the gross or net income from the 'specified unlawful activity'".[10] In 2008, the Supreme Court, relying on the rule of lenity to construe what was deemed an ambiguous statute in favor of the defendant, held that the term "proceeds" means "profits" rather than "receipts". [11] In response to that decision, however, Congress amended ss.1956 and 1957 to define "proceeds" as "any property derived from or obtained or retained, directly or indirectly, through some form of unlawful activity, including the gross receipts of such activity".[12]

---

[9] See 18 USC § 1957(a). The term "criminally derived property" means "any property constituting, or derived from, proceeds obtained from a criminal offense". 18 USC § 1957(f)(2).

[10] See Carolyn L. Hart, "Money Laundering", (2014) 51 Am. Crim. L. Rev. 1449 at 1461.

[11] See *United States v Santos*, (2008) 553 U.S. 507 at 524. In the absence of a statutory definition, the Court, voting 4-1-4, held in its plurality decision that it was required to follow the Rule of Lenity and adopt the "defendant-friendly" definition that "proceeds" constitutes only net "profits". In a vigorous dissent, four justices argued that, in light of the contextual and customary usage of the word, as well as the difficulties of proof associated with determining what factors to consider in calculating net profits realised from an unlawful activity, the term "proceeds" must necessarily constitute gross receipts. Casting the deciding vote, Justice Stevens agreed with the plurality that "proceeds" under the statute should be interpreted as "profits" in a prosecution under s.1956(a)(1) where the "specified unlawful activity" is operating a gambling business. When following a plurality decision, lower courts must adhere to the narrowest possible grounds for judgment, since no one opinion received a majority vote. See *Marks v United States* (1977) 430 U.S. 188 at 193. After the decision, the former Deputy Chief for Legal Policy of the Asset Forfeiture and Money Laundering Section of the Criminal Division of the DOJ wrote that the decision "upset decades of money laundering case law built on the assumption that 'proceeds' meant 'gross receipts'", and that the case had produced a "wave of litigation in which the courts have struggled to apply *Santos*". Stefan D. Cassella, "*United States v Santos*: The US Supreme Court Rewrites the Money Laundering Statute", (2009) 12 J. of Money Laundering Control 221 at 222.

[12] See 18 USC §§ 1956(c)(9), 1957(f)(3) (2012).

In *Cuellar v United States*,[13] another case viewed as being likely to complicate money laundering prosecutions, the Supreme Court required proof that a criminal defendant intended to conceal the funds in a s.1956 action. Cuellar, a Mexican national, was charged with violating 18 USC § 1956(a)(2)(B)(i) after attempting to transport $81,000 of illegal drug proceeds across the US border by hiding the cash in a secret compartment in his vehicle. The defendant argued that the Department of Justice (DOJ) failed to prove, as required by s.1956, that the underlying reason for transporting the cash was to conceal the proceeds.[14] The Supreme Court agreed with the defendant and held that the evidence of concealment related only to the manner of transportation, and that the DOJ had failed to demonstrate that the reason the defendant was transporting the money was for the purpose of concealing the funds.[15]

Since the Supreme Court decided *Cuellar*, federal circuit courts have required that the government prove that the transportation of money was for the purpose of concealment, including in instances in which the transportation of the funds is carried out through the use of electronic wire transfers.[16] Nevertheless, while merely concealing proceeds is not sufficient to violate s.1956, one circuit has recognized that a jury may still "infer the requisite design to conceal based on circumstantial evidence."[17] As a result, *Cuellar* does not appear to have imposed particularly onerous limitations on the US government's ability to prosecute money laundering offenses.

---

[13] *Cuellar v United States* (2008) 553 U.S. 550.

[14] *Cuellar* at 561–563.

[15] *Cuellar* at 568.

[16] See e.g. *United States v Demmitt*, (2013) 706 F.3d 665 at 678 (5th Cir.); *United States v Brown*, (2008) 553 F.3d 768 at 786 (5th Cir.) (recognizing that while one "mere act of structuring could not support a concealment conviction", numerous acts of structuring "are more clearly designed to conceal the nature of the moneys" and support a money laundering conviction).

[17] See *United States v Day*, (2012) 700 F.3d 713 at 724 (4th Cir.) (finding that while "no such circumstantial evidence existed" in *Cuellar*, in the instant case circumstantial evidence tended to show that the defendant not only knew that his conduct would "have the effect of concealing the location, nature, and source of his unlawful proceeds", but that he undertook concealment efforts "for precisely that purpose").

In addition to the direct criminalisation of money laundering under the MLCA,[18] US AML law consists of a series of extensive record-keeping, reporting, and due diligence obligations imposed on US financial institutions in an effort to prevent and detect financial crimes, including money laundering.[19] These obligations include record-keeping regarding

---

[18] Section 1956(e) expressly grants authority to the US DOJ, the US Department of the Treasury, the US Department of Homeland Security, and the US Postal Service to investigate violations of the MLCA. Further, the government may choose to bring a civil penalty action against one who violates the MLCA instead of instituting criminal proceedings. See § 1956(b). On the other hand, there is no private right of action for money laundering under the MLCA and therefore no mechanism for private individuals to bring suit. See e.g. *United States v Bergman*, (2013) 550 F. App'x 651 at 655 (10th Cir.) (recognizing that 18 USC § 1956 "does not provide a private cause of action"); *Philips v Deutsche Bank Nat. Trust Co*, No. 10 CV 5883, 2010 WL 5246032, at *1 (C.D. Cal. 16 December 2010) (finding "no private right of action" under 18 USC § 1956 and dismissing plaintiff's claim); *Dubai Islamic Bank v Citibank*, (2000) 126 F. Supp. 2d 659 at 668 (S.D.N.Y.) ("18 USC § 1956 does not give rise to a private right of action."). However, the failure to maintain a viable and credible AML compliance programme can result in civil liability under the Anti-Terrorism Act, 18 USC § 2331 and what follows (the ATA).

[19] See e.g. Currency and Foreign Transactions Reporting Act, Pub. L. No. 91-508, 84 Stat. 1114 (1970). Title II of the Currency and Foreign Transactions Reporting Act, commonly referred to as the Bank Secrecy Act, authorises the Secretary of the Treasury to require certain reports or records which "have a high degree of usefulness in criminal, tax, or regulatory investigations or proceedings". 31 USC § 5311 (2001). These reporting and record-keeping requirements have largely been prescribed through regulations issued by the Treasury Department. In the US legal system, legislation enacted by Congress can authorise an executive branch department to issue regulations, which have the force of law, in order to effectuate the purposes of the legislation. Typically, the process involves the executive department issuing proposed regulations for public comment, and then ultimately implementing final regulations. See 2 Am. Jur. 2d *Administrative Law* §§ 127, 147–152 (2003).

Complying with requirements set forth in federal regulations can be difficult, as is especially clear in the context of mergers and acquisitions. The Federal Reserve approves bank merger and acquisition applications based on several factors, including the efficacy of "Bank Secrecy Act/anti-money-laundering compliance programs". Board of Governors of the Federal Reserve System, *Semiannual Report on Banking Applications Activity: July 1–December 31, 2014*, at 2 (April 2015), *http://www.federalreserve.gov/bankinforeg/201504-semiannual-report-on-banking-applications-activity.pdf* [Accessed 1 October 2015]. In recent years, federal inquiries have delayed merger transactions sought by at least two US banks. For example, Bancorp South has twice extended its merger agreements with two smaller institutions and experienced a year-and-a-half delay due, in part, to regulatory concerns over its AML compliance programme. Rachel Louise Ensign, "Waiting Game: Bancorp South Deals Hit with New Delays", *Wall Street Journal* (1 July 2015), *http://blogs.wsj.com/moneybeat/2015/07/01/waiting-game-bancorpsouth-deals-hit-with-new-delays* [Accessed 1 October 2015]. Similar AML regulatory concerns continue to delay the approval of M&T Bank's acquisition of Hudson

customer information and transactions, reporting to the government certain cash and currency transactions, and reporting to the government certain suspicious transactions.

10.1.2 Pre-PATRIOT Act proposals

Prior to the 11 September attacks, numerous proposals had been made by executive branch officials and in Congress to strengthen US AML law. For example, the US National Money Laundering Strategy, released in March 2000 by the Treasury and Justice Departments (the 2000 National Strategy), pro-posed a new framework for AML enforcement, including the extension of AML regulations to a variety of previously unregulated financial actors.[20] The 2000 National Strategy also called for the Treasury Department to be granted authority to take action "against those jurisdictions, foreign financial institutions, or types of transactions that pose particular money laundering threats",[21] and advocated greater scrutiny of customers, including senior foreign political figures and their associates, and of transactions that posed a heightened risk of money laundering and other financial crimes.[22]

The Treasury Department and DOJ's 2001 National Money Laundering Strategy, finalised in the weeks before the 11 September attacks, emphasised many of those same initiatives and also advocated increasing restrictions for certain activities, such as correspondent banking by foreign financial institutions.[23]

City Bancorp, an agreement reached in 2012. Chelsey Dulaney, "M&T Bank, Hudson City Extend Merger Timeline to Oct. 31", *Wall Street Journal* (17 April 2015), *http://www.wsj.com/articles/m-t-bank-hudson-city-extend-merger-timeline-to-oct-31-1429274409* [Accessed 1 October 2015].

[20] See Dep't of Treasury & Dep't of Justice, *The National Money Laundering Strategy for 2000*, at 40 (2000), *http://www.treasury.gov/press-center/press-releases/Documents/ml2000.pdf* [Accessed 6 October 2015].

[21] *The National Money Laundering Strategy for 2000* at 58.

[22] *The National Money Laundering Strategy for 2000* at 33–35; 73–75.

[23] See Dep't of Treasury & Dep't of Justice, "The 2001 National Money Laundering Strategy" (2001), *http://www.treasury.gov/resource-center/sanctions/OFAC-Enforcement/Documents/ml2001.pdf* [Accessed 28 October 2015] For a description of the various AML bills introduced in Congress during this time, see generally David Meister, "Accounts Owned by Foreign Officials: Automatic Red Flags?" J. Investment Compliance, 22 June 2001, at 35. See also Norton and Shams, "Money

10.2   The PATRIOT Act

Following the 11 September attacks, virtually all AML proposals that had been under discussion for several years were enacted in a matter of weeks as part of the PATRIOT Act. Primarily collected in Title III of the PATRIOT Act, separately titled the International Money Laundering Abatement and Anti-Terrorist Financing Act of 2001, many of the PATRIOT Act's AML measures[24] explicitly targeted money laundering at foreign financial institutions and by foreign entities and persons. One of the Act's stated purposes was "to increase the strength of [US] measures to prevent, detect, and prosecute international money laundering and the financing of terrorism".[25] Among the Act's findings were that money laundering "provide[d] the financial fuel that permit[ted] transnational criminal enterprises to conduct and expand their operations to the detriment of the safety and security of American citizens",[26] and that US AML efforts were "impeded by outmoded and inadequate statutory provisions that [made] investigations, prosecutions, and forfeitures more difficult, particularly in cases in which money laundering involve[d] foreign persons, foreign banks, or foreign countries".[27]

The PATRIOT Act added various elements to US AML law in an effort to address those perceived weaknesses. In many instances, those provisions granted US authorities significant powers to regulate access by foreign entities and individuals to the US financial system, effectively exerting US influence over activities overseas.[28] The PATRIOT Act also significantly

---

laundering law and terrorist financing: post-September 11 responses—let us step back and take a deep breath?" (2002) 36 Int'l Lawyer 103.

24 For an overview of these changes, see generally William J. Sweet Jr., Saul M. Pilchen and Stacie E. McGinn, "Summary of the USA PATRIOT Act of 2001 Anti-Money Laundering Provisions", (2001) 1289 PLI/Corp. 55.

25 See PATRIOT Act § 302(b)(1), Pub. L. No. 107-56, 115 Stat. 272, 297 (2001).

26 See PATRIOT Act § 302(a)(1), 115 Stat. at 296.

27 See PATRIOT Act § 302(a)(8), 115 Stat. at 297.

28 Title III also provides for the explicit extension of a number of these obligations to a variety of financial institutions in the US that previously had not been subject to AML regulation, including insurance companies, money wiring agencies, futures commission merchants, securities broker-dealers, and credit unions. See PATRIOT Act §§ 321, 356, 115 Stat. at 315 and 324.

amended the US money laundering statutes in such a way as to target overseas activity. The remainder of this Chapter will address the provisions of the PATRIOT Act with extra-territorial effect and will discuss recent developments in US AML law.[29]

---

[29] Although the subject of this Chapter is mostly limited to federal US AML law, it bears noting that the criminal laws and regulatory regimes of states often track federal law. For example, the Manhattan District Attorney's Office in New York City—now under Cyrus R. Vance Jr., and previously under his predecessor, Robert M. Morgenthau—has been particularly active in investigating possible international money laundering involving funds that pass through financial institutions with a presence in Manhattan. See Christopher M. Matthews, "Manhattan DA Charges NY Broker-Dealer in International Fraud", *Wall Street Journal* (20 May 2015), *http://www.wsj.com/articles/manhattan-da-charges-ny-broker-dealer-in-international-fraud-1432144347* [Accessed 1 October 2015]. ("[The prosecution] highlights the efforts of the district attorney's office to pursue increasingly complex and international cases that are more frequently handled by … federal counterparts blocks away at the … US attorney's office."). As the Manhattan District Attorney's Office has become more involved in AML investigations, it has also benefited from greater co-operation with foreign law enforcement agencies. For example, in November 2014, Mr Vance and Adrian Leppard, Commissioner of the City of London Police, signed a Memorandum of Understanding formalizing a new personnel sharing programme that will provide for six-month staff exchanges between the two offices. Manhattan DA's Office, *District Attorney Vance Hosts Fifth Annual Financial Crimes and Cybersecurity Symposium at the Federal Reserve Bank of New York* (19 November 2014), *http://manhattanda.org/press-release/district-attorney-vance-hosts-5th-annual-financial-crimes-and-cybersecurity-symposium-/* [Accessed 1 October 2015]. The plan aims to facilitate "joint investigations and intelligence-sharing" regarding cybercrime and financial crime in New York and London.

Additionally, the New York State Department of Financial Services (the NYDFS), created in 2011, has aggressively pursued financial institutions operating with New York banking licences. For example, in 2012, the NYDFS fined Standard Chartered $340 million on the ground that it had allegedly engaged in prohibited conduct with respect to transactions with certain Iranian customers. *Consent Order, In re Matter of Standard Chartered Bank* (21 September 2012), *http://www.dfs.ny.gov/about/ea/ea120921.pdf* [Accessed 19 October 2015]. NYDFS also required that Standard Chartered install an independent monitor to review its money-laundering risk controls and ensure that proper measures be taken to prevent future improper transactions. *Statement From Benjamin M Lawsky, Superintendent of Financial Services, Regarding Standard Chartered Bank* (14 August 2012), *http://www.dfs.ny.gov/about/press/pr1208141.htm* [Accessed 1 October 2015]. Then, in 2014, the NYDFS fined Standard Chartered an additional $300 million for alleged continued failings of its AML compliance programme. See Press Release, *NYDFS Announces Standard Chartered Bank to Suspend Dollar Clearing for High-Risk Clients in Hong Kong* (19 August 2014), *http://www.dfs.ny.gov/about/press/pr1408191.htm* [Accessed 1 October 2015]. In 2015, Commerzbank was penalized $610 million by the NYDFS for alleged failures in its compliance programme. (In total, Commerzbank paid $1.45 billion to resolve parallel investigations by the NYDFS, the DOJ, the Federal Reserve, and others.) Among other issues

10.2.1 Amendments to federal money laundering statutes

The PATRIOT Act significantly increased the extra-territorial reach of the MLCA. The Act expanded the list of "offenses against a foreign nation" which can constitute "specified unlawful activities" for the purpose of triggering the MLCA.[30] These offences include bribery of a public official,[31] or the misappropriation, theft, or embezzlement of public funds by or for the benefit of a public official; smuggling or export control violations; and any offence with respect to which the US would be obligated by a multilateral treaty either to extradite the alleged offender or to submit the case for prosecution, if the offender were found within the US.[32] Moreover, expansive

---

identified, the NYDFS alleged that Commerzbank's New York compliance staff believed that bank employees overseas were not sufficiently cooperative in aiding investigations of red flags for money laundering, which led the New York compliance staff to simply "clear" the alert. Press Release, *NYDFS Announces Commerzbank To Pay $1.45 Billion, Terminate Employees, Install Independent Monitor For Banking Law Violations* (12 March 2015), *http://www.dfs.ny.gov/about/press/pr1503121.htm* [Accessed 1 October 2015].

[30] See PATRIOT Act § 315, 115 Stat. at 309–310 (codified as amended at 18 USC § 1956(c)(7)(B) (2012)).

[31] Foreign bribery became a predicate offense for federal money laundering crimes in 1992, with the addition of "a felony violation of the Foreign Corrupt Practices Act" to the list of predicate offenses. See Marian Hagler, "International Money Laundering and U.S. Law: A Need to 'Know-Your-Partner'", (2004) 31 Syracuse J. Int'l L. & Com. 227 at 247. Until 1998, however, an FCPA violation required "the use of mails or other means of interstate commerce", and "seemed to invite circumvention through the careful orchestration of payment schemes offshore." Hagler at 247. The FCPA was expanded in 1998 to reach the conduct of US persons occurring wholly abroad, as well as the conduct of other persons taking place in the United States (including those that did not use a "means of interstate commerce"). Hagler at 247. However, the FCPA remained (as it continues to remain) limited to the specific conduct prohibited by its terms, "which are largely independent of considerations of the anti-bribery laws of the foreign official's home country". Hagler at 247. The PATRIOT Act expanded the role of foreign bribery as a predicate for federal money laundering far beyond the purview of the FCPA by allowing violations of foreign anti-bribery laws to serve as a predicate offense. See Mark Pieth, Lucinda A. Low and Nicola Bonucci (eds), *The OECD Convention on Bribery: A Commentary* 2nd edn, (Cambridge University Press: 2014). ("By allowing US money laundering cases to be based on foreign bribery that is not an FCPA violation, [the PATRIOT Act] greatly expand[ed] the scope of corrupt activities that can serve as predicate offences under the US money laundering laws.").

[32] See PATRIOT Act § 315, 115 Stat. at 309–310 (codified as amended at 18 USC § 1956(c)(7)(B) (2012)). In 2006, legislators added to this list offenses for human trafficking and sexual exploitation. See 18 USC § 1956(c)(7)(vii) (2012).

judicial interpretation of the US wire fraud statute,[33] the violation of which is a "specified unlawful activity", has expanded the extra-territorial reach of the MLCA and the nature of "specified unlawful activities" that may be the subject of a US AML prosecution. A 2005 US Supreme Court decision, for example, held that a scheme to defraud a foreign government of its tax revenues was a violation of the wire fraud statute and therefore an appropriate predicate for a money laundering charge.[34]

---

[33] 18 USC § 1343 (2008).

[34] *Pasquantino v United States*, (2005) 544 U.S. 349. At issue in *Pasquantino* was whether the defendants' alleged scheme to smuggle liquor from the US to Canada without paying the required excise taxes could be punished under the wire fraud statute. See *Pasquantino* at 352. The court found that the elements of wire fraud, a predicate act to a money laundering charge, were met because "the right to tax revenue is property in Canada's hands", *Pasquantino* at 356, and "[t]his … was a scheme 'designed to defraud by representations'", *Pasquantino* at 357. Further, the court found that the common-law revenue rule, which prevents enforcement of the right to foreign tax revenue of one sovereign in the courts of another sovereign, did not bar application of the wire fraud statute in this case because the suit was "not a suit that recovers foreign tax liability, like a suit to enforce a judgment" but was "a criminal prosecution brought by the United States in its sovereign capacity to punish domestic criminal conduct". See *Pasquantino* at 359–369.
In *United States v Yusuf*, (2008) 536 F.3d 178 (3d Cir.), the Third Circuit determined that unpaid taxes retained pursuant to a violation of the wire fraud statute "constitute 'proceeds' of mail fraud for purposes of supporting a charge of federal money laundering". *Yusuf* at 189. Therefore, under *Pasquantino* and *Yusuf*, conduct that defrauds a foreign government of foreign tax revenue that would subject an actor to criminal liability under the wire fraud statute would also support a charge of money laundering for the amount of unpaid taxes, provided that the other requisite elements of the money laundering statutes are met.
While not a wire fraud case, the Ninth Circuit held in *United States v Chao Fan Xu*, (2013) 706 F.3d 965 at 987 (9th Cir.), that *Pasquantino* also applies to conspiracies to defraud foreign governments under 18 USC § 1956(h). The defendants were charged with conspiring to engage in a monetary transaction over $10,000 derived from a specified unlawful activity, in this case allegations of fraud and theft from the Bank of China. The Government did not offer evidence tracing the proceeds of the Bank of China fraud directly to the money transported into the US, but the court still found it sufficient that "significant objective acts" showed that "Defendants *agreed* to transfer to the United States more than $10,000 *in fraudulent proceeds*." *Xu* at 980 (emphasis in original). In affirming the conviction, the court rejected the defendants' argument that the trial court impermissibly enforced Chinese law and found that defendants' foreign fraud scheme was "a means to violate United States laws", thereby providing an appropriate "predicate to enforcement of the money laundering statute". *Xu* at 987 (citing *Pasquantino v United States*, (2005) 544 U.S. 349 at 369).

Section 318 of the PATRIOT Act makes it clear that laundering money through foreign banks, not simply their US-sited agencies and branches, is within the scope of the MLCA, subject to satisfying the jurisdictional requirement set forth in s.317 below.[35] Prior to the adoption of s.318, it was not clear whether laundering money through the offshore offices of foreign banks was a crime under US law.[36] Section 318 resolves that confusion by broadening the definition of "financial institution" to include "any foreign bank, as defined in s.1 of the International Banking Act of 1978 (12 USC § 3101)".[37]

Section 317 grants US federal courts long-arm jurisdiction in MLCA actions against foreign money launderers, including any foreign financial institution that maintains a bank account at a US financial institution, provided that the foreign financial institution has been served with process pursuant to the laws of the appropriate foreign jurisdiction or the US Federal Rules of Civil Procedure.[38] Importantly, those provisions relate to obtaining personal jurisdiction over a foreign person in cases where subject matter jurisdiction already is established by other provisions of the MLCA.[39] Despite earlier speculation by commentators that those provisions of s.317 might confer jurisdiction over foreign financial institutions even where the activity proscribed by the MLCA occurs "entirely outside the US",[40] at least one US federal court has declined to construe s.317 so broadly, and limited the extra-territorial application of

---

[35] See PATRIOT Act § 318, 115 Stat. at 311 (codified as amended at 18 USC § 1956(c)(6) (2012)); Charles Doyle, Cong. Research Serv., "The USA PATRIOT Act: A Legal Analysis" at 35–36 (2002), *http://fpc.state.gov/documents/organization/10092.pdf* [Accessed 1 October 2015]. ("[S]ection 318 expands 18 USC § 1956 to cover financial transactions conducted in foreign financial institutions.").

[36] See Doyle, "The USA PATRIOT Act: A Legal Analysis" at 36 n.71 (citing H.R. Rep. No. 107-250, at 38 (2000)).

[37] PATRIOT Act § 318, 115 Stat. at 311 (codified as amended at 18 USC § 1956(c)(6)(B) (2012)).

[38] See PATRIOT Act § 317, 115 Stat. at 310 (codified as amended at 18 USC § 1956(b)(2) (2012)).

[39] *United States v Lloyds TSB Bank PLC*, (2009) 639 F. Supp. 2d 314 at 317 (S.D.N.Y.).

[40] Norton and Shams, "Money laundering law and terrorist financing: post-September 11 responses—let us step back and take a deep breath?", (2002) 36 Int'l Lawyer 103 at 108.

the MLCA to instances where the unlawful conduct occurred in part in the US or where the conduct was by a US citizen.[41]

Section 320 amends the civil forfeiture law to allow the US government to seize property "within the jurisdiction of the [US], constituting, derived from, or traceable to, any proceeds obtained directly or indirectly from an offense against a foreign nation, or any property used to facilitate such an offense", if the offence (i) involves controlled substances, or any of the offences listed in 18 USC § 1956(c)(7)(B)[42]; (ii) would be punishable by a foreign nation by death or imprisonment for a term exceeding one year; and (iii) would be punishable under US law by imprisonment for a term exceeding one year.[43]

---

[41] See *Lloyds TSB Bank*, (2009) 639 F. Supp. 2d 314 at 316–324. In *Lloyds*, the United States District Court for the Southern District of New York dismissed an AML civil enforcement action against Lloyds TSB Bank PLC, a UK-based banking institution. The complaint alleged a fraud scheme perpetrated by two Cypriots who maintained and laundered unlawful proceeds through accounts at Lloyds' Geneva branch. Importantly, Lloyds' interaction with the alleged transactions was limited to transfers in Europe, and only the alleged co-conspirators' actions took place in the United States. See *Lloyds* at 318 and 324. In granting the defendant's motion to dismiss, the court found that the long-arm jurisdiction provision of s.317, codified at 18 USC § 1956(b)(2), was "irrelevant" to the issue of subject matter jurisdiction before the court. See *Lloyds* at 317. Rather, the MLCA afforded extra-territorial application only in the limited instances set forth in 18 USC §§ 1956(f), 1957. In that case, the district court held that there was no subject matter jurisdiction because there was an insufficient connection between the United States and the unlawful conduct. See *Lloyds* at 324. In an unpublished order in *United States v Bank of Cyprus*, the same federal district court judge dismissed the government's complaint for lack of subject matter jurisdiction for the reasons set forth in *Lloyds*, which was its companion case. Order, *United States v Bank of Cyprus Public Co*, No. 07-CV-9234 (S.D.N.Y. 31 March 2009) (finding that the "decisive facts of the two cases are indistinguishable, and the governing law is the same for each").

[42] The offences listed in 18 USC § 1956(c)(7)(B) include kidnapping, robbery, extortion, murder, destruction of property, fraud by or against a foreign bank, bribery of a public official, embezzlement of public funds, smuggling or export control violations, and human trafficking or sexual exploitation. The civil forfeiture law was subsequently amended in 2006 to include offences relating to trafficking in nuclear, chemical, biological, or radiological weapons technology or material. See 18 USC § 981(a)(1)(B)(i) (2012).

[43] PATRIOT Act § 320, 18 USC § 981(a)(1)(B) (2012). For example, in *United States v Item 1: A 1990 Jeep Cherokee*, (2005) 147 F. App'x 775 (10th Cir.), the 10th Circuit upheld forfeiture of proceeds traceable to the importation of hashish into Canada. See *A 1990 Jeep Cherokee* at 778. That court also rejected the defendant's constitutional challenges to Section 981(a)(1)(B) on Commerce Clause and Article III standing grounds. See *A 1990 Jeep Cherokee* at 777–778.

Under s.323, the government may seek a restraining order freezing assets in the US in order to satisfy a civil or criminal forfeiture under foreign law.[44] Further, the Act subjects foreign entities or persons to forfeiture proceedings in the US if they commit an offence in violation of foreign law that would have subjected them to forfeiture under US law if their act had been committed in the US.[45] Finally, s.323 relaxes the notice requirement for the forfeiture proceeding so that the foreign nation need only establish that it "took steps" to give notice, instead of providing the defendant with actual notice.[46]

In addition, along with ss.320 and 323, s.806 permits the US government to seize and forfeit all assets, foreign or domestic, (i) belonging to "any individual, entity, or organization engaged in planning or perpetrating any act of domestic or international terrorism ... against the United States, [or] citizens or residents of the United States", (ii) acquired or maintained "with the intent and for the purpose of supporting, planning, conducting, or concealing" an act of terrorism "against the United States, [or] citizens or residents of the United States", or (iii) "derived from, involved in, or used or intended to be used to commit" such an act.[47] In 2006, Congress further amended civil forfeiture laws to permit the seizure and forfeiture of assets belonging to an individual, entity, or organization that is "engaged in planning or perpetrating any act of international terrorism against any

---

[44] See PATRIOT Act § 323, 28 USC § 2467(d)(3)(A)(i) (2010); see also *In re Seizure of Approximately $12,116,153.16 & Accrued Interest in U.S. Currency*, (2012) 903 F. Supp. 2d 19 at 33 and 38 (D.D.C.) (holding US assets could be restrained in support of Brazilian criminal prosecution, and rejecting argument that due process under the Fifth Amendment required a pre-restraint hearing). Note that Congress further amended 28 USC § 2467(d)(3) in 2010 by passing the Preserving Foreign Criminal Assets for Forfeiture Act, Pub. I. No. 111–342, 124 Stat. 3607 (22 December 2010), which clarified that the judgment of a foreign court need not be final prior to restraining US assets.

[45] See 28 USC at § 2467(a)(2)(A).

[46] See 28 USC at §§ 2467(b)(1)(C) and 2647(d)(1)(D).

[47] See PATRIOT Act § 806, 115 Stat. at 378 (current version at 18 USC § 981(a)(1)(G) (2012)); see also *United States v Saade*, No. 11-CR-111, 2013 WL 6847034, at *1 (S.D.N.Y. 30 December 2013) (upholding forfeiture action over Eighth Amendment excessive fines challenge after defendant was found guilty of conspiring to acquire and sell to the Taliban anti-aircraft missiles).

international organization or against any foreign Government".[48] In order to qualify under that new basis for civil
forfeiture, some act in furtherance of planning or perpetrating
an act of international terrorism must have occurred within the
US.[49]

10.2.2 Interbank and correspondent bank accounts

A significant AML development in the PATRIOT Act relates to
the regulation of accounts held by foreign financial institutions
in the US. Those accounts, known as "interbank" and
"correspondent" accounts, are the chief portals through which
the PATRIOT Act attempts to project US AML law extra-
territorially.[50]

An "interbank account" is defined as an "account" [51] held by
one financial institution at another financial institution primarily for the purpose of facilitating customer transactions, such
transactions being denominated in the currency used in the
jurisdiction where the account is located.[52] The PATRIOT Act
defines a "correspondent account" as "an account established
to receive deposits from, make payments on behalf of a foreign
financial institution, or handle other financial transactions
related to such institution".[53] The legislative history of the
PATRIOT Act indicates that, for the purposes of its forfeiture

---

[48] 18 USC § 981(a)(1)(G)(iv) (2012).

[49] 18 USC § 981(a)(1)(G)(iv) (2012).

[50] Kern Alexander, "Extraterritorial US Banking Regulation and International
      Terrorism: The PATRIOT Act and the International Response", (2002) 3 J. Int'l
      Banking Reg. 307 at 313.

[51] "Account" is defined as "a formal banking or business relationship established to
      provide regular services, dealings, and other financial transactions". See
      PATRIOT Act § 311(a), 31 USC § 5318A(e)(1)(A) (2006). In response to questions
      regarding the definition of "account" as a relationship that provides "regular"
      services, the Treasury Department clarified that "most isolated or occasional
      transactions that a … financial institution conducts with a foreign bank would
      not constitute a correspondent account". See *Anti-Money Laundering
      Requirements—Correspondent Accounts for Foreign Shell Banks; Recordkeeping and
      Termination of Correspondent Accounts for Foreign Banks*, 67 Fed Reg 60 at 562 and
      564 (26 September 2002).

[52] 18 USC § 984(c)(2)(B) (2000); PATRIOT Act § 319(a), 18 USC § 981(k) (2012).

[53] See PATRIOT Act § 311(b), 31 USC § 5318A(e)(1)(B) (2006).

provisions, the terms "interbank account" and "correspondent account" are synonymous and interchangeable.[54]

10.2.2.1 Seizure of funds in US interbank accounts

In arguably its most expansive provision, the PATRIOT Act authorises DOJ to seize funds held in the name of a foreign bank in an interbank account at a US "covered financial institution"[55] if the proceeds from unlawful activities have been deposited into an offshore account at the foreign bank.[56] Under s.319(a), funds deposited abroad "shall be deemed to have been deposited into the interbank account in the US, and any restraining order, seizure warrant, or arrest warrant *in rem* regarding the funds may be served on the covered financial institution, and funds in the interbank account, up to the value of the funds deposited into the [offshore] account at the foreign bank, may be restrained, seized, or arrested".[57] Those funds will then be forfeited to the US if the government can establish, by a preponderance of the evidence, that the foreign bank received property "subject to forfeiture"—including the proceeds of "specified unlawful activities"—in the offshore account at the foreign bank.[58] Moreover, under s.319(a), the Government does not have to demonstrate that the funds to be forfeited are "directly traceable" to the funds deposited in the foreign bank; funds are treated as fungible, and the language of

---

[54] See H.R. Rep. No. 107-250, at 9 and 104 (2001) (noting that, for the purposes of civil forfeiture, "'correspondent account' has the meaning given to the term 'interbank account'"); see also *Abelesz v OTP Bank*, (2012) 692 F.3d 638 at 657 (7th Cir.) (explaining that "[i]nterbank accounts, *also known as correspondent accounts*, are used by foreign banks to offer services in jurisdictions where the banks have no physical presence" (emphasis added)); *United States v Union Bank for Sav. & Inv. (Jordan)*, (2007) 487 F.3d 8 at 15 (1st Cir.).

[55] See note 5.

[56] See PATRIOT Act § 319(a), 18 USC § 981(k) (2012). Under Section 981(a)(1), this expansive forfeiture authority applies to property, real or personal, constituting the proceeds of conduct violating various federal statutes. This conduct includes, but is not limited to, the "specified unlawful activity" defined in s.1956(c)(7).

[57] See PATRIOT Act § 319(a), 18 USC § 981(k) (2012).

[58] See 18 USC § 983(c)(1) (2009) (providing burden of proof in forfeiture proceedings).

the statute relieves the government of any need to show any relationship between the assets forfeited and the criminally derived proceeds.[59]

In order to contest a forfeiture proceeding under the PATRIOT Act, the person or entity contesting the seizure must be an "owner" of the funds.[60] The owner of the funds is deemed to be the person who was the owner of the funds that were deposited into the offshore account at the foreign bank at the time of the deposit, not the foreign bank or any intermediary institution involved in the transfer of the funds.[61] Therefore, the foreign bank from which the funds are being seized may not contest the forfeiture unless the basis of the forfeiture is a purported wrongdoing committed by the foreign bank, or the foreign bank establishes, by a preponderance of the evidence, that the underlying funds at issue had been withdrawn from the foreign bank account prior to the seizure of funds from the interbank account, thereby satisfying the bank's obligation to its depositor.[62]

To date, only one US federal appellate court has considered the extent to which a foreign bank is an "owner" of forfeited funds for the purpose of contesting the forfeiture. In *United States v Union Bank for Savings & Investment (Jordan)*, the court rejected Union Bank's arguments claiming ownership[63] and held that a

---

[59] 18 USC § 981(k)(1)(A)(2) (2012).

[60] 18 USC at § 981(k)(3).

[61] See *Union Bank*, 487 F.3d at 16; see generally Ian M. Comisky & Matthew D. Lee, "The USA PATRIOT Act Has Broad Implications for Financial Institutions", (2002) J. Tax'n Fin. Institutions, May/June 2002, at 23.

[62] See PATRIOT Act § 319(a), 18 USC § 981(k)(4)(B); *United States v Sum of $70,990,605*, (2015) 305 F.R.D. 20 at 24 (D.D.C.) (holding that bank could not establish statutory standing unless it could "satisfy one of the two exceptions to [the] definition of 'owner' excluding foreign financial institutions"). The *Sum of $70,990,605* court considered the seizure of $10.1 million from Afghanistan International Bank's (AIB) interbank account at Standard Chartered in New York in connection with the alleged wire fraud of an AIB customer. *Sum of $70,990,605* at 22–23. Post-restraint, the court held that the US only had to answer those of AIB's interrogatories relating to the two exceptions from the definition of "owner" in 18 USC § 981(k). See *Sum of $70,990,605* at 25–27. Interrogatories relating to the "actual owner" of funds in AIB's interbank account were deemed immaterial.

[63] See *Union Bank*, 487 F.3d at 18 (rejecting argument that "because no recourse or set-off was possible in this case, [Union Bank] discharged its obligations and

bank is only the "owner" of seized funds to the extent it has discharged its obligations arising from *all* accounts held by the depositor of the illicit funds and not only those obligations arising under the particular account into which such illicit funds were deposited.[64] Therefore, because the amount of funds still on deposit in the alleged wrongdoer's accounts exceeded the total amount of funds seized from Union Bank's correspondent account, the court held that Union Bank was not an "owner" of the funds for the purpose of challenging the forfeiture regardless of whether or not the bank could seek recovery from the depositor under local law.[65]

In another reported interbank forfeiture case, the offshore customer moved to vacate the forfeiture in the district court that had ordered it. The customer in question, Soulbury Limited (Soulbury), first argued that venue was improper because the court ordering the forfeiture was not located in the district where the account was sited, and also argued that because funds were no longer held by the bank, but had been transferred to the bank's nominee for investment in securities, the forfeiture was invalid.[66] Instead of addressing Soulbury's motion on the merits, however, the district court granted the government's motion for summary judgment against Soulbury on fugitive disentitlement grounds.[67] The US Court of Appeals

---

should be deemed the owner of the seized funds"). The court also rejected Union Bank's argument that its obligation to the depositor should only be measured against any funds held in the specific account into which the purportedly illicit funds were deposited without regard to whether the depositor held funds in an additional account. See *Union Bank* at 20.

[64] *Union Bank* at 11 ("[W]e hold that for purposes of section 981(k), obligations include amounts in any account held at the time of the seizure by anyone who was an owner of the funds at the time they were deposited.").

[65] See *Union Bank* at 19–20 ("Whether or not the bank is correct that it lacks recourse or set-off rights in this case, it has not explained why, as a general matter, banks are not in a position to protect themselves by contract or other means, so as to give the foreign depositor the appropriate incentive to appear.").

[66] See *United States v $6,976,934.65 Plus Interest Deposited into Royal Bank of Scot. Int'l, Acct. No. 2029-56141070, Held in the Name of Soulbury Ltd, and Prop. Traceable Thereto,* (2007) 478 F. Supp. 2d 30 (D.D.C.).

[67] See *United States v $6,976,934.65 Plus Interest Deposited into Royal Bank of Scot. Int'l, Acct. No. 2029-56141070, Held in the Name of Soulbury Ltd., and Prop. Traceable Thereto,* (2007) 520 F. Supp. 2d 188 (D.D.C.). Mr William Scott, the majority owner of Soulbury, had been charged in 1998 with the money laundering violation that gave rise to the forfeiture in the first place, and had never returned to the US to

for the District of Columbia Circuit reversed, concluding that there was a material question of fact as to whether the government had met its burden of showing that each element of the Fugitive Disentitlement Act (the FDA) could be applied to the majority shareholder of Soulbury so as to bar Soulbury's challenge of the interbank forfeiture in question.[68]

At least one commentator has pointed out, and the *Union Bank* case demonstrates, that forfeitures under s.319(a) create the possibility of double liability for the foreign financial institution because the Act may allow the US government to seize funds from the foreign institution's interbank account without relieving the foreign institution of its obligation to its depositors under local law.[69] The remedy in such an instance is an appeal to the discretion of the Attorney General, who is authorised to suspend or terminate a forfeiture proceeding if she determines that a conflict of law exists between US law and the laws of the jurisdiction in which the foreign bank is located, that termination of the proceeding would not harm the national interests of the US, and that termination would be in the interests of justice.[70] Should the Attorney General ever decline to exercise such discretion, it remains to be seen whether a financial institution could successfully assert a constitutional challenge under either the Fifth Amendment Due Process Clause or the Eighth Amendment prohibition against excessive fines.[71]

---

contest the criminal charge. The Fugitive Disentitlement Act (FDA), 28 USC § 2466, was based on a doctrine that developed at common law and was intended to deal with the "unseemly spectacle" of "a criminal defendant who, facing both incarceration and forfeiture for his misdeeds, attempts to invoke from a safe distance only so much of a US court's jurisdiction as might secure him the return of alleged criminal proceeds while carefully shielding himself from the possibility of a penal sanction". *Collazos v United States*, (2004) 368 F.3d 190 at 200 (2d Cir.). The FDA is expressly made applicable in a forfeiture context, and can be used against a corporation "if any majority shareholder", as was Scott, would be prevented from challenging the same forfeiture. See 28 USC § 2466.

[68] See *United States v $6,976,934.65, Plus Interest Deposited into Royal Bank of Scotland Int'l, Account No. 2029-56141070, Held in Name of Soulbury Ltd*, (2009) 554 F.3d 123 at 125 (D.C. Cir.).

[69] See Comisky and Lee, "The USA PATRIOT Act Has Broad Implications for Financial Institutions", (2002) J. Tax'n Fin. Institutions, May/June 2002.

[70] See PATRIOT Act § 319(a), 18 USC § 981(k)(1)(B) (2012).

[71] One financial institution has argued that a forfeiture under s.319(a) violates the

Section 319(a) represents an effort by the US to create a powerful incentive for foreign financial institutions seeking access to the US financial system to strengthen their AML practices in order to reduce the risk that funds will be seized from their accounts at US financial institutions. The DOJ has instituted forfeiture actions under s.319(a) against funds in US-based correspondent bank accounts of numerous foreign banks, including banks in Andorra, Belize, Bolivia, Cambodia, China, Guernsey, Haiti, India, Israel, Japan, Jordan, South Korea, Kuwait, Lebanon, Liechtenstein, Nigeria, Oman, Pakistan, Singapore, Taiwan, the UAE, and Yemen.[72]

In a report to the US Congress dated 13 May 2003, the DOJ described a case involving a lawyer accused of defrauding his US clients who fled to Belize in January 2001 after depositing some of the proceeds from his scheme into accounts maintained with two Belizean banks.[73] Although the government of Belize initially agreed to freeze the funds at those Belizean banks at the request of the US prosecutors, a Belizean court

---

Due Process Clause of the Fifth Amendment because the statute "fails to provide sufficient guidance regarding the definitions of 'foreign bank' and 'discharged all or part of its obligation', thereby rendering it unconstitutionally vague". BNP Paribas Reply Memorandum of Law in Support of Its Motion to Vacate Warrants of Arrest and Dismiss the Action at 24, *United States v All Funds on Deposit in Any & All U.S. Interbank Accts. Maintained at the Bank of N.Y. by BNP Paribas*, No. 04 CV 2343 (E.D.N.Y. 8 July 2005). The institution also argued that such a forfeiture is an arbitrary deprivation of property. *BNP Paribas* at 2. The case settled prior to a court finding on the merits of the arguments.

The only federal appellate court to address a challenge to interbank forfeiture under the Eighth Amendment found such forfeitures constitutional. See *Union Bank*, 487 F.3d at 23 ("A forfeiture under section 981(k) ... is not intended to punish the foreign bank at all, at least when the foreign bank is not a statutory owner ... Congress's evident intent was to use the foreign bank merely as an intermediary to reach the foreign depositor ... [T]he forfeiture does not treat the bank as an object of punishment, and hence the Eighth Amendment does not limit the government's ability to extract funds from the bank's interbank account in the first instance.").

[72] Jack de Kluiver, "International Forfeiture Cooperation", (2013) 61(5) US Attorneys' Bull (September), 36 at 43 *http://www.justice.gov/sites/default/files/usao/legacy/2013/09/16/usab6105.pdf* [Accessed 1 October 2015].

[73] Letter from Jamie E. Brown, Acting Assistant Attorney General of the Legal Affairs Division of the Department of Justice, to F. James Sensenbrenner Jr., Chairman, Comm. on the Judiciary, US House of Representatives, and John Conyers Jr., Ranking Minority Member, Comm. on the Judiciary, US House of Representatives 24–25 (13 May 2003), *http://www.justice.gov/archive/ll/subs/congress/hjcpatriotwcover051303final.pdf* [Accessed 1 October 2015].

lifted the freeze and prohibited the Belizean Government from further assisting US law enforcement agencies. According to the DOJ report, efforts to break the impasse failed and the lawyer withdrew a portion of the funds from the accounts in Belize. Following the passage of the PATRIOT Act, a seizure warrant was served in the US pursuant to s.319(a), and the US took possession of funds in the Belizean bank's interbank account in the United States in an equivalent amount to the funds remaining in the accounts in Belize. In a more recent case, the US seized $16.2 million from the UBS correspondent account of Wegelin & Co, a Swiss bank that later pleaded guilty to conspiring with US taxpayers to conceal $1.2 billion from the Internal Revenue Service (the IRS).[74]

Those cases demonstrate that the DOJ will not limit use of the s.319(a) seizure power to cases involving terrorism.[75] As one spokesperson for the DOJ has commented, "[w]hen tools are available, yes, we'll use them. There is no wording in the law that limits this provision to terrorism. And given the complex connection between terrorism and money-laundering and other criminal activity, such as drug trafficking, we think it is appropriate to use the law to track down proceeds of illegal activity generally".[76] DOJ commentary also acknowledges that "the use of this power could very well adversely affect US

---

[74] Press Release, Dep't of Justice, *Swiss Bank Indicted on U.S. Tax Charges* (28 January 2013), *http://www.justice.gov/opa/pr/swiss-bank-indicted-us-tax-charges* [Accessed 1 October 2015].

[75] Prosecutors do continue to use s.319(a)'s seizure provisions to pursue money launderers with links to terrorism. For example, in August 2012, the government seized $150 million from the US correspondent account of Banque Libano Française SAL (BLF) as a substitute for an equal amount held in escrow at BLF in Lebanon for Lebanese financial institutions accused of laundering money for Hizballah. See Press Release, Federal Bureau of Investigation, *US Government Seizes $150 Million in Connection with Hizballah-Related Money Laundering Scheme* (20 August 2012), *https://www.fbi.gov/newyork/press-releases/2012/u.s.-government-seizes-150-million-in-connection-with-hizballah-related-money-laundering-scheme* [Accessed 1 October 2015]. ("We will use every resource at our disposal to separate terrorists and narco-traffickers, and the banks that work with them, from their illicit funds, even those hidden in foreign accounts.").

[76] "To Seize or Not to Seize", *Washington Times*, 2 June 2003, at A18. See also de Kluiver, "International Forfeiture Cooperation", at 43 ("Importantly, even though [s.319(a)] was enacted as part of the PATRIOT Act, its application is not limited to terrorism cases. Section [319(a)'s] capabilities apply to money laundering forfeitures and the forfeiture of proceeds of all specified unlawful activities.").

bilateral or multilateral law enforcement relations".[77] Accordingly, use of s.319(a) must be formally approved by the Asset Forfeiture and Money Laundering Section (AFMLS) of the Criminal Division of the DOJ and "will be granted only in extraordinary cases in which the government of the nation in which the foreign account is located is unable or unwilling to provide assistance" and "should be considered only as a last resort".[78]

10.2.2.1.1 Possible statute of limitations defence to seizure of US interbank account funds

The statute of limitations for bringing a forfeiture action pursuant to US law may be tolled (i.e. suspended) for the period of time that the property is "absent" from the US.[79] Therefore, in forfeiture cases involving the seizure of funds in non-US bank accounts, that tolling period may effectively give the Government an indefinite amount of time to institute a forfeiture action against the property.[80] In 2008, however, a US federal appellate court was presented with the question of whether, following the adoption of s.319(a), the tolling provision is applicable to funds seized from a US interbank account pursuant to s.319(a).[81] Without deciding the issue,[82] the court noted that the language of s.319(a) provides that funds

---

[77] Linda M. Samuel, "Developments in International Forfeiture and Money Laundering Cooperation", (2007) 55(6) US Attorneys' Bull. 51 at 56. *http://www.justice.gov/sites/default/files/usao/legacy/2007/12/21/usab5506.pdf* [Accessed 1 October 2015].

[78] Dep't of Justice, *Asset Forfeiture Policy Manual* 139 (2013), *http://www.justice.gov/sites/default/files/criminal-afmls/legacy/2014/05/23/policy-manual-2013rev.pdf* [Accessed 1 October 2015].

[79] See 19 USC § 1621 (2000).

[80] See *United States v All Assets Held In Account No. 80020796,* No. 13 CV 1832, 2015 WL 1285791, at *5 (D.D.C. 19 March 2015) (quoting *United States v All Funds in Account Nos. 747.034/278, 747.009/278 & 747.714/278 Banco Espanol de Credito, Spain,* (2002) 295 F.3d 23 at 27 (D.C. Cir.)) ("[O]ur reading tolls the running of the limitations period indefinitely for bringing actions against drug proceeds located in foreign countries ... [G]iven the uncertainties of foreign cooperation, Congress may not have wanted to force the Government to bring forfeiture proceedings within five years to recover such property.").

[81] See *United States v All Funds & Other Personal Prop., Silverado Found,* (2008) 277 F. App'x 607, 609–610 (7th Cir.).

[82] The court did not address the merits of the depositor's claims contesting the forfeiture. Instead the court held that the depositor's plea agreement with the

deposited into a foreign bank account are "deemed to have been deposited into the interbank account in the United States".[83] What the court did not decide was whether, given that language, the forfeited assets should be considered legally absent for the purposes of the tolling statute.[84] If tolling does not apply to funds subject to forfeiture in an interbank account, then the statute of limitations will run as if the funds were deposited directly into a US bank account.[85]

10.2.2.2 *Record-keeping and US subpoena power*

Beginning with the passage of the Bank Secrecy Act (the BSA) in 1970, the US government has required US financial institutions to maintain detailed account records and to file certain reports with respect to all accounts, including correspondent accounts.[86] The PATRIOT Act amended the BSA to require that US financial institutions maintain additional records relating to correspondent accounts held for foreign banks and make them available to US authorities on demand. In particular, US financial institutions that maintain correspondent accounts for foreign financial institutions must maintain records that identify the owner(s) of the foreign financial institution[87] as well as the name and address of a US resident authorised by the foreign financial institution to

---

Government, in which he agreed not to challenge any civil forfeiture proceedings, precluded the depositor from contesting the forfeiture on any of the grounds raised. *All Funds* at 609 ("Because [the depositor] validly waived any challenge to the district court's ruling favoring the government's forfeiture efforts, we must dismiss [his] appeal, as we would dismiss any appeal that violates a plea agreement.").

[83] See 18 USC § 981(k)(1)(A) (2012).

[84] See *All Funds*, 277 F. App'x at 609 ("We note that because [depositor]'s plea agreement requires us to dismiss this appeal, we need not reach [his] argument that the government initiated the forfeiture suit beyond the statute of limitations.").

[85] The current statute provides: "No suit or action ... shall be instituted unless such suit or action is commenced within five years after the time when the alleged offence was discovered, or in the case of forfeiture, within two years after the time when the involvement of the property in the alleged offense was discovered". 19 USC § 1621 (2000).

[86] See "To Seize or Not to Seize", *Washington Times*, 2 June 2003, at A18.

[87] The covered financial institution need not maintain a record of the owner(s) of the foreign financial institution where (i) the shares of the foreign financial institution are publicly traded, or (ii) the foreign financial institution already has

accept service of legal process for records regarding the offshore accounts making use of the correspondent account for US dollar transactions.[88] The US financial institution must provide this information within seven days of a request by a federal law enforcement officer.[89]

Under s.319(b), the Secretary of the Treasury or the Attorney General "may issue a summons or subpoena to any foreign bank that maintains a correspondent account in the United States and request records related to such correspondent account, including records maintained outside of the United States relating to the deposit of funds into the foreign bank".[90] US financial institutions must terminate any correspondent relationship with a foreign bank within 10 business days after receipt of a written notice from either the Secretary or the Attorney General that the foreign financial institution has failed to comply with the subpoena or summons or to contest the subpoena or summons in the US courts.[91] Failure of a US financial institution to terminate all correspondent relationships after such written notice may result in assessment of a civil penalty of up to $10,000 per day until the correspondent relationship is terminated.[92]

Significantly, no substantive limitations on this subpoena power exist in s.319(b) or elsewhere in the PATRIOT Act, suggesting that the subpoenas may be issued for any law enforcement or regulatory purpose and not just as part of AML or anti-terrorism initiatives.[93] However, certain procedural protections are in place; in order to issue or enforce a subpoena under s.319(b), a prosecutor must obtain prior approval from

---

on file with the Federal Reserve a Form FR Y-7, which contains certain ownership information. See 31 CFR § 1010.630(a)(2).

[88] PATRIOT Act § 319(b), 31 USC § 5318(k) (2014).

[89] See 31 CFR § 1010.670(c).

[90] PATRIOT Act § 319(b), 31 USC § 5318(k)(3) (2014).

[91] PATRIOT Act § 319(b), 31 USC § 5318(k)(3) (2014).

[92] PATRIOT Act § 319(b), 31 USC at § 5318(k)(3)(c)(iii).

[93] See Joseph B. Tompkins Jr., "The Impact of the USA PATRIOT Act of 2001 on Non-U.S. Banks" (2002), *http://www.imf.org/external/np/leg/sem/2002/cdmfl/eng/tompki.pdf* [Accessed 1 October 2015].

the DOJ's Office of International Affairs (OIA)[94] by establishing to OIA's satisfaction "an extraordinary need for the subject evidence, and show[ing] that no other method is likely to result in compliance".[95]

The PATRIOT Act also states that a US financial institution has only 120 hours to comply with a request by its "appropriate Federal banking agency"[96] for information related to AML compliance by a covered financial institution or a customer of such an institution. The time limit applies to information and account documentation for any account opened, maintained, administered, or managed in the US by the financial institution, including accounts of foreign entities or individuals.[97]

The record-keeping and document production requirements imposed on foreign financial institutions with correspondent accounts at US financial institutions[98] are another example of the US effort to extend the reach of its AML regime, in this instance by effectively treating foreign financial institutions as domestic financial institutions in respect of their obligation to provide documents to the US government. In effect, the US is requiring foreign financial institutions that maintain US correspondent accounts to open their related records to scrutiny by US regulators, even where those records are maintained abroad.

Moreover, s.314 of the Act provides US financial institutions as well as US regulators and law enforcement officials with increased access to client information from other financial

---

[94] See Dep't of Justice, *United States Attorneys' Manual* § 9-13.525, *http://www. justice.gov/usam/usam-9-13000-obtaining-evidence* [Accessed 1 October 2015].

[95] Corey J. Smith, "Obtaining Foreign Evidence Outside of the Mutual Legal Assistance Treaty Process", 2007(5) US Attorneys' Bull. 27 at 30. *http://www.justice. gov/sites/default/files/usao/legacy/2007/04/20/usab5502.pdf* [Accessed 1 October 2015].

[96] The term "appropriate Federal banking agency" has the same meaning as in s.3 of the Federal Deposit Insurance Act, 12 USC § 1813, which includes the Office of the Comptroller of the Currency, the Federal Deposit Insurance Corporation, and the Board of Governors of the Federal Reserve System.

[97] PATRIOT Act § 319(b)(2), 31 USC § 5318(k)(2) (2014).

[98] 31 USC § 5318(i) (2014); 31 CFR 1010.610(a); 31 CFR 1010.610(b).

institutions.[99] Under that provision, the Secretary of the Treasury has promulgated regulations encouraging the sharing of information between the government and financial institutions, as well as among financial institutions themselves, in an effort to combat money laundering and terrorism.[100] In particular, the regulations promulgated under s.314(a) allow federal, state, local, or foreign law enforcement agencies to request information from financial institutions through a submission to the Treasury Department's Financial Crimes Enforcement Network (FinCEN),[101] provided that "each individual, entity, or organization about which the Federal law enforcement agency is seeking information is engaged in, or is reasonably suspected ... of engaging in, terrorist activity or money laundering".[102] That resource enables law enforcement agencies to reach out to more than 43,000 points of contact at more than 22,000 financial institutions. As of 7 July 2015, 2,535 requests have been processed under s.314(a) and have yielded

---

[99] PATRIOT Act § 314, 31 USC § 5311 (2001) (Historical and Statutory Notes).

[100] The Treasury Department published final rules implementing s.314 on 26 September 2002. See *Special Information Sharing Procedures to Deter Money Laundering and Terrorist Activity*, 31 CFR pt. 1010. In specifying procedures for sharing information, the Treasury Department specifically announced that a financial institution or association of financial institutions receiving information from another financial institution or association may use the information received to assist in compliance with any requirement set forth in the Treasury Department's regulations adopted under Title III of the PATRIOT Act. See *Special Information Sharing Procedures to Deter Money Laundering and Terrorist Activity*. Moreover, voluntary reporting to another financial institution does not relieve an institution of its obligation to file a suspicious activity report.

[101] On 10 February 2010, Treasury Department regulations were amended to allow certain foreign law enforcement agencies, as well as state and local law enforcement agencies, to initiate s.314(a) queries. See *Expansion of Special Information Sharing Procedures to Deter Money Laundering and Terrorist Activity*, 75 Fed. Reg. 6560 (10 February 2010). A foreign law enforcement agency qualifies for access to the 314(a) programme if it "is from a jurisdiction that is party to a treaty that provides, or in the determination of FinCEN is from a jurisdiction that otherwise allows, law enforcement agencies in the United States access to information comparable to that obtained under this section". 31 CFR § 1010.520(a)(2). At present, law enforcement agencies of the European Union are permitted to initiate s.314(a) queries by virtue of the Mutual Legal Assistance Treaty between the US and EU. See Reider-Gordon, "US and International Anti-Money Laundering Developments", (2011) 45 Int'l Law. 365 at 366.

[102] 31 CFR § 1010.520(b).

productive leads to law enforcement, including the identification of new accounts and transactions for further investigation.[103]

Section 314(b) enables US financial institutions, upon notice to the Secretary, to voluntarily share information with each other "regarding individuals, entities, organizations, and countries suspected of possible terrorist or money laundering activities".[104] While such disclosures would, under ordinary circumstances, violate financial institutions' confidentiality obligations under US law, the Act contains a safe harbour provision that expressly protects institutions participating in s.314(b) information sharing from liability for the disclosure of the information and any failure to provide notice of the disclosure "to the person who is the subject of such disclosure, or any other person identified in the disclosure".[105] Some commentators have noted that s.314(b) and the implementing regulations may raise problematic issues for foreign financial institutions subject to obligations under the confidentiality laws of their own jurisdictions.[106] At least among US financial

---

[103] FinCEN, *FinCEN's 314(a) Fact Sheet* (7 July 2015), *http://www.fincen.gov/statutes_regs/patriot/pdf/314afactsheet.pdf* [Accessed 1 October 2015]. FinCEN reports that, of that number, 2,055 requests pertained to money laundering investigations, while 480 requests pertained to terrorism-related investigations. Ibid. Based on feedback from law enforcement agencies using the s.314(a) programme, FinCEN estimates that each s.314(a) request identifies, on average, 8.2 new bank accounts and 16.2 new transactions that can be used as leads for further investigation into complex money laundering or terrorism finance schemes.

[104] PATRIOT Act § 314(b), 31 USC § 5311 (2001).

[105] PATRIOT Act § 314(b), 31 USC § 5311 (2001). In order for an institution to avail itself of the protection from liability in s.314(b), "a financial institution or an association must notify [the government] of its intent to engage in information sharing and that it has established and will maintain adequate procedures to protect the security and confidentiality of the information". Fed. Fin. Insts. Examination Council, *Bank Secrecy Act/Anti-Money Laundering Examination Manual* 95 (2014), *https://www.ffiec.gov/bsa_aml_infobase/documents/BSA_AML_Man_2014.pdf* [Accessed 1 October 2015]. See also 31 CFR § 1010.540(b)(5).

[106] Bruce Zagaris, "Treasury New Rules for Information Sharing Have Important International Implications", (2002) 18 Int'l Enforcement L. Rep. 174; see also Ian Comins, "Banking on the USA PATRIOT Act", (2002) Cayman Fin. Rev. (Winter). Section 203 of the PATRIOT Act, though not one of Title III's AML provisions, may also have implications for the confidentiality of foreign customer information. This provision amends the Federal Rules of Criminal Procedure to allow for the disclosure of matters involving "foreign intelligence or counterintelligence" to "any Federal law enforcement, intelligence, protective, immigration, national

---

institutions, though, s.314(b) communications have brought several benefits to law enforcement and, in particular, have helped financial institutions file "more comprehensive and complete" suspicious activity reports (SARs).[107] The volume of

defense, or national security official in order to assist the official receiving that information in the performance of his official duties". PATRIOT Act § 203(a)(1), codified at Fed. R. Crim. P. 6(e)(3)(C); see also 50 USC § 3003(2) (providing an expansive definition of foreign intelligence as "information relating to the capabilities, intentions, or activities of foreign governments or elements thereof, foreign organizations, or foreign persons"). Under s.203, information gathered and presented to a grand jury for one purpose or in the context of one potential law enforcement action could then be used by an agency of the US government for a different purpose, so long as the information relates to a foreign person or entity. See Tompkins, "The Impact of the USA PATRIOT Act of 2001 on Non-U.S. Banks", note 93, at 13–17.

[107] FinCEN, *Section 314(b) Fact Sheet* (2013), *http://www.fincen.gov/statutes_regs/patriot/ pdf/314bfactsheet.pdf* [Accessed 1 October 2015] (explaining the benefits of s.314(b) voluntary information sharing). Banks, bank holding companies, and their subsidiaries are required by federal law to file a SAR under a variety of circumstances, including where they detect transactions or attempted transactions in excess of $5,000 that the bank or affiliate knows, suspects, or has reason to know "may involve potential money laundering or other illegal activity." Fed. Fin. Insts. Examination Council, *Bank Secrecy Act/Anti-Money Laundering Examination Manual* 60 (2014) at *https://www.ffiec.gov/bsa_aml_infobase/documents/BSA_ AML_Man_2014.pdf* [Accessed 1 October 2015] (identifying federal regulations establishing the SAR requirement). In August 2015, FinCEN proposed a rule that would require certain investment advisers to report suspicious activity as well. FinCEN, *FinCEN Proposes AML Regulations for Investment Advisers* (25 August 2015), *http://www.fincen.gov/news_room/nr/pdf/20150825.pdf* [Accessed 1 October 2015]. Because the proposed rule has been put out for comment, it is unknown whether or when it will be finalized and, if it is, what its exact terms will be.
FinCEN, while not itself an investigatory body, is the repository for SARs filed with the US government and maintains them for law enforcement use. See Skerry, "Financial Counter-intelligence: How Changes to the US Anti-Money Laundering Regime Can Assist US Counter-intelligence Efforts", (2013) 53 Santa Clara L. Rev. 205 at 224. It also provides interpretive guidance to financial institutions on how to identify and report suspicious activity. See Skerry at 226–227. The financial sector produces a high volume of SARs, with the most recent data reflecting approximately 1.4 million SARs filed per year. FinCEN, SAR Stats, July 2014, at 1, *http://www.fincen.gov/news_room/rp/files/SAR01/SAR_ Stats_proof_2.pdf* [Accessed 1 October 2015].
SAR requirements in the US are constantly evolving. In 2014, following the legalization of marijuana in Washington State and Colorado, FinCEN released guidelines on how financial institutions are to provide services to marijuana-related businesses. The FinCEN guidance requires financial institutions to file a SAR even if they only provide indirect financial services to a marijuana business. FinCEN, "BSA Expectations Regarding Marijuana-Related Businesses" (14 February 2014), *http://www.fincen.gov/statutes_regs/guidance/pdf/FIN-2014-G001.pdf* [Accessed 1 October 2015]; see also Christopher L. Allen, "Reefer Madness: New Treasury Guidance for Banks Providing Financial Services to Marijuana Sellers",

such communications is not publicly available, but the number of SARs filed with federal law enforcement agencies that attribute the discovery of suspicious activity at least in part to inter-institution communications has grown substantially in recent years—from just 2 in 2002 to 3,671 in 2012.[108] While the majority of s.314(b) SARs have been and continue to be filed by banks,[109] the Act allows a wide variety of financial institutions to participate in the information sharing programme, and in recent years securities firms and broker-dealers have become more involved.[110] The participation of more and diverse institutions in the s.314(b) programme should allow financial institutions to more effectively identify and report suspicious activities relating to money laundering and other criminal activities.[111] At the same time, financial institutions should note that regulators are also placing increasing scrutiny on instances in which there has been a failure to file a SAR.[112]

(2014) 68 Consumer Fin. L.Q. Rep. 28 at 30. Thus, a bank must file a SAR if it provided financial services to another financial institution which in turn offered its services to marijuana-related accounts, or if it provided services to a landlord that leases property to a marijuana business. Furthermore, the guidance indicates that financial institutions that do business with clients engaged in the marijuana trade in states where such activity is legal are not guaranteed "safe harbor". The DOJ has explicitly stated that neither its own guidance nor any state or local law "provides a legal defense to a violation of federal law, including any civil or criminal violation of the Controlled Substances Act, the money laundering and unlicensed money transmitter statutes, or the [BSA], including the obligation of financial institutions to conduct customer due diligence." Press Release, Dep't of Justice, *Statement of Michael C. Ormsby and Jenny A. Durkan, United States Attorneys for the Eastern and Western Districts of Washington* (14 February 2014), *http://www. justice.gov/usao-edwa/pr/statement-michael-c-ormsby-and-jenny-durkan-united-states-attorneys-eastern-and-western* [Accessed 1 October 2015]; Dep't of Justice, *Guidance Regarding Marijuana Enforcement* (29 August 2013), *http://www.justice.gov/iso/opa/ resources/3052013829132756857467.pdf* [Accessed 1 October 2015].

[108] FinCEN, *The SAR Activity Review: Trends, Tips & Issues* (May 2013), at 41, *http://www.fincen.gov/news_room/rp/files/sar_tti_23.pdf* [Accessed 1 October 2015].

[109] FinCEN has published this type of communication as an example of the success of the s.314(b) programme. See e.g. FinCEN, *SARs and 314(b) Call Lead to Guilty Plea in Ponzi Scheme* (October 2011), *http://www.fincen.gov/law_enforcement/ss/html/ Issue%2020-story8.html* [Accessed 1 October 2015] (explaining how information sharing between two banks led to filing of SAR and indictment of individual on mail fraud charges).

[110] FinCEN, *The SAR Activity Review: Trends, Tips & Issues* at 42.

[111] FinCEN, *The SAR Activity Review: Trends, Tips & Issues* at 42–43.

[112] In January 2014, JP Morgan and the US Attorney's Office for the Southern District of New York entered into a deferred prosecution agreement (DPA) in which JP Morgan was alleged to have failed to file a SAR in connection with the Bernie

10.2.2.3   Regulation of shell bank accounts

The PATRIOT Act also attempts to eliminate access to the US financial system by foreign banks that do not maintain a physical presence in any country, commonly known as "shell banks". Section 313 prohibits covered financial institutions from establishing, maintaining, administering, or managing correspondent accounts for "shell banks".[113] In addition, it calls for the Secretary of the Treasury to set forth regulations outlining the "reasonable steps" that must be taken by a US financial institution in order to ensure that any correspondent account for a foreign financial institution is not being used by the foreign bank to provide banking services to a foreign shell bank indirectly.[114] To date, the regulations have provided limited guidance on the ways in which institutions may achieve compliance with this provision, but they do provide a "safe harbor" from liability if institutions require the foreign banks for which they maintain correspondent accounts to complete a model certification appended to the regulations.[115] In an important exception to the provision's broad prohibition, s.313 exempts shell banks that are affiliated with a US or

---

Madoff Ponzi scheme. Pursuant to the DPA, JP Morgan paid a $1.7 billion penalty. According to the allegations set forth in the charging instrument filed in connection with this resolution, JP Morgan's London desk began to find Madoff's trading activity suspicious as early as the Fall of 2007, when an analyst wrote a memorandum about the trades that resulted in JP Morgan filing a report with the United Kingdom's Serious Organised Crime Agency. According to the allegations, these concerns were not raised with compliance in the United States, and therefore did not result in the filing of a SAR. The US Attorney's Office accused JP Morgan of lacking adequate communication and failing to implement a satisfactory BSA/AML compliance programme. Deferred Prosecution Agreement, JPMorgan Chase Bank, N.A. (6 January 2014), *http://www.justice.gov/sites/ default/files/usao-sdny/legacy/2015/03/25/JPMC%20DPA%20Packet%20(Fully%20 Executed%20w%20Exhibits).pdf* [Accessed 1 October 2015]. The FBI Assistant Director-in-Charge, George Venizelos, stated, "[i]n order to avoid these types of disasters in the future—we all need to be invested in making our markets safer and more equitable. The FBI can't do it alone. Traders, compliance officers, analysts, bankers, and executives are the gatekeepers of the financial industry. We need their help protecting our markets". Dep't of Justice, *Press Release* (7 January 2014), *http://www.justice.gov/usao-sdny/pr/manhattan-us-attorney-and-fbi-assistant-director-charge-announce-filing-criminal* [Accessed 1 October 2015].

[113] PATRIOT Act § 313, 31 USC § 5318(j) (2014).
[114] PATRIOT Act § 313, 31 USC § 5318(j)(2).
[115] See 31 CFR § 1010.630(b).

foreign financial institution and subject to supervision by a banking authority in the jurisdiction that regulates the affiliated financial institution.[116]

A *Section-by-Section Analysis*, published by the Treasury Department with its regulations implementing s.313, also clarifies the "reasonable steps" needed to ensure that correspondent accounts are not being used indirectly to provide banking services to foreign shell banks. In particular, it elaborates on the certification needed to demonstrate compliance with the prohibition on the indirect provision of correspondent accounts to foreign shell banks, as required under 31 USC § 5318(j)(2).[117] The analysis states:

> "[A] foreign bank could certify that it is not using a correspondent account with a covered financial institution to provide banking services to any foreign shell bank, *without in turn asking each of its foreign bank customers to provide it with a similar certification*. To interpret this requirement otherwise would lead to an endless chain of certifications."[118]

As with s.319, foreign branches of US federally insured banks will be treated as "foreign banks", not "covered financial institutions", and thus are not directly subject to the regulations relating to shell banks under s.313.[119] The result is that

---

[116] An "affiliate" is defined as a foreign bank that is "controlled by or is under common control with a depository institution, credit union, or a foreign bank". 31 USC § 5318(j)(4)(A). "Control" is defined as "[1] [o]wnership, control, or power to vote 50 per cent or more of any class of voting securities or other voting interests of another company; or [2] [c]ontrol in any manner [of] the election of a majority of the directors (or individuals exercising similar functions) of another company". 31 CFR § 1010.605(n)(2)(ii).

[117] For the model certification, see appendix A to 31 CFR § 1060.30, available at *http://www.fincen.gov/statutes_regs/frn/pdf/CISADA_Certification.pdf* [Accessed 1 October 2015].

[118] Anti-Money Laundering Requirements—Correspondent Accounts for Foreign Shell Banks; Recordkeeping and Termination of Correspondent Accounts for Foreign Banks, 67 Fed. Reg. 60 at 562 and 568 n.27 (emphasis added).

[119] Anti-Money Laundering Requirements—Correspondent Accounts for Foreign Shell Banks; Recordkeeping and Termination of Correspondent Accounts for Foreign Banks, 67 Fed. Reg. 60 at 565.

such US federally insured banks are required to perform due diligence on their own foreign branches and may accept certifications from them.

10.2.2.4 Due diligence for correspondent and private bank accounts

Section 312 of the PATRIOT Act requires US financial institutions to perform due diligence and, in some cases, enhanced due diligence, with regard to private banking accounts established or maintained for non-US persons and correspondent accounts established or maintained for foreign financial institutions.[120]

10.2.2.4.1 General due diligence obligations

Regulations implementing s.312 require US financial institutions to conduct general due diligence through policies, procedures, and controls "reasonably designed" to enable the detection and reporting of any known or suspected money laundering activity.[121] For private banking accounts maintained by non-US persons, US institutions must determine the identity of all nominal and beneficial owners of the account; determine the sources of funds deposited and their expected use; and review the activity of the account to ensure that it is consistent with information obtained about the source of the

---

[120] See PATRIOT Act § 312(a), 31 USC § 5318(i)(1) (2014) (requiring "appropriate, specific, and, where necessary, enhanced, due diligence policies, procedures, and controls that are reasonably designed to detect and report instances of money laundering through those accounts"). The Act defines "private banking account" as "an account (or any combination of accounts) that (i) requires a minimum aggregate deposit of funds or other assets of not less than $1,000,000; (ii) is established on behalf of 1 or more individuals who have a direct or beneficial ownership interest in the account; and (iii) is assigned to, or is administered or managed by, in whole or in part, an officer, employee, or agent of a financial institution acting as liaison between the financial institution and the direct or beneficial owner of the account". PATRIOT Act § 312(a), 31 USC § 5318(i)(4)(B).

[121] See 31 CFR §§ 1010.610, 1010.620 (implementing due diligence requirements for private and correspondent accounts); see generally FinCEN, *Fact Sheet: Section 312 of the USA PATRIOT Act Final Regulation and Notice of Proposed Rulemaking* (2005), *http://www.fincen.gov/news_room/rp/rulings/html/312factsheet.html* [Accessed 1 October 2015].

funds and the account's stated purpose.[122] For correspondent accounts maintained by foreign financial institutions, US institutions must assess the money-laundering risk posed by the account based on the consideration of certain enumerated risk factors and adopt risk-based policies, procedures, and controls to review the account's activity with an eye towards detecting suspicious money laundering activity.[123]

10.2.2.4.2 Enhanced due diligence obligations

In special circumstances, US financial institutions must conduct enhanced due diligence against accounts held by foreign individuals and foreign financial institutions. The enhanced due diligence obligations with respect to private banking accounts take effect where a "senior foreign political official" acts as either a nominal or beneficial owner of the account.[124] In such instances, US institutions must employ enhanced scrutiny reasonably designed to detect and report transactions that may involve the proceeds of "foreign corruption".[125]

---

[122] See 31 CFR §1010.620(b). Recently, FinCEN expanded its requirement that financial institutions identify beneficial ownership for new legal entity customers. In doing so, FinCEN set out a two-pronged definition of beneficial ownership, requiring both ownership and control. Under the new rule, a covered financial institution must identify "each individual who owns 25 per cent or more of the equity interests" of the legal entity customer and also one individual who exercises significant managerial control over the legal entity customer. 79 Fed. Reg. 45 at 158 (4 August 2014).

[123] See 31 CFR §1010.610(a).

[124] See PATRIOT Act § 312, 31 USC § 5318(i)(3)(B). A "senior foreign political figure" is defined as "(i) [a] current or former: (A) [s]enior official in the executive, legislative, administrative, military, or judicial branches of a foreign government (whether elected or not); (B) [s]enior official of a major foreign political party; or (C) [s]enior executive of a foreign government-owned commercial enterprise; (ii) [a] corporation, business or other entity that has been formed by, or for the benefit of, any such individual; (iii) [a]n immediate family member of any such individual; and (iv) [a] person who is widely and publicly known (or is actually known by the relevant covered financial institution) to be a close associate of such individual". 31 CFR § 1010.605.

[125] 31 CFR § 1010.620(c)(1). "Proceeds of foreign corruption" are defined as any asset or property that is acquired by, through, or on behalf of a senior foreign political figure through misappropriation, theft, or embezzlement of public funds, the unlawful conversion of property of a foreign government, or through acts of bribery or extortion, and shall include any other property into which any such assets have been transformed or converted. 31 CFR § 1010.620(c)(2).

The enhanced due diligence requirements for correspondent accounts require greater scrutiny of accounts maintained for three categories of foreign financial institutions: (i) those operating under an offshore banking licence[126]; (ii) those operating under a banking licence issued by a foreign country designated as "non-co-operative" with AML principles by an intergovernmental group or organisation of which the US is a member—usually the Financial Action Task Force (FATF)—and with which the US representative concurs;[127] and (iii) those operating under a banking licence issued by a foreign country designated by the Secretary of the Treasury as warranting special measures due to money laundering concerns.[128]

As applied to these particular types of correspondent accounts, enhanced due diligence requires compliance by a US financial institution with several additional obligations. First, the US institution must engage in greater scrutiny of the foreign bank, including obtaining information relating to the foreign bank's own AML policies; monitoring transactions to, from, and through the correspondent account; and obtaining information about the identity of any person with authority to direct transactions through any correspondent account that is a "payable-through account".[129] Second, the US institution must determine whether the foreign bank itself "maintains correspondent accounts for other foreign banks" and, if so, take

---

[126] Section 312 defines the term "offshore banking license" to mean a "license to conduct banking activities which, as a condition of the license, prohibits the licensed entity from conducting banking activities with the citizens of, or with the local currency of, the country which issued the license". PATRIOT Act § 312, 31 USC § 5318(i)(4)(A) (2014).

[127] 31 CFR § 1010.610(c)(2); see also AML Programs; Special Due Diligence Programs for Certain Foreign Accounts, 31 CFR § 103.176(b)–(c) ("The [FATF] is the only intergovernmental organization of which the United States is a member that has designated countries as non-cooperative with international anti-money laundering principles ... The United States has concurred with all FATF designations to date.") The FATF is comprised of 34 member-states and two regional organizations. FATF, *About Us, http://www.fatf-gafi.org/pages/aboutus/membersandobservers/* [Accessed 1 October 2015].

[128] PATRIOT Act § 312, 31 USC § 5318(i)(2)(A) (2014).

[129] 31 CFR § 1010.610(b). A "payable-through account" means "a correspondent account maintained by a covered financial institution for a foreign bank by means of which the foreign bank permits its customers to engage, either directly or through a subaccount, in banking activities usual in connection with the business of banking in the United States". 31 CFR § 1010.610(b)(1)(iii)(B).

reasonable steps to obtain information relevant to assess and mitigate money laundering risks associated with those other foreign banks.[130] Finally, the US institution must determine, "for any correspondent account established or maintained for a foreign bank whose shares are not publicly traded, the identity of each owner of the foreign bank and the nature and extent of each owner's ownership interest".[131]

The US relies on the FATF for its list of whom to monitor for enhanced due diligence requirements, particularly with respect to correspondent accounts. While the US Treasury Secretary maintains authority to identify foreign jurisdictions warranting special scrutiny, the US is a member-state of the FATF and adopts the intergovernmental body's determinations of foreign jurisdictions "non-co-operative" with AML principles.[132] The FATF publishes a list identifying foreign jurisdictions possessing strategic AML deficiencies and against whom Member States should apply enhanced due diligence (EDD) or enact counter-measures, which entails due diligence along with other reporting and banking requirements.[133] In March 2015, as it has done on many prior occasions, the US Department of the Treasury issued an advisory to US financial institutions that endorsed the FATF's "non-co-operative" designations and urged EDD against the correspondent accounts of foreign banks from those jurisdictions.[134]

---

[130] 31 CFR § 1010.610(b)(2).

[131] 31 CFR § 1010.610(b)(3)(i).

[132] See FATF, *High-Risk and Non-Cooperative Jurisdictions*, *http://www.fatf-gafi.org/topics/high-riskandnon-cooperativejurisdictions* [Accessed 1 October 2015].

[133] See FATF, *High-Risk and Non-Cooperative Jurisdictions*. As of February 2015, the FATF has identified Iran and the Democratic People's Republic of North Korea as jurisdictions requiring counter-measures, and has identified Algeria, Ecuador, and Myanmar as jurisdictions warranting enhanced due diligence. See FATF, Public Statement (27 February 2015), *http://www.fatf-gafi.org/topics/high-riskandnon-cooperativejurisdictions/documents/public-statement-february-2015.html* [Accessed 1 October 2015]. Separately, the FATF publishes a list of jurisdictions possessing strategic AML deficiencies but that have provided a high-level political commitment to adopt an action plan in cooperation with the FATF. See FATF, *Improving Global AML/CFT Compliance: On-Going Process* (27 February 2015), *http://www.fatf-gafi.org/topics/high-riskandnon-cooperativejurisdictions/documents/fatf-compliance-february-2015.html* [Accessed 1 October 2015].

[134] See FinCEN, *Advisory on the FATF-Identified Jurisdictions with AML/CFT Deficiencies* (16 March 2015), *http://www.fincen.gov/statutes_regs/guidance/pdf/FIN-2014-A009.pdf* [Accessed 1 October 2015]. With respect to those jurisdictions identified

10.2.3 Special measures applicable to foreign jurisdictions and foreign financial institutions of primary money laundering concern

Section 311 of the PATRIOT Act empowers the Secretary of the Treasury, upon finding that reasonable grounds exist for concluding that a foreign jurisdiction, institution, class of transaction, or type of account is of "primary money laundering concern", to require domestic financial institutions and financial agencies to take certain "special measures" against the entity or matter of primary money laundering concern, including compliance with narrow but powerful economic sanctions.[135] Designations under s.311 entail a two-step process.

First, the Secretary of the Treasury, in consultation with the Secretary of State and the Attorney General, must make the preliminary designation of "primary money laundering concern".[136] For foreign jurisdictions, the Secretary may consider certain "jurisdictional factors" enumerated by the Act, such as evidence that organised criminal groups or international terrorists have transacted business there as well as the substance and quality of the jurisdiction's AML laws.[137] For foreign financial institutions, the Secretary may consider certain "institutional factors" enumerated by the Act, such as

---

by the FATF as AML deficient but nevertheless cooperative, FinCEN reminded US financial institutions of their general due diligence obligations under s.312 of the PATRIOT Act. See *Advisory on the FATF-Identified Jurisdictions with AML/CFT Deficiencies* at 4–5.

[135] See PATRIOT Act § 311, 31 USC §§ 5318A(a)(1), 5318A(b) (2006); see generally Stephen Heifetz and Evan Sherwood, "Those Other Economic Sanctions: Section 311 Special Measures", (2014) 131 Banking L.J. 688. Section 311 also empowers the Secretary to impose this designation against "classes of transactions" outside of the US as well as certain "types of accounts". See Heifetz and Sherwood. However, FinCEN—the unit within the Department of the Treasury tasked with making these designations—has thus far only passed special measures against foreign jurisdictions and financial institutions. See FinCEN, *Section 311 Special Measures*, http://www.fincen.gov/statutes_regs/patriot/section311.html [Accessed 1 October 2015].

[136] See PATRIOT Act § 311, 31 USC § 5318A(c).

[137] See PATRIOT Act § 311, 31 USC § 5318A(c)(2)(A) (enumerating seven "potentially relevant factors" for jurisdictions, to be considered together with any other such information as the Secretary may determine relevant).

the extent to which certain financial institutions are used to facilitate or promote money laundering in and through the foreign jurisdiction.[138]

Second, after a designation has been made, s.311 permits the Secretary of the Treasury to impose one or more of five "special measures" on financial institutions and agencies operating within the US, including branches and agencies of non-US banks whose dealings relate to the jurisdiction or institution of primary money laundering concern.[139] The first four measures entail various record keeping and investigation requirements, including (i) the establishment of additional record-keeping and reporting procedures on domestic financial institutions with respect to the "primary money laundering concern";[140] (ii) the collection and maintenance of information concerning the identities and addresses of the beneficial owners of any accounts opened in the US by a foreign person involving the designated area of concern[141]; (iii) the identification and acquisition of additional information on any customers of foreign financial institutions that open or maintain "payable-through accounts" for their customers at US financial institutions[142]; and (iv) similar requirements for foreign financial institutions that open or maintain "correspondent accounts" for their customers at US financial institutions.[143] The fifth measure is the most powerful, allowing the Secretary to require the prohibition or imposition of conditions on the opening or maintaining of correspondent accounts or payable-through accounts "by any domestic financial institution or domestic financial agency for or on behalf of a foreign banking institution".[144] Following due consultation with various governmental and regulatory entities, the Secretary may impose the first four of these measures by means of an order

---

[138] See PATRIOT Act § 311, 31 USC § 5318A(c)(2)(B) (enumerating three "potentially relevant factors" for institutions, to be considered together with any other such information as the Secretary may determine relevant).

[139] See PATRIOT Act § 311, 31 USC § 5318A(b).

[140] See PATRIOT Act § 311, 31 USC § 5318A(b)(1)(A).

[141] See PATRIOT Act § 311, 31 USC § 5318A(b)(2).

[142] See PATRIOT Act § 311, 31 USC § 5318A(b)(3).

[143] See PATRIOT Act § 311, 31 USC § 5318A(b)(4).

[144] See PATRIOT Act § 311, 31 USC § 5318A(b)(5).

accompanied by a notice of rulemaking.[145] The fifth measure may only become effective through the formal rulemaking process, which involves notice and a comment period.[146]

A Treasury Department official has described the sweeping nature of s.311:

---

[145] Factors to consider in selecting "special measures" include "[1] whether similar action has been or is being taken by other nations or multilateral groups; [2] whether the imposition of any particular special measure would create a significant competitive disadvantage, including any undue cost or burden associated with compliance, for financial institutions organized or licensed in the United States; [3] the extent to which the action or the timing of the action would have a significant adverse systemic impact on the international payment, clearance, and settlement system, or on legitimate business activities involving the particular jurisdiction, institution, class of transactions, or type of account; and [4] the effect of the action on United States national security and foreign policy". See PATRIOT Act § 311, 31 USC § 5318A(a)(4)(B).

[146] Currently, the Treasury Department has final rules instituting the fifth measure of s.311 against one jurisdiction, Burma, and two financial institutions, Commercial Bank of Syria and Banco Delta Asia. See 31 CFR §§ 1010.651, 653, 655. Other final rules had been promulgated, but later rescinded, against the jurisdictions of Nauru and Ukraine as well as against financial institutions such as Asia Wealth Bank, Myanmar Mayflower Bank, and VEF Banka. See FinCEN, *Section 311 Special Measures,* *http://www.fincen.gov/statutes_regs/patriot/section311.html* [Accessed 1 October 2015]. Between 2011 and 2015, though, FinCEN has provided notice of other proposed rulemakings for sanctions against Iran as well as seven additional financial institutions: Lebanese Canadian Bank, JSC CredexBank, Kassem Rmeiti & Co. Foreign Exchange, Halawi Exchange Co., Liberty Reserve SA, FBME Bank, and Banca Privada d'Andorra. See FinCEN, *Section 311 Special Measures.* Final rules have not yet been adopted.

It was previously unclear to what extent a financial institution must take affirmative steps to identify and subsequently terminate the existence of any "indirect accounts" (i.e. a correspondent account that a foreign bank uses to provide services indirectly to an institution of money laundering concern) to be in compliance with a final rule instituting s.311's fifth measure. Such "nested" relationships can present difficulties because it may not be readily apparent that an account is being operated on behalf of an institution of money laundering concern. The final rule promulgated against Burma clarified the extent of these obligations, noting that a financial institution need not specifically review every account maintained for foreign banks to be in compliance with a final rule under s.311, but rather banks are only required to terminate a correspondent account if the bank obtains *actual knowledge* through the due diligence procedures already in place that a foreign bank is using an account to provide banking services indirectly to a financial institution of money laundering concern. Imposition of Special Measures Against Burma, 31 CFR § 1010.651 ("[T]his section does not itself impose an independent obligation on covered financial institutions ... Instead, [it applies] if covered financial institutions become aware, through due diligence that is otherwise appropriate or required under existing anti-money laundering obligations, that a foreign bank is using its correspondent account to provide banking services indirectly to a Burmese banking institution.").

"This is an extremely powerful tool ... It can be directed against a country, an institution, or a practice ... We have used this extremely powerful tool ... and stand ready in appropriate circumstances to use it again. While we are mindful of the fact that such measures should be used sparingly, and not generally as a first resort, we will not hesitate to use these extraordinary special powers again if the circumstance warrants its use."[147]

Section 311's process for implementing special measures against an institution or jurisdiction may serve as the catalyst for such institution or jurisdiction to reform its AML regime.[148]

---

[147] Remarks by Michael Dawson, Deputy Assistant Sec'y, Critical Infrastructure Prod. and Compliance Policy, Dep't of the Treasury, to the Bankers' Ass'n for Fin. & Trade (Wash., DC, 15 July 2003).

[148] The designations of Ukraine and Nauru as jurisdictions of primary money laundering concern under s.311 were subsequently revoked in response to significant legislative reforms in those jurisdictions. See Revocation of Designation of Ukraine as Primary Money Laundering Concern, 68 Fed. Reg. 19,071 (17 April 2003); Withdrawal of the Notice of Proposed Rulemaking Against the Republic of Nauru, 73 Fed. Reg. 21,179 (18 April 2008) (noting legislative reforms that "address[ed] the deficiencies in [Nauru's] anti-money laundering regime"); see also Withdrawal of the Finding of Primary Money Laundering Concern and the Notice of Proposed Rulemaking Against Multibanka, 71 Fed. Reg. 39,606, 39,608 (13 July 2006) ("Multibanka has been forthcoming in addressing the concerns that we identified in the notice of proposed rulemaking and has instituted measures to guard against money laundering abuses"). In rare instances, designations may result in the revocation of licences for financial institutions. See *Withdrawal of Final Rules Against Myanmar Mayflower Bank and Asia Wealth Bank*, 77 Fed. Reg. 59 at 747 and 748 (1 October 2012) ("Subsequent to the issuance of the final rule related to the Banks, the Government of Burma revoked the licences of the Banks in 2005 and neither financial institution currently exists.").

10.3   Recent developments in US AML law

10.3.1   *Addressing demand-side corruption: AML charges as a supplement to the FCPA in prosecuting foreign officials*

Although the Foreign Corrupt Practices Act (the FCPA) criminalises the offer of a bribe to a foreign official, it "does not criminalize the receipt of a bribe by a foreign official".[149] US AML law, however, enables prosecutors to criminally charge those who accept bribes. As a result, the DOJ has brought money laundering charges against foreign officials in conjunction with FCPA and money laundering prosecutions of US citizens, and as the predicate crime for seeking forfeitures under 18 USC § 981.

For example, in a recent case involving Telecommunications D'Haiti, S.A.M. (Haiti Teleco), a state-owned company in Haiti, the DOJ secured FCPA and money laundering convictions of the co-owners of a Florida-based telecommunications company, as well as money laundering convictions of Jean Rene Duperval, Robert Antoine and Patrick Joseph, the Haitian officials they bribed.[150] The 11th Circuit ultimately upheld the convictions of the co-owners and Duperval, rejecting arguments that the money-laundering conviction presented a merger problem by punishing the same conduct as the underlying FCPA offense, and that Haiti Teleco was not an instrumentality of the Haitian Government (which would have meant that Duperval was not a "foreign official" within the meaning of the FCPA).[151] Duperval received a nine-year sentence, while Antoine and Joseph, who each had pled guilty, were sentenced to 18 months and one year and one day in prison respectively. In November 2013, in a prior prosecution brought on a similar theory, Maria Gonzalez, a former Venezuelan government official who accepted bribes while

---

[149] See *United States v Blondek*, (1990) 741 F. Supp. 116 at 117 (N.D. Tex.); sub nom. *United States v Castle*, (1991) 925 F.2d 831 (5th Cir.).

[150] See *United States v Duperval*, (2015) 777 F.3d 1324 at 1338 (11th Cir.).

[151] See *Duperval*, at 1333–1334; *United States v Esquenazi*, (2014) 752 F.3d 912, 935–936 (11th Cir.), *cert. denied*, 135 S. Ct. 293.

working at Banco de Desarrollo Economico y Social de Venezuela, a state-owned economic development bank in Venezuela, pled guilty in the Southern District of New York to money laundering charges related to the bribery scheme.[152]

10.3.2 Virtual Currency

A notable addition to the AML landscape over the last several years relates to the development of "digital" or "virtual" currency. Virtual currency is not legal tender, but can be transferred between entities or individuals as a substitute for legal tender, and can be converted into real currency at online "exchanges".[153] The most popular digital currency currently in use is "Bitcoin", which operates as a "peer-to-peer, decentralized network administered by the network's users", and utilises a public "ledger" to verify transactions without the need for a central authority or clearing house for digital transactions, such as a government, bank, or traditional financial or credit institution.[154]

Three features in particular make virtual currencies, such as Bitcoin, potentially attractive vehicles for money laundering. First, users can transfer financial instruments to one another without the assistance of a third-party bank or financial institution.[155] Additionally, money launderers may find useful "the relative 'speed and ease with which [virtual currency] transactions can be carried out'".[156] Finally, virtual currencies offer users a degree of anonymity.[157] As Assistant Attorney

---

[152] See Press Release, Dep't of Justice, *High-Ranking Bank Official at Venezuelan State Development Bank Pleads Guilty to Participating in Bribery Scheme* (18 November 2013), *http://www.justice.gov/opa/pr/high-ranking-bank-official-venezuelan-state-development-bank-pleads-guilty-participating* [Accessed 1 October 2015]. As of October 2015, Gonzalez had not been sentenced.

[153] Treasury Dep't, *2015 National Money Laundering Risk Assessment* 57.

[154] Kavid Singh, "The New Wild West: Preventing Money Laundering in the Bitcoin Network", (2015) 13 Nw. J. Tech. & Intell. Prop. 37 at 40. For a more detailed description of how Bitcoin works, see Singh at 40–45.

[155] Nicholas J. Ajello, Note, "Fitting a Square Peg in a Round Hole: Bitcoin, Money Laundering, and the Fifth Amendment Privilege against Self-Incrimination", (2015) 80 Brook L. Rev. 435 at 446.

[156] Ajello at 447.

[157] Ajello at 446–447 (stating that although every Bitcoin transfer is published on "the public ledger", Bitcoin does not maintain records that link a public address

General Leslie Caldwell explained during a speech to the ABA in June 2015, "many criminals like virtual currency systems because these systems conduct transfers quickly, securely and with a perceived level of anonymity".[158] Indeed, for some virtual currencies, an e-mail address is the only piece of information needed to set up an account.[159] In conjunction with anonymising "onion routers" such as "Tor", which create anonymous communications through several layers of encryption,[160] Bitcoin and similar virtual currencies are perceived to have contributed to the growth of the "Dark Net", where black market goods, such as drugs, weapons, and child pornography, can be sold anonymously and digital proceeds instantly laundered back into traditional currency.[161]

The first major case illustrating the government's approach to digital currency money laundering was the 2007 indictment of E-Gold Limited and its owners, the proprietors of the gold-backed digital currency "E-Gold", by AFMLS and the Computer Crime and Intellectual Property Section (CCIPS) of the Criminal Division of the DOJ.[162] Charges against E-Gold Limited were brought under s.1960 of the BSA and the MLCA based on allegations that the company allowed its users

---

to an individual or organization). Additionally, it is relatively easy to obtain a public address, and Bitcoin users typically have multiple public addresses, "thereby muddying the evidentiary waters and making it very difficult for law enforcement to efficiently and properly investigate potential money laundering violations".

[158] Remarks of Leslie R. Caldwell, Assistant Attorney General, Dep't of Justice, Criminal Division, at the ABA's National Institute on Bitcoin and Other Digital Currencies (26 June 2015).

[159] Remarks of Leslie R. Caldwell, Assistant Attorney General, Dep't of Justice, Criminal Division, at the ABA's National Institute on Bitcoin and Other Digital Currencies (26 June 2015).

[160] Tor is "an outgrowth of '[T]he [O]nion [R]outing' (TOR) project" (alluding to the peeling back of an onion's layers), which was originally funded by the U.S. Naval Research Laboratory. Lawrence Trautman, "Virtual Currencies; Bitcoin & What Now After Liberty Reserve, Silk Road, and Mt. Gox?", (2014) 20 Rich. J.L. & Tech. 13 at 23. The Tor system masks a user's identity by distributing a transaction "'over several places on the Internet, so that no single point can link you to your destination.'" Trautman at n.45 (quoting "The Solution: A Distributed, Anonymous Network", Tor Project).

[161] Stephen Small, "Bitcoin: The Napster of Currency", (2015) 37 Hous. J. Int'l L. 581 at 592–596; Trautman at 23.

[162] Ajello, at 448; see *United States v E-Gold Ltd*, (2008) 550 F. Supp.2d 82 (D.D.C.).

anonymity, maintained a staff without professional financial expertise, and did not respond to customer complaints regarding fraud.[163] The defendants argued that E-Gold Limited did not qualify as a "money services business" because E-Gold was not "currency" under the meaning of s.1960, and thus they could not be held liable for failing to obtain a licence.[164] The court rejected that argument, concluding that the legislative intent was to regulate "financial institutions", not just "currency transmitters" or "financial institutions that engage in currency transactions".[165] In 2008, E-Gold Limited and three associated individuals pled guilty to money laundering and operating an unlicensed money transmitting business.[166]

In March 2013, FinCEN released an interpretive guidance report to clarify how the BSA's regulations apply to persons "creating, obtaining, distributing, exchanging, accepting, or transmitting virtual currencies".[167] The guidance explained that although a user of virtual currency does not qualify as a money services business, an administrator or exchanger of virtual currency is a money services business, and therefore must comply with FinCEN's registration, reporting, and record-keeping regulations unless a limitation or exemption applies.[168]

---

[163] Ajello at 449 (quoting Derek A. Dion, Note, "I'll Gladly Trade You Two Bits on Tuesday for a Byte Today: Bitcoin, Regulating Fraud in the E-Conomy of Hacker-Cash", (2013) U. Ill. J.L. Tech. & Pol'y 165 at 167.

[164] *United States v E-Gold Ltd*, 550 F.Supp. 2d at 88.

[165] *United States v E-Gold Ltd* at 95.

[166] Remarks of Leslie R. Caldwell, Assistant Attorney General, Dep't of Justice, Criminal Division, at the ABA's National Institute on Bitcoin and Other Digital Currencies (26 June 2015). 18 USC § 1960 imposes penalties on anyone who knowingly operates an unlicensed "money services business".

[167] FinCEN, Dep't of the Treasury, Fin-2013-G001, *Application of FinCEN's Regulations to Persons Administering, Exchanging, or Using Virtual Currencies* (2013) http://www.fincen.gov/statutes_regs/guidance/pdf/FIN-2013-G001.pdf [Accessed 1 October 2015], at 2.

[168] Fin-2013-G001, *Application of FinCEN's Regulations to Persons Administering, Exchanging, or Using Virtual Currencies* at 1. The guidance defines a user as someone who "obtains virtual currency to purchase goods or services". By contrast, an exchanger is "engaged as a business in the exchange of virtual currency for real currency, funds, or other virtual currency", and an administrator is "engaged as a business in issuing (putting into circulation) a virtual currency" and has the authority to redeem the virtual currency by withdrawing it

The FinCEN guidance also clarified that the law does not view real currency and convertible virtual currencies differently and, accordingly, digital currency exchanges are not exempt from the BSA or the MLCA.[169] FinCEN's guidance has provoked varying responses from the digital currency community. While some feel that the guidance is the prelude to a federal crackdown on Bitcoin, others see the guidance as an indication that FinCEN is not interested in heavily regulating the virtual currency economy at all.[170]

Subsequent to *E-Gold*, the most important digital currency provider criminal case was against Liberty Reserve and a number of its executives (many of whom had also been involved with E-Gold) in 2013.[171] Liberty Reserve, an online digital currency service similar to E-Gold Limited, was based in Costa Rica.[172] Before it was shut down by the Government, Liberty Reserve had accumulated more than one million users worldwide, who collectively conducted approximately $6 billion in transactions (consisting largely of credit card fraud, investment fraud, identity theft, computer hacking, child pornography, and narcotics trafficking) using "Liberty Reserve Dollars" and "Liberty Reserve Euros," the service's digital currencies, which were tied to the value of the US dollar and the Euro, respectively.[173] The DOJ charged Liberty Reserve with conspiracy to commit money laundering, conspiracy to operate an unlicensed money transmitting business, and operation of an unlicensed money transmitting business,[174] and several top executives ultimately pled guilty to money laundering and operating an unlicensed money transmitting

---

from circulation. Fin-2013-G001, *Application of FinCEN's Regulations to Persons Administering Exchanging, or Using Virtual Currencies* at 2.

[169] "Application of FinCEN's Regulations to Persons Administering, Exchanging, or Using Virtual Currencies" at 3.

[170] Ajello, "Fitting a Square Peg in a Round Hole: Bitcoin, Money Laundering, and the Fifth Amendment Privilege against Self-Incrimination", (2015) 80 Brook L. Rev. 435 at 450–451.

[171] Trautman, "Virtual Currencies; Bitcoin & What Now After Liberty Reserve, Silk Road, and Mt. Gox?", (2014) 20 Rich. J.L. & Tech. 13 at 85.

[172] Treasury Dep't, *2015 National Money Laundering Risk Assessment* at 57.

[173] Remarks of Leslie R. Caldwell, Assistant Attorney General, Dep't of Justice, Criminal Division, at the ABA's National Institute on Bitcoin and Other Digital Currencies (26 June 2015).

[174] Trautman at 85.

business.[175] Acting Assistant Attorney General Mythili Raman stated that the Liberty Reserve prosecution demonstrated the DOJ's determination "to pursue purported major money laundering facilitators, even those who hide offshore".[176]

In 2015, FinCEN initiated the first civil enforcement action against a virtual currency exchanger, fining Ripple Labs Inc. and its wholly owned subsidiary, XRP II, LLC, $700,000 for selling its virtual currency, XRP, without registering as a money services business.[177]

10.3.3 Prosecutions related to offshore tax evasion, internet gambling, and terrorist financing

10.3.3.1 Offshore tax evasion

Regulators have recently shown a strong interest in pursuing financial institutions for allowing tax evaders to harbour their assets offshore. Prosecutors are therefore looking into bank accounts in jurisdictions with strict bank secrecy laws, such as the Cayman Islands, Liechtenstein, the Bahamas, and Switzerland.[178] Although preventing tax evasion is not strictly an element of an AML compliance programme, a financial institution can be held liable for facilitating such unlawful activity, and an AML compliance programme with strong due diligence requirements and information sharing can help to root it out.[179] Under authority provided by the BSA, FinCEN manages the submission of Foreign Bank and Financial

---

[175] Remarks of Leslie R. Caldwell, Assistant Attorney General, Dep't of Justice, Criminal Division, at the ABA's National Institute on Bitcoin and Other Digital Currencies (26 June 2015).

[176] Remarks of Acting Assistant Attorney General Mythili Raman before the Senate Committee on Homeland Security and Governmental Affairs (18 November 2013), *http://www.hsgac.senate.gov/download/?id=ac50a1af-cc98-4b04-be13-a7522ea7a70d* [Accessed 1 October 2015].

[177] See FinCEN, Press Release, *FinCEN Fines Ripple Labs Inc. in First Civil Enforcement Action Against a Virtual Currency Exchanger* (5 May 2015), *http://www.fincen.gov/news_room/nr/html/20150505.html* [Accessed 1 October 2015].

[178] Devlin Barrett, "U.S. Broadens Hunt for Tax Evaders", *Wall Street Journal* (27 May 2014).

[179] Rui Tavares, "Relationship Between Money Laundering, Tax Evasion and Tax Havens", European Union Special Committee on Organised Crime, Corruption

Account Reports, which are required by the IRS for US persons holding foreign financial accounts exceeding $10,000 at any time during the calendar year.[180]

One federal investigation focused on allegations that Swiss banking institution UBS "help[ed] its American clients hide as much as $20 billion in assets offshore, thereby evading at least $300 million in taxes".[181] An issue in the investigation was whether "qualified intermediary agreements"[182] with the IRS were inappropriately used to provide US clients with offshore banking services.[183] The US concern was whether financial institutions had assisted US investors in avoiding IRS reporting requirements and tax obligations.[184] The investigation led to UBS being charged in 2009 with conspiracy to defraud the IRS and its entering into a DPA with the US Attorney's Office for the Southern District of Florida. Pursuant to the DPA, UBS agreed to pay $780 million and to strengthen its compliance programme by hiring additional staff and developing "enhanced controls to identify, prevent, detect, and correct" any compliance failures.[185]

More recently, in 2014, Credit Suisse Group AG pled guilty to conspiracy to aid and assist US taxpayers in filing false income

---

and Money Laundering 2012–2013 (January 2013), *http://www.europarl.europa.eu/meetdocs/2009_2014/documents/crim/dv/tavares_ml_/tavares_ml_en.pdf* [Accessed 1 October 2015], at 4–5.

[180] FinCEN, *BSA Electronic Filing Requirements for Report of Foreign Bank and Financial Accounts* (June 2014), *http://www.fincen.gov/forms/files/FBAR%20Line%20Item%20Filing%20Instructions.pdf* [Accessed 1 October 2015].

[181] Lynnley Browning, "U.S. Tightens Oversight of Foreign Banks", *New York Times* (16 October 2008), at B8.

[182] Such agreements allow financial institutions to assume certain documentation and withholding responsibilities related to accounts held by non-US investors in exchange for simplified information reporting to the IRS related to such accounts. See Internal Revenue Serv., Dep't of Treasury, *Qualified Intermediary Frequently Asked Questions*, *http://www.irs.gov/Businesses/International-Businesses/Qualified-Intermediary-Frequently-Asked-Questions* [Accessed 1 October 2015].

[183] See Bernie Becker, "Facing Inquiry, UBS Halts Offshore Banking for U.S. Clients", Int'l Herald Trib. (19 July 2008), at 15.

[184] Lynnley Browning, "IRS Aims to Give Teeth to a Program Meant to Counter Offshore Tax Avoidance", *New York Times* (15 July 2008), at C3.

[185] Deferred Prosecution Agreement, *United States v UBS AG*, No. 09-CR-60033 (S.D. Fla. 18 February 2009).

tax returns and other documents with the IRS.[186] In doing so, Credit Suisse became the first major multi-national financial institution to plead guilty to a crime at the "parent" level in over a decade.[187] As part of the guilty plea, Credit Suisse agreed to pay a total of $2.6 billion in fines, including $1.8 billion to the DOJ for the US Treasury, $100 million to the Federal Reserve, and $715 million to the NYDFS. The resolution also required Credit Suisse to implement pro-grammes to ensure compliance with US law, including reporting requirements under the Foreign Account Tax Com-pliance Act and relevant tax treaties.[188]

10.3.3.2 Internet gambling prosecutions

Another example of the potential extra-territorial reach of the US AML laws can be seen in prosecutions for internet gambling crimes, which have been paired in several instances with criminal charges of money laundering. In the prosecution that led to the Soulbury interbank forfeiture discussed above, for example, the substantive crime supporting the forfeiture was money laundering in aid of an Antiguan internet gambling operation. After securing the interbank forfeiture on 21 December 2003, the Justice Department obtained a second indictment charging William Scott and his wife, the owners of Soulbury, and their internet gambling platform, WorldWide Telesports, with conspiracy to promote a gambling enterprise and to violate the Wire Wager Act.[189] Those gambling charges were coupled with a count alleging a money laundering

---

[186] Andrew Grossman, "Credit Suisse Pleads Guilty in Criminal Tax Case", *Wall Street Journal* (19 May 2014), *http://www.wsj.com/articles/SB10001424052702304422704579571732769356894* [Accessed 1 October 2015].

[187] Remarks at the Advanced Compliance and Ethics Workshop, Principal Deputy Assistant Attorney General Marshall L. Miller, Dep't of Justice, Criminal Division (7 October 2014), *http://www.justice.gov/opa/speech/remarks-principal-deputy-assistant-attorney-general-criminal-division-marshall-l-miller-0* [Accessed 1 October 2015].

[188] Dep't of Justice, Press Release, *Credit Suisse Pleads Guilty to Conspiracy to Aid and Assist U.S. Taxpayers in Filing False Returns* (19 May 2014), *http://www.justice.gov/opa/pr/credit-suisse-pleads-guilty-conspiracy-aid-and-assist-us-taxpayers-filing-false-returns* [Accessed 1 October 2015].

[189] Indictment, *United States v Scott*, CR05-122 (7 April 2005) (alleging a conspiracy to violate 18 USC §§ 1952, 1084).

conspiracy and three counts of money laundering by transferring funds offshore from locations inside the US with the
intention of promoting internet gambling.[190]

Another prosecution that graphically illustrates the intersec-
tion of internet gambling and money laundering was one
brought against the founders and principal executive officers
of Neteller Limited, a company based on the Isle of Man that
was alleged to provide payment services to 80 per cent of the
internet gambling operations in the world. Messrs Stephen
Lawrence and Eric Lefebvre, both Canadian citizens, were
charged with conspiracy to commit money laundering by
transferring funds offshore with the intent to promote internet
gambling in violation of both the Wire Wager Act and a statute
making it a federal crime to use interstate commerce to violate
state anti-gambling laws.[191] Neteller itself subsequently pled
guilty to a felony information charging it with conspiracy to
operate an unlicensed money-transmitting business and conspiracy to promote internet gambling, and also entered into a
deferred prosecution agreement with the DOJ in which it
agreed to forfeit $136 million.[192] Lawrence and Lefebvre each
also pled guilty to similar conspiracy charges, agreed jointly to

---

[190] Indictment, *United States v Scott*, CR05-122 (7 April 2005) (alleging violations of 18
USC §§ 1956(a)(2)(A), 1956(h)). As indicated above, Soulbury was unable to
challenge the civil forfeiture on the merits because the district court had granted
summary judgment based solely on the FDA. *United States v $6,976,934.65*, (2009)
554 F.3d 123 at 133 (D.C. Cir.). The court ultimately reversed the district court's
grant of summary judgment in favor of the government and remanded for
further proceedings. Scott entered into a consent order of forfeiture in 2012, in
which he forfeited nearly $7 million. Press Release, Dep't of Justice, *Department of
Justice Forfeits Nearly $7 Million in Proceeds of Unlawful Offshore Gambling and
Money Laundering Following Guilty Plea by William Paul Scott* (14 December 2012),
*http://www.justice.gov/opa/pr/department-justice-forfeits-nearly-7-million-proceeds-
unlawful-offshore-gambling-and-money* [Accessed 1 October 2015].

[191] Press Release, US Attorney's Office for the Southern District of NY, Dep't of
Justice, *U.S. Charges Two Founders of Payment Services Company with Laundering
Billions of Dollars of Internet Gambling Proceeds* (16 January 2007), *http://www.justice.
gov/archive/usao/nys/pressreleases/January07/netellerarrestspr.pdf* [Accessed 1 October
2015].

[192] See "Neteller Settles a Case", *Wall Street Journal*, 19 July 2007, at C6; Sophie
Brodie, "Neteller £12.3m in the Red After Its Forced US Withdrawal", *Daily
Telegraph* (London) (24 August 2007), at City Section p.5.

forfeit $100 million,[193] and were each sentenced to 45 days' imprisonment and one year supervised release along with the imposed fine.[194]

The Unlawful Internet Gambling Enforcement Act (UIGEA) was passed in 2006 with the aim of regulating internet gambling via the transmission of funds through financial institutions. The principal objective of UIGEA is to stop the flow of funds to and from internet gambling businesses by making it unlawful for an internet gambling business to "knowingly accept" most forms of payment "in connection with the participation of another person in unlawful Internet gambling."[195] UIGEA's final rules designate the payment systems that could be used to facilitate unlawful internet gambling[196] and require operators of these systems to use "adequate due diligence" when assessing the risk of a commercial customer using the account for unlawful internet gambling.[197]

The most notable enforcement of UIGEA to date came on 15 April 2011, when prosecutors in the Southern District of New York unsealed an indictment against several founders of Full Tilt Poker, PokerStars, and Absolute Poker, all offshore companies, alleging that they had violated UIGEA by operating an unlawful internet gambling business as in the United States, and charging them with bank fraud and money laundering in connection with the illegal processing of money

---

[193] See Brodie, "Neteller £12.3m in the Red After Its Forced US Withdrawal", *Daily Telegraph* (London) (24 August 2007), at City Section p.5.

[194] *United States v Lawrence*, No. 07-CR-597 (S.D.N.Y. 23 September 2011).

[195] 31 USC §§ 5363, 5366 (2006). The statute does not define "unlawful Internet gambling"; rather, it relies on federal and state gambling laws to make that determination. 31 USC § 5362(10)(A) (2006).

[196] The designated payments systems are automated clearinghouse systems, card systems, check collection systems, money transmitting businesses to the extent they engage in the transmission of funds and permit customers to initiate transactions remotely, and wire transfer systems. 31 CFR § 132.3.

[197] The Federal Reserve has advised that the most "efficient" means of implementing these due diligence requirements is to incorporate them into existing account opening procedures as regulated by the BSA, but notes that the BSA and UIGEA are separate regulations. Federal Reserve, *Regulation GG: Prohibition on Funding of Unlawful Internet Gambling, http://www.federalreserve.gov/bankinforeg/regggcg.htm#f9* [Accessed 1 October 2015].

transfers.[198] The DOJ seized the sites' domain names and pursued a civil forfeiture action for the proceeds of the companies' alleged money laundering.[199] PokerStars ultimately entered into a settlement agreement, pursuant to which it forfeited $547 million.[200]

10.3.3.3 Terrorist financing enforcement actions

The financing of terrorist activities has long been targeted both by prosecutors and civil litigants, and certain of these efforts have been linked to claims based on the alleged failure to maintain a viable and credible AML compliance programme.

In several cases brought more than a decade ago, some of which remain pending, foreign financial institutions were sued for treble damages by victims of terrorist attacks under the ATA. In those actions, the plaintiffs alleged that the financial institutions in question aided and abetted or knowingly provided material support to foreign terrorist organisations, or provided or collected funds knowing that such funds would be used for terrorist activities. A common thread linking the complaints in those actions were allegations that the institutions failed to have in place or to comply with rigorous AML programmes designed to prevent and detect terrorist financial activity and other criminal activity.[201] In *Weiss v National*

---

[198] Federal Bureau of Investigation, Press Release, *Manhattan U.S. Attorney Announces $731 Million Settlement of Money Laundering and Forfeiture Complaint with PokerStars and Full Tilt Poker* (31 July 2012), *https://www.fbi.gov/newyork/press-releases/2012/manhattan-u.s.-attorney-announces-731-million-settlement-of-money-laundering-and-forfeiture-complaint-with-pokerstars-and-full-tilt-poker* [Accessed 1 October 2015].

[199] Matt Richtel, "U.S. Cracks Down on Online Gambling", *New York Times* (15 April 2011), *http://www.nytimes.com/2011/04/16/technology/16poker.html* [Accessed 1 October 2015]. Django Gold, "PokerStars Pays $731M, Acquires Full Tilt In DOJ Settlement", Law 360 (31 July 2012), *http://www.law360.com/articles/365430/pokerstars-pays-731m-acquires-full-tilt-in-doj-settlement* [Accessed 1 October 2015].

[200] Django Gold, "PokerStars Pays $731M, Acquires Full Tilt In DOJ Settlement", Law 360 (31 July 2012).

[201] See First Amended Complaint 402–418, *Weiss v Nat'l Westminster Bank Plc*, No. 05-CV-4622 (E.D.N.Y. 5 January 2006); First Amended Complaint 79–105, *Almog v Arab Bank, PLC*, No. 04-CV-5564 (E.D.N.Y. 25 February 2005); First Amended Complaint 133–163, *Licci v Lebanese Canadian Bank, SAL*, No. 08-07253-GBD (S.D.N.Y. 22 January 2009); *Weiss v Nat'l Westminster Bank, Plc*, (2006) 453 F. Supp. 2d 609 (E.D.N.Y.); *Almog v Arab Bank Plc*, (2007) 471 F. Supp. 2d 257 (E.D.N.Y.);

Westminster Bank Plc,[202] plaintiffs brought suit against National Westminster Bank, Plc (NatWest), alleging that its London office had processed transactions for alleged foreign terrorist organisations with links to Hamas, which had been designated by the Treasury Department's Office of Foreign Assets Control (OFAC) as a Specially Designated Global Terrorist (SDGT). Some transactions were conducted by affiliates of Hamas that only appeared on Israeli designated terrorist lists. NatWest argued that the provision of basic banking services did not satisfy the degree of knowledge necessary to establish liability under the ATA, and that it had no obligation to consult the Israeli lists. In rejecting NatWest's arguments, at least in part, the court measured NatWest's conduct against what it referred to as "international banking norms".[203]

The court found these "international banking norms" in the written principles issued by FATF and in the Wolfsberg Principles for the Suppression of Terror Financing, and concluded, in the context of a motion to dismiss (where a plaintiff's allegations are accepted as true), that if NatWest had followed these principles, it would have found the organisations at issue identified on all publicly available terrorist lists, and would not have engaged in the financial transactions at

---

Licci v Am. Exp. Bank Ltd, (2010) 704 F. Supp. 2d 403, 404 (S.D.N.Y.); aff'd in part sub nom. *Licci ex rel. Licci v Lebanese Canadian Bank, SAL*, (2012) 672 F.3d 155 (2d Cir.) and *vacated in part in conformance with answer to certified question Licci ex rel. Licci v Lebanese Canadian Bank, SAL*, (2013) 732 F.3d 161 (2d Cir.); *Linde v Arab Bank Plc*, No. 04-CV-2799, 2015 WL 1565479 (E.D.N.Y. 8 April 2015). Those allegations are designed to satisfy the burden of proof under the knowledge requirement of the ATA that the bank knowingly supplied material support to terrorists or collected funds knowing that such funds would be used for terrorist activity. See *Boim v Holy Land Found. for Relief & Dev.*, (2008) 549 F.3d 685 at 693 (7th Cir.) ("To give money [or material support] to an organization that commits terrorist acts is not intentional misconduct unless one either knows that the organization engages in such acts or is deliberately indifferent to whether it does or not, meaning that one knows there is a substantial probability that the organization engages in terrorism but one does not care."); Compare with *Boim* at 702 ("As long as A either knows or is reckless in failing to discover that donations to B end up with Hamas, A is liable ... [T]o set the knowledge and causal requirement higher than we have done in this opinion would be to invite money laundering [and] the proliferation of affiliated organizations.").

[202] *Weiss v National Westminster Bank Plc* (2006) 453 F. Supp. 2d 609 (S.D.N.Y.).

[203] *Weiss*, 453 F. Supp. 2d at 619.

issue.[204] Accordingly, while there may be no private right of action for money laundering under the MLCA,[205] the Know Your Customer (KYC) and transaction monitoring programmes that financial institutions are required to have in place to prevent money laundering have been used to measure knowledge and conduct in suits where financial institutions are alleged to have aided and abetted or otherwise assisted the conduct of the principal wrongdoers.

Following a jury trial in which several actions brought under the ATA were consolidated, the jury returned a verdict on liability against Arab Bank Plc, based on allegations that it had provided material support to Hamas, which had claimed credit for a number of terrorist attacks that formed the basis for the plaintiffs' claims.[206] On Arab Bank's motion to set aside the verdict and for a new trial, the district court upheld the jury's verdict in an opinion issued on 8 April 2015.[207]

In its defence, Arab Bank had argued that it should not be held liable for "the millions of routine, automated transactions that [the Bank] process[es] even when proper compliance requirements are followed".[208] In rejecting Arab Bank's arguments, the district court stated that plaintiffs had provided "volumes of damning circumstantial evidence that [Arab Bank] knew its customers were terrorists".[209] The court also rejected Arab

---

[204] See *Weiss* at 625–631. In 2013, a US District Court granted NatWest summary judgment on the ground that the evidence did not demonstrate that it had acted with deliberate indifference so as to have "knowingly provide[d] material support or resources to a foreign terrorist organization" within the meaning of the ATA, but the Second Circuit thereafter vacated the judgment and remanded the case to the district court, reasoning that the district court had "imposed on Plaintiffs a more onerous burden with respect to NatWest's scienter" than the ATA requires. See *Weiss v National Westminster Bank Plc*, (2013) 936 F. Supp. 2d 100 at 103 (E.D.N.Y.), *vacated and remanded*, (2014) 768 F.3d 202 at 209 (2d Cir.).

[205] See discussion at fn.18.

[206] The following cases were consolidated under the caption of *Linde v Arab Bank Plc*, No. 04-CV-2799: *Philip Litle v Arab Bank Plc*, No. 04-CV-5449; *Oran Almog v Arab Bank Plc*, No. 04-CV-5564; *Robert L. Coulter, Sr v Arab Bank Plc*, No. 05-CV-365; *Gila Afriat-Kurtzer v Arab Bank Plc*, No. 05-CV-388; *Michael Bennett v Arab Bank Plc*, No. 05-CV-3183; *Arnold Roth v Arab Bank Plc*, No. 05-CV-3738; *Stewart Weiss v Arab Bank Plc*, No. 06-CV-1623.

[207] *Linde v Arab Bank Plc*, No. 04-CV-5564, 2015 WL 1565479 (E.D.N.Y. 8 April 2015).

[208] Tania Karas, "After 10 Years, a Jury Gets Arab Bank Case", (2014) 252 N.Y. L.J. 1.

[209] Stephanie Clifford, "Judge Removes Two Attacks from Arab Bank Terror Case",

Bank's heavy reliance on government watch lists, such as OFAC's lists of Specially Designated Nationals (SDNs) or SDGTs, as insufficient to shield it from liability. The court described Arab Bank's state of mind as constituting wilful ignorance because a "well-known Hamas figure could enter the bank [and] be recognized as such by every employee there," but not be treated as a terrorist, the transactions of which were to be blocked, if he was not on an OFAC or other watch list.[210]

To a significant extent, Arab Bank's compliance programme was very much on trial. When the head of compliance for its New York branch characterized Arab Bank as an "eminently compliant financial institution", and attempted to describe its compliance programmes in "glowing terms", the plaintiffs were permitted to use portions of a FinCEN assessment to impeach his testimony. As the court noted:

> "FinCEN's investigation ... found the Bank's compliance programs lacking in several critical respects. FinCEN's factual findings included that 'Arab Bank—New York did not file the majority of its suspicious activity reports regarding terrorist financing until after the Office of the Comptroller of the Currency commenced a review of its funds transfer activity in July 2004,' and 'Arab Bank—New York failed to review information in its possession that would have shown it was clearing funds transfers for individuals and entities dealing with subsequently designated terrorists and terrorists organizations, failed to analyze this information, and failed to file Suspicious Activity Reports.'"[211]

Arab Bank's defence was handicapped, perhaps significantly, because of discovery sanctions imposed following its failure to produce information allegedly protected by foreign bank secrecy laws. On 14 August 2015, three days before the jury

---

New York Times (9 April 2015), at A24. In its opinion, the court found that the bank was not liable for two of the 24 terrorist attacks at issue.

[210] Stephanie Clifford, "Judge Removes Two Attacks from Arab Bank Terror Case", *New York Times* (9 April 2015), at A24.

[211] *Linde v Arab Bank Plc*, 2015 WL 1565479, at *49.

trial to determine damages was set to begin, the parties reached a confidential settlement agreement and it is unknown whether there will be further litigation with respect to any issues in the case.[212]

At least one court has noted that "non-compliance with banking laws and industry standards alone will not render a bank negligently liable for the violent attacks committed by a terrorist organization who benefitted, in some general, nondescript manner, from monies passing through the bank during the performance of routine banking services."[213] The Second Circuit affirmed this court's dismissal of plaintiffs' claims against American Express Bank, which maintained a correspondent account for a Lebanese financial institution, Lebanese Canadian Bank, SAL (Lebanese Canadian Bank), that allegedly facilitated transactions for a Hezbollah affiliate.[214]

The above cases accentuate the importance of having in place viable and credible KYC, AML, and anti-terrorist financing programmes.[215]

---

[212] Andrew Keshner, "Arab Bank, Terrorism Plaintiffs Reach Settlement", N.Y. L.J. (17 August 2015), *http://www.newyorklawjournal.com/printerfriendly/id= 1202734838201* [Accessed 1 October 2015].

[213] *Licci*, (2010) 704 F. Supp.2d at 410 (S.D.N.Y.).

[214] *Licci*, (2012) 672 F.3d 155 at 158 (2d Cir.). Although the US Court of Appeals for the Second Circuit dismissed the case against American Express Bank, it remanded the case against Lebanese Canadian Bank for further proceedings. *Licci*, (2013) 732 F.3d 161 at 174 (2d Cir.). On remand, the district court dismissed the claim against Lebanese Canadian Bank for lack of personal jurisdiction. (2010) 704 F. Supp. 2d 403 (S.D.N.Y.). On plaintiffs' appeal, the Second Circuit certified to the New York Court of Appeals, the highest appellate court in the New York state court system, the question as to whether simply maintaining a correspondent account with a New York bank was sufficient to establish jurisdiction over a foreign bank with no presence in New York under New York's long-arm statute. (2012) 673 F.3d 50 (2d Cir.). When the New York Court of Appeals answered the certified question in the affirmative, (2012) 20 N.Y.3d 327, the Second Circuit went on to conclude that subjecting Lebanese Canadian Bank to jurisdiction in New York with respect to transactions in the correspondent account was consistent with due process, and reversed the dismissal on jurisdictional grounds. (2012) 732 F.3d 161 (2d Cir.). In April 2015, the case against Lebanese Canadian Bank, SAL was dismissed on collateral estoppel grounds; it is currently on appeal to the Second Circuit. Memorandum and Order, *Licci v Lebanese Canadian Bank, SAL*, No. 08-CV-7523 (S.D.N.Y. 14 April 2015).

[215] In a recent development that underscores the importance of corporate compliance programmes to the DOJ's analysis of what, if any, actions to take with

Terrorist financing cases also draw impetus from the sanctions programmes administered by OFAC. OFAC issues and enforces regulations promulgated under laws that provide for the imposition of economic sanctions on countries, entities, or persons in order to further US foreign policy and national security objectives, including the International Emergency Economic Powers Act[216] (IEEPA), pursuant to which sanctions against Iran, Syria, and Sudan, among others, have been promulgated, and the Trading with the Enemy Act[217] (TWEA), pursuant to which sanctions against Cuba have been promulgated. Under OFAC-administered laws, Presidential Executive Orders, and the regulations promulgated thereunder, banks, among others, are required, inter alia, to block transactions and freeze funds of specified countries, entities, and persons who appear on OFAC's lists of SDNs or SDGTs.[218]

---

respect to companies whose employees have engaged in misconduct, the Fraud Section of the Criminal Division of the DOJ announced in July 2015 that it would be hiring a compliance counsel who would serve as a corporate specialist assisting prosecutors in differentiating between companies that have good compliance programs and those that do not. Joel Schectman, "Compliance Counsel to Help DOJ Decide Whom to Prosecute", *Wall Street Journal* (30 July 2015), *http://blogs.wsj.com/riskandcompliance/2015/07/30/compliance-counsel-to-help-doj-decide-whom-to-prosecute* [Accessed 1 October 2015]. According to Andrew Weissmann, the Chief of the Fraud Section, "[t]his is an effort to place greater resources and expertise to separate out the companies that really don't get it—those with sham or paper programs—from those that do get it." Mr. Weissmann has indicated that, among other matters, this compliance counsel will "benchmark with various companies in a variety of different industries to make sure we have realistic expectations ... and tough-but-fair ones in various industries. It doesn't do anyone good to have people wasting their compliance dollars on areas that are low risk."

[216] 50 USC §§ 1701–1707.

[217] 12 USC § 95a–b; 50 USC App. §§ 1–44.

[218] On July 14, 2015, Iran and the US entered into the Joint Comprehensive Plan of Action (the JCPOA). Under the JCPOA, the US agreed to lift all nuclear-related sanctions against Iran in exchange for Iran agreeing to limit its nuclear programme. Although the agreement's terms lay out a gradual implementation period, the proposed lifted sanctions will include those on the Iranian rial, the provision of US banknotes to the Government of Iran, and the purchase, subscription to, and facilitation of the issuance of Iranian sovereign debt. See *Joint Comprehensive Plan of Action* at 12–13 (14 July 2015), *http://www.state.gov/documents/organization/245317.pdf* [Accessed 1 October 2015]. The JCPOA must be approved by the US Congress before the US lifts its sanctions.

In addition, in an effort to improve relations with Cuba, the US Department of the Treasury and the US Department of Commerce recently published amendments to existing sanctions against Cuba. Along with loosened travel restrictions and re-established diplomatic relations, US financial institutions are

A financial institution is responsible for ensuring that it does not conduct business with sanctioned entities and that it blocks any transactions with such entities. Although sanctions programmes do not strictly fall under AML regulations, "since the OFAC Sanctions lists include alleged money launderers and terrorists and [the] PATRIOT Act requirements mandate that certain financial institutions vet customer names against the OFAC list, institutions often consider the OFAC program to be a subset of their overall AML program".[219] OFAC sanctions compliance will sometimes fall within the same department as AML compliance, although the two compliance units will utilise different manuals, software, and personnel. Indeed, OFAC has promulgated procedures by which to report potential sanctions violations as well as guidelines for implementing an OFAC compliance programme, and the elements of such a programme overlap with AML compliance programme requirements.[220]

The DOJ and other US regulators have aggressively pursued financial institutions that have allegedly acted in violation of economic sanctions imposed on countries designated as state sponsors of terror, producing record forfeitures. In 2009, Lloyds TSB Bank entered into DPAs with both the DOJ and the Manhattan District Attorney's Office, and agreed to forfeit $350 million in connection with banking transactions it was alleged to have executed for clients located in Iran.[221] The alleged

---

now permitted to open correspondent accounts at Cuban financial institutions and authorise some remittances to Cuba. Dep't of Treasury, *Fact Sheet: Treasury and Commerce Announce Regulatory Amendments to Cuba Sanctions* (15 January 2015), *http://www.treasury.gov/press-center/press-releases/Pages/jl9740.aspx* [Accessed 1 October 2015]; see also President Barack Obama, *Statement by the President on the Re-Establishment of Diplomatic Relations with Cuba* (1 July 2015), *https://www. whitehouse.gov/the-press-office/2015/07/01/statement-president-re-establishment-diplomatic-relations-cuba* [Accessed 1 October 2015].

[219] Protiviti, *Guide to US Anti-Money Laundering Requirements* (5th edn) at 12, *http://www.protiviti.com/en-US/Documents/Resource-Guides/Guide-to-US-AML-Requirements-5thEdition-Protiviti.pdf* [Accessed 1 October 2015].

[220] See Protiviti, *Guide to US Anti-Money Laundering Requirements* (5th edn) at 295–296; "OFAC FAQs: Sanctions Compliance", *http://www.treasury.gov/resource-center/faqs/Sanctions/Pages/faq_compliance.aspx#start* [Accessed 1 October 2015].

[221] *Lloyds TSB Bank Plc Agrees to Forfeit $350 Million in Connection with Violations of the International Emergency Economic Powers Act* (9 January 2009), *http://www.justice. gov/archive/opa/pr/2009/January/09-crm-023.html* [Accessed 1 October 2015].

transactions were made in violation of US regulations issued by OFAC under the aegis of IEEPA, which prohibits the exportation of services, including correspondent banking services such as funds transfers, to Iran.[222] In order to circumvent such regulations, Lloyds allegedly removed client-identifying information from wire transfer instructions, a process known as "stripping", to avoid detection by electronic filters designed to flag prohibited transactions for investigation or rejection by US correspondent banks.[223] Lloyds' stripping of wire transfer instructions thus caused its US correspondent banks to transfer funds to or from parties located in Iran in violation of OFAC regulations, and also resulted in the falsification of business records of banks located in New York in violation of New York state law.[224]

In a recent and significant sanctions prosecution, BNP Paribas SA (BNP Paribas) pled guilty on 9 July 2014 to IEEPA and TWEA violations. On 1 May 2015, BNP Paribas was sentenced to five years' probation and agreed to forfeit $8.8 billion on top of a $140 million fine.[225] BNP Paribas admitted to knowing and wilful violations of US sanctions against Iran, Sudan, and Cuba and to using "cover payments", stripping, and highly compli-cated transactional structures to conceal the involvement of sanctioned entities in US dollar transactions.[226] The DOJ

---

[222] 31 CFR § 560.204.

[223] See Exhibit A of Exhibit 1 to Joint Motion for Approval of Deferred Prosecution Agreement and Exclusion of Time Under the Speedy Trial Act, *United States v Lloyds TSB Bank PLC*, No. 09-CR-007 (D.D.C. 9 January 2009).

[224] See New York Penal Law § 175.10.

[225] Press Release, Dep't of Justice, *BNP Paribas Sentenced for Conspiring to Violate the International Emergency Economic Powers Act and the Trading with the Enemy Act* (1 May 2015), http://www.justice.gov/opa/pr/bnp-paribas-sentenced-conspiring-violate-international-emergency-economic-powers-act-and [Accessed 1 October 2015].

[226] Statement of Facts, *United States v BNP Paribas* (28 June 2014), http://www.justice.gov/sites/default/files/opa/legacy/2014/06/30/statement-of-facts.pdf [Accessed 1 October 2015]. Like BNP Paribas, ING Bank, N.V. (ING Bank) and two HSBC affiliates (HSBC) entered into deferred prosecution agreements with the DOJ in which they admitted to violating OFAC sanctions by processing US dollar transactions in which the involvement of Cuba, among other sanctioned countries, was concealed. Press Release, Dep't of Justice, *ING Bank N.V. Agrees to Forfeit $619 million for Illegal Transactions with Cuban and Iranian Entities* (12 June 2012), http://www.justice.gov/opa/pr/ing-bank-nv-agrees-forfeit-619-million-illegal-transactions-cuban-and-iranian-entities-0 [Accessed 1 October 2015]; Press Release, Dep't of Justice, *HSBC Holdings Plc. and HSBC Bank USA N.A. Admit to*

alleged that BNP processed over $6 billion for Sudanese financial institutions while deliberately omitting references to Sudan in payment messages and moving money through "satellite banks" (unaffiliated banks outside of both Sudan and the US) to evade detection by US authorities.[227] The DOJ also alleged that internal communications between senior compliance officers and other BNP Paribas employees demonstrated an awareness that their Sudanese banking customers "play[ed] a pivotal part in the support of the Sudanese government" and that BNP Paribas's actions could be "interpreted as supporting the leaders in place" despite the government's support for terrorism and human rights abuse, most notably in the Darfur crisis.[228]

Anti-Money Laundering and Sanctions Violations, Forfeit $1.256 Billion in Deferred Prosecution Agreement (11 December 2012), *http://www.justice.gov/opa/pr/hsbc-holdings-plc-and-hsbc-bank-usa-na-admit-anti-money-laundering-and-sanctions-violations* [Accessed 1 October 2015].

Those resolutions and the admissions they contained were utilised by plaintiffs with a terrorist judgment entered under 28 USC § 1605A against Cuba in the amount of $2.9 billion to allege the basis for a RICO claim against BNP Paribas, ING Bank and HSBC predicated on alleged wire fraud and money laundering violations. See e.g. *Villoldo v BNP Paribas S.A*, No. 14-CV-9930 (S.D.N.Y. 16 December 2014). The plaintiffs in *Villoldo* alleged that, but for the admitted concealment of Cuba's involvement in the numerous wire transfers and other transactions that were the subject of the plea agreements, the proceeds of the transactions would have been blocked and thus available for execution in satisfaction of the *Villoldo* judgment. The proceeds of the wire transfers were alleged to constitute the proceeds of sanctions violations, hence the proceeds of "specified unlawful activity". See 18 USC § 1956.

On 21 July 2015, the court dismissed the *Villoldo* RICO claims for failure to allege an injury to business or property, and to show causation. Because the banks' transactions involving Cuba occurred before the Villoldos obtained their judgment against it, they could not, the court held, claim the requisite injury to a property interest. A civil RICO claim also requires a showing that the wrongful conduct alleged was the proximate cause of the claimed injury. The *Villoldo* court held that the banks' actions could not be viewed as the proximate cause of the Villoldos' claimed inability to collect on their judgment because Cuba's failure to pay was an intervening direct cause of the injury. Order, *Villoldo v BNP Paribas S.A.*, No. 14-CV-9930 (S.D.N.Y. 21 July 2015) (appeal pending).

[227] *Villoldo v BNP Paribas S.A*, No. 14-CV-9930.
[228] *Villoldo v BNP Paribas S.A*, No. 14-CV-9930.

10.3.4 Recent trends in resolution terms and in targets of AML enforcement actions

10.3.4.1 Use of monitors as basis for continued oversight of post-resolution compliance

In recent years, the US government has at times required corporate entities, as a condition to resolving AML and other charges, to submit to oversight by independent monitors. DPAs and non-prosecution agreements (NPAs) have also become an important tool of the US government in its efforts to hold institutions accountable for corporate misconduct and promote compliance with the law without unnecessarily exposing financial institutions to disproportionate adverse collateral consequences that could result from a criminal conviction.[229] While provisions in those negotiated resolutions have often required "self-reporting by the company" in order to have some basis for measuring its progress toward greater regulatory compliance, the Government has at times required institutions to submit to the oversight of an independent third-party monitor for a fixed period of time.[230]

A notable recent experience with a monitorship resulted from the 2012 DPA entered into between the DOJ and HSBC Bank USA, which resolved allegations of AML and sanctions violations.[231] Federal prosecutors alleged, in part, that HSBC

---

[229] In 2014, the DOJ and SEC entered into 20 DPAs and 10 NPAs with companies as a means of resolving allegations of corporate misconduct. See Joseph Warin, "2014 Year-End Update on Corporate Deferred Prosecution and Non-Prosecution Agreements" (18 January 2015), *http://corpgov.law.harvard.edu/2015/01/18/2014-year-end-update-on-corporate-deferred-prosecution-and-non-prosecution-agreements* [Accessed 1 October 2015].

[230] See Warin. Recent analysis shows that, in 2014, "of the 30 NPAs and DPAs issued ..., 19 required some form of monitoring, including self-reporting and, in three instances, traditional independent monitors."

[231] In a four-count criminal information, federal prosecutors alleged that HSBC willfully failed to maintain an effective anti-money laundering programme, wilfully failed to engage in due diligence on correspondent accounts held on behalf of foreign persons, and wilfully facilitated transactions in violation of economic sanctions against Iran, Libya, Sudan, Burma, and Cuba. See Information, *United States v HSBC Bank USA, N.A.*, No. 12-CR-763, 2012 WL 6120591 (E.D.N.Y. 11 December 2012) (alleging violations of 31 USC §§ 5318(h), 5318(i), and two statutes codifying US economic sanctions).

USA failed to conduct due diligence on suspicious transactions and activities initiated by other HSBC affiliates, in particular HSBC Mexico.[232] Prosecutors further alleged that between 2006 and 2009, over $670 billion in wire transfers and over $9.4 billion in purchases of US dollars from HSBC Mexico went unmonitored and led the bank to become the "preferred financial institution for drug cartels and money launderers."[233] By entering into a DPA with the US government, HSBC avoided a criminal conviction,[234] but in exchange it agreed to forfeit $1.256 billion to federal and state authorities and to pay an additional $665 million in civil monetary penalties to the Federal Government.[235] Moreover, as part of the terms of the

---

[232] *Statement of Facts* at 4, *http://www.justice.gov/sites/default/files/opa/legacy/2012/12/11/ dpa-attachment-a.pdf* [Accessed 1 October 2015].

[233] Statement of Facts, *United States v HSBC Bank USA N.A.*, No. 12-CR-763 (E.D.N.Y. 11 December 2012); see also Dep't of Justice, *HSBC Holdings Plc. and HSBC Bank USA N.A. Admit to Anti-Money Laundering and Sanctions Violations, Forfeit $1.256 Billion in Deferred Prosecution Agreement* (11 December 2012), *http://www. justice.gov/opa/pr/hsbc-holdings-plc-and-hsbc-bank-usa-na-admit-anti-money- laundering-and-sanctions-violations* [Accessed 1 October 2015].

[234] Although traditionally courts have not taken an active interest in reviewing the terms of DPAs negotiated by the parties, two recent cases illustrate instances of greater judicial scrutiny of such agreements. In *HSBC Bank USA*, the district court judge took the unusual step of inquiring as to whether "the DPA adequately reflects the seriousness of the offense behavior and why accepting the DPA would yield a result consistent with the goals of the federal sentencing scheme". *United States v HSBC Bank USA, N.A.*, No. 12-CR-763, 2013 WL 3306161, at *1 (E.D.N.Y. 1 July 2013). The court rejected both parties' contention that it lacked authority to approve or disapprove the DPA and concluded that "[b]y placing a criminal matter on the docket of a federal court, the parties have subjected their DPA to the legitimate exercise of that court's [supervisory] authority". *United States v HSBC Bank USA* at *5–6. In the end, the court still decided to approve the DPA, "subject to a continued monitoring of its execution and implementation". *United States v HSBC Bank USA* at *7. In a more recent case, however, a different district court judge adopted a similar stance on its supervisory authority and then rejected the parties' DPA, concluding that its terms were "grossly disproportionate to the gravity" of the defendant's conduct. *United States v Fokker Services B.V.*, No. 14-CR-121, 2015 WL 729291, at *4–6 (D.D.C. 5 February 2015). While it remained open to approving a modified agreement, the court indicated that, at a minimum, fines should exceed the amount of revenue generated from the alleged misconduct, the probationary period should exceed 18 months, and the defendant should appoint an independent monitor to oversee compliance. *United States v Fokker Services B.V.* at *6. Both the Government and Fokker are appealing the district court's decision to the DC Circuit.

[235] See Deferred Prosecution Agreement, *United States v HSBC Bank USA, N.A.*, 2012 WL 6120512 (E.D.N.Y. 11 December 2012); see also Jessica Silver-Greenberg, "HSBC to Pay Record Fine to Settle Money-Laundering Charges", *New York Times* (11 December 2012), *http://dealbook.nytimes.com/2012/12/11/hsbc-to-pay-record-fine-*

resolution, HSBC agreed to appoint an independent monitor for a five-year period to oversee implementation of AML compliance efforts.[236]

In 2012, Standard Chartered reached resolutions with federal and state authorities concerning alleged violations of OFAC sanctions.[237] Specifically, the bank agreed to pay $227 million in penalties and forfeiture pursuant to DPAs entered into with the DOJ and the Manhattan District Attorney's Office, and paid a $100 million penalty to the Federal Reserve, a $132 million penalty to OFAC,[238] and a $340 million penalty to the NYDFS. In addition, pursuant to the agreement with the NYDFS, the bank agreed to subject itself to the oversight of an independent monitor for a two-year period.[239] Following the monitor's identification of various alleged deficiencies in the bank's AML programme, Standard Chartered entered into a new consent order with the NYDFS in August 2014, whereby the bank agreed to pay an additional $300 million civil monetary penalty, to temporarily suspend portions of its US dollar clearing operations, and to extend the monitorship for an additional two years.[240]

---

to-settle-money-laundering-charges [Accessed 1 October 2015]. The $665 million in civil monetary penalties encompassed payments to the Federal Reserve and to the Office of the Comptroller of the Currency.

[236] The length of the monitorship was unusual as most monitorships are 2–3 years in length.

[237] See Information, *United States v Standard Chartered Bank*, 2012 WL 6097343 (D.D.C. 8 December 2012); *Consent Order, In re Matter of Standard Chartered Bank* (21 September 2012), *http://www.dfs.ny.gov/about/ea/ea120921.pdf* [Accessed 1 October 2015]. The Information alleged that Standard Chartered processed financial transactions with entities affiliated with Iran, Sudan, Libya, and Burma.

[238] See Deferred Prosecution Agreement, *United States v Standard Chartered Bank*, No. 12-CR-262, 2012 WL 6097335 (D.D.C. 7 December 2012); Press Release, Manhattan DA, "Standard Chartered Bank Reaches $327 Million Settlement for Illegal Transactions" (10 December 2012), *http://manhattanda.org/press-release/standard-chartered-bank-reaches-327-million-settlement-illegal-transactions* [Accessed 19 October 2015].

[239] *Consent Order 8–10, In re Matter of Standard Chartered Bank* (21 September 2012), *http://www.dfs.ny.gov/about/ea/ea120921.pdf* [Accessed 1 October 2015].

[240] See *Consent Order 1–5, In re Matter of Standard Chartered Bank* (19 August 2014), *http://www.dfs.ny.gov/about/ea/ea140819.pdf* [Accessed 1 October 2015]. In that same year, Standard Chartered also voluntarily agreed with federal and state prosecutors to a three-year extension of the DPAs. See Notice on Consent of Amendment to Deferred Prosecution Agreement, *United States v Standard Chartered Bank*, *http://www.mainjustice.com/wp-admin/documents-databases/208-1-U.*

The experiences of HSBC and Standard Chartered are but two examples of the significant roles monitors can be asked to play in the ongoing oversight of financial institutions as part of law enforcement and regulatory resolutions with banks in connection with AML, sanctions and other investigations.

10.3.4.2 Recent enforcement actions seeking compliance officer liability for AML violations

Another recent trend in AML enforcement actions has been the emergence of potential individual liability for compliance officers of corporate entities that have allegedly engaged in AML violations. As some commentators have noted, prosecutors have long had the authority to seek civil penalties against financial institutions and any of their directors, officers, or employees, but they "rarely sought such penalties against individual officers".[241] However, two recent cases may signal a shift in that approach and suggest the possibility for more findings of individual liability in future AML investigations.

First, in February 2014, the Financial Industry Regulatory Authority (FINRA) determined that Brown Brothers Harriman & Co (BBH) was responsible for "substantial anti-money laundering compliance failures" due, in part, to its alleged inability to adequately "monitor and detect suspicious penny stock transactions".[242] In addition to imposing an $8 million penalty on the company, FINRA also announced that Harold Crawford, BBH's Global AML Compliance Officer, would be fined $25,000 and suspended for one month.[243]

S.-v.-Standard-Chartered-Bank—Filing—Dec.-9-2014.pdf [Accessed 19 October 2015]; Half Year Report 2015, Standard Chartered Bank, at 103 (30 June 2015).

[241] Greg Marshall & Erin Sullivan, "Avoiding Personal Liability Amidst Heightened AML Enforcement", *Inside Counsel* (3 March 2015), http://www.insidecounsel.com/2015/03/03/avoiding-personal-liability-amidst-heightened-aml [Accessed 1 October 2015].

[242] FINRA, "FINRA Fines Brown Brothers Harriman a Record $8 Million for Substantial Anti-Money Laundering Compliance Failures" (5 February 2014), https://www.finra.org/newsroom/2014/finra-fines-brown-brothers-harriman-record-8-million-substantial-anti-money-laundering [Accessed 1 October 2015].

[243] FINRA, "FINRA Fines Brown Brothers Harriman a Record $8 Million for Substantial Anti-Money Laundering Compliance Failures" (5 February 2014).

A second enforcement action, in December 2014, again resulted in compliance officer liability, but imposed a significantly higher penalty. Following an earlier probe into MoneyGram International Inc., FinCEN assessed a $1 million civil money penalty against Thomas Haider, who had served as the company's Chief Compliance Officer from 2003 to 2008, and also sought to have Haider barred from participating in the financial industry for a term of years to be determined.[244] In support of its sanctions, FinCEN alleged that Haider failed to implement an effective AML programme and file timely SARs with the government.[245] While the penalty imposed was severe, FinCEN contended that it was justified by Haider's "wilful violations" of AML regulations, which "created an environment where fraud and money laundering thrived and dirty money rampaged through the very system he was charged with protecting".[246]

10.3.4.3 Recent enforcement actions seeking third-party consultant liability for AML violations

In addition to compliance officers, third-party consultants have recently become the target of AML enforcement actions as a result of perceived deficiencies in their reporting to financial regulators on behalf of corporate clients under investigation. Since 2013, at least three major consulting firms have been fined by the NYDFS as a result of their work in AML investigations. In a June 2013 resolution with Deloitte LLP arising from its consulting services provided to Standard

---

[244] FinCEN, *FinCEN Assesses $1 Million Penalty and Seeks to Bar Former MoneyGram Executive from Financial Industry* (18 December 2014), *http://www.fincen.gov/news_room/nr/html/20141218.html* [Accessed 1 October 2015]. FinCEN immediately filed a suit in federal court to enforce the penalty and enjoin Haider from employment in the financial industry.

[245] Complaint at 3, *United States Department of Treasury v Thomas Haider* (S.D.N.Y. 18 December 2014), *http://www.fincen.gov/news_room/ea/files/USAO_SDNY_Complaint.pdf* [Accessed 1 October 2015].

[246] FinCEN, *FinCEN Assesses $1 Million Penalty and Seeks to Bar Former MoneyGram Executive from Financial Industry* (18 December 2014). MoneyGram itself had forfeited $100 million in 2012 after the DOJ concluded that it had engaged in AML violations. See Rachel Louise Ensign, "Former MoneyGram Compliance Chief Faces Penalty", *Wall Street Journal* (18 December 2014), *http://www.wsj.com/articles/regulator-expected-to-set-penalty-on-former-moneygram-compliance-officer-1418924616* [Accessed 1 October 2015].

Chartered Bank, the NYDFS imposed a $10 million fine and required the company to refrain from conducting new business with certain New York banks for a one-year period.[247] Although the NYDFS found "no evidence that [Deloitte] intentionally helped or conspired with the bank to launder money", it did find that the consulting firm omitted "critical information" in a report submitted to regulators following an independent review of the bank.[248] Another consultant to Standard Chartered, Promontory Financial Group, was hired as an independent monitor to provide a historical transaction review, but allegedly "made changes to 'soften' and 'tone down' the language in its reports" or removed other information.[249] Promontory recently agreed to pay a $15 million penalty and accepted a six-month suspension from new consulting projects that required New York state authorization.[250]

In August 2014, the NYDFS imposed a $25 million penalty and two-year ban from conducting certain business activities with New York banks on PricewaterhouseCoopers.[251] The NYDFS alleged that the consulting firm "improperly alter[ed]" an independent report summarizing alleged sanctions violations committed by the Bank of Tokyo-Mitsubishi UFJ, in particular by allegedly agreeing to client recommendations to either "delete or water down a number of important issues".[252] As AML investigations continue to proliferate, members of the

---

[247] Karen Freifeld, "Deloitte to Pay NY $10 Million for Misconduct over Standard Chartered", Reuters (18 June 2013), *http://www.reuters.com/article/2013/06/18/us-deloitte-stanchart-ny-idUSBRE95H0VC20130618* [Accessed 1 October 2015].

[248] Karen Freifeld, "Deloitte to Pay NY $10 Million for Misconduct over Standard Chartered", Reuters (18 June 2013).

[249] NY Dep't of Fin. Servs., *Report on Investigation of Promontory Financial Group, LLC* (August 2015), *http://www.dfs.ny.gov/reportpub/promontory_inv_rpt_2015.pdf* [Accessed 1 October 2015].

[250] Christopher M. Matthews, "Promontory to Pay $15 Million in Settlement of Standard Chartered Case", *Wall Street Journal* (18 August 2015), *http://www.wsj.com/articles/promontory-settles-with-ny-regulator-on-standard-chartered-investigation-1439923453* [Accessed 1 October 2015].

[251] Ben Protess, "Altered Bank Study Draws Fine for Giant Auditor PwC", *New York Times* (18 August 2014), *http://dealbook.nytimes.com/2014/08/18/new-york-regulator-announces-settlement-with-pricewaterhousecoopers* [Accessed 1 October 2015].

[252] Ben Protess, "Altered Bank Study Draws Fine for Giant Auditor PwC", *New York Times* (18 August 2014).

bank consulting industry may find themselves subject to closer scrutiny and potential liability for alleged omissions in independent reports distributed to regulators.

10.4 Conclusion

The 11 September attacks prompted a rapid expansion and evolution of US AML law, much of it targeted at conduct overseas. The regulations promulgated under the authority of the PATRIOT Act, along with expansive judicial interpretations of federal criminal statutes, have provided US regulators and law enforcement with greater extra-territorial reach. Under the Obama administration, the Federal Government has continued that trend as it has implemented its domestic and foreign policies. It remains to be seen whether that trend will be altered after a new administration takes the reins in January 2017.

Index

This index has been prepared using Sweet and Maxwell's Legal Taxonomy. Main index entries conform to keywords provided by the Legal Taxonomy except where references to specific documents or non-standard terms (denoted by quotation marks) have been included. These keywords provide a means of identifying similar concepts in other Sweet and Maxwell publications and online services to which keywords from the Legal Taxonomy have been applied. Readers may find some minor differences between terms used in the text and those which appear in the index. Suggestions to *sweetandmaxwell.taxonomy@thomson.com*.

All indexing is to heading number